SIMPSONS™ COMICS
BEACH BLANKET BONGO

SIMPSONS COMICS BEACH BLANKET BONGO

Bongo Comics Group books may be purchased for educational, business,
or sales promotional use. For information, please call or write
P.O. Box 1963, Santa Monica, CA 90406-1963

FIRST EDITION

ISBN-13: 978-1-892849-18-2
ISBN: 1-892849-18-6

07 08 09 10 11 QWM 10 9 8 7 6 5 4 3 2 1

Publisher: Matt Groening
Creative Director: Bill Morrison
Managing Editor: Terry Delegeane
Director of Operations: Robert Zaugh
Art Director: Nathan Kane
Art Director Special Projects: Serban Cristescu
Production Manager: Christopher Ungar
Legal Guardian: Susan A. Grode

Trade Paperback Concepts and Design: Serban Cristescu

HarperCollins Editors: Hope Innelli, Jeremy Cesarec

Contributing Artists:
Karen Bates, John Costanza, Serban Cristescu, Mike DeCarlo, Luis Escobar,
Chia-Hsien Jason Ho, James Huang, Brian Iles, Nathan Kane, Kim Le, Scott McRae,
Bill Morrison, Joey Nilges, Phyllis Novin, Phil Ortiz, Andrew Pepoy, Ryan Rivette,
Mike Rote, Howard Shum, Steve Steere Jr., Chris Ungar, Art Villanueva

Contributing Writers:
Elma Blackburn, Ian Boothby, Tony DiGerolamo,
Chuck Dixon, Jesse L. McCann, Gail Simone, Seran Williams, Chris Yambar

PRINTED IN CANADA

TABLE OF CONTENTS

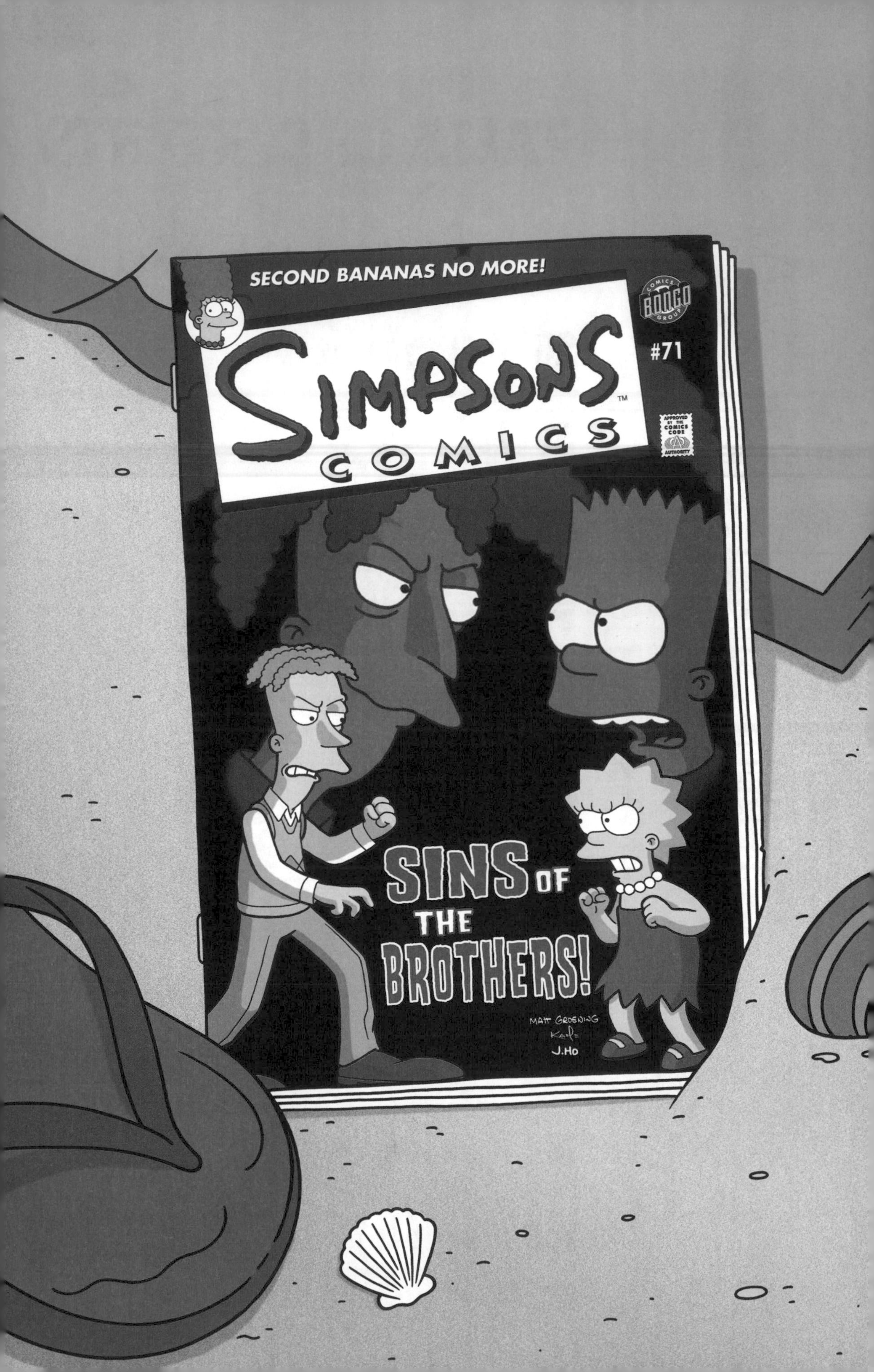
SECOND BANANAS NO MORE!
SIMPSONS COMICS
#71
APPROVED BY THE COMICS CODE AUTHORITY
SINS OF THE BROTHERS!
MATT GROENING
J.HO

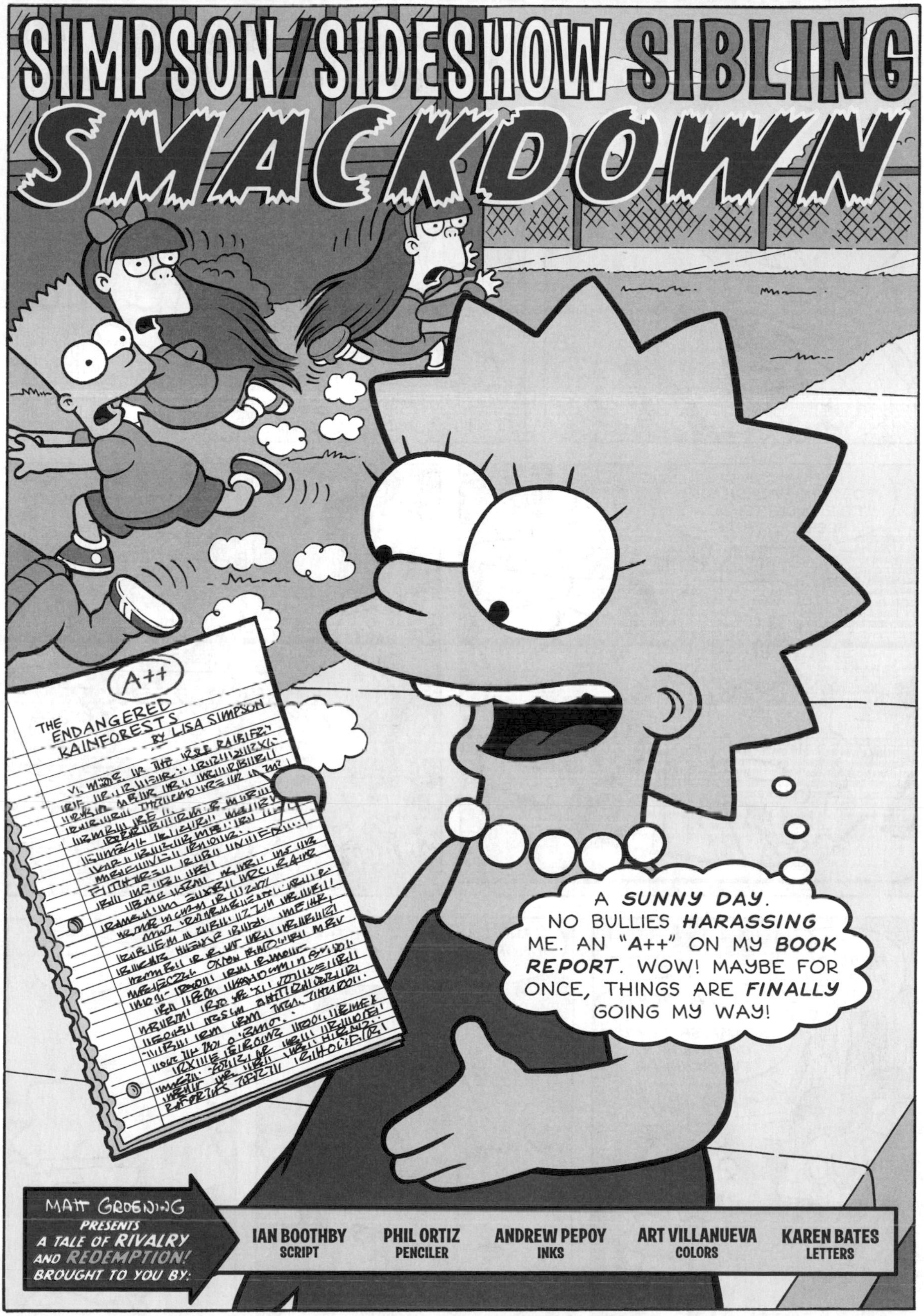
SIMPSON/SIDESHOW SIBLING
SMACKDOWN
A++
THE ENDANGERED RAINFORESTS
BY LISA SIMPSON
A SUNNY DAY. NO BULLIES HARASSING ME. AN "A++" ON MY BOOK REPORT. WOW! MAYBE FOR ONCE, THINGS ARE FINALLY GOING MY WAY!
MATT GROENING PRESENTS A TALE OF RIVALRY AND REDEMPTION! BROUGHT TO YOU BY:
IAN BOOTHBY SCRIPT
PHIL ORTIZ PENCILER
ANDREW PEPOY INKS
ART VILLANUEVA COLORS
KAREN BATES LETTERS

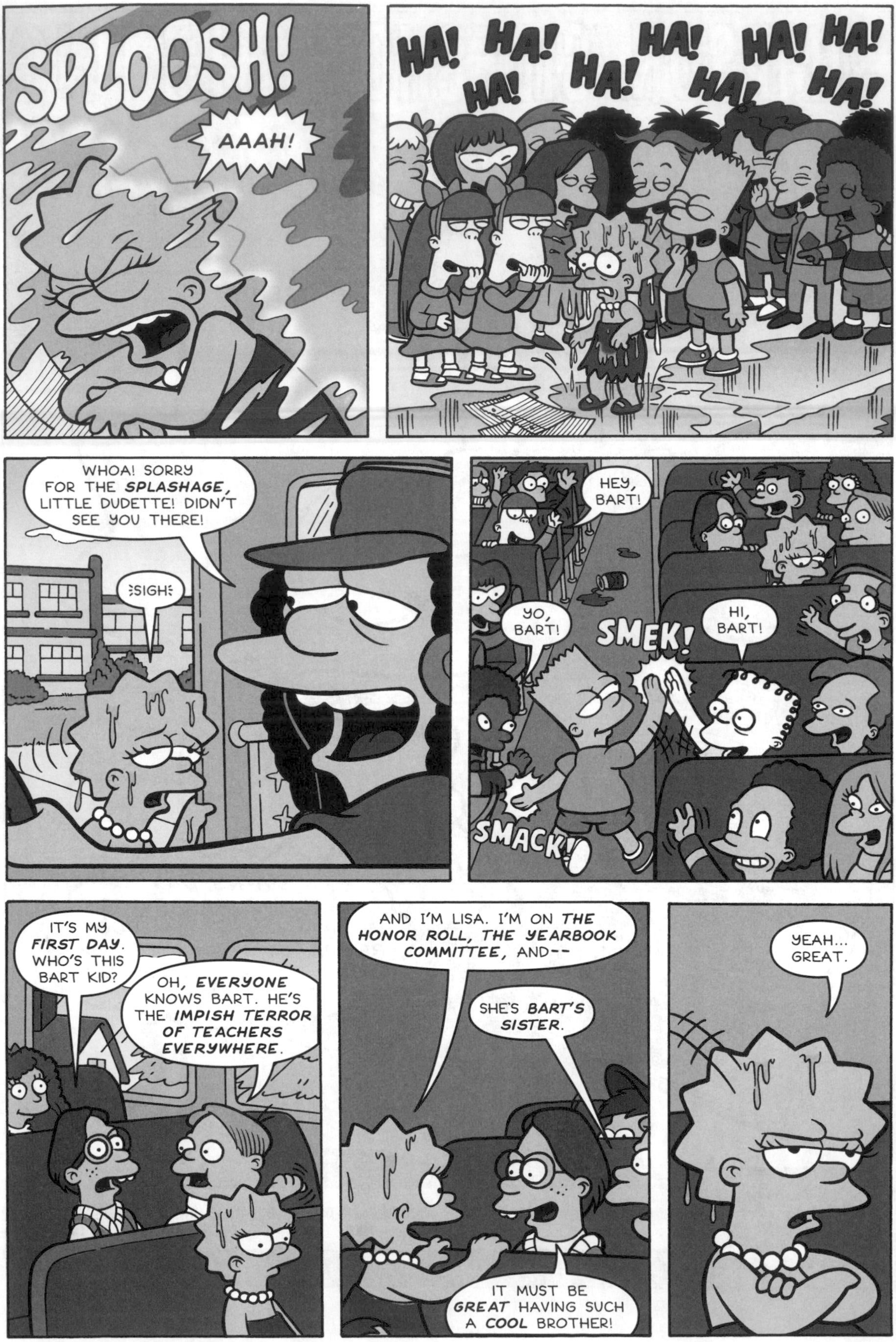
SPLOOSH!
AAAH!
HA! HA! HA! HA! HA! HA! HA! HA! HA! HA!
WHOA! SORRY FOR THE *SPLASHAGE*, LITTLE DUDETTE! DIDN'T SEE YOU THERE!
SIGH
HEY, BART!
YO, BART!
SMEK!
HI, BART!
SMACK!
IT'S MY *FIRST DAY*. WHO'S THIS BART KID?
OH, *EVERYONE* KNOWS BART. HE'S THE *IMPISH TERROR OF TEACHERS EVERYWHERE*.
AND I'M LISA. I'M ON *THE HONOR ROLL, THE YEARBOOK COMMITTEE*, AND--
SHE'S *BART'S SISTER*.
IT MUST BE *GREAT* HAVING SUCH A *COOL* BROTHER!
YEAH... GREAT.

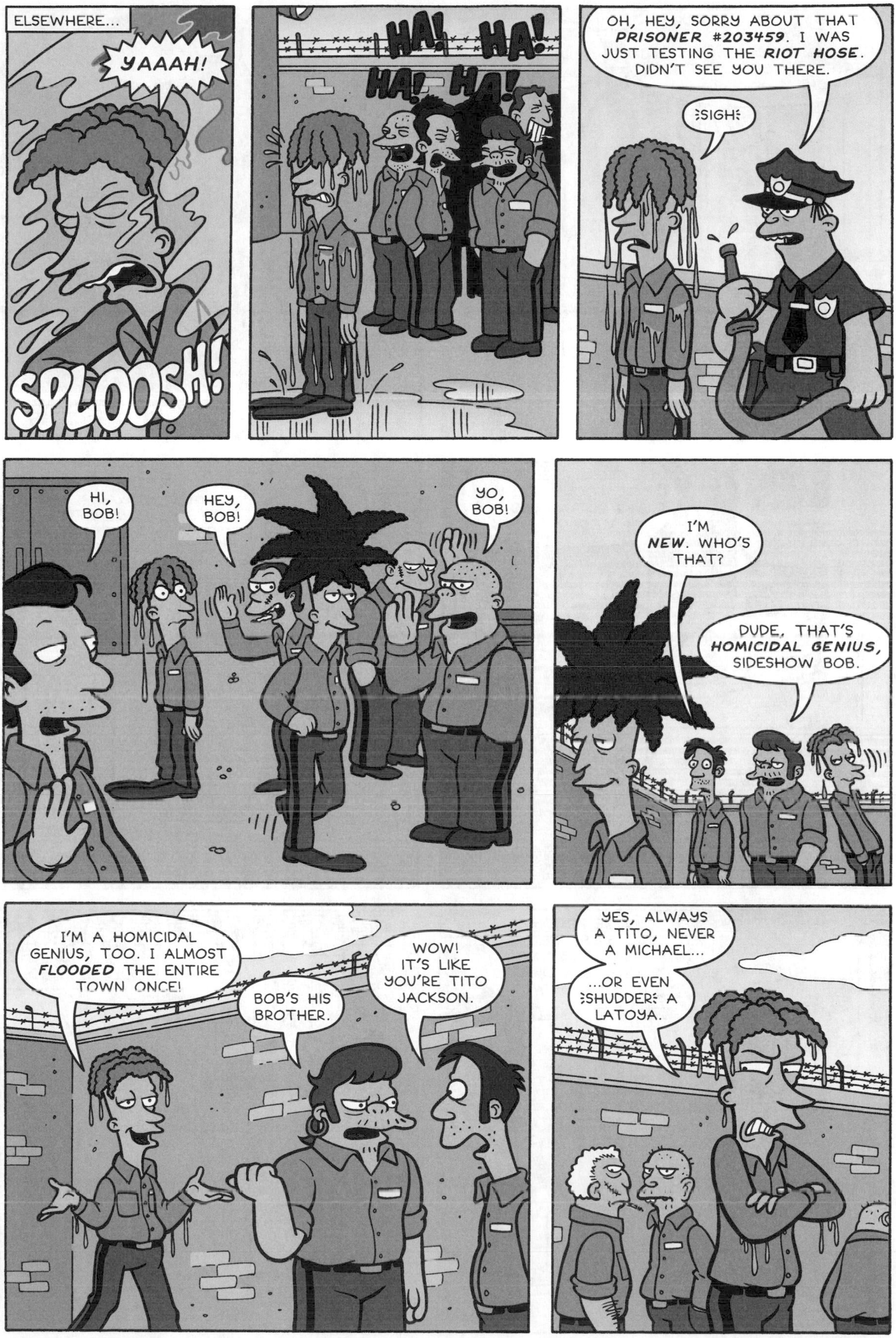
ELSEWHERE...
YAAAH!
SPLOOSH!
HA! HA! HA! HA!
OH, HEY, SORRY ABOUT THAT PRISONER #203459. I WAS JUST TESTING THE RIOT HOSE. DIDN'T SEE YOU THERE.
:SIGH:
HI, BOB!
HEY, BOB!
YO, BOB!
I'M NEW. WHO'S THAT?
DUDE, THAT'S HOMICIDAL GENIUS, SIDESHOW BOB.
I'M A HOMICIDAL GENIUS, TOO. I ALMOST FLOODED THE ENTIRE TOWN ONCE!
BOB'S HIS BROTHER.
WOW! IT'S LIKE YOU'RE TITO JACKSON.
YES, ALWAYS A TITO, NEVER A MICHAEL...
...OR EVEN :SHUDDER: A LATOYA.

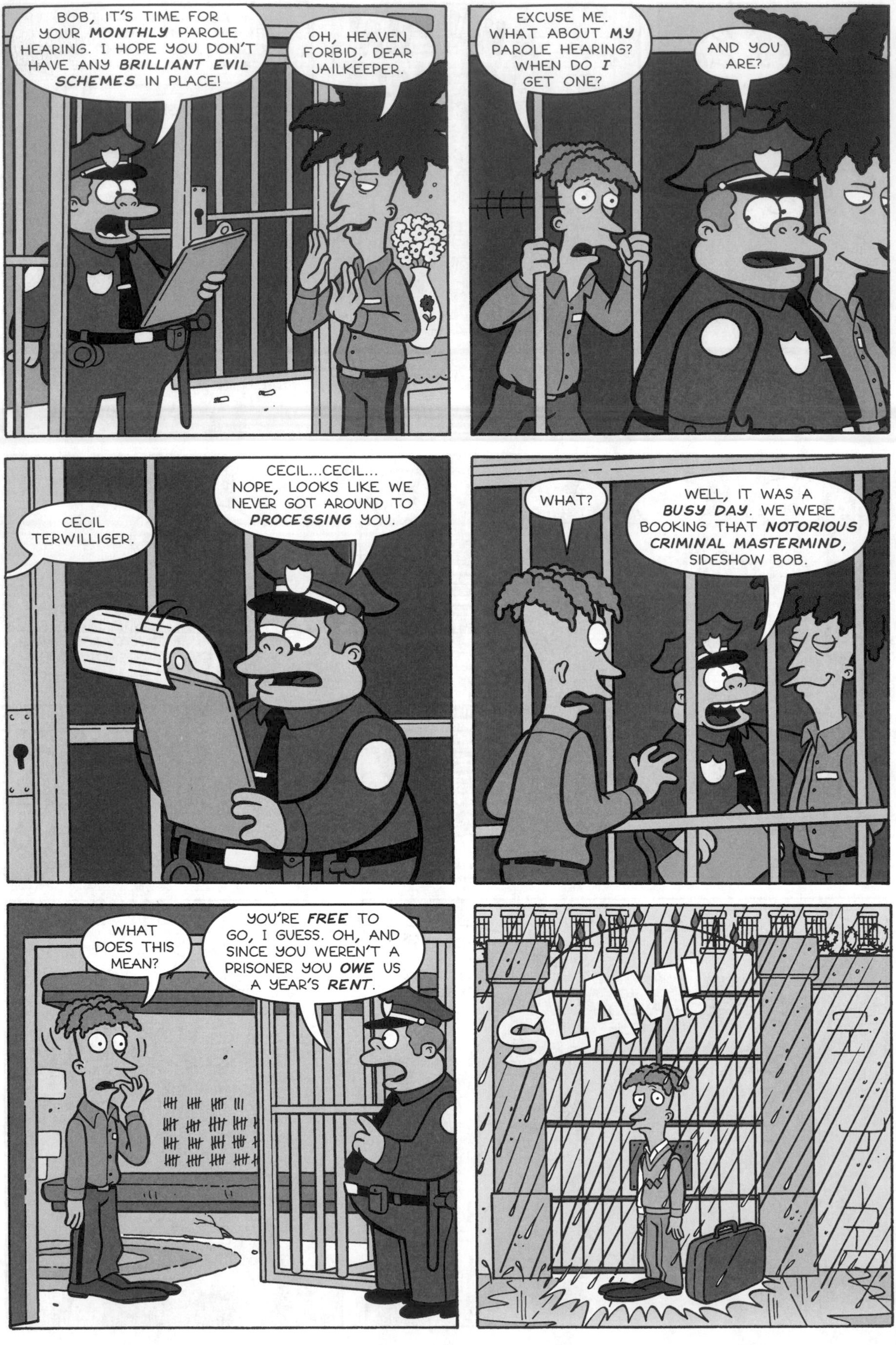

BOB, IT'S TIME FOR YOUR **MONTHLY** PAROLE HEARING. I HOPE YOU DON'T HAVE ANY **BRILLIANT EVIL SCHEMES** IN PLACE!
OH, HEAVEN FORBID, DEAR JAILKEEPER.
EXCUSE ME. WHAT ABOUT **MY** PAROLE HEARING? WHEN DO **I** GET ONE?
AND YOU ARE?
CECIL TERWILLIGER.
CECIL...CECIL... NOPE, LOOKS LIKE WE NEVER GOT AROUND TO **PROCESSING** YOU.
WHAT?
WELL, IT WAS A **BUSY DAY**. WE WERE BOOKING THAT **NOTORIOUS CRIMINAL MASTERMIND,** SIDESHOW BOB.
WHAT DOES THIS MEAN?
YOU'RE **FREE** TO GO, I GUESS. OH, AND SINCE YOU WEREN'T A PRISONER YOU **OWE** US A YEAR'S **RENT**.
SLAM!

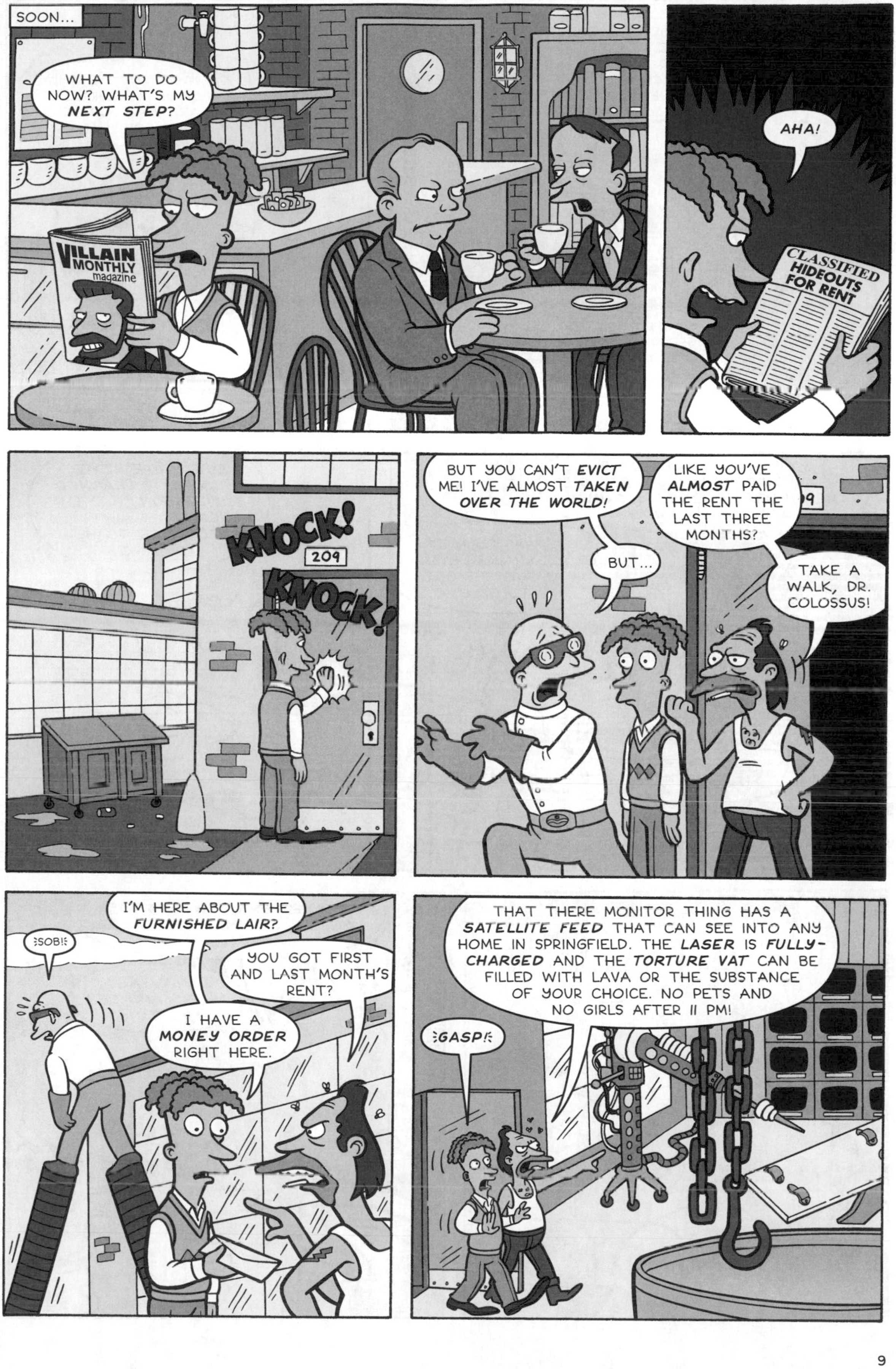
SOON...
WHAT TO DO NOW? WHAT'S MY NEXT STEP?
VILLAIN MONTHLY magazine
AHA!
CLASSIFIED HIDEOUTS FOR RENT
KNOCK! KNOCK!
209
BUT YOU CAN'T EVICT ME! I'VE ALMOST TAKEN OVER THE WORLD!
LIKE YOU'VE ALMOST PAID THE RENT THE LAST THREE MONTHS?
BUT...
TAKE A WALK, DR. COLOSSUS!
I'M HERE ABOUT THE FURNISHED LAIR?
SOB!
YOU GOT FIRST AND LAST MONTH'S RENT?
I HAVE A MONEY ORDER RIGHT HERE.
THAT THERE MONITOR THING HAS A SATELLITE FEED THAT CAN SEE INTO ANY HOME IN SPRINGFIELD. THE LASER IS FULLY-CHARGED AND THE TORTURE VAT CAN BE FILLED WITH LAVA OR THE SUBSTANCE OF YOUR CHOICE. NO PETS AND NO GIRLS AFTER 11 PM!
GASP!

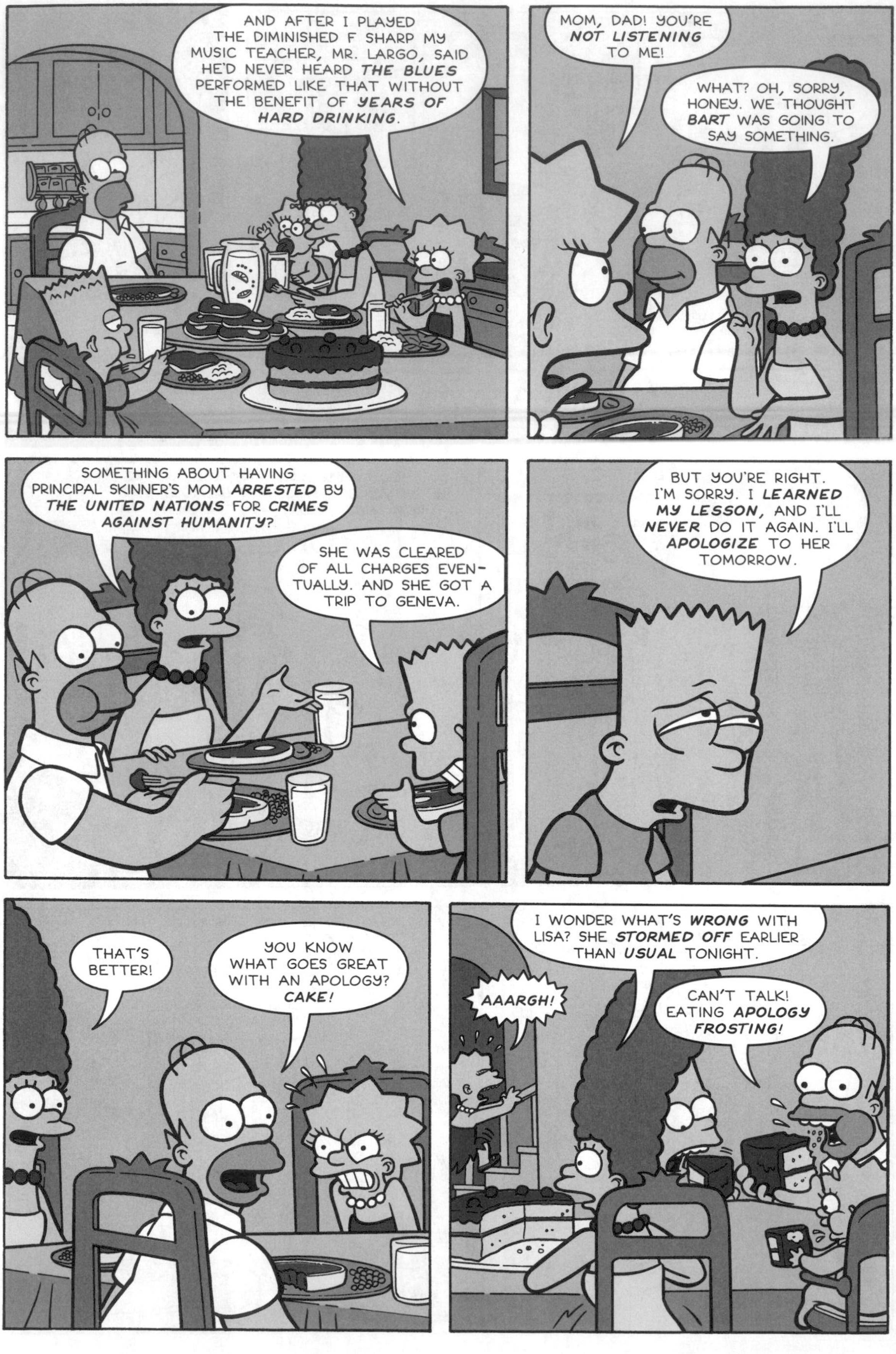
AND AFTER I PLAYED THE DIMINISHED F SHARP MY MUSIC TEACHER, MR. LARGO, SAID HE'D NEVER HEARD **THE BLUES** PERFORMED LIKE THAT WITHOUT THE BENEFIT OF **YEARS OF HARD DRINKING**.
MOM, DAD! YOU'RE **NOT LISTENING** TO ME!
WHAT? OH, SORRY, HONEY. WE THOUGHT **BART** WAS GOING TO SAY SOMETHING.
SOMETHING ABOUT HAVING PRINCIPAL SKINNER'S MOM **ARRESTED** BY **THE UNITED NATIONS** FOR **CRIMES AGAINST HUMANITY**?
SHE WAS CLEARED OF ALL CHARGES EVEN-TUALLY. AND SHE GOT A TRIP TO GENEVA.
BUT YOU'RE RIGHT. I'M SORRY. I **LEARNED MY LESSON,** AND I'LL **NEVER** DO IT AGAIN. I'LL **APOLOGIZE** TO HER TOMORROW.
THAT'S BETTER!
YOU KNOW WHAT GOES GREAT WITH AN APOLOGY? **CAKE!**
I WONDER WHAT'S **WRONG** WITH LISA? SHE **STORMED OFF** EARLIER THAN **USUAL** TONIGHT.
AAARGH!
CAN'T TALK! EATING **APOLOGY FROSTING!**

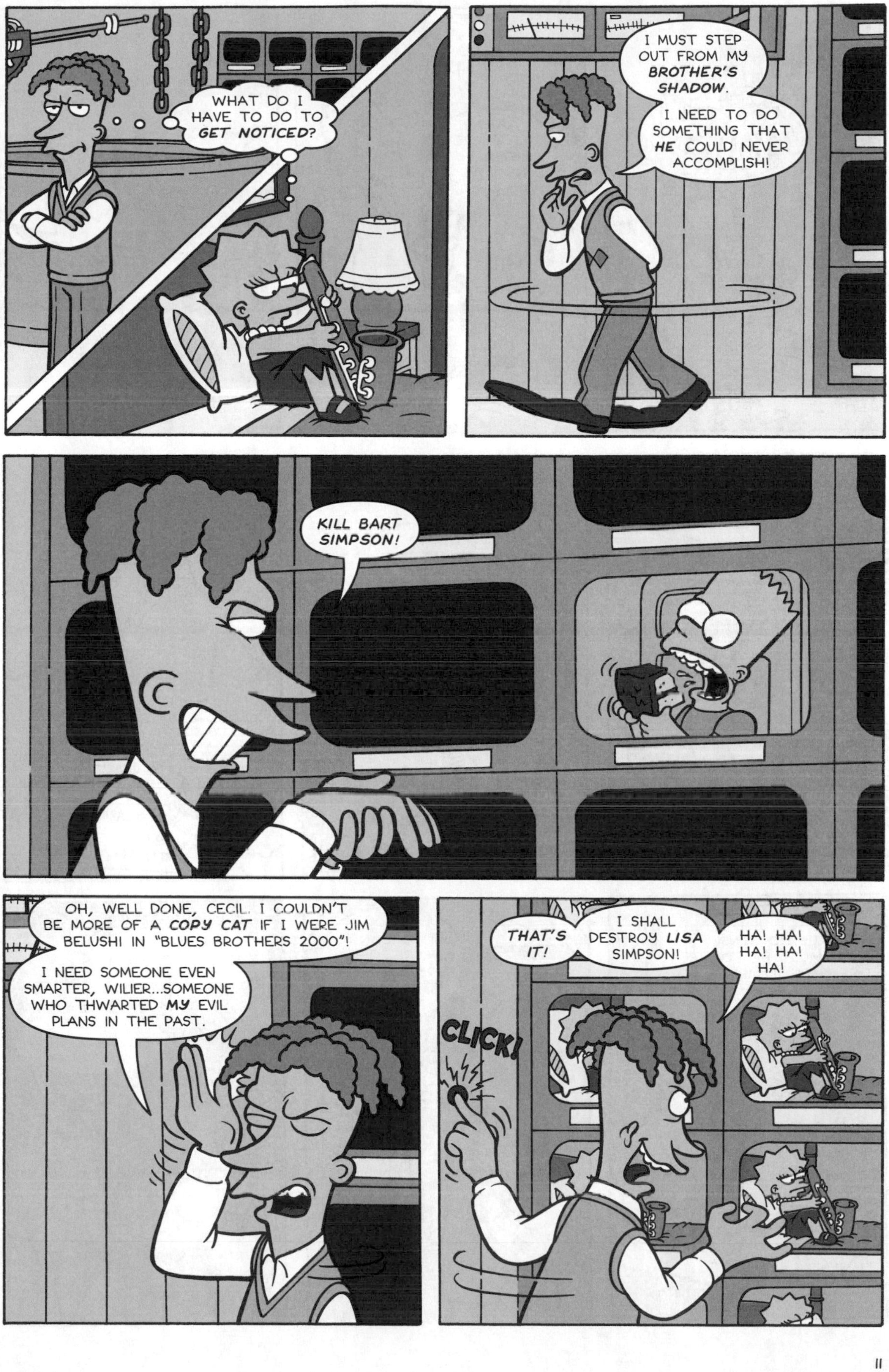
WHAT DO I HAVE TO DO TO GET NOTICED?
I MUST STEP OUT FROM MY BROTHER'S SHADOW.
I NEED TO DO SOMETHING THAT HE COULD NEVER ACCOMPLISH!
KILL BART SIMPSON!
OH, WELL DONE, CECIL. I COULDN'T BE MORE OF A COPY CAT IF I WERE JIM BELUSHI IN "BLUES BROTHERS 2000"!
I NEED SOMEONE EVEN SMARTER, WILIER...SOMEONE WHO THWARTED MY EVIL PLANS IN THE PAST.
THAT'S IT!
I SHALL DESTROY LISA SIMPSON!
HA! HA! HA! HA! HA!
CLICK!

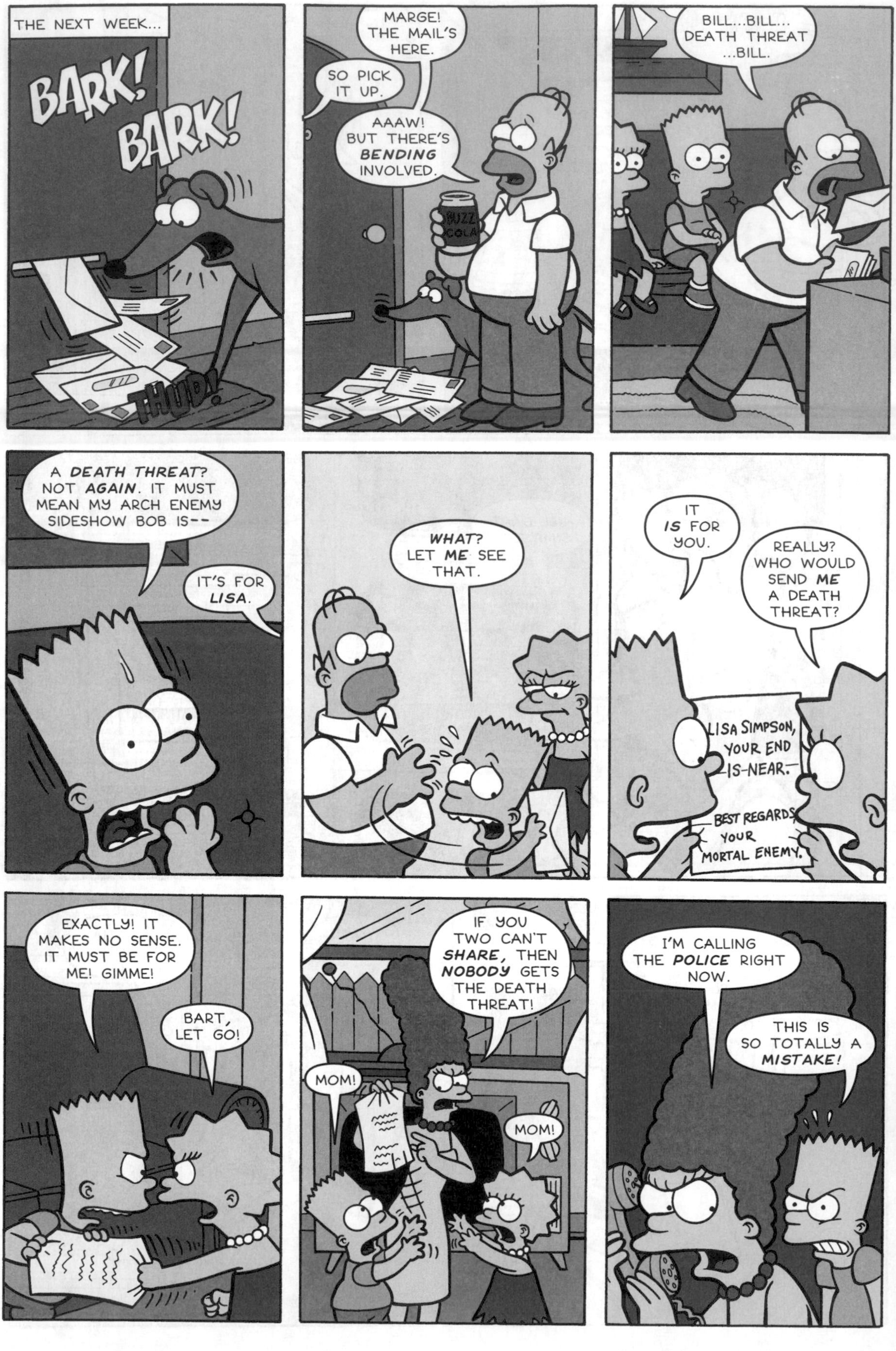
THE NEXT WEEK...
BARK! BARK!
THUD!
MARGE! THE MAIL'S HERE.
SO PICK IT UP.
AAAW! BUT THERE'S BENDING INVOLVED.
BUZZ COLA
BILL...BILL... DEATH THREAT ...BILL.
A DEATH THREAT? NOT AGAIN. IT MUST MEAN MY ARCH ENEMY SIDESHOW BOB IS--
IT'S FOR LISA.
WHAT? LET ME SEE THAT.
IT IS FOR YOU.
REALLY? WHO WOULD SEND ME A DEATH THREAT?
LISA SIMPSON, YOUR END IS NEAR.
BEST REGARDS YOUR MORTAL ENEMY.
EXACTLY! IT MAKES NO SENSE. IT MUST BE FOR ME! GIMME!
BART, LET GO!
IF YOU TWO CAN'T SHARE, THEN NOBODY GETS THE DEATH THREAT!
MOM!
MOM!
I'M CALLING THE POLICE RIGHT NOW.
THIS IS SO TOTALLY A MISTAKE!

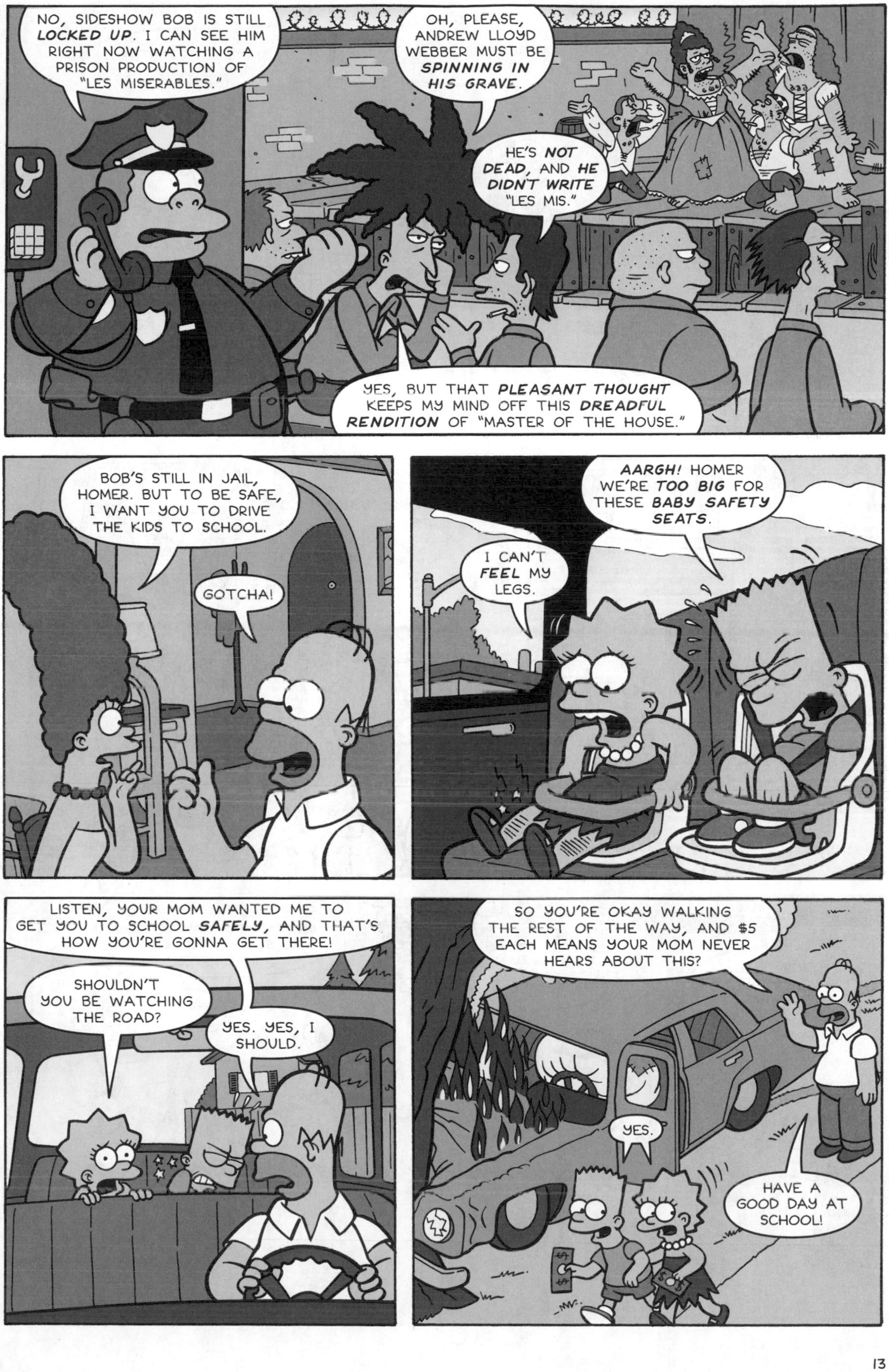
NO, SIDESHOW BOB IS STILL LOCKED UP. I CAN SEE HIM RIGHT NOW WATCHING A PRISON PRODUCTION OF "LES MISERABLES."
OH, PLEASE, ANDREW LLOYD WEBBER MUST BE SPINNING IN HIS GRAVE.
HE'S NOT DEAD, AND HE DIDN'T WRITE "LES MIS."
YES, BUT THAT PLEASANT THOUGHT KEEPS MY MIND OFF THIS DREADFUL RENDITION OF "MASTER OF THE HOUSE."
BOB'S STILL IN JAIL, HOMER. BUT TO BE SAFE, I WANT YOU TO DRIVE THE KIDS TO SCHOOL.
GOTCHA!
AARGH! HOMER WE'RE TOO BIG FOR THESE BABY SAFETY SEATS.
I CAN'T FEEL MY LEGS.
LISTEN, YOUR MOM WANTED ME TO GET YOU TO SCHOOL SAFELY, AND THAT'S HOW YOU'RE GONNA GET THERE!
SHOULDN'T YOU BE WATCHING THE ROAD?
YES. YES, I SHOULD.
SO YOU'RE OKAY WALKING THE REST OF THE WAY, AND $5 EACH MEANS YOUR MOM NEVER HEARS ABOUT THIS?
YES.
HAVE A GOOD DAY AT SCHOOL!

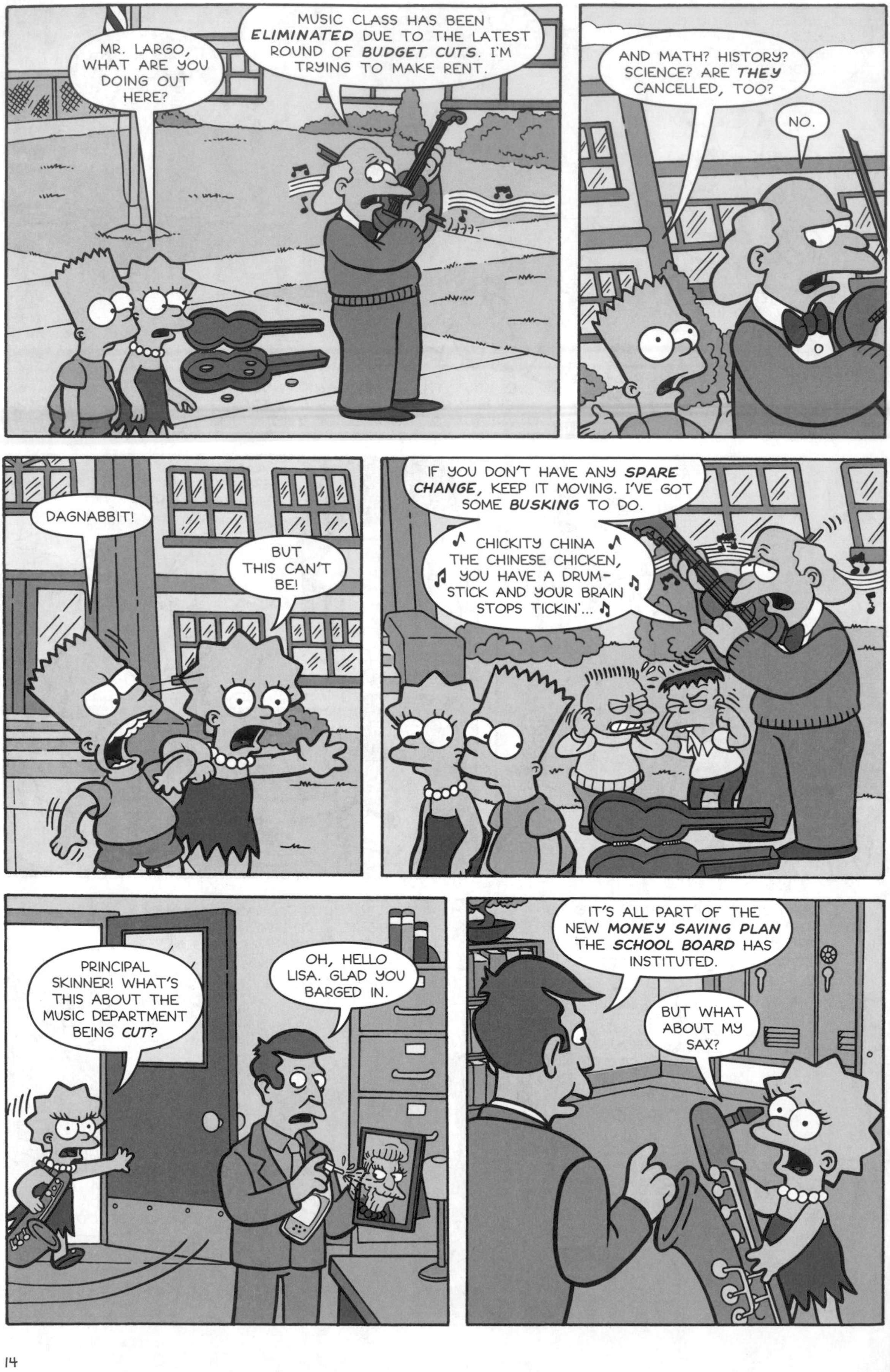
MR. LARGO, WHAT ARE YOU DOING OUT HERE?
MUSIC CLASS HAS BEEN ELIMINATED DUE TO THE LATEST ROUND OF BUDGET CUTS. I'M TRYING TO MAKE RENT.
AND MATH? HISTORY? SCIENCE? ARE THEY CANCELLED, TOO?
NO.
DAGNABBIT!
BUT THIS CAN'T BE!
IF YOU DON'T HAVE ANY SPARE CHANGE, KEEP IT MOVING. I'VE GOT SOME BUSKING TO DO.
♪ CHICKITY CHINA THE CHINESE CHICKEN, ♪ YOU HAVE A DRUMSTICK AND YOUR BRAIN STOPS TICKIN'... ♪
PRINCIPAL SKINNER! WHAT'S THIS ABOUT THE MUSIC DEPARTMENT BEING CUT?
OH, HELLO LISA. GLAD YOU BARGED IN.
IT'S ALL PART OF THE NEW MONEY SAVING PLAN THE SCHOOL BOARD HAS INSTITUTED.
BUT WHAT ABOUT MY SAX?

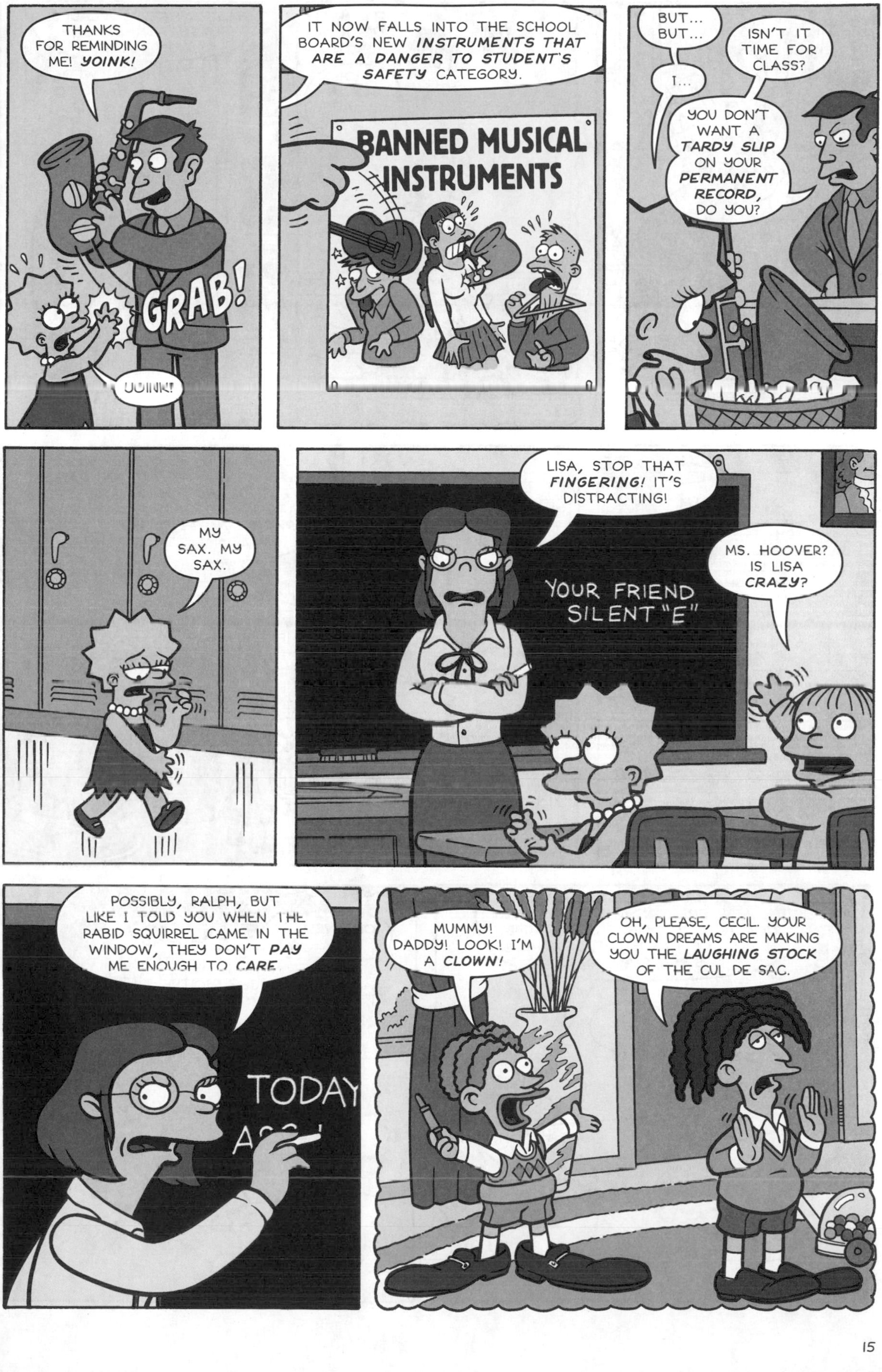
THANKS FOR REMINDING ME! YOINK!
GRAB!
IT NOW FALLS INTO THE SCHOOL BOARD'S NEW INSTRUMENTS THAT ARE A DANGER TO STUDENT'S SAFETY CATEGORY.
BANNED MUSICAL INSTRUMENTS
BUT... BUT...
I...
ISN'T IT TIME FOR CLASS?
YOU DON'T WANT A TARDY SLIP ON YOUR PERMANENT RECORD, DO YOU?
MY SAX. MY SAX.
LISA, STOP THAT FINGERING! IT'S DISTRACTING!
YOUR FRIEND SILENT "E"
MS. HOOVER? IS LISA CRAZY?
POSSIBLY, RALPH, BUT LIKE I TOLD YOU WHEN THE RABID SQUIRREL CAME IN THE WINDOW, THEY DON'T PAY ME ENOUGH TO CARE.
TODAY
MUMMY! DADDY! LOOK! I'M A CLOWN!
OH, PLEASE, CECIL. YOUR CLOWN DREAMS ARE MAKING YOU THE LAUGHING STOCK OF THE CUL DE SAC.

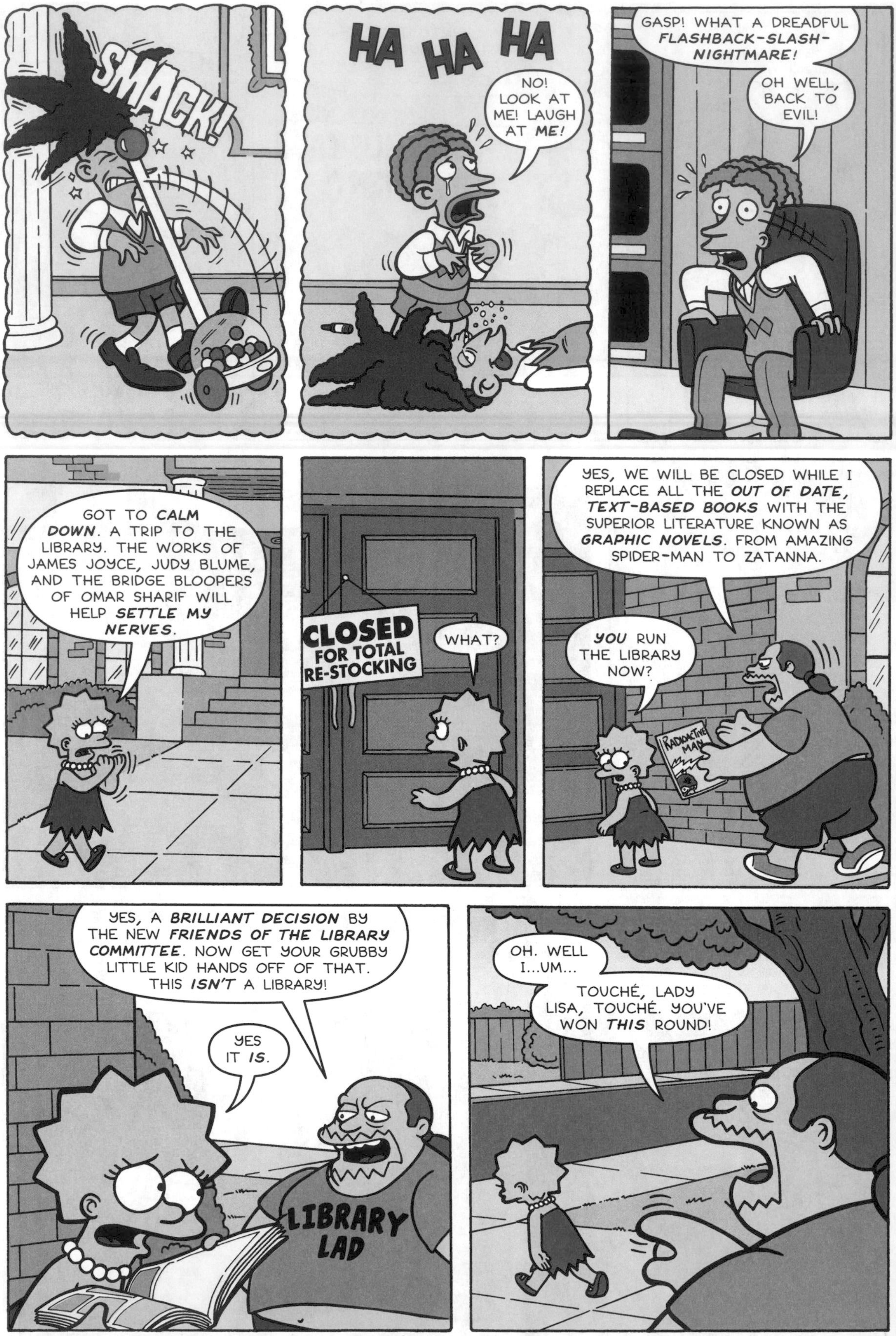
SMACK!
HA HA HA
NO! LOOK AT ME! LAUGH AT ME!
GASP! WHAT A DREADFUL FLASHBACK-SLASH-NIGHTMARE!
OH WELL, BACK TO EVIL!
GOT TO CALM DOWN. A TRIP TO THE LIBRARY. THE WORKS OF JAMES JOYCE, JUDY BLUME, AND THE BRIDGE BLOOPERS OF OMAR SHARIF WILL HELP SETTLE MY NERVES.
CLOSED FOR TOTAL RE-STOCKING
WHAT?
YES, WE WILL BE CLOSED WHILE I REPLACE ALL THE OUT OF DATE, TEXT-BASED BOOKS WITH THE SUPERIOR LITERATURE KNOWN AS GRAPHIC NOVELS. FROM AMAZING SPIDER-MAN TO ZATANNA.
YOU RUN THE LIBRARY NOW?
RADIOACTIVE MAN
YES, A BRILLIANT DECISION BY THE NEW FRIENDS OF THE LIBRARY COMMITTEE. NOW GET YOUR GRUBBY LITTLE KID HANDS OFF OF THAT. THIS ISN'T A LIBRARY!
YES IT IS.
LIBRARY LAD
OH. WELL I...UM...
TOUCHÉ, LADY LISA, TOUCHÉ. YOU'VE WON THIS ROUND!

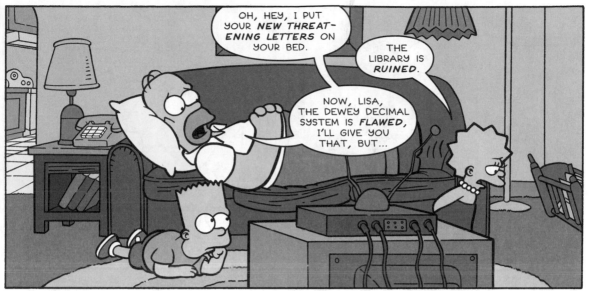

OH, HEY, I PUT YOUR *NEW THREATENING LETTERS* ON YOUR BED.

THE LIBRARY IS *RUINED*.

NOW, LISA, THE DEWEY DECIMAL SYSTEM IS *FLAWED*, I'LL GIVE YOU THAT, BUT...

I DON'T GET IT! WHY WOULD SIDESHOW BOB SEND LETTERS TO *YOU* TO GET TO *ME*?

MAYBE THIS ISN'T ABOUT *YOU*. MAYBE HE'S AFTER *ME*!

HA, HA! YEAH, RIGHT!

WHAT? I'M NOT *IMPORTANT ENOUGH* TO HAVE A *MORTAL ENEMY*?

EXACTLY.

GRRRRRR. LET'S JUST WATCH "ITCHY AND SCRATCHY." I NEED TO RELAX.

HEY, HEY, KIDS! ITCHY AND SCRATCHY HAVE BEEN PERMANENTLY PUT ON *HIATUS*.

AND IT'S NOT BECAUSE SOMEONE'S *BLACKMAILING* ME WITH PICTURES FROM MY VACATION IN BANGKOK.

IN ITS PLACE, HERE'S SOMETHING JUST AS GOOD FROM ENGLAND. P.G. WODEHOUSE'S "JEEVES AND WOOSTER"!

I SAY, JEEVES, I'M IN A PICKLE. I HAVE A DATE WITH BOTH CECILY AND BEATRICE ON THE DAY I'M SUPPOSED TO MARRY THE QUEEN.

YOU, SIR, ARE A *BLOODY IDIOT*.

RATS! IT'S BASED ON ONE OF THE *LATER* NOVELS!

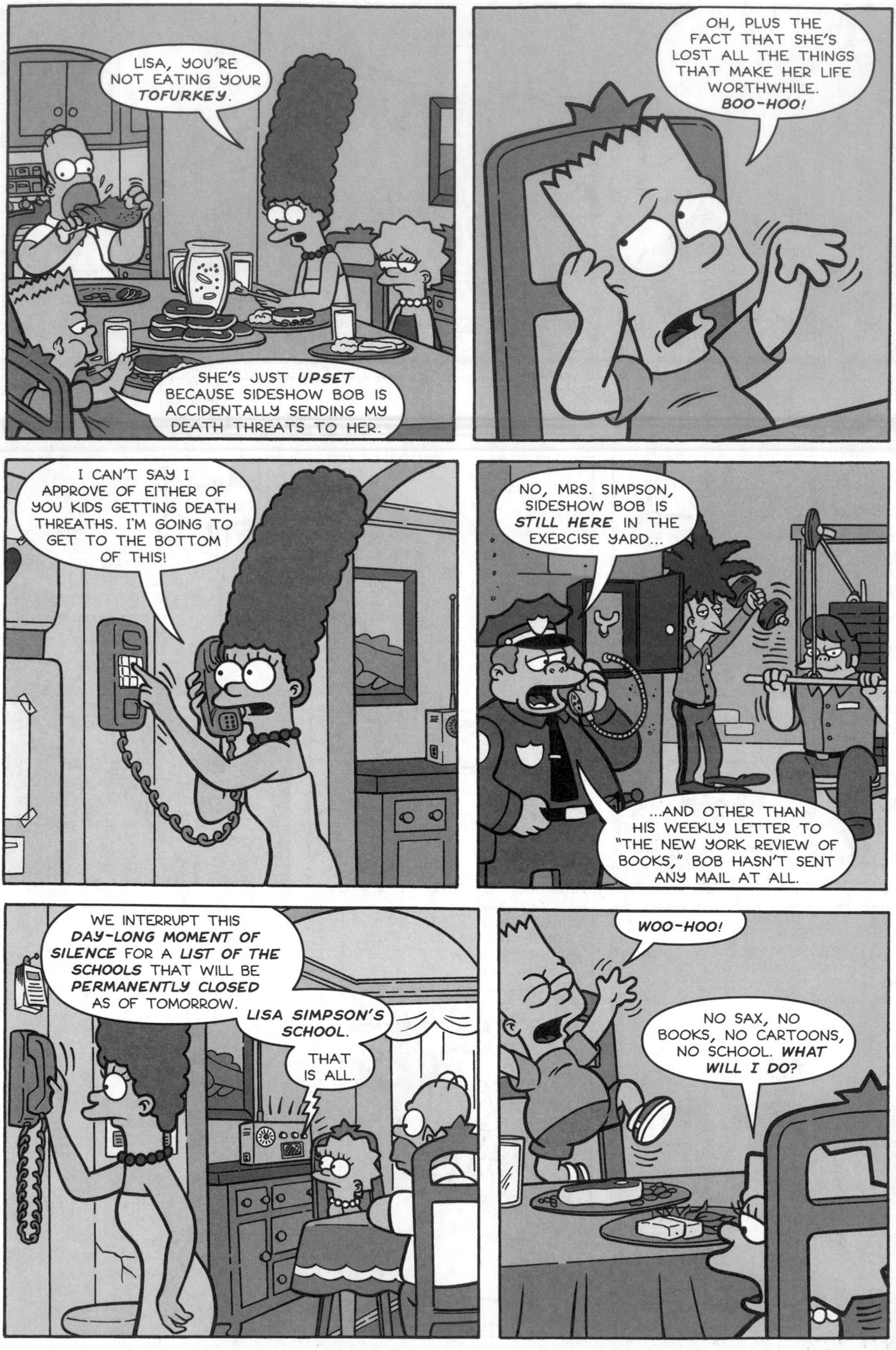
LISA, YOU'RE NOT EATING YOUR TOFURKEY.
SHE'S JUST UPSET BECAUSE SIDESHOW BOB IS ACCIDENTALLY SENDING MY DEATH THREATS TO HER.
OH, PLUS THE FACT THAT SHE'S LOST ALL THE THINGS THAT MAKE HER LIFE WORTHWHILE. BOO-HOO!
I CAN'T SAY I APPROVE OF EITHER OF YOU KIDS GETTING DEATH THREATHS. I'M GOING TO GET TO THE BOTTOM OF THIS!
NO, MRS. SIMPSON, SIDESHOW BOB IS STILL HERE IN THE EXERCISE YARD...
...AND OTHER THAN HIS WEEKLY LETTER TO "THE NEW YORK REVIEW OF BOOKS," BOB HASN'T SENT ANY MAIL AT ALL.
WE INTERRUPT THIS DAY-LONG MOMENT OF SILENCE FOR A LIST OF THE SCHOOLS THAT WILL BE PERMANENTLY CLOSED AS OF TOMORROW.
LISA SIMPSON'S SCHOOL.
THAT IS ALL.
WOO-HOO!
NO SAX, NO BOOKS, NO CARTOONS, NO SCHOOL. WHAT WILL I DO?

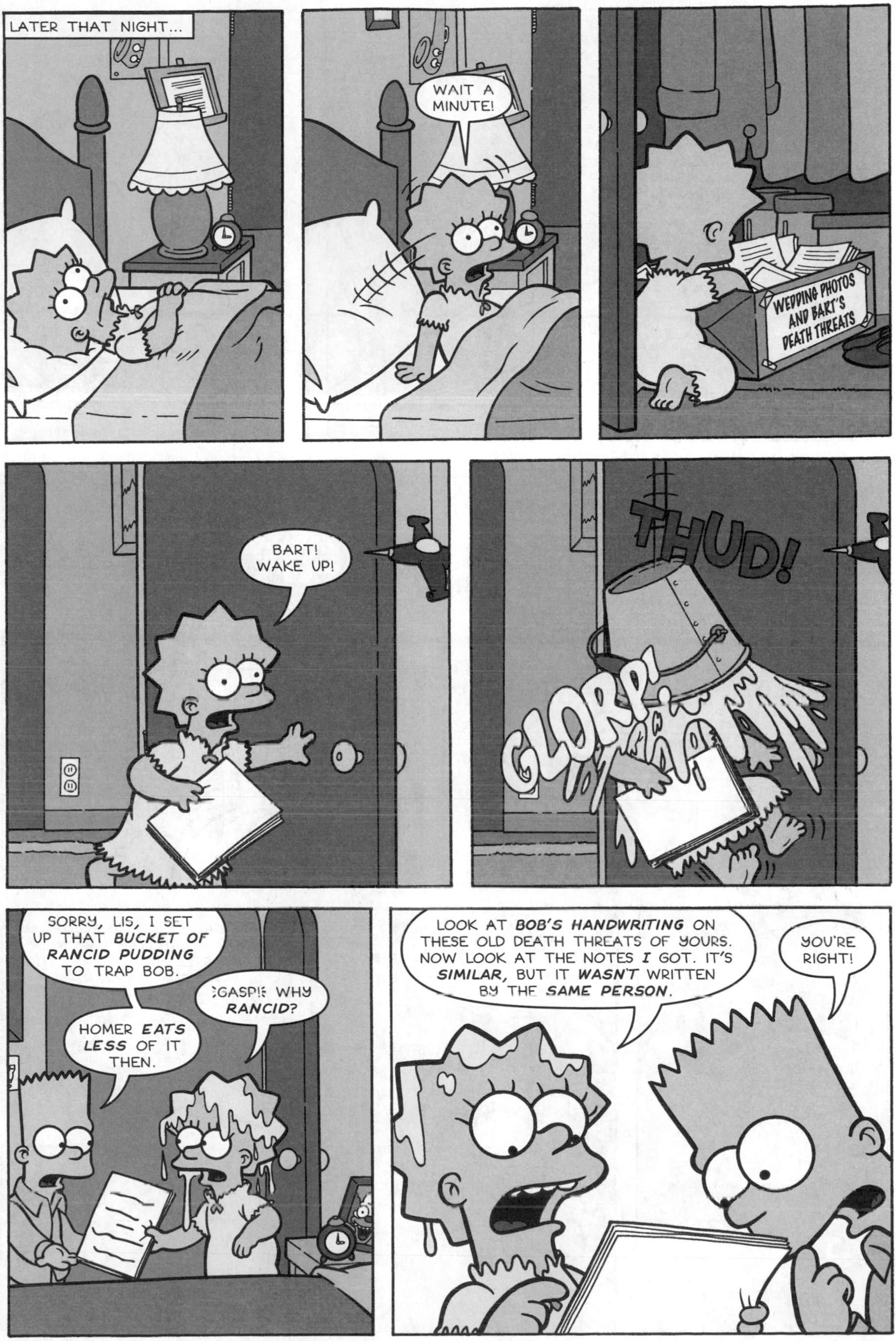
LATER THAT NIGHT...
WAIT A MINUTE!
WEDDING PHOTOS AND BART'S DEATH THREATS
BART! WAKE UP!
THUD!
GLORP!
SORRY, LIS, I SET UP THAT BUCKET OF RANCID PUDDING TO TRAP BOB.
¡GASP!¡ WHY RANCID?
HOMER EATS LESS OF IT THEN.
LOOK AT BOB'S HANDWRITING ON THESE OLD DEATH THREATS OF YOURS. NOW LOOK AT THE NOTES I GOT. IT'S SIMILAR, BUT IT WASN'T WRITTEN BY THE SAME PERSON.
YOU'RE RIGHT!

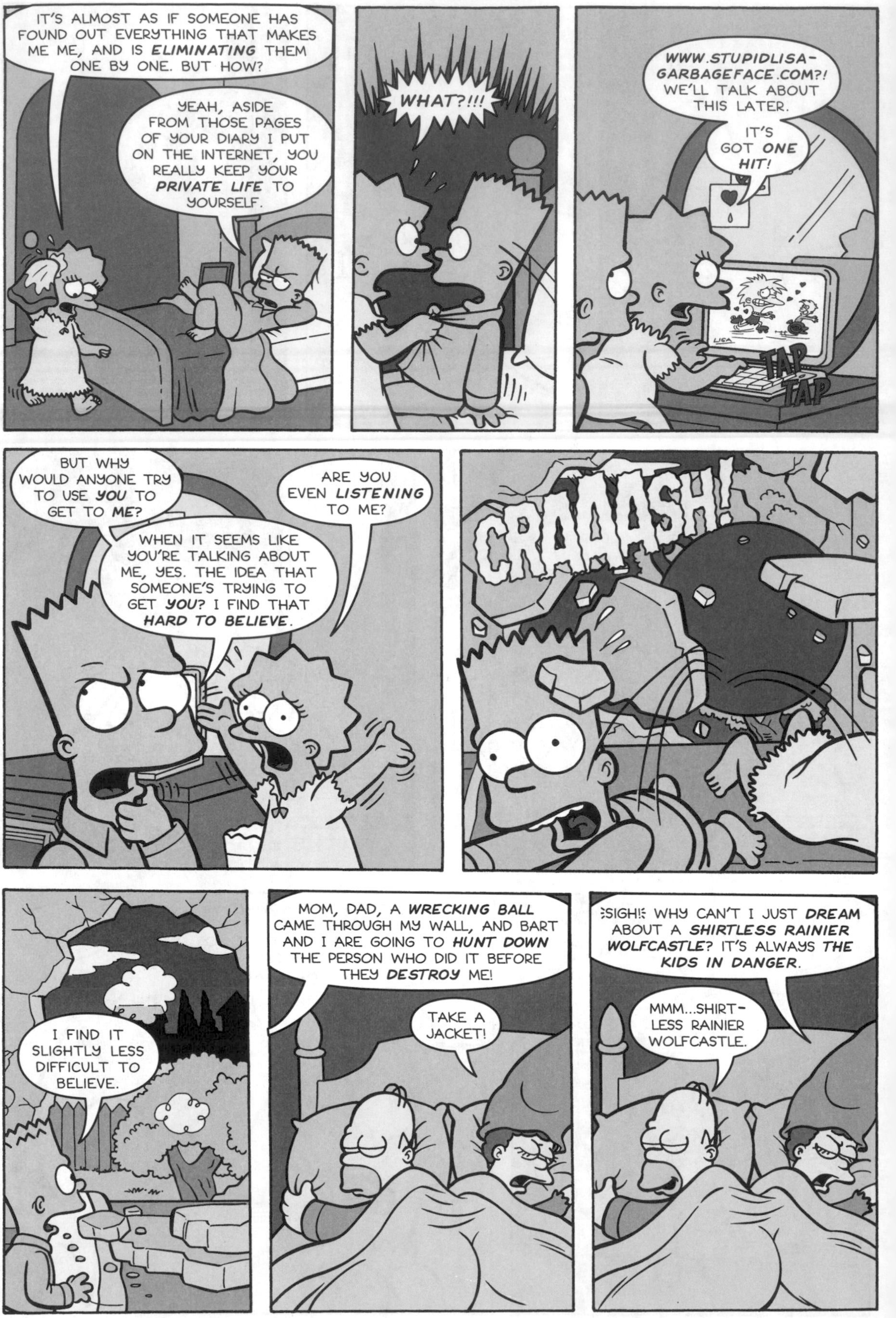
IT'S ALMOST AS IF SOMEONE HAS FOUND OUT EVERYTHING THAT MAKES ME ME, AND IS ELIMINATING THEM ONE BY ONE. BUT HOW?
YEAH, ASIDE FROM THOSE PAGES OF YOUR DIARY I PUT ON THE INTERNET, YOU REALLY KEEP YOUR PRIVATE LIFE TO YOURSELF.
WHAT?!!!
WWW.STUPIDLISA-GARBAGEFACE.COM?! WE'LL TALK ABOUT THIS LATER.
IT'S GOT ONE HIT!
LISA
TAP TAP
BUT WHY WOULD ANYONE TRY TO USE YOU TO GET TO ME?
WHEN IT SEEMS LIKE YOU'RE TALKING ABOUT ME, YES. THE IDEA THAT SOMEONE'S TRYING TO GET YOU? I FIND THAT HARD TO BELIEVE.
ARE YOU EVEN LISTENING TO ME?
CRAAASH!
I FIND IT SLIGHTLY LESS DIFFICULT TO BELIEVE.
MOM, DAD, A WRECKING BALL CAME THROUGH MY WALL, AND BART AND I ARE GOING TO HUNT DOWN THE PERSON WHO DID IT BEFORE THEY DESTROY ME!
TAKE A JACKET!
SIGH! WHY CAN'T I JUST DREAM ABOUT A SHIRTLESS RAINIER WOLFCASTLE? IT'S ALWAYS THE KIDS IN DANGER.
MMM...SHIRT-LESS RAINIER WOLFCASTLE.

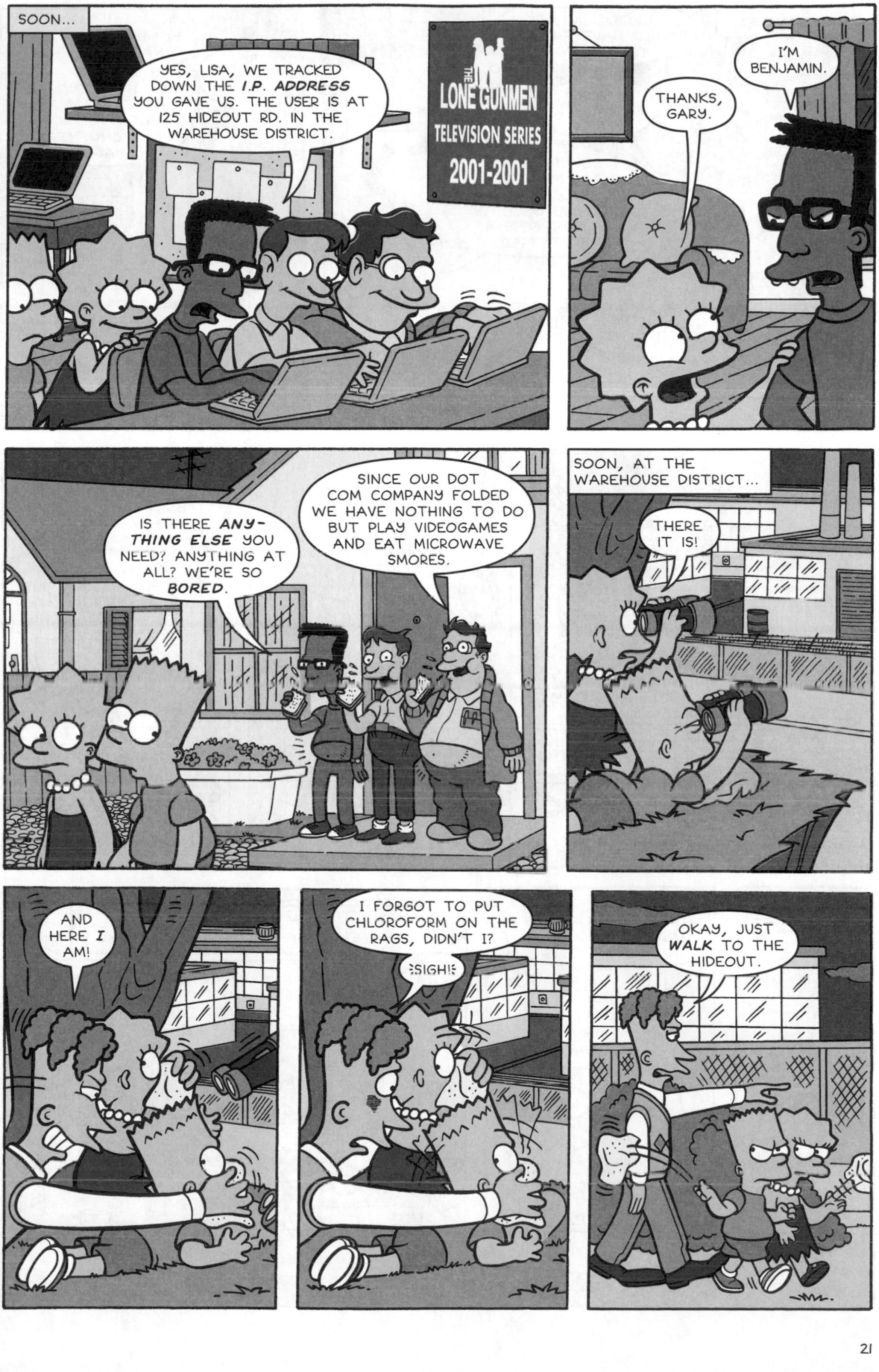
SOON...
YES, LISA, WE TRACKED DOWN THE I.P. ADDRESS YOU GAVE US. THE USER IS AT 125 HIDEOUT RD. IN THE WAREHOUSE DISTRICT.
THE LONE GUNMEN TELEVISION SERIES 2001-2001
THANKS, GARY.
I'M BENJAMIN.
IS THERE ANYTHING ELSE YOU NEED? ANYTHING AT ALL? WE'RE SO BORED.
SINCE OUR DOT COM COMPANY FOLDED WE HAVE NOTHING TO DO BUT PLAY VIDEOGAMES AND EAT MICROWAVE SMORES.
SOON, AT THE WAREHOUSE DISTRICT...
THERE IT IS!
AND HERE I AM!
I FORGOT TO PUT CHLOROFORM ON THE RAGS, DIDN'T I?
SIGH!
OKAY, JUST WALK TO THE HIDEOUT.

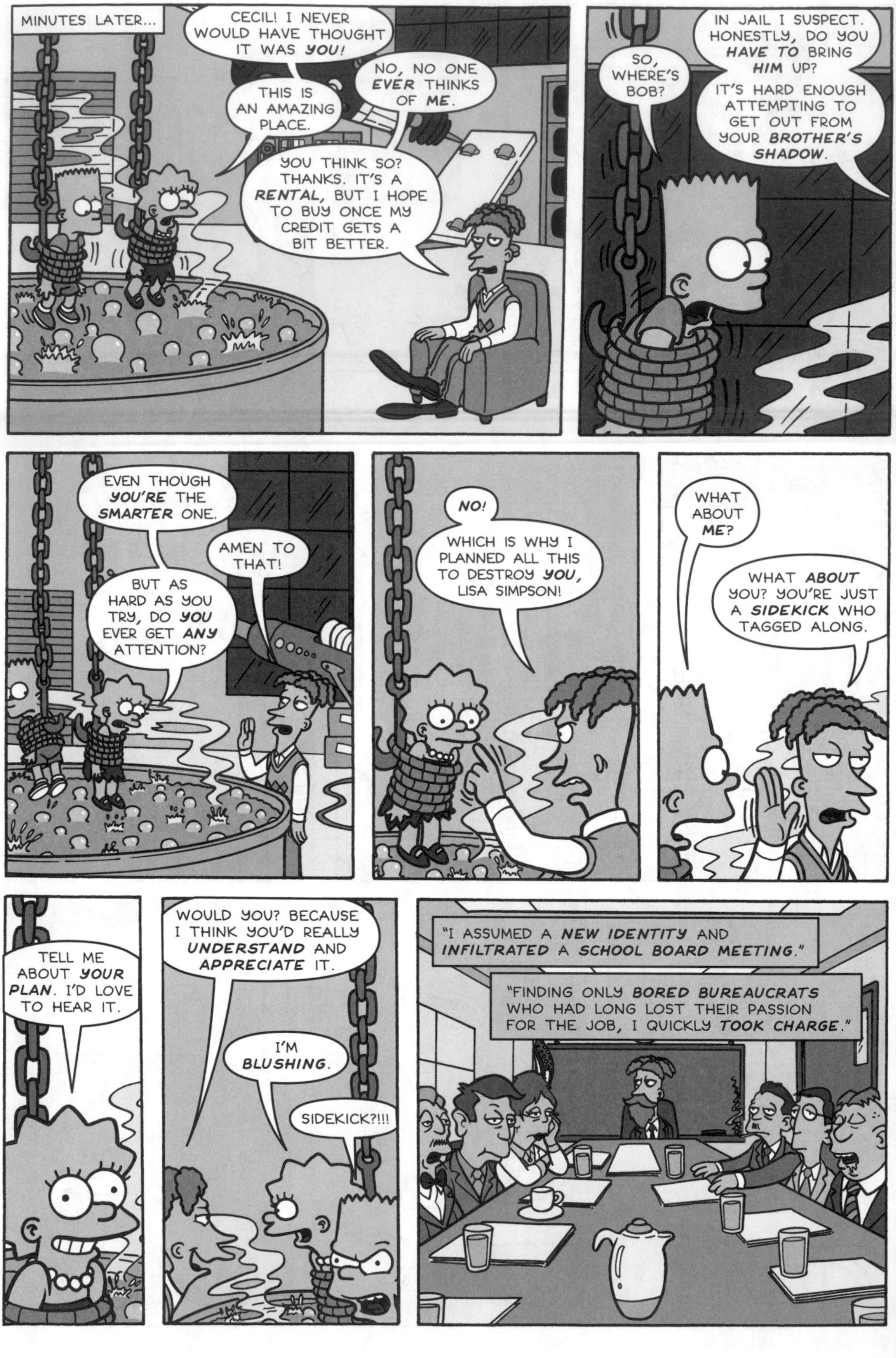
MINUTES LATER...
CECIL! I NEVER WOULD HAVE THOUGHT IT WAS YOU!
THIS IS AN AMAZING PLACE.
NO, NO ONE EVER THINKS OF ME.
YOU THINK SO? THANKS. IT'S A RENTAL, BUT I HOPE TO BUY ONCE MY CREDIT GETS A BIT BETTER.
SO, WHERE'S BOB?
IN JAIL I SUSPECT. HONESTLY, DO YOU HAVE TO BRING HIM UP?
IT'S HARD ENOUGH ATTEMPTING TO GET OUT FROM YOUR BROTHER'S SHADOW.
EVEN THOUGH YOU'RE THE SMARTER ONE.
AMEN TO THAT!
BUT AS HARD AS YOU TRY, DO YOU EVER GET ANY ATTENTION?
NO!
WHICH IS WHY I PLANNED ALL THIS TO DESTROY YOU, LISA SIMPSON!
WHAT ABOUT ME?
WHAT ABOUT YOU? YOU'RE JUST A SIDEKICK WHO TAGGED ALONG.
TELL ME ABOUT YOUR PLAN. I'D LOVE TO HEAR IT.
WOULD YOU? BECAUSE I THINK YOU'D REALLY UNDERSTAND AND APPRECIATE IT.
I'M BLUSHING.
SIDEKICK?!!!
"I ASSUMED A NEW IDENTITY AND INFILTRATED A SCHOOL BOARD MEETING."
"FINDING ONLY BORED BUREAUCRATS WHO HAD LONG LOST THEIR PASSION FOR THE JOB, I QUICKLY TOOK CHARGE."

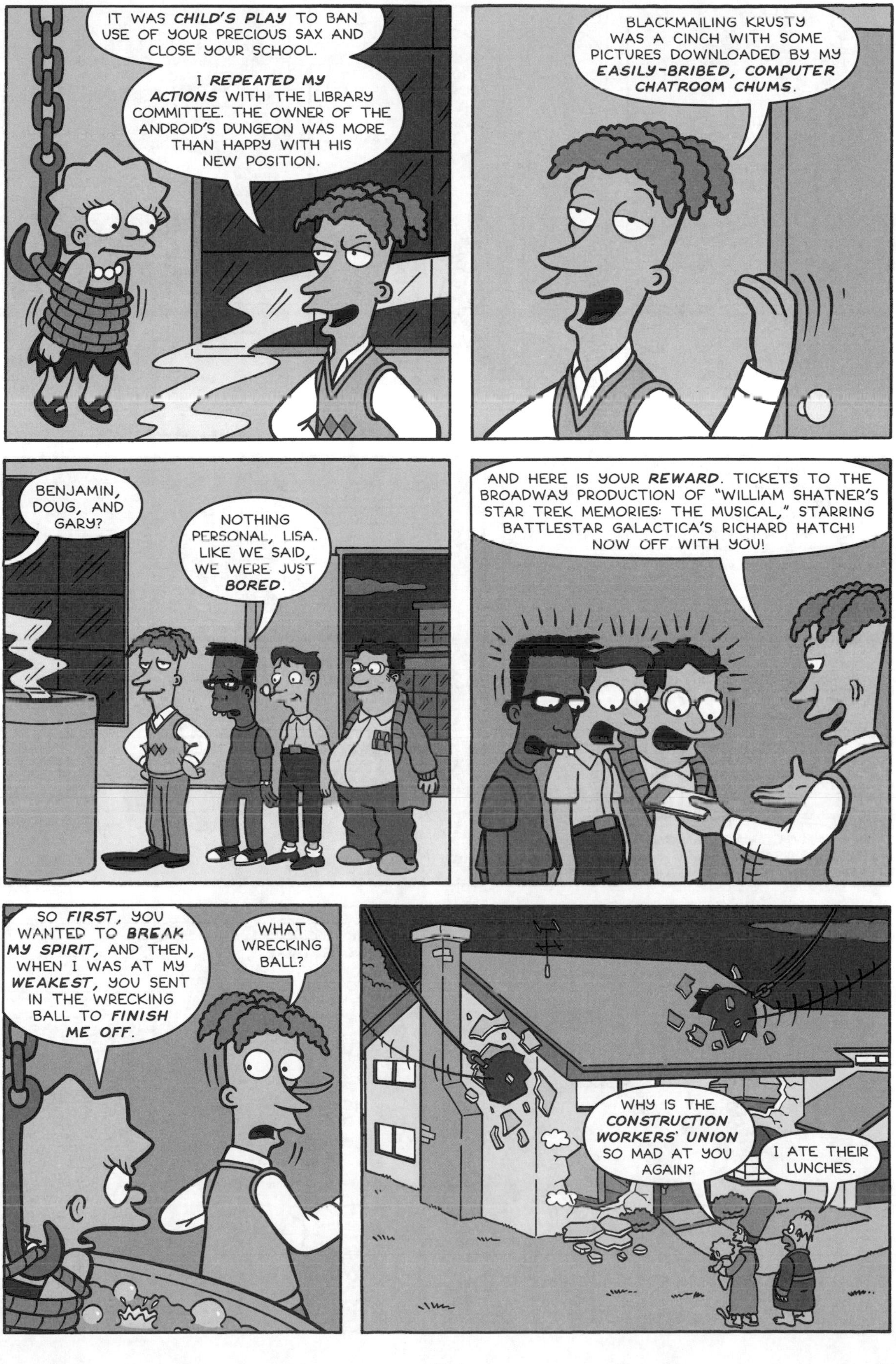
IT WAS CHILD'S PLAY TO BAN USE OF YOUR PRECIOUS SAX AND CLOSE YOUR SCHOOL.
I REPEATED MY ACTIONS WITH THE LIBRARY COMMITTEE. THE OWNER OF THE ANDROID'S DUNGEON WAS MORE THAN HAPPY WITH HIS NEW POSITION.
BLACKMAILING KRUSTY WAS A CINCH WITH SOME PICTURES DOWNLOADED BY MY EASILY-BRIBED, COMPUTER CHATROOM CHUMS.
BENJAMIN, DOUG, AND GARY?
NOTHING PERSONAL, LISA. LIKE WE SAID, WE WERE JUST BORED.
AND HERE IS YOUR REWARD. TICKETS TO THE BROADWAY PRODUCTION OF "WILLIAM SHATNER'S STAR TREK MEMORIES: THE MUSICAL," STARRING BATTLESTAR GALACTICA'S RICHARD HATCH! NOW OFF WITH YOU!
SO FIRST, YOU WANTED TO BREAK MY SPIRIT, AND THEN, WHEN I WAS AT MY WEAKEST, YOU SENT IN THE WRECKING BALL TO FINISH ME OFF.
WHAT WRECKING BALL?
WHY IS THE CONSTRUCTION WORKERS' UNION SO MAD AT YOU AGAIN?
I ATE THEIR LUNCHES.

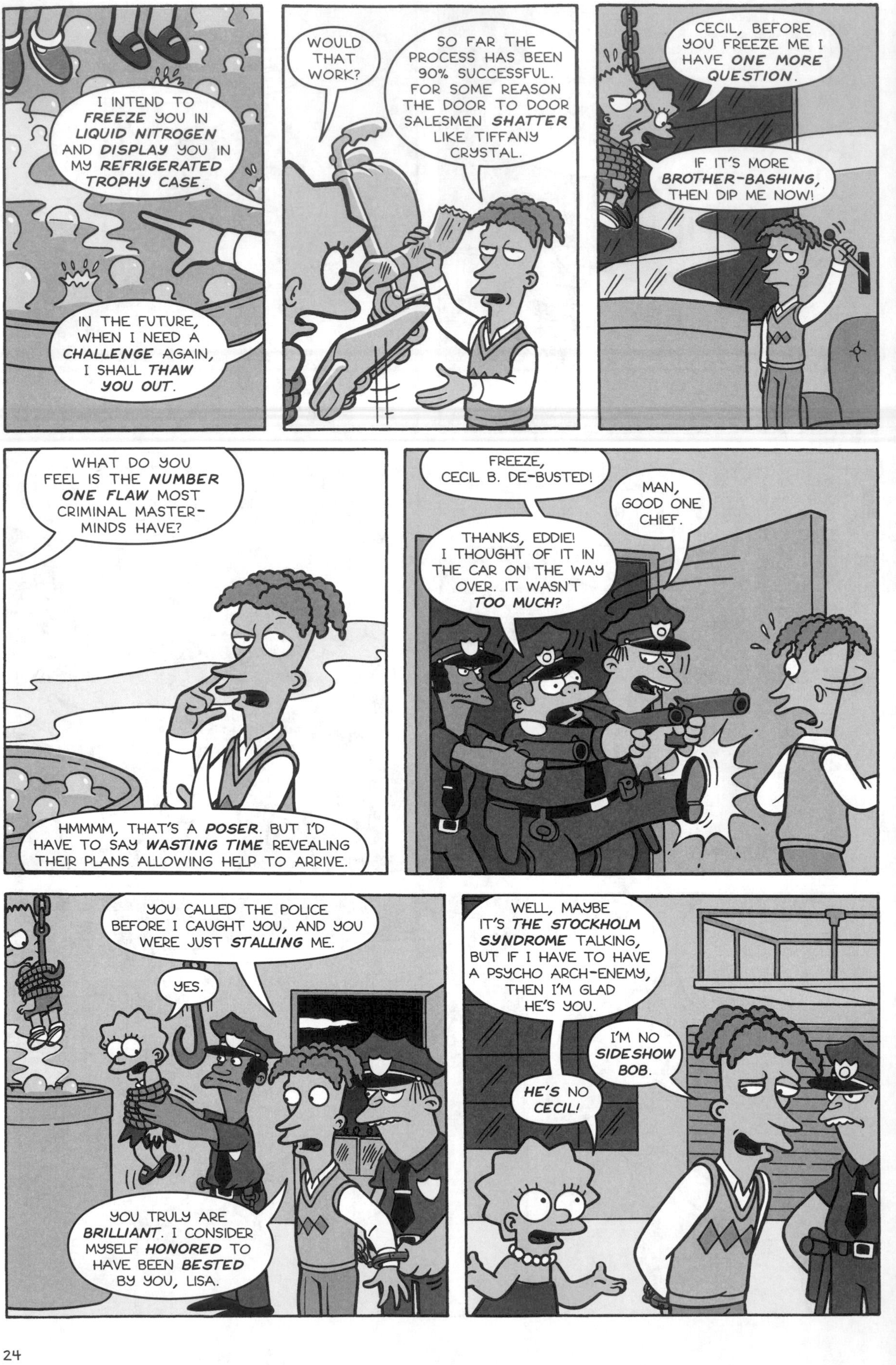
I INTEND TO FREEZE YOU IN LIQUID NITROGEN AND DISPLAY YOU IN MY REFRIGERATED TROPHY CASE.
IN THE FUTURE, WHEN I NEED A CHALLENGE AGAIN, I SHALL THAW YOU OUT.
WOULD THAT WORK?
SO FAR THE PROCESS HAS BEEN 90% SUCCESSFUL. FOR SOME REASON THE DOOR TO DOOR SALESMEN SHATTER LIKE TIFFANY CRYSTAL.
CECIL, BEFORE YOU FREEZE ME I HAVE ONE MORE QUESTION.
IF IT'S MORE BROTHER-BASHING, THEN DIP ME NOW!
WHAT DO YOU FEEL IS THE NUMBER ONE FLAW MOST CRIMINAL MASTER-MINDS HAVE?
HMMMM, THAT'S A POSER. BUT I'D HAVE TO SAY WASTING TIME REVEALING THEIR PLANS ALLOWING HELP TO ARRIVE.
FREEZE, CECIL B. DE-BUSTED!
THANKS, EDDIE! I THOUGHT OF IT IN THE CAR ON THE WAY OVER. IT WASN'T TOO MUCH?
MAN, GOOD ONE CHIEF.
YOU CALLED THE POLICE BEFORE I CAUGHT YOU, AND YOU WERE JUST STALLING ME.
YES.
YOU TRULY ARE BRILLIANT. I CONSIDER MYSELF HONORED TO HAVE BEEN BESTED BY YOU, LISA.
WELL, MAYBE IT'S THE STOCKHOLM SYNDROME TALKING, BUT IF I HAVE TO HAVE A PSYCHO ARCH-ENEMY, THEN I'M GLAD HE'S YOU.
I'M NO SIDESHOW BOB.
HE'S NO CECIL!

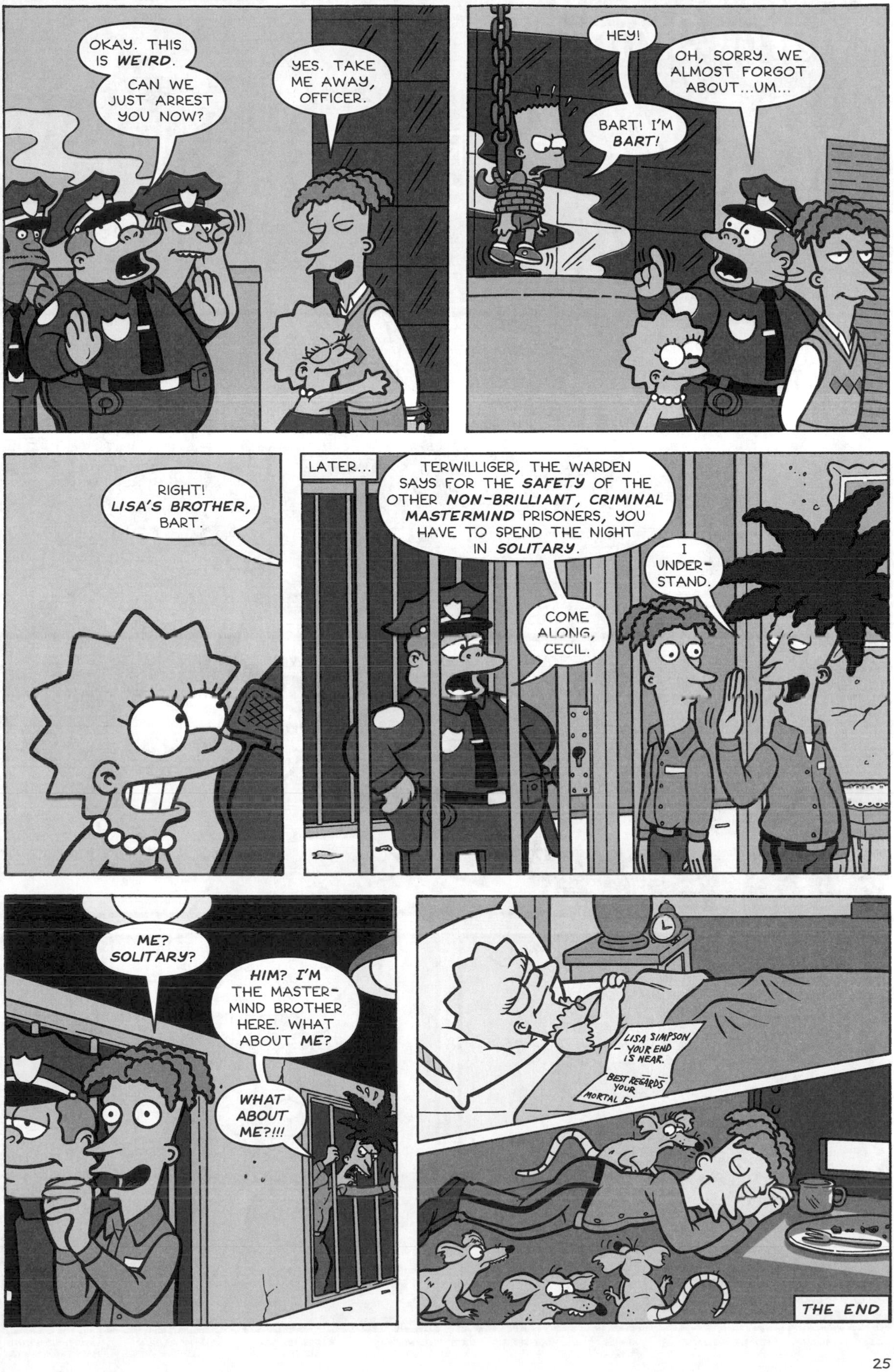
OKAY. THIS IS WEIRD.
CAN WE JUST ARREST YOU NOW?
YES. TAKE ME AWAY, OFFICER.
HEY!
BART! I'M BART!
OH, SORRY. WE ALMOST FORGOT ABOUT...UM...
RIGHT! LISA'S BROTHER, BART.
LATER...
TERWILLIGER, THE WARDEN SAYS FOR THE SAFETY OF THE OTHER NON-BRILLIANT, CRIMINAL MASTERMIND PRISONERS, YOU HAVE TO SPEND THE NIGHT IN SOLITARY.
COME ALONG, CECIL.
I UNDERSTAND.
ME? SOLITARY?
HIM? I'M THE MASTERMIND BROTHER HERE. WHAT ABOUT ME?
WHAT ABOUT ME?!!!
LISA SIMPSON - YOUR END IS NEAR.
BEST REGARDS YOUR MORTAL
THE END

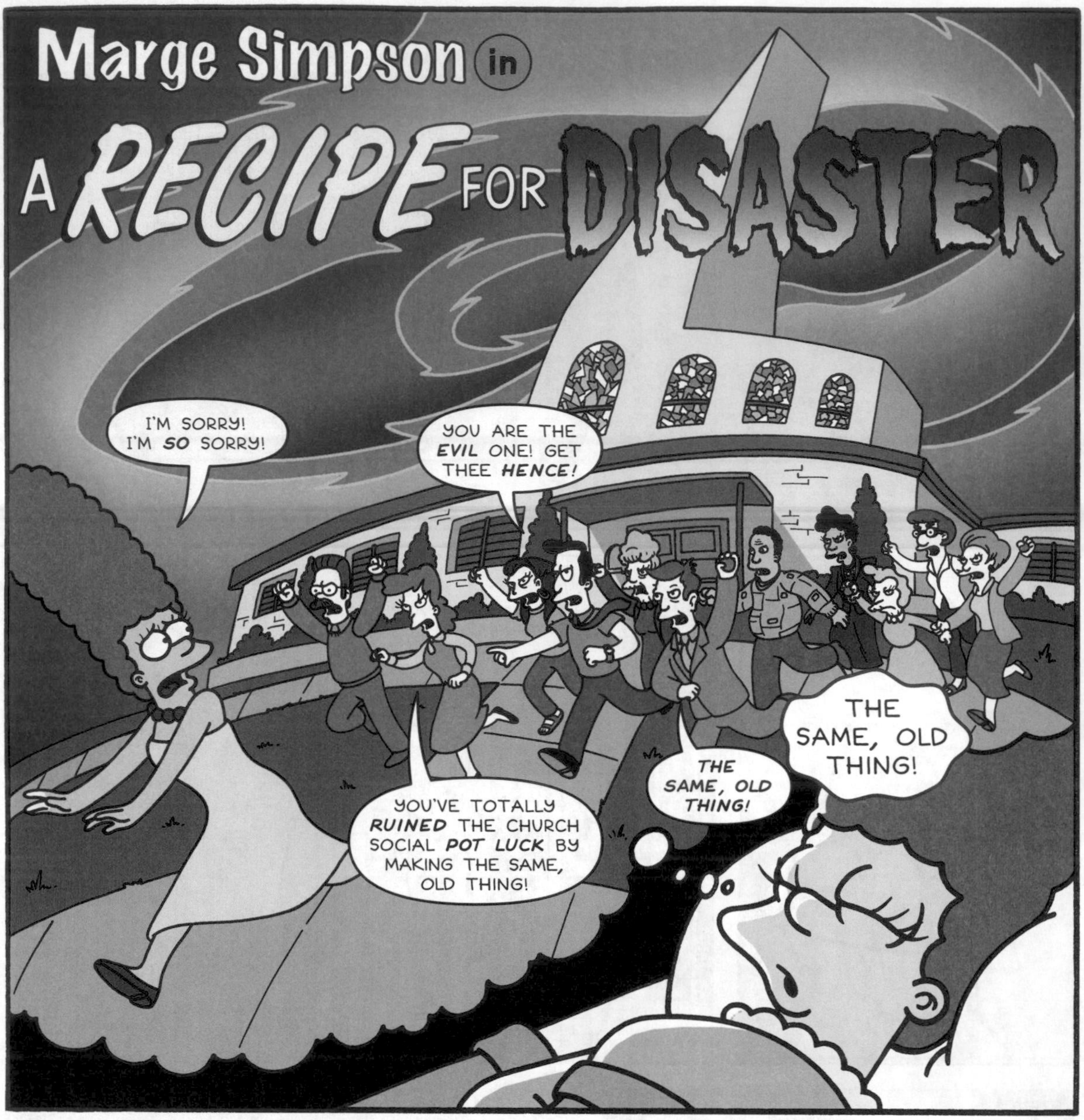
Marge Simpson in
A RECIPE FOR DISASTER
I'M SORRY! I'M SO SORRY!
YOU ARE THE EVIL ONE! GET THEE HENCE!
YOU'VE TOTALLY RUINED THE CHURCH SOCIAL POT LUCK BY MAKING THE SAME, OLD THING!
THE SAME, OLD THING!
THE SAME, OLD THING!

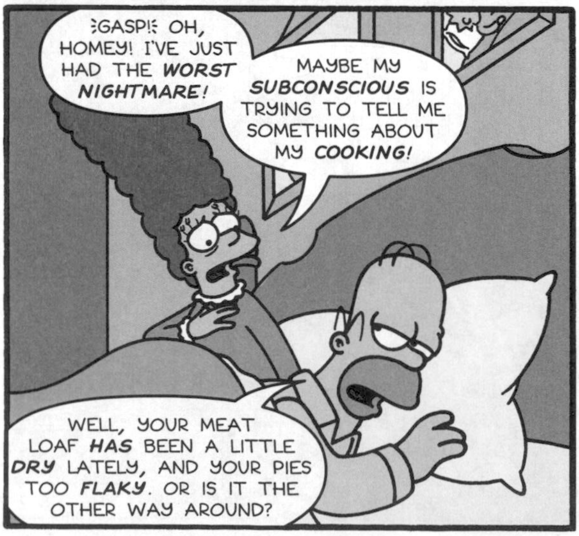
:GASP!: OH, HOMEY! I'VE JUST HAD THE WORST NIGHTMARE!
MAYBE MY SUBCONSCIOUS IS TRYING TO TELL ME SOMETHING ABOUT MY COOKING!
WELL, YOUR MEAT LOAF HAS BEEN A LITTLE DRY LATELY, AND YOUR PIES TOO FLAKY. OR IS IT THE OTHER WAY AROUND?

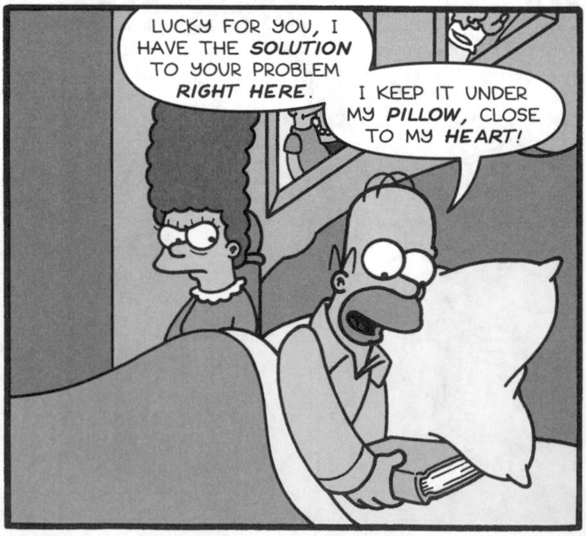
LUCKY FOR YOU, I HAVE THE SOLUTION TO YOUR PROBLEM RIGHT HERE.
I KEEP IT UNDER MY PILLOW, CLOSE TO MY HEART!

JESSE L. MCCANN & SERAN WILLIAMS SCRIPT · KIM LE PENCILS · MIKE ROTE INKS · ART VILLANUEVA COLORS · KAREN BATES LETTERS · BILL MORRISON EDITOR · MATT GROENING HAPPY HOMEMAKER

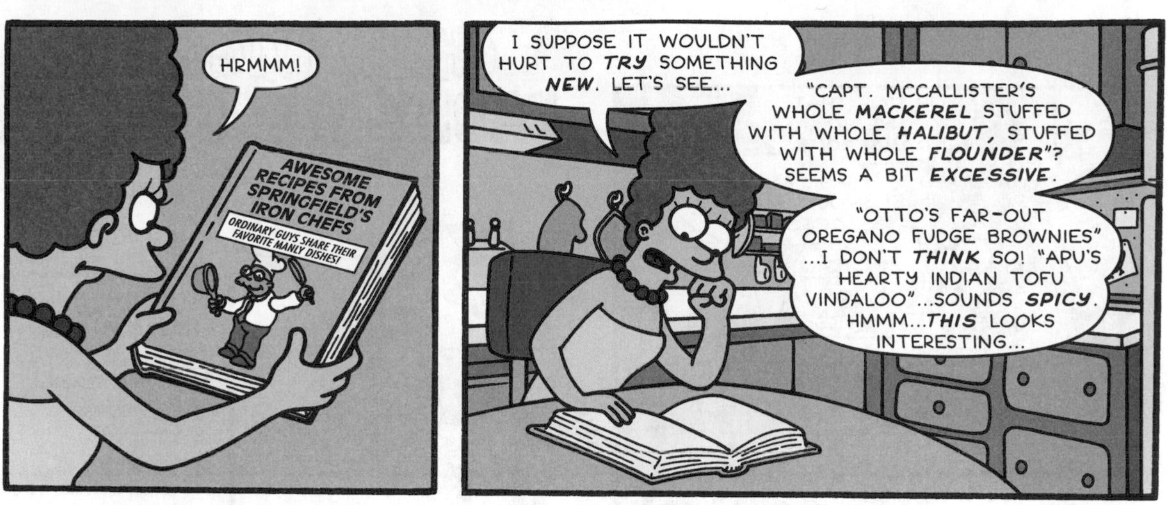
HRMMM!
AWESOME RECIPES FROM SPRINGFIELD'S IRON CHEFS
ORDINARY GUYS SHARE THEIR FAVORITE MANLY DISHES!
I SUPPOSE IT WOULDN'T HURT TO TRY SOMETHING NEW. LET'S SEE...
"CAPT. MCCALLISTER'S WHOLE MACKEREL STUFFED WITH WHOLE HALIBUT, STUFFED WITH WHOLE FLOUNDER"? SEEMS A BIT EXCESSIVE.
"OTTO'S FAR-OUT OREGANO FUDGE BROWNIES" ...I DON'T THINK SO! "APU'S HEARTY INDIAN TOFU VINDALOO"...SOUNDS SPICY. HMMM...THIS LOOKS INTERESTING...

GROUNDSKEEPER WILLIE'S HAWAIIAN HAGGIS LUAU SURPRISE

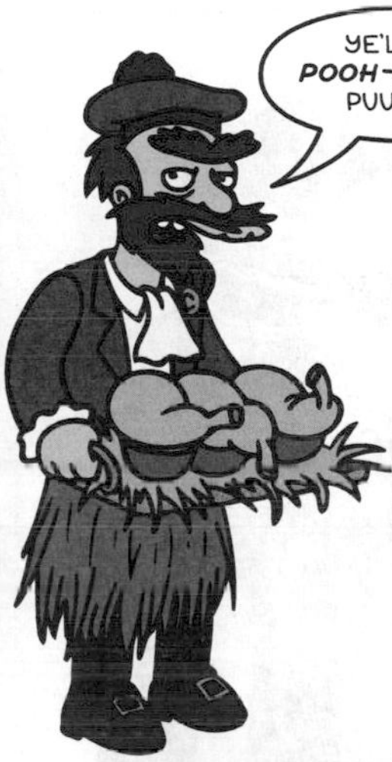
YE'LL NOT POOH-POOH MY PUU PUUS!

INGREDIENTS:
4 medium sheep's plucks (that's a stomach bag, yeh noodle-headed newbie!)
2 lb. dry oatmeal
1 lb. suet
1 lb. lamb's liver
2 1/2 cups stock (any kind will do)
1 large chopped onion
1/2 tsp. cayenne pepper, jamaica pepper and salt
1 over-ripened pineapple
4 coconuts, sawed in two
1 raw turnip (to eat while yeh cook)

1.

PREPARATION:
Boil liver and parboil the onion, then mince them together. Lightly brown the oatmeal. Mix all ingredients together. Fill each sheep's pluck with the mixture, pressing it down to remove all the air.

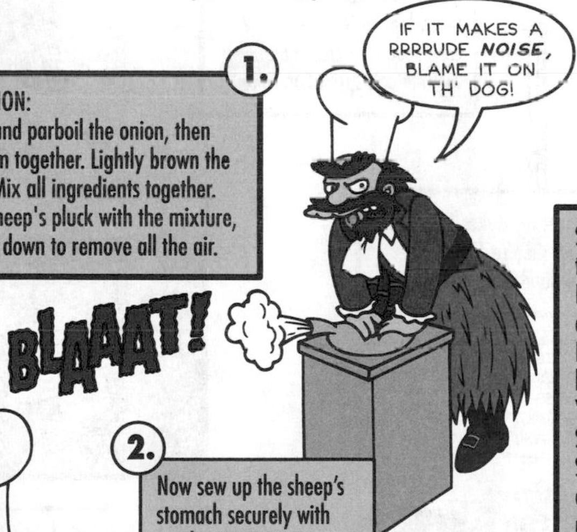
IF IT MAKES A RRRRUDE NOISE, BLAME IT ON TH' DOG!
BLAAAT!

2.

Now sew up the sheep's stomach securely with synthetic cat gut.

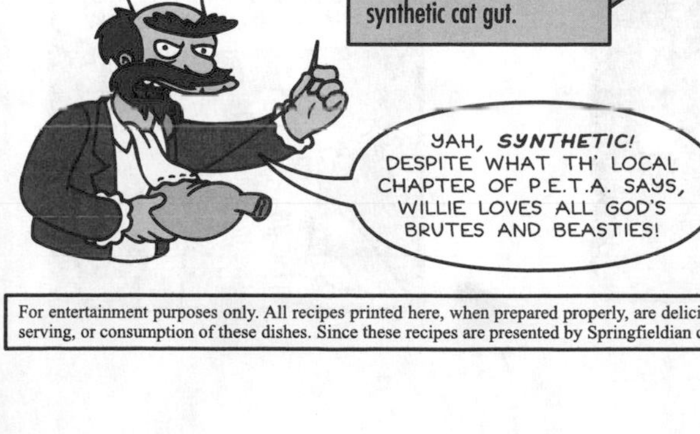
YAH, SYNTHETIC! DESPITE WHAT TH' LOCAL CHAPTER OF P.E.T.A. SAYS, WILLIE LOVES ALL GOD'S BRUTES AND BEASTIES!

3.

Prick wee holes in the haggis in several places so that it does not burst. Place haggis in boiling water and boil slowly in a large metal pot for 4-5 hours.

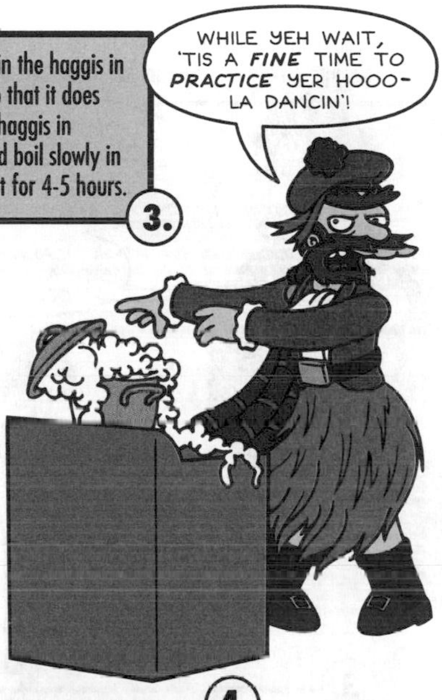
WHILE YEH WAIT, 'TIS A FINE TIME TO PRACTICE YER HOOO-LA DANCIN'!

4.

Stuff one pluck per coconut, glue the coconut halves back together. Invite a dozen friends over for an "authentic" Highland Luau. Dress them in grass skirts and leis. Play "Bang the Coconut on Yer Head," a traditional Scottish/Hawaiian party game. Surprise! The first one to crack open the coconut with their noggin gets to eat the haggis!

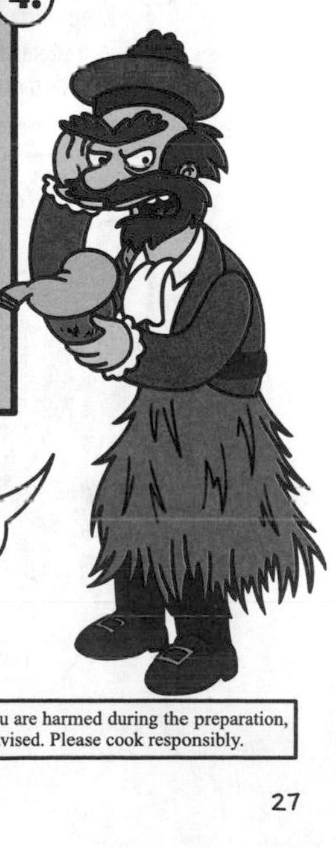
A WEE NIP WILL CURE TH' RESULTIN' HEAD-ACHES!

Serves approximately 12.

CHIEF WIGGUM'S PADDY-WAGON-CAKE

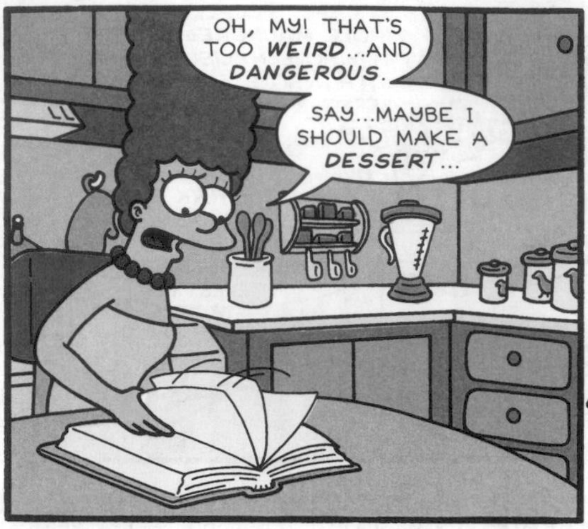
OH, MY! THAT'S TOO WEIRD...AND DANGEROUS.
SAY...MAYBE I SHOULD MAKE A DESSERT...

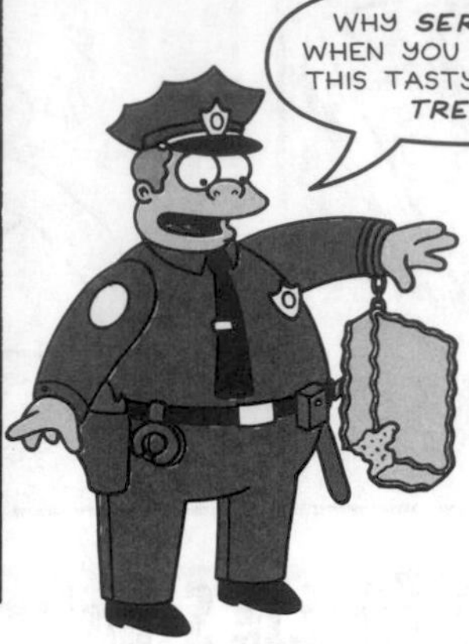
WHY SERVE TIME WHEN YOU CAN SERVE THIS TASTY NOVELTY TREAT?

INGREDIENTS:
1 (18.25 ounce) package white cake mix
5 tablespoons crème de menthe flavoring
1 (16 ounce) can chocolate syrup
1 (8 ounce) container frozen whipped topping, thawed
1 pair freshly scrubbed handcuffs, key set aside

PREPARATION:
Prepare 1 box white cake mix as directed, except substitute 3 tablespoons crème de menthe flavoring for 3 tablespoons water. Pour into 13x9 inch pan and drop handcuffs into batter.

1.

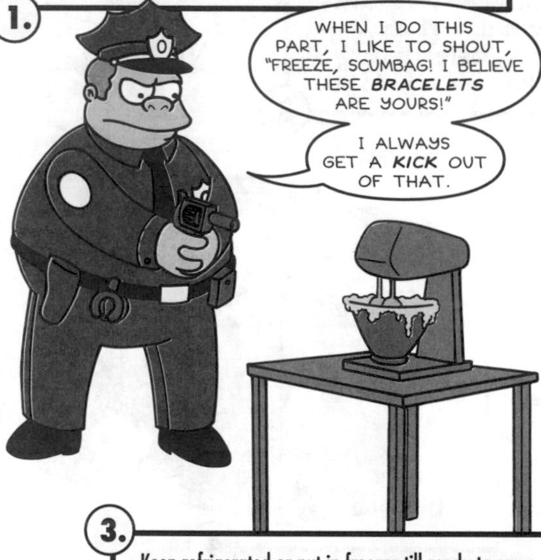
WHEN I DO THIS PART, I LIKE TO SHOUT, "FREEZE, SCUMBAG! I BELIEVE THESE BRACELETS ARE YOURS!"
I ALWAYS GET A KICK OUT OF THAT.

2.

Bake according to cake package directions. Remove from oven and while hot, poke holes in cake with fork, then pour chocolate syrup over the top. Refrigerate until cool, about one hour. After cooling, mix whipped topping with 2 tablespoons of crème de menthe and spread on cake.

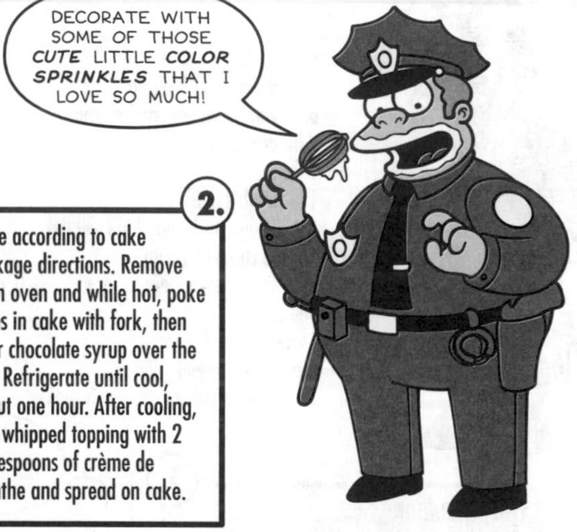
DECORATE WITH SOME OF THOSE CUTE LITTLE COLOR SPRINKLES THAT I LOVE SO MUCH!

3.

Keep refrigerated or put in freezer till ready to serve. Makes 1-13x19 inch sheet cake. Tell whoever finds the 'cuffs that they're "Busted." Ha! It's a great party joke, especially at political fund-raisers!

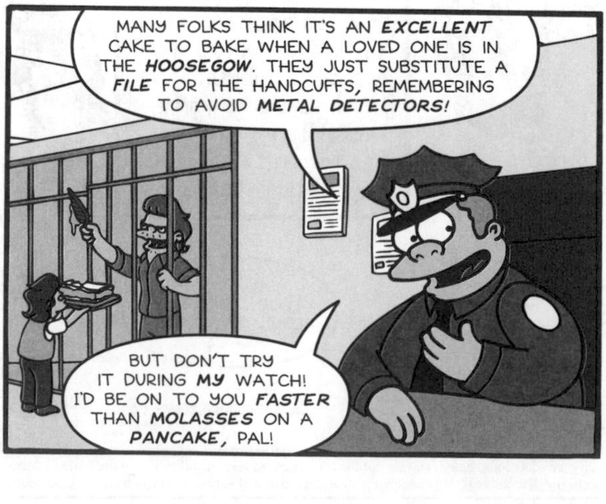
MANY FOLKS THINK IT'S AN EXCELLENT CAKE TO BAKE WHEN A LOVED ONE IS IN THE HOOSEGOW. THEY JUST SUBSTITUTE A FILE FOR THE HANDCUFFS, REMEMBERING TO AVOID METAL DETECTORS!
BUT DON'T TRY IT DURING MY WATCH! I'D BE ON TO YOU FASTER THAN MOLASSES ON A PANCAKE, PAL!

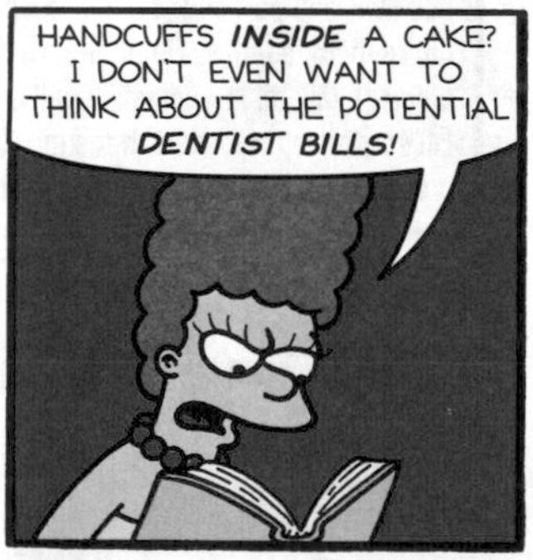
HANDCUFFS INSIDE A CAKE? I DON'T EVEN WANT TO THINK ABOUT THE POTENTIAL DENTIST BILLS!

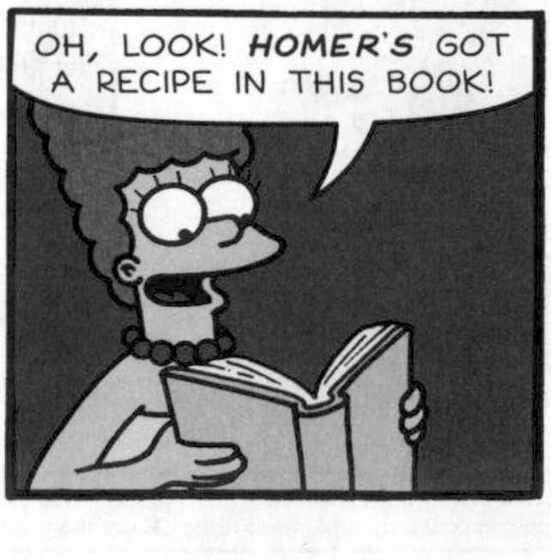
OH, LOOK! HOMER'S GOT A RECIPE IN THIS BOOK!

HOMER'S BEER BISCUITS

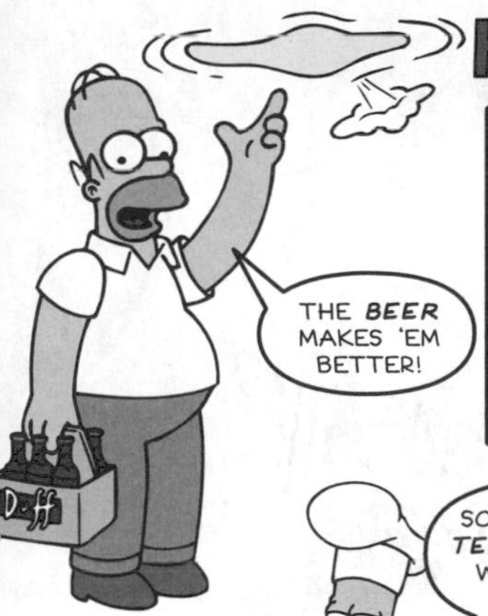
THE BEER MAKES 'EM BETTER!

INGREDIENTS:
1 case of Duff Beer
2 cups sifted all-purpose flour
4 tsp baking powder
1 tsp salt
1/4 cup shortening
3/4 cup milk

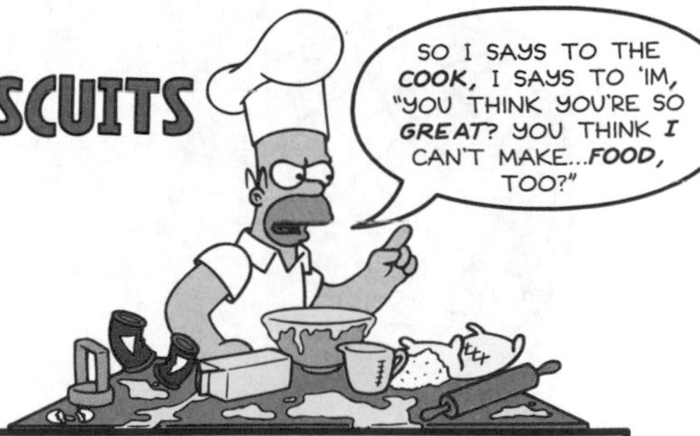
SO I SAYS TO THE COOK, I SAYS TO 'IM, "YOU THINK YOU'RE SO GREAT? YOU THINK I CAN'T MAKE...FOOD, TOO?"

1.

PREPARATION:
Drink a can of Duff. Sift dry ingredients together. Cut in shortening. Drink half of a can of Duff. Pour the rest of the can of Duff into the mixture. Drink another can of Duff so you won't regret wasting the previous half-can of Duff. Turn out the dough on a lightly floured board. Knead about 1/2 minute. During this 1/2 minute, why not enjoy another Duff?

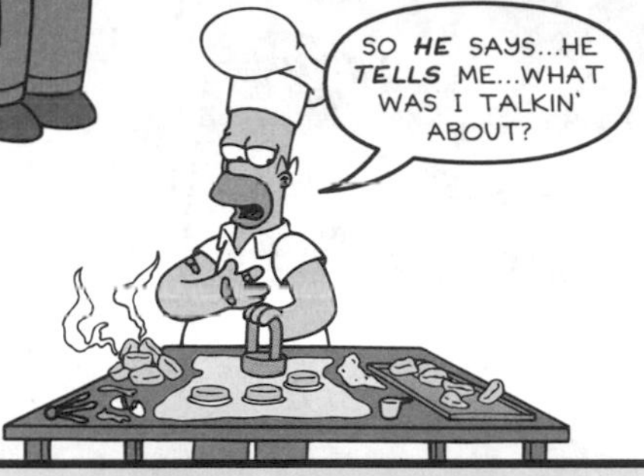
SO HE SAYS...HE TELLS ME...WHAT WAS I TALKIN' ABOUT?

2.

Roll out dough 1/2 inch thick. Cut with floured biscuit cutter. You'll probably wound yourself with the cutter, so it's time for another wonderful Duff! Place dough cut-outs on baking sheet and bake in 475° f oven 12-15 minutes. Now, open a Duff and wait.

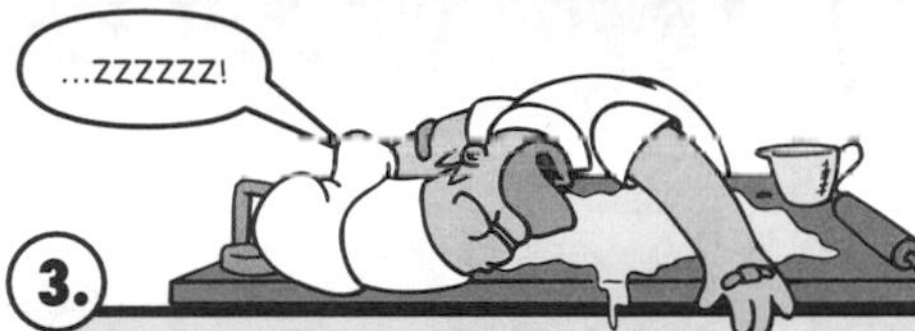
...ZZZZZZ!

3.

Invite some friends over, but make sure they bring their own Duff. By the time you're done with all that hot and strenuous phone-calling, you'll probably need another Duff. If you forget the biscuits and they burn, throw them out and drink the rest of the Duff. If the biscuits turn out good, serve them with something thirst-quenching. I recommend a cold and friendly stein of Duff!

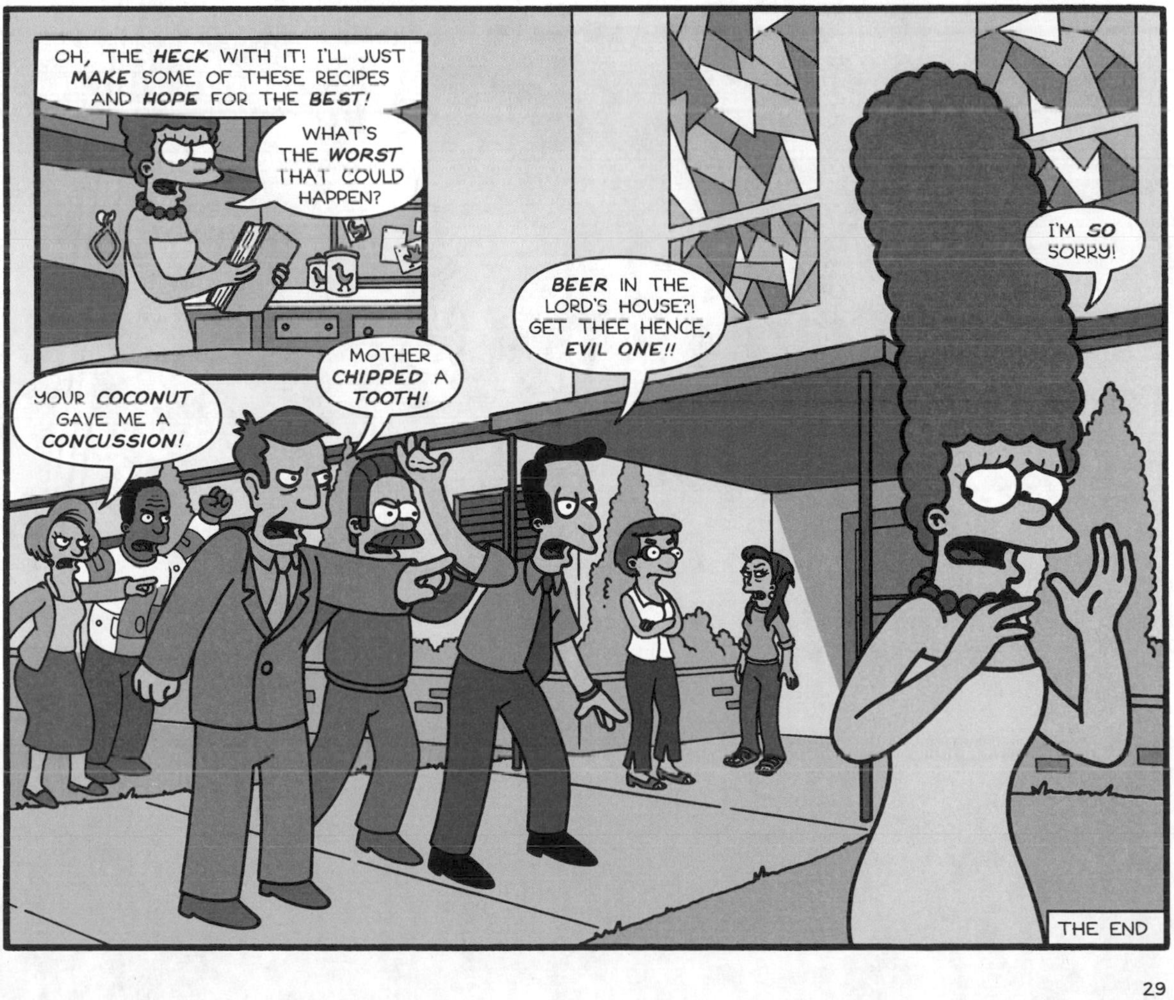
OH, THE HECK WITH IT! I'LL JUST MAKE SOME OF THESE RECIPES AND HOPE FOR THE BEST!
WHAT'S THE WORST THAT COULD HAPPEN?
YOUR COCONUT GAVE ME A CONCUSSION!
MOTHER CHIPPED A TOOTH!
BEER IN THE LORD'S HOUSE?! GET THEE HENCE, EVIL ONE!!
I'M SO SORRY!
THE END

DOWN IN THE DUMPS? READ THIS COMIC!

BONGO COMICS GROUP

SIMPSONS™ COMICS

#72

APPROVED BY THE COMICS CODE AUTHORITY

PIZZA

HOMER'S RUN
CRASH!
SMASH!
SMASH!
KA-BASH!
IAN BOOTHBY SCRIPT
LUIS ESCOBAR PENCILS
STEVE STEERE, JR. INKS
ART VILLANUEVA COLORS
KAREN BATES LETTERS
BILL MORRISON EDITOR
MATT GROENING FULLY VESTED
IT'S ARMAGEDDON, PEOPLE!
RUN FOR YOUR LIVES!

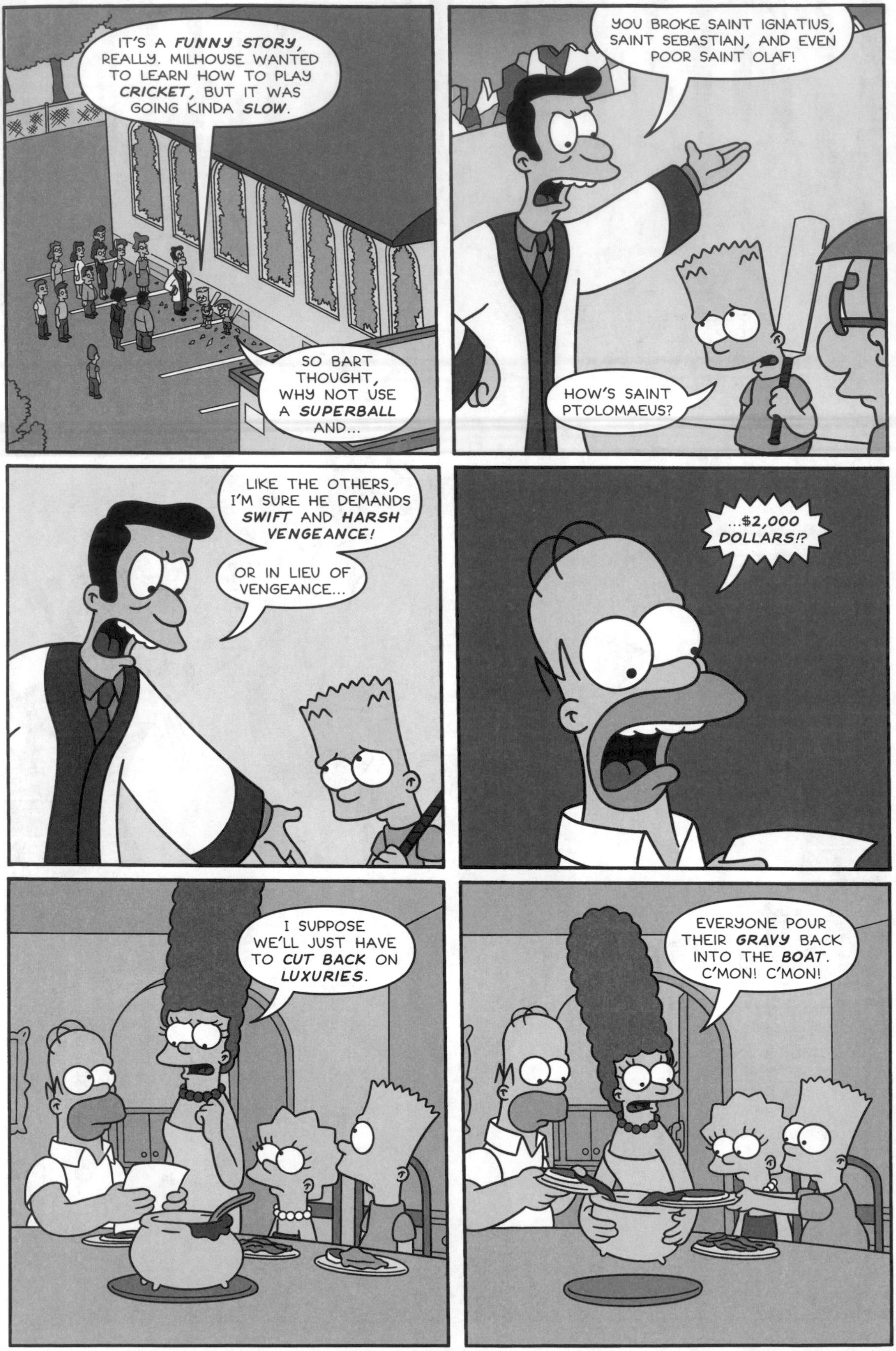
IT'S A FUNNY STORY, REALLY. MILHOUSE WANTED TO LEARN HOW TO PLAY CRICKET, BUT IT WAS GOING KINDA SLOW.
SO BART THOUGHT, WHY NOT USE A SUPERBALL AND...
YOU BROKE SAINT IGNATIUS, SAINT SEBASTIAN, AND EVEN POOR SAINT OLAF!
HOW'S SAINT PTOLOMAEUS?
LIKE THE OTHERS, I'M SURE HE DEMANDS SWIFT AND HARSH VENGEANCE!
OR IN LIEU OF VENGEANCE...
...$2,000 DOLLARS!?
I SUPPOSE WE'LL JUST HAVE TO CUT BACK ON LUXURIES.
EVERYONE POUR THEIR GRAVY BACK INTO THE BOAT. C'MON! C'MON!

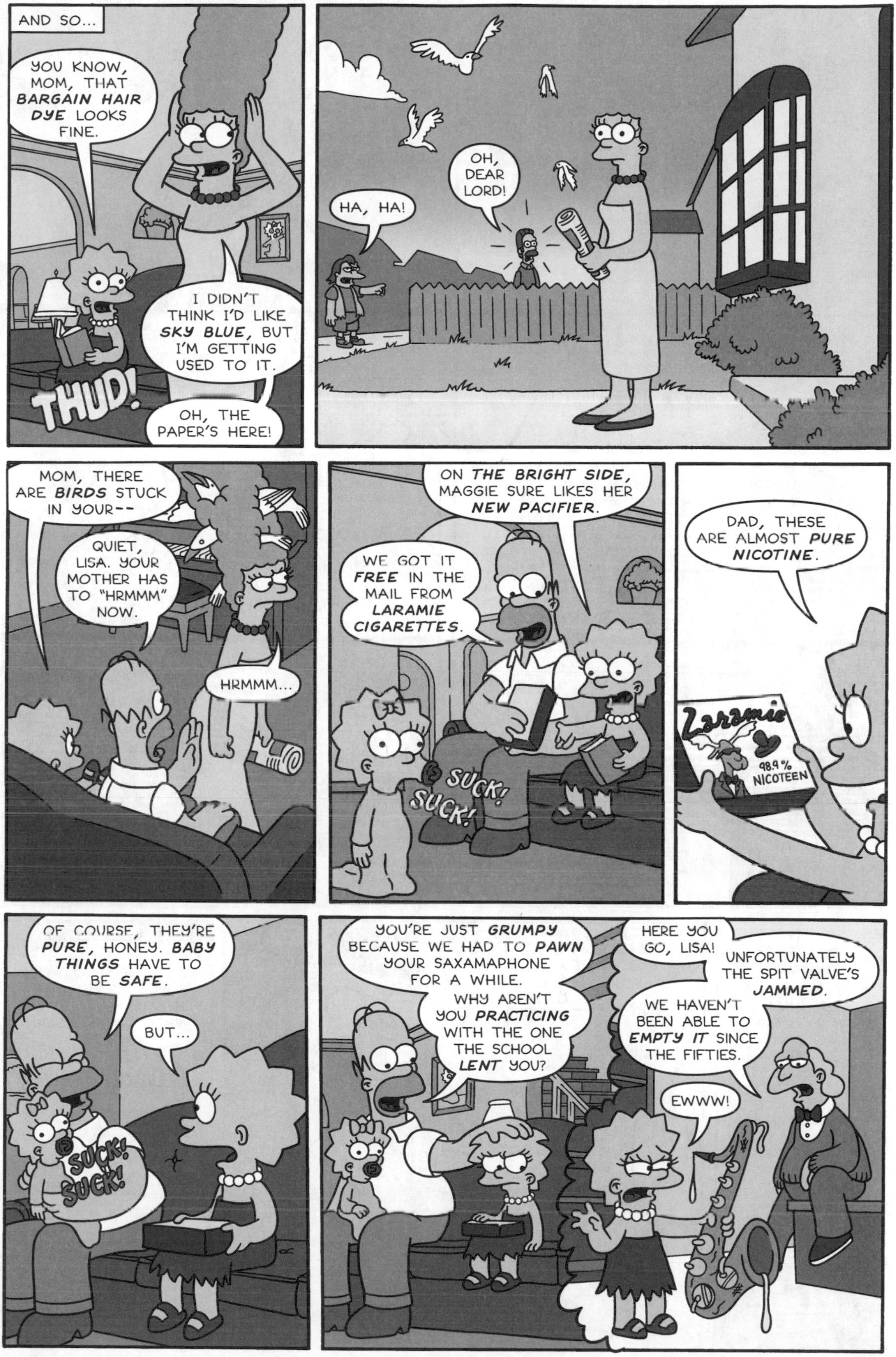

AND SO...
YOU KNOW, MOM, THAT BARGAIN HAIR DYE LOOKS FINE.
I DIDN'T THINK I'D LIKE SKY BLUE, BUT I'M GETTING USED TO IT.
THUD!
OH, THE PAPER'S HERE!
HA, HA!
OH, DEAR LORD!
MOM, THERE ARE BIRDS STUCK IN YOUR--
QUIET, LISA. YOUR MOTHER HAS TO "HRMMM" NOW.
HRMMM...
ON THE BRIGHT SIDE, MAGGIE SURE LIKES HER NEW PACIFIER.
WE GOT IT FREE IN THE MAIL FROM LARAMIE CIGARETTES.
SUCK! SUCK!
DAD, THESE ARE ALMOST PURE NICOTINE.
Laramie
98.9% NICOTEEN
OF COURSE, THEY'RE PURE, HONEY. BABY THINGS HAVE TO BE SAFE.
BUT...
SUCK! SUCK!
YOU'RE JUST GRUMPY BECAUSE WE HAD TO PAWN YOUR SAXAMAPHONE FOR A WHILE.
WHY AREN'T YOU PRACTICING WITH THE ONE THE SCHOOL LENT YOU?
HERE YOU GO, LISA!
UNFORTUNATELY THE SPIT VALVE'S JAMMED.
WE HAVEN'T BEEN ABLE TO EMPTY IT SINCE THE FIFTIES.
EWWW!

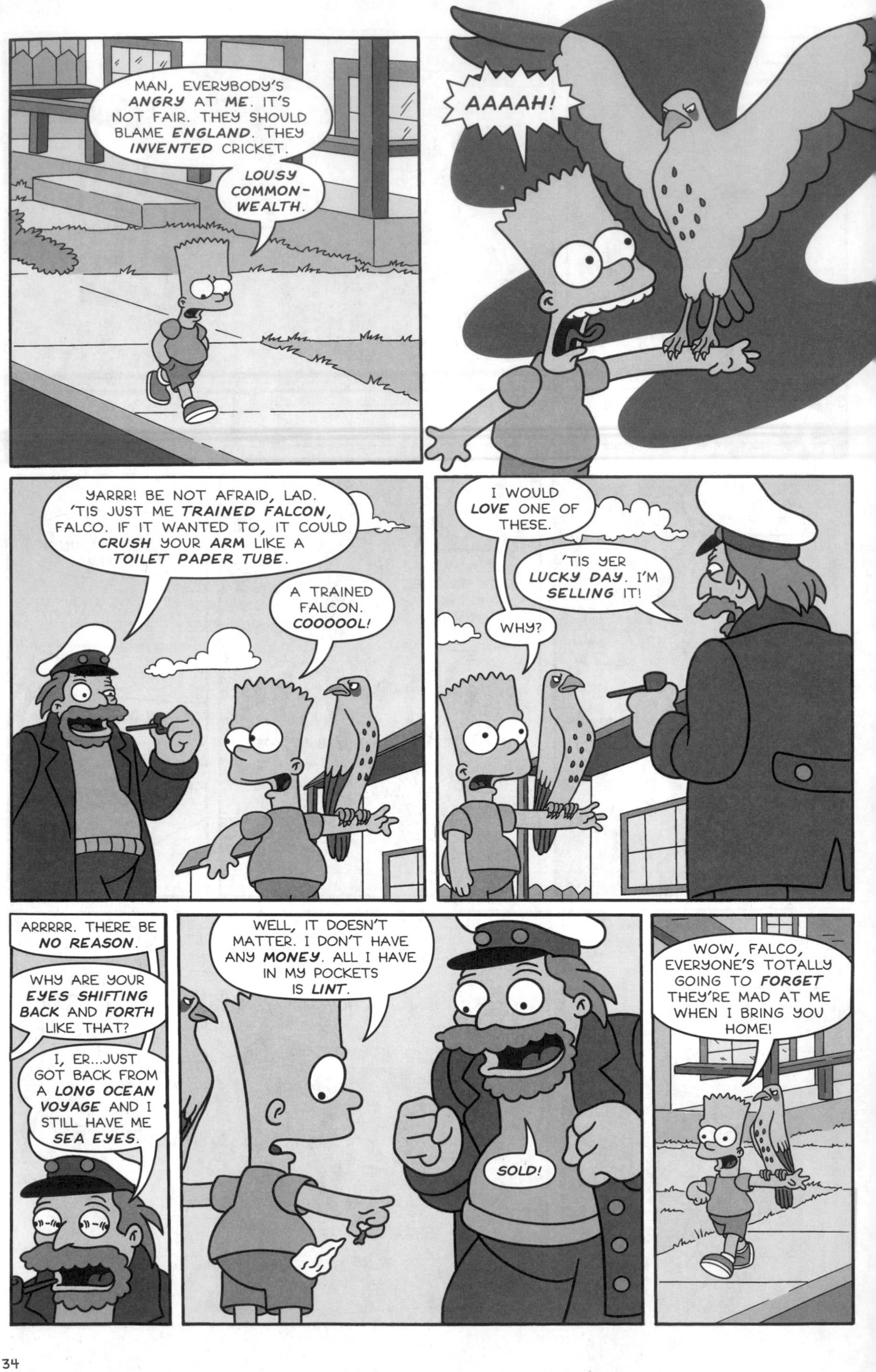
MAN, EVERYBODY'S ANGRY AT ME. IT'S NOT FAIR. THEY SHOULD BLAME ENGLAND. THEY INVENTED CRICKET.
LOUSY COMMON-WEALTH.
AAAAH!
YARRR! BE NOT AFRAID, LAD. 'TIS JUST ME TRAINED FALCON, FALCO. IF IT WANTED TO, IT COULD CRUSH YOUR ARM LIKE A TOILET PAPER TUBE.
A TRAINED FALCON. COOOOOL!
I WOULD LOVE ONE OF THESE.
'TIS YER LUCKY DAY. I'M SELLING IT!
WHY?
ARRRRR. THERE BE NO REASON.
WHY ARE YOUR EYES SHIFTING BACK AND FORTH LIKE THAT?
I, ER...JUST GOT BACK FROM A LONG OCEAN VOYAGE AND I STILL HAVE ME SEA EYES.
WELL, IT DOESN'T MATTER. I DON'T HAVE ANY MONEY. ALL I HAVE IN MY POCKETS IS LINT.
SOLD!
WOW, FALCO, EVERYONE'S TOTALLY GOING TO FORGET THEY'RE MAD AT ME WHEN I BRING YOU HOME!

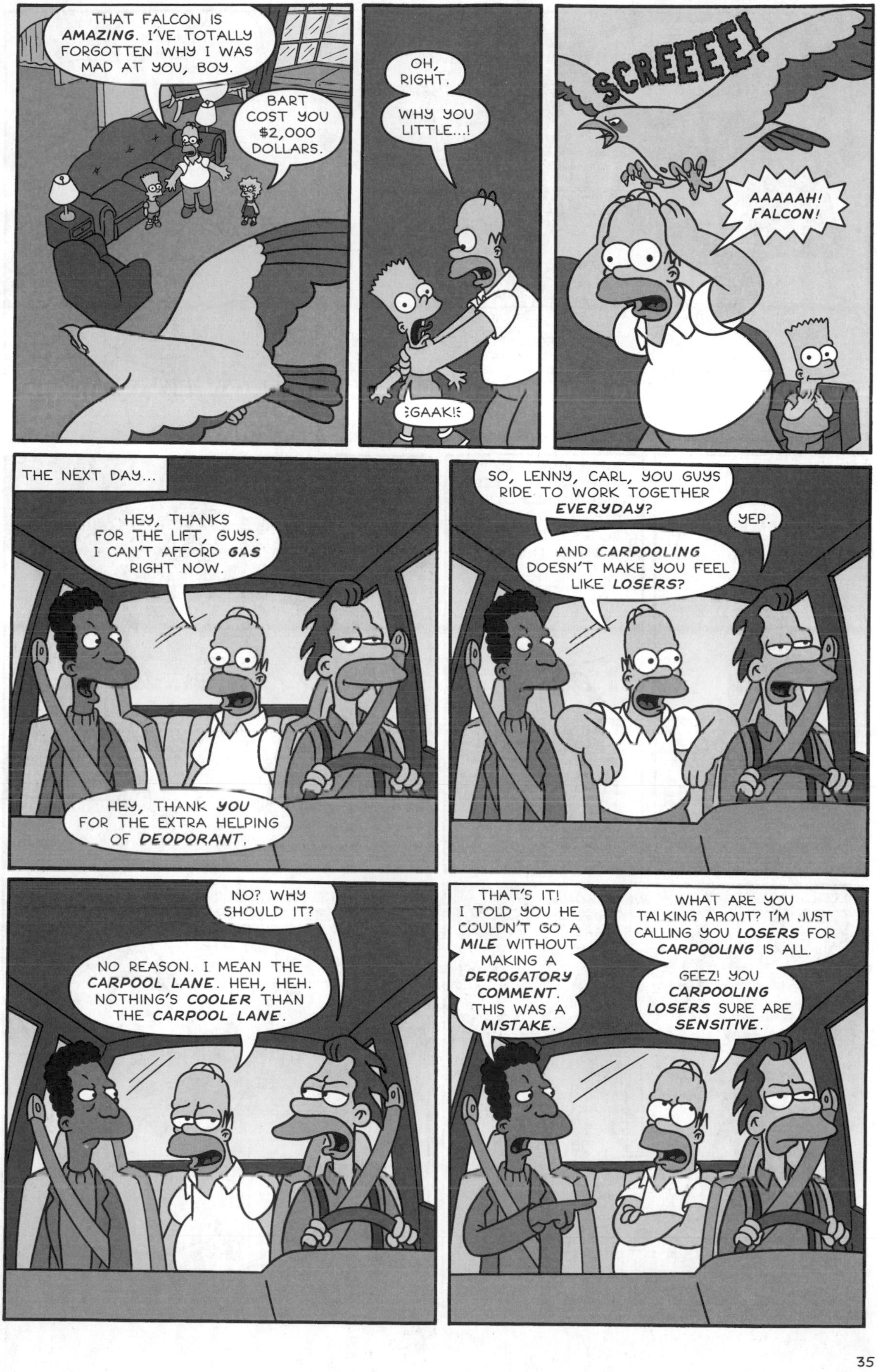
THAT FALCON IS AMAZING. I'VE TOTALLY FORGOTTEN WHY I WAS MAD AT YOU, BOY.
BART COST YOU $2,000 DOLLARS.
OH, RIGHT.
WHY YOU LITTLE...!
GAAK!
SCREEEE!
AAAAAH! FALCON!
THE NEXT DAY...
HEY, THANKS FOR THE LIFT, GUYS. I CAN'T AFFORD GAS RIGHT NOW.
HEY, THANK YOU FOR THE EXTRA HELPING OF DEODORANT.
SO, LENNY, CARL, YOU GUYS RIDE TO WORK TOGETHER EVERYDAY?
YEP.
AND CARPOOLING DOESN'T MAKE YOU FEEL LIKE LOSERS?
NO? WHY SHOULD IT?
NO REASON. I MEAN THE CARPOOL LANE. HEH, HEH. NOTHING'S COOLER THAN THE CARPOOL LANE.
THAT'S IT! I TOLD YOU HE COULDN'T GO A MILE WITHOUT MAKING A DEROGATORY COMMENT. THIS WAS A MISTAKE.
WHAT ARE YOU TALKING ABOUT? I'M JUST CALLING YOU LOSERS FOR CARPOOLING IS ALL.
GEEZ! YOU CARPOOLING LOSERS SURE ARE SENSITIVE.

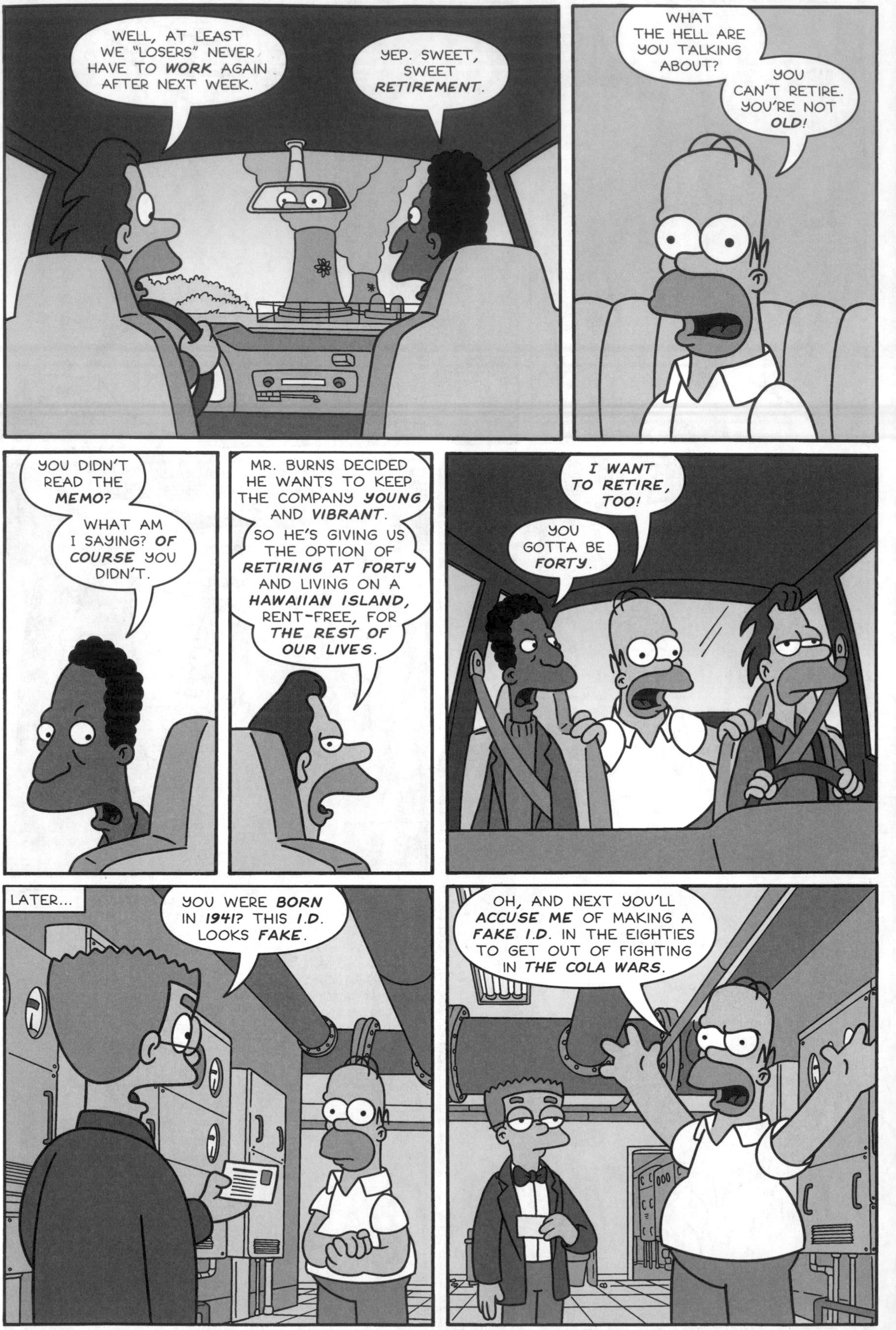
WELL, AT LEAST WE "LOSERS" NEVER HAVE TO WORK AGAIN AFTER NEXT WEEK.
YEP. SWEET, SWEET RETIREMENT.
WHAT THE HELL ARE YOU TALKING ABOUT?
YOU CAN'T RETIRE. YOU'RE NOT OLD!
YOU DIDN'T READ THE MEMO?
WHAT AM I SAYING? OF COURSE YOU DIDN'T.
MR. BURNS DECIDED HE WANTS TO KEEP THE COMPANY YOUNG AND VIBRANT.
SO HE'S GIVING US THE OPTION OF RETIRING AT FORTY AND LIVING ON A HAWAIIAN ISLAND, RENT-FREE, FOR THE REST OF OUR LIVES.
I WANT TO RETIRE, TOO!
YOU GOTTA BE FORTY.
LATER...
YOU WERE BORN IN 1941? THIS I.D. LOOKS FAKE.
OH, AND NEXT YOU'LL ACCUSE ME OF MAKING A FAKE I.D. IN THE EIGHTIES TO GET OUT OF FIGHTING IN THE COLA WARS.

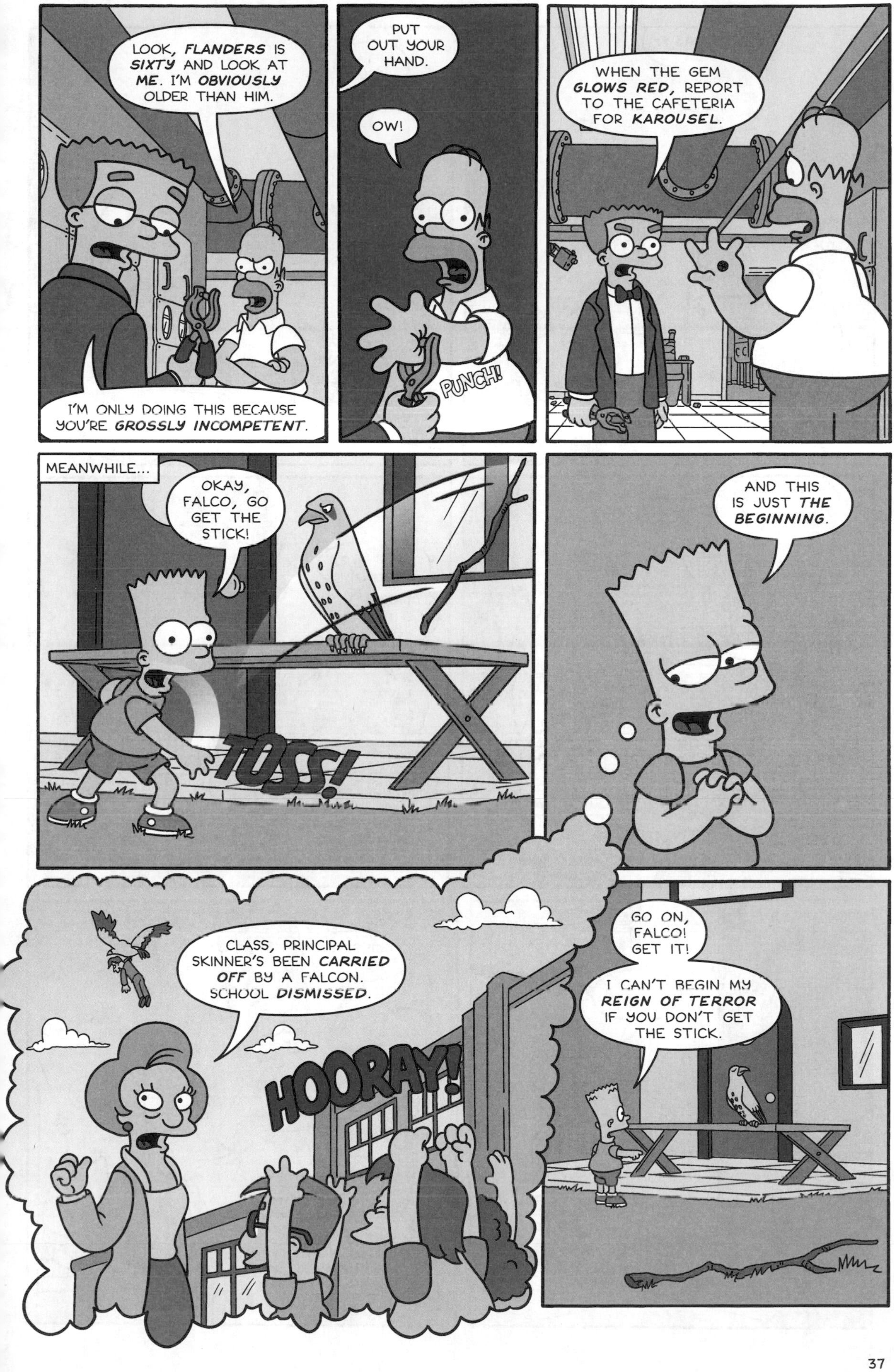
LOOK, FLANDERS IS SIXTY AND LOOK AT ME. I'M OBVIOUSLY OLDER THAN HIM.
I'M ONLY DOING THIS BECAUSE YOU'RE GROSSLY INCOMPETENT.
PUT OUT YOUR HAND.
OW!
PUNCH!
WHEN THE GEM GLOWS RED, REPORT TO THE CAFETERIA FOR KAROUSEL.
MEANWHILE...
OKAY, FALCO, GO GET THE STICK!
TOSS!
AND THIS IS JUST THE BEGINNING.
CLASS, PRINCIPAL SKINNER'S BEEN CARRIED OFF BY A FALCON. SCHOOL DISMISSED.
HOORAY!
GO ON, FALCO! GET IT!
I CAN'T BEGIN MY REIGN OF TERROR IF YOU DON'T GET THE STICK.

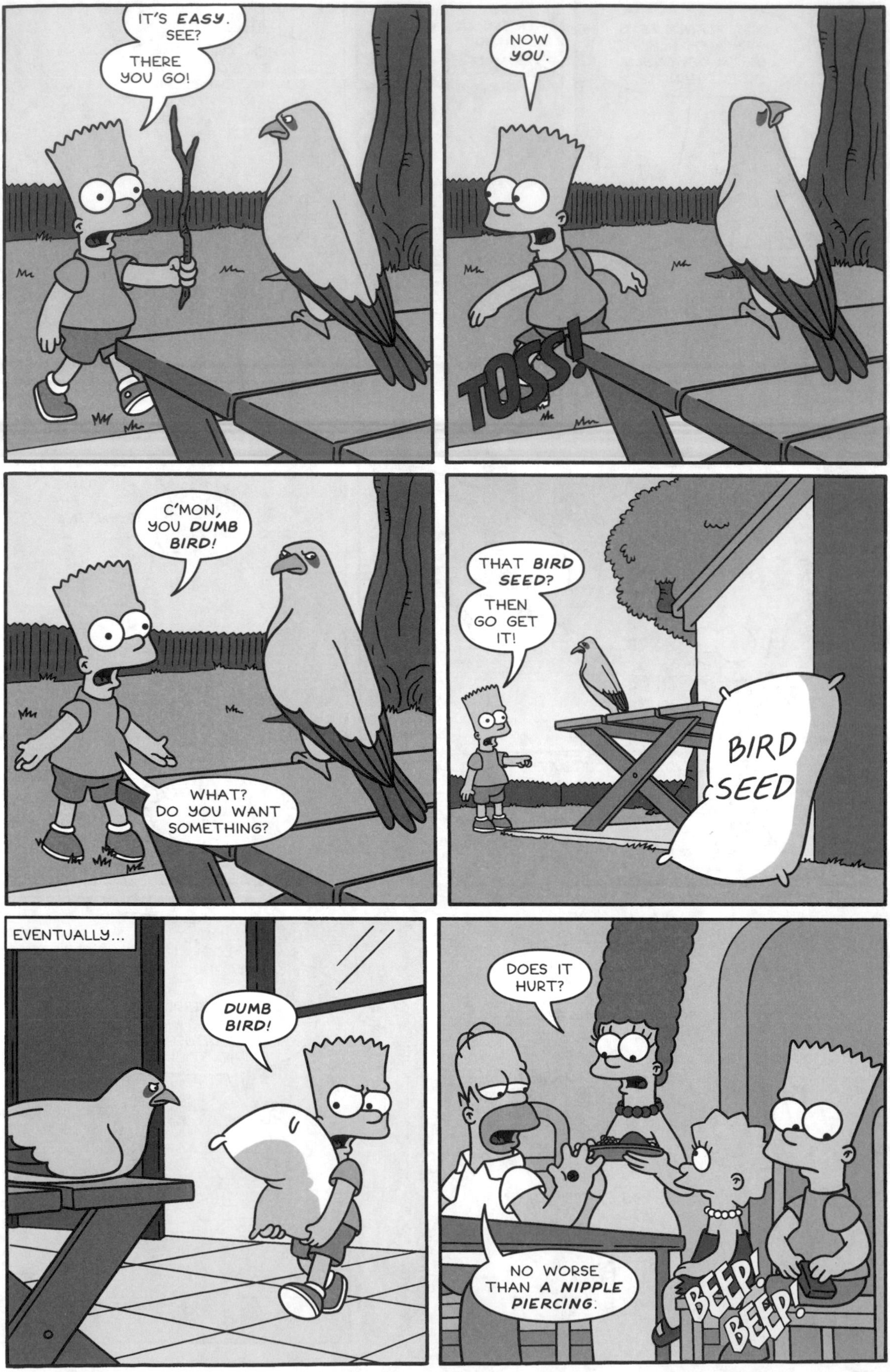
IT'S EASY. SEE?
THERE YOU GO!
NOW YOU.
TOSS!
C'MON, YOU DUMB BIRD!
WHAT? DO YOU WANT SOMETHING?
THAT BIRD SEED?
THEN GO GET IT!
BIRD SEED
EVENTUALLY...
DUMB BIRD!
DOES IT HURT?
NO WORSE THAN A NIPPLE PIERCING.
BEEP! BEEP!

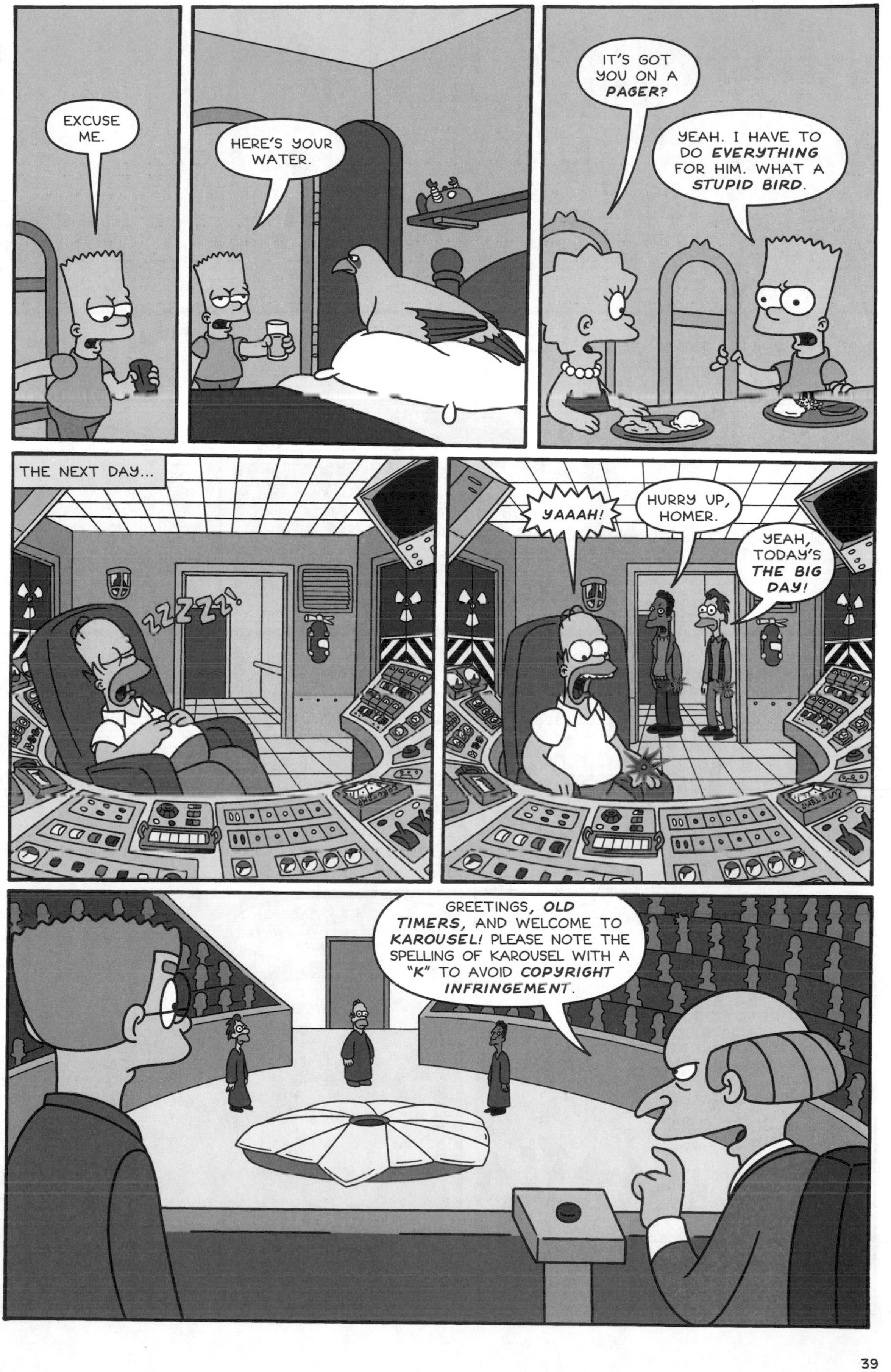
EXCUSE ME.
HERE'S YOUR WATER.
IT'S GOT YOU ON A PAGER?
YEAH. I HAVE TO DO EVERYTHING FOR HIM. WHAT A STUPID BIRD.
THE NEXT DAY...
ZZZZZ!
YAAAH!
HURRY UP, HOMER.
YEAH, TODAY'S THE BIG DAY!
GREETINGS, OLD TIMERS, AND WELCOME TO KAROUSEL! PLEASE NOTE THE SPELLING OF KAROUSEL WITH A "K" TO AVOID COPYRIGHT INFRINGEMENT.

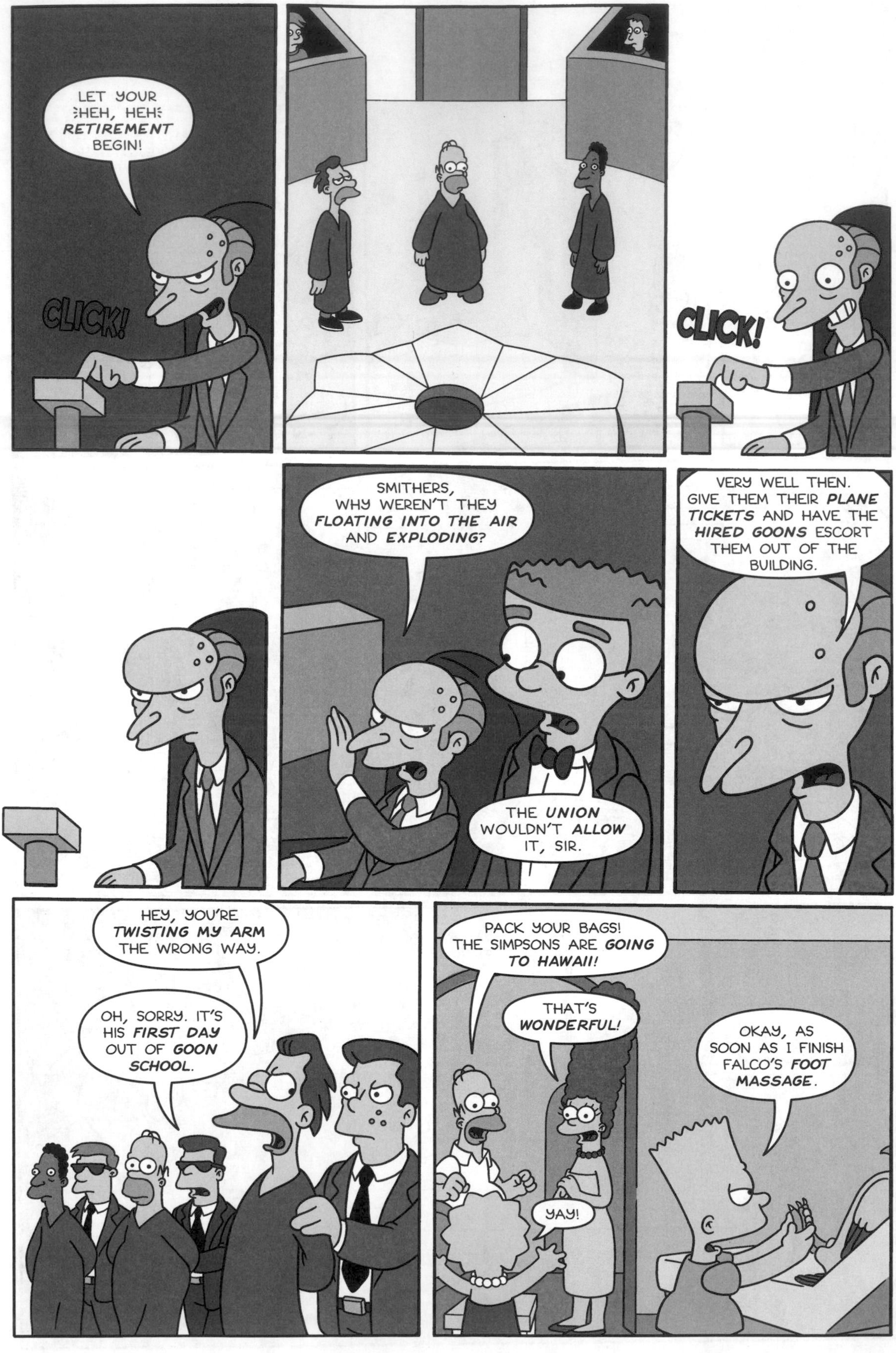
LET YOUR HEH, HEH RETIREMENT BEGIN!
CLICK!
CLICK!
SMITHERS, WHY WEREN'T THEY FLOATING INTO THE AIR AND EXPLODING?
THE UNION WOULDN'T ALLOW IT, SIR.
VERY WELL THEN. GIVE THEM THEIR PLANE TICKETS AND HAVE THE HIRED GOONS ESCORT THEM OUT OF THE BUILDING.
HEY, YOU'RE TWISTING MY ARM THE WRONG WAY.
OH, SORRY. IT'S HIS FIRST DAY OUT OF GOON SCHOOL.
PACK YOUR BAGS! THE SIMPSONS ARE GOING TO HAWAII!
THAT'S WONDERFUL!
YAY!
OKAY, AS SOON AS I FINISH FALCO'S FOOT MASSAGE.

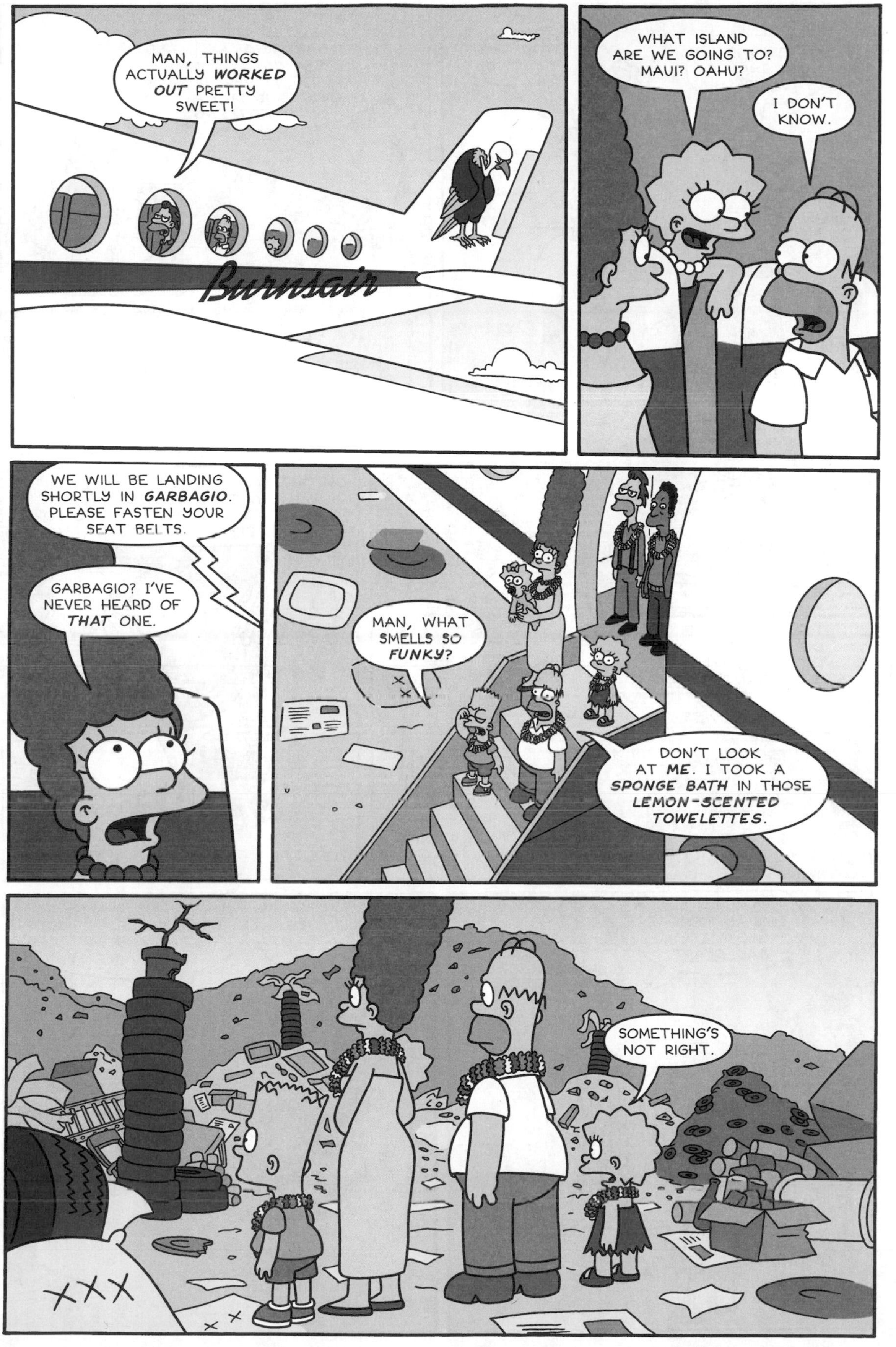
MAN, THINGS ACTUALLY WORKED OUT PRETTY SWEET!
Burnsair
WHAT ISLAND ARE WE GOING TO? MAUI? OAHU?
I DON'T KNOW.
WE WILL BE LANDING SHORTLY IN GARBAGIO. PLEASE FASTEN YOUR SEAT BELTS.
GARBAGIO? I'VE NEVER HEARD OF THAT ONE.
MAN, WHAT SMELLS SO FUNKY?
DON'T LOOK AT ME. I TOOK A SPONGE BATH IN THOSE LEMON-SCENTED TOWELETTES.
SOMETHING'S NOT RIGHT.

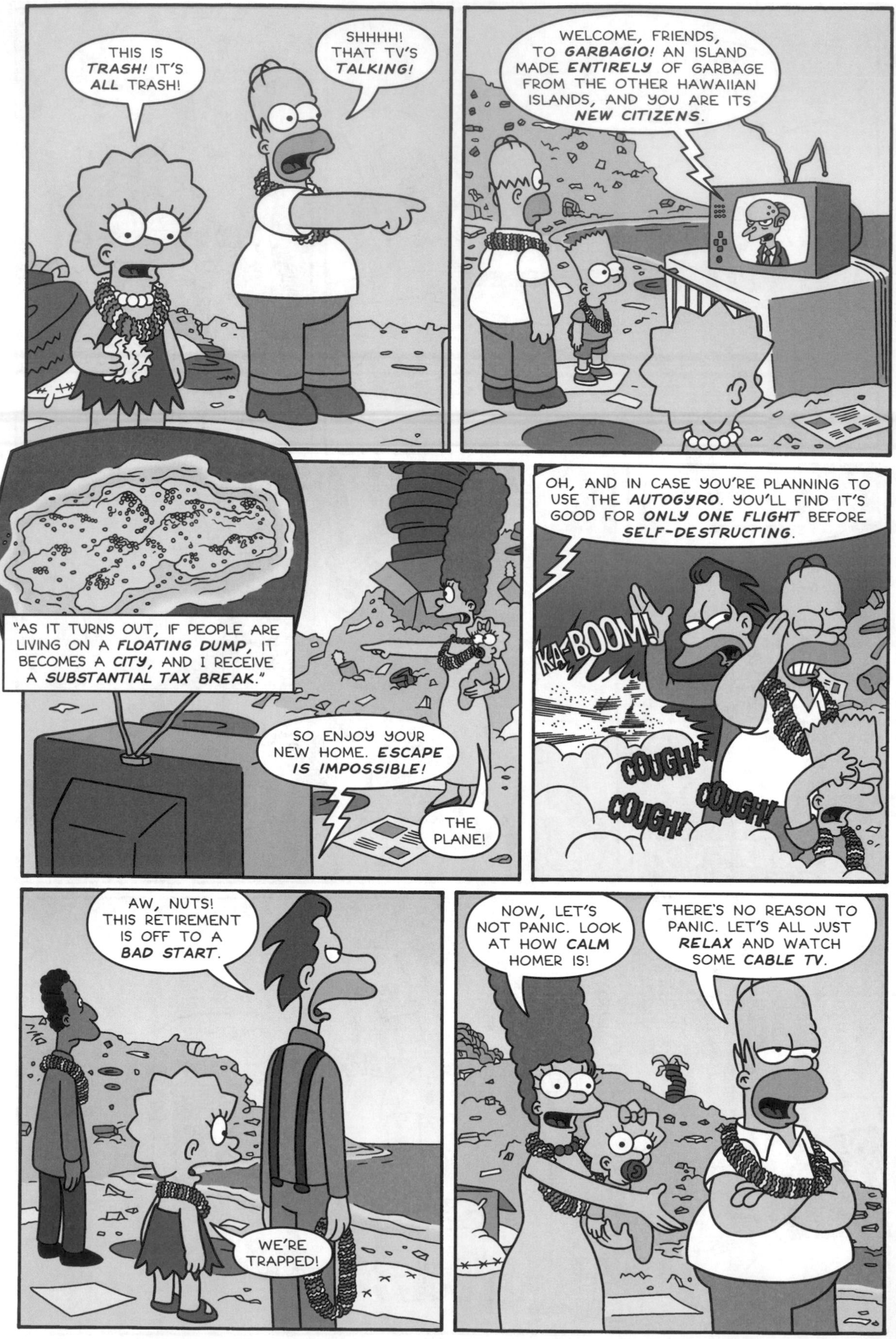
THIS IS TRASH! IT'S ALL TRASH!
SHHHH! THAT TV'S TALKING!
WELCOME, FRIENDS, TO GARBAGIO! AN ISLAND MADE ENTIRELY OF GARBAGE FROM THE OTHER HAWAIIAN ISLANDS, AND YOU ARE ITS NEW CITIZENS.
"AS IT TURNS OUT, IF PEOPLE ARE LIVING ON A FLOATING DUMP, IT BECOMES A CITY, AND I RECEIVE A SUBSTANTIAL TAX BREAK."
SO ENJOY YOUR NEW HOME. ESCAPE IS IMPOSSIBLE!
THE PLANE!
OH, AND IN CASE YOU'RE PLANNING TO USE THE AUTOGYRO. YOU'LL FIND IT'S GOOD FOR ONLY ONE FLIGHT BEFORE SELF-DESTRUCTING.
KA-BOOM!
COUGH!
COUGH!
COUGH!
AW, NUTS! THIS RETIREMENT IS OFF TO A BAD START.
WE'RE TRAPPED!
NOW, LET'S NOT PANIC. LOOK AT HOW CALM HOMER IS!
THERE'S NO REASON TO PANIC. LET'S ALL JUST RELAX AND WATCH SOME CABLE TV.

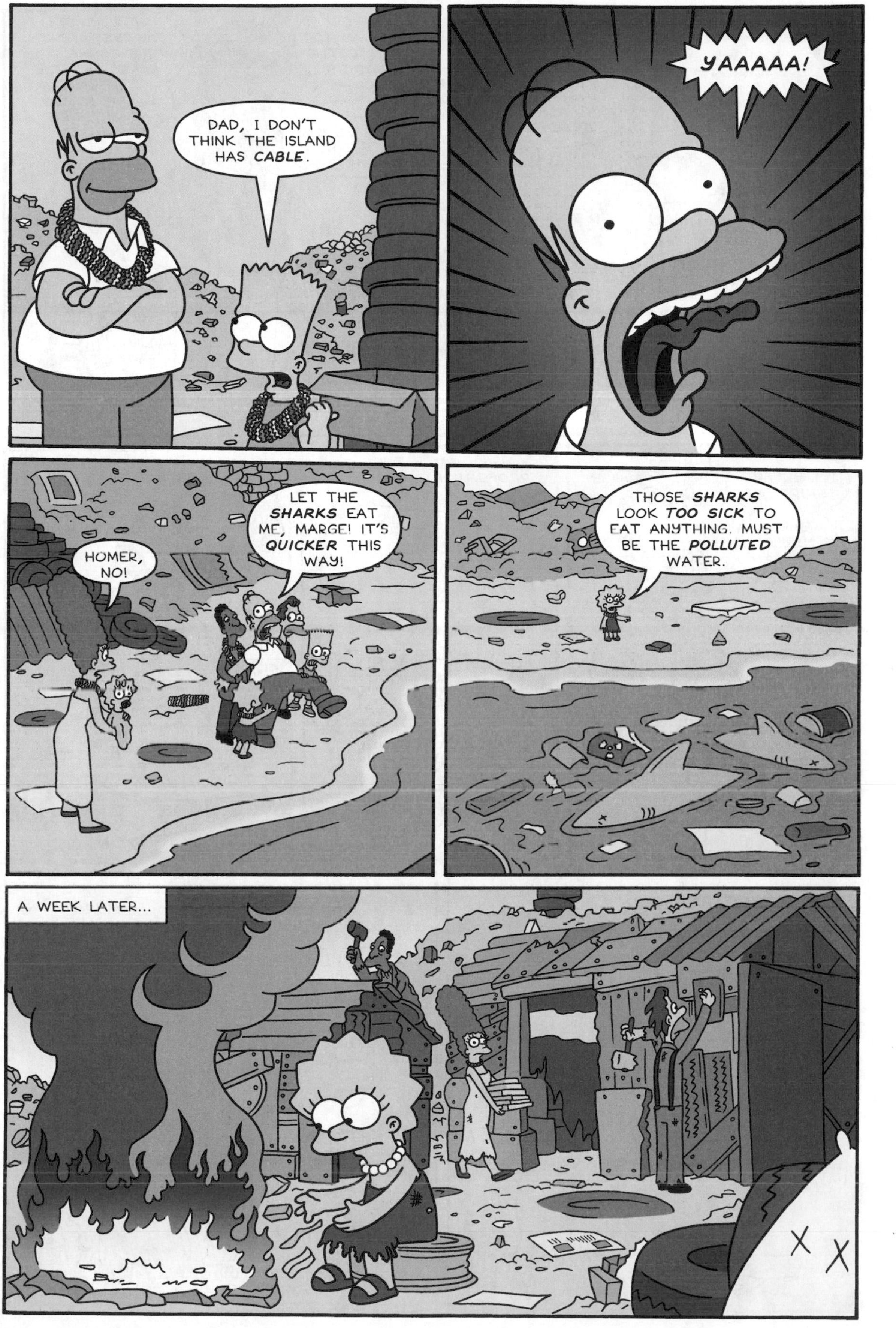
DAD, I DON'T THINK THE ISLAND HAS CABLE.
YAAAAA!
HOMER, NO!
LET THE SHARKS EAT ME, MARGE! IT'S QUICKER THIS WAY!
THOSE SHARKS LOOK TOO SICK TO EAT ANYTHING. MUST BE THE POLLUTED WATER.
A WEEK LATER...

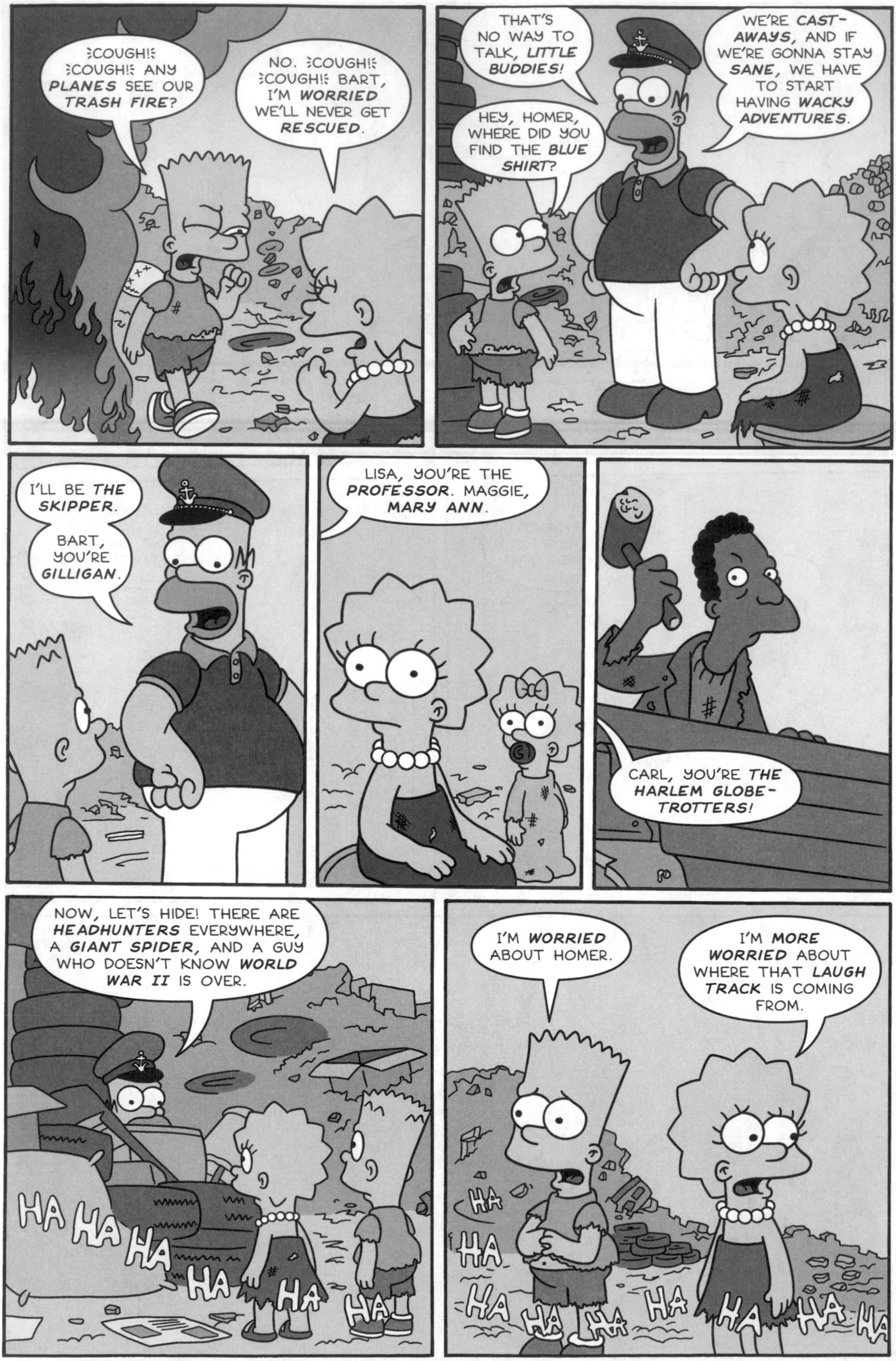
¡COUGH!¡ ¡COUGH!¡ ANY PLANES SEE OUR TRASH FIRE?
NO. ¡COUGH!¡ ¡COUGH!¡ BART, I'M WORRIED WE'LL NEVER GET RESCUED.
THAT'S NO WAY TO TALK, LITTLE BUDDIES!
HEY, HOMER, WHERE DID YOU FIND THE BLUE SHIRT?
WE'RE CAST-AWAYS, AND IF WE'RE GONNA STAY SANE, WE HAVE TO START HAVING WACKY ADVENTURES.
I'LL BE THE SKIPPER.
BART, YOU'RE GILLIGAN.
LISA, YOU'RE THE PROFESSOR. MAGGIE, MARY ANN.
CARL, YOU'RE THE HARLEM GLOBE-TROTTERS!
NOW, LET'S HIDE! THERE ARE HEADHUNTERS EVERYWHERE, A GIANT SPIDER, AND A GUY WHO DOESN'T KNOW WORLD WAR II IS OVER.
HA HA HA HA HA HA
I'M WORRIED ABOUT HOMER.
I'M MORE WORRIED ABOUT WHERE THAT LAUGH TRACK IS COMING FROM.
HA HA HA HA HA HA HA HA HA HA

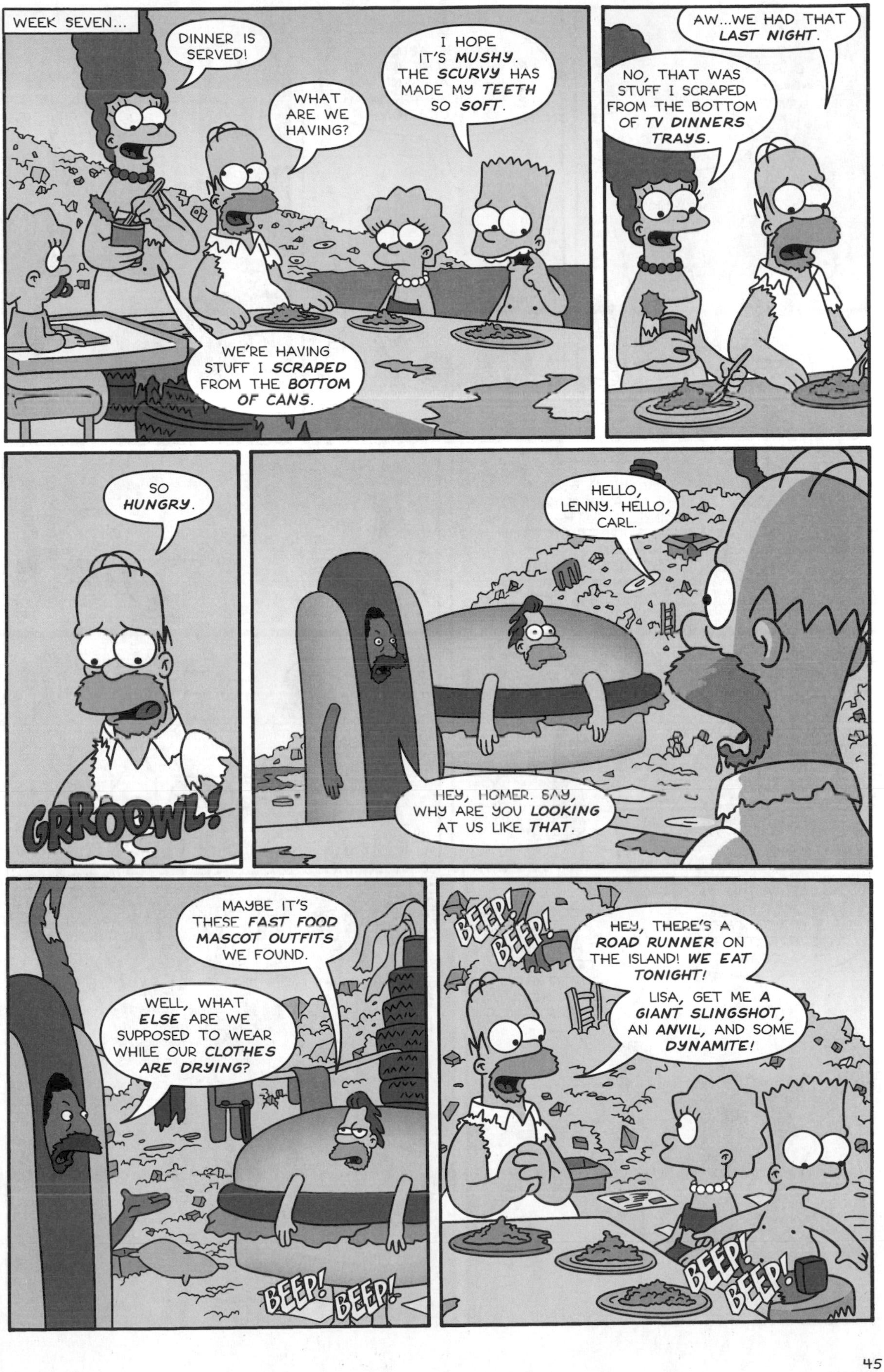
WEEK SEVEN...
DINNER IS SERVED!
WHAT ARE WE HAVING?
I HOPE IT'S MUSHY. THE SCURVY HAS MADE MY TEETH SO SOFT.
WE'RE HAVING STUFF I SCRAPED FROM THE BOTTOM OF CANS.
AW...WE HAD THAT LAST NIGHT.
NO, THAT WAS STUFF I SCRAPED FROM THE BOTTOM OF TV DINNERS TRAYS.
SO HUNGRY.
GRROOWL!
HELLO, LENNY. HELLO, CARL.
HEY, HOMER. SAY, WHY ARE YOU LOOKING AT US LIKE THAT.
MAYBE IT'S THESE FAST FOOD MASCOT OUTFITS WE FOUND.
WELL, WHAT ELSE ARE WE SUPPOSED TO WEAR WHILE OUR CLOTHES ARE DRYING?
BEEP! BEEP!
BEEP! BEEP!
HEY, THERE'S A ROAD RUNNER ON THE ISLAND! WE EAT TONIGHT!
LISA, GET ME A GIANT SLINGSHOT, AN ANVIL, AND SOME DYNAMITE!
BEEP! BEEP!

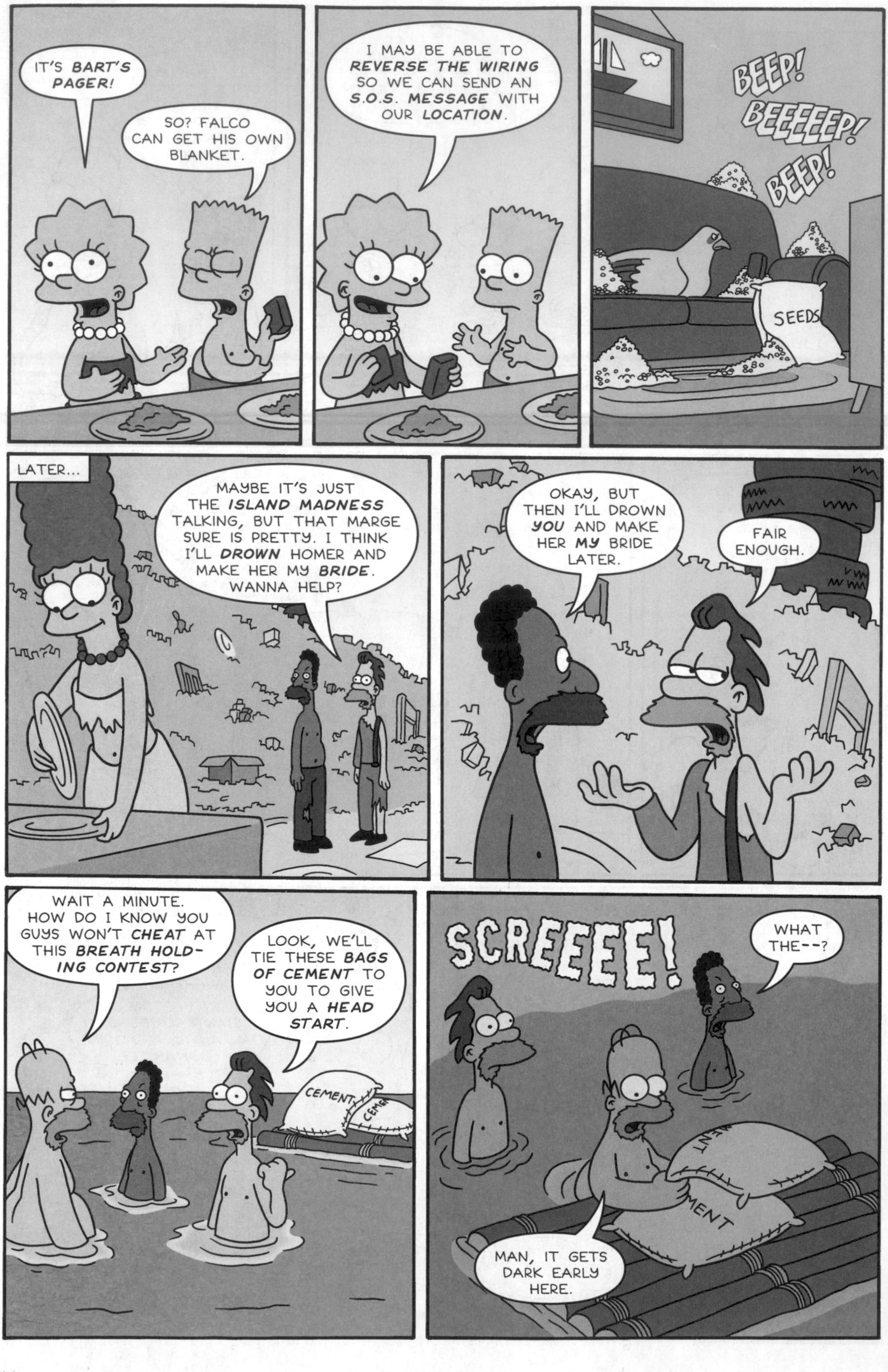
IT'S BART'S PAGER!
SO? FALCO CAN GET HIS OWN BLANKET.
I MAY BE ABLE TO REVERSE THE WIRING SO WE CAN SEND AN S.O.S. MESSAGE WITH OUR LOCATION.
BEEP! BEEEEEP! BEEP!
SEEDS
LATER...
MAYBE IT'S JUST THE ISLAND MADNESS TALKING, BUT THAT MARGE SURE IS PRETTY. I THINK I'LL DROWN HOMER AND MAKE HER MY BRIDE. WANNA HELP?
OKAY, BUT THEN I'LL DROWN YOU AND MAKE HER MY BRIDE LATER.
FAIR ENOUGH.
WAIT A MINUTE. HOW DO I KNOW YOU GUYS WON'T CHEAT AT THIS BREATH HOLDING CONTEST?
LOOK, WE'LL TIE THESE BAGS OF CEMENT TO YOU TO GIVE YOU A HEAD START.
CEMENT
SCREEEE!
WHAT THE--?
MAN, IT GETS DARK EARLY HERE.

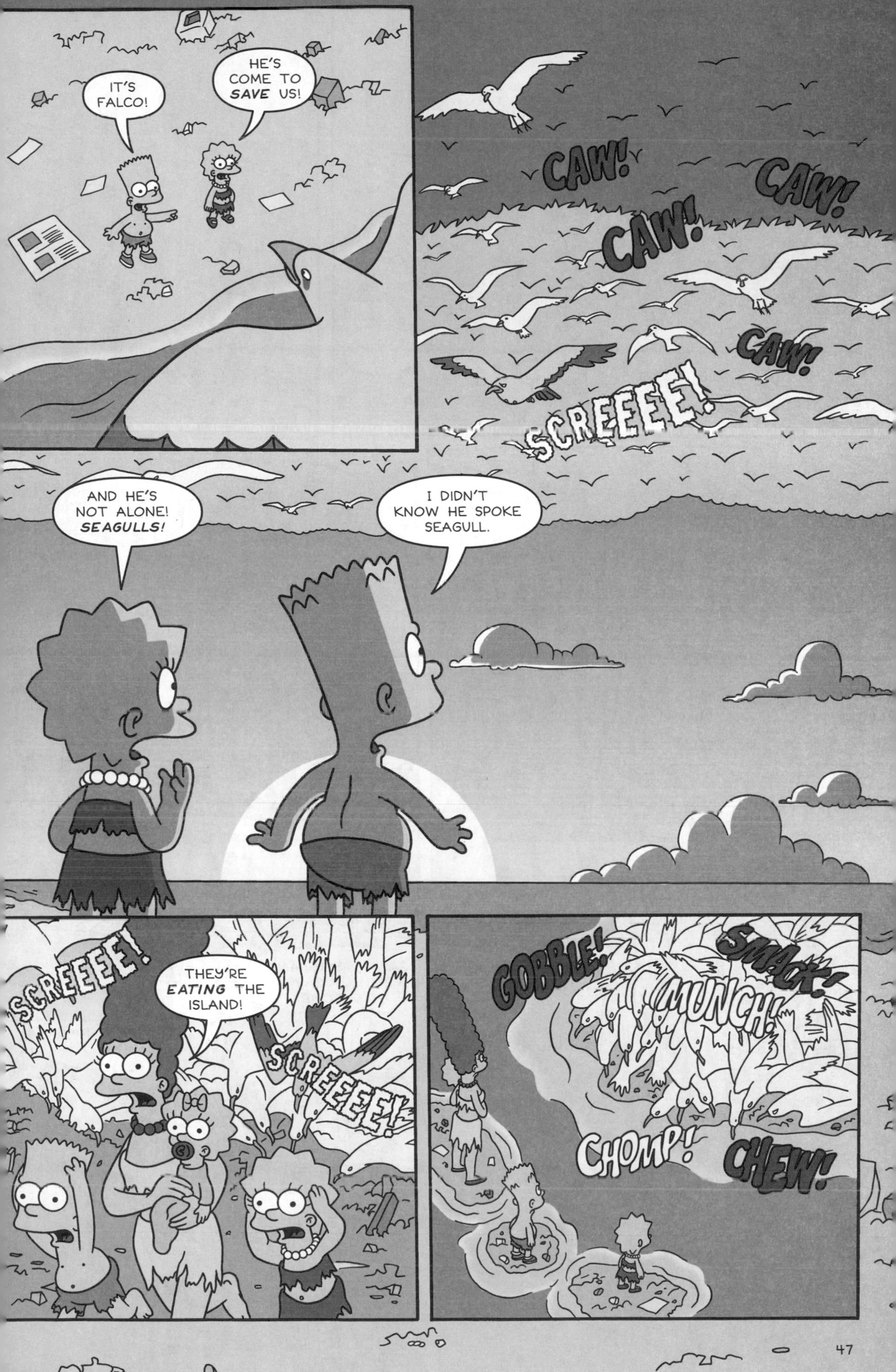
IT'S FALCO!
HE'S COME TO SAVE US!
CAW!
CAW!
CAW!
CAW!
SCREEEEE!
AND HE'S NOT ALONE! SEAGULLS!
I DIDN'T KNOW HE SPOKE SEAGULL.
SCREEEEE!
THEY'RE EATING THE ISLAND!
SCREEEEE!
GOBBLE!
SMACK!
MUNCH!
CHOMP!
CHEW!

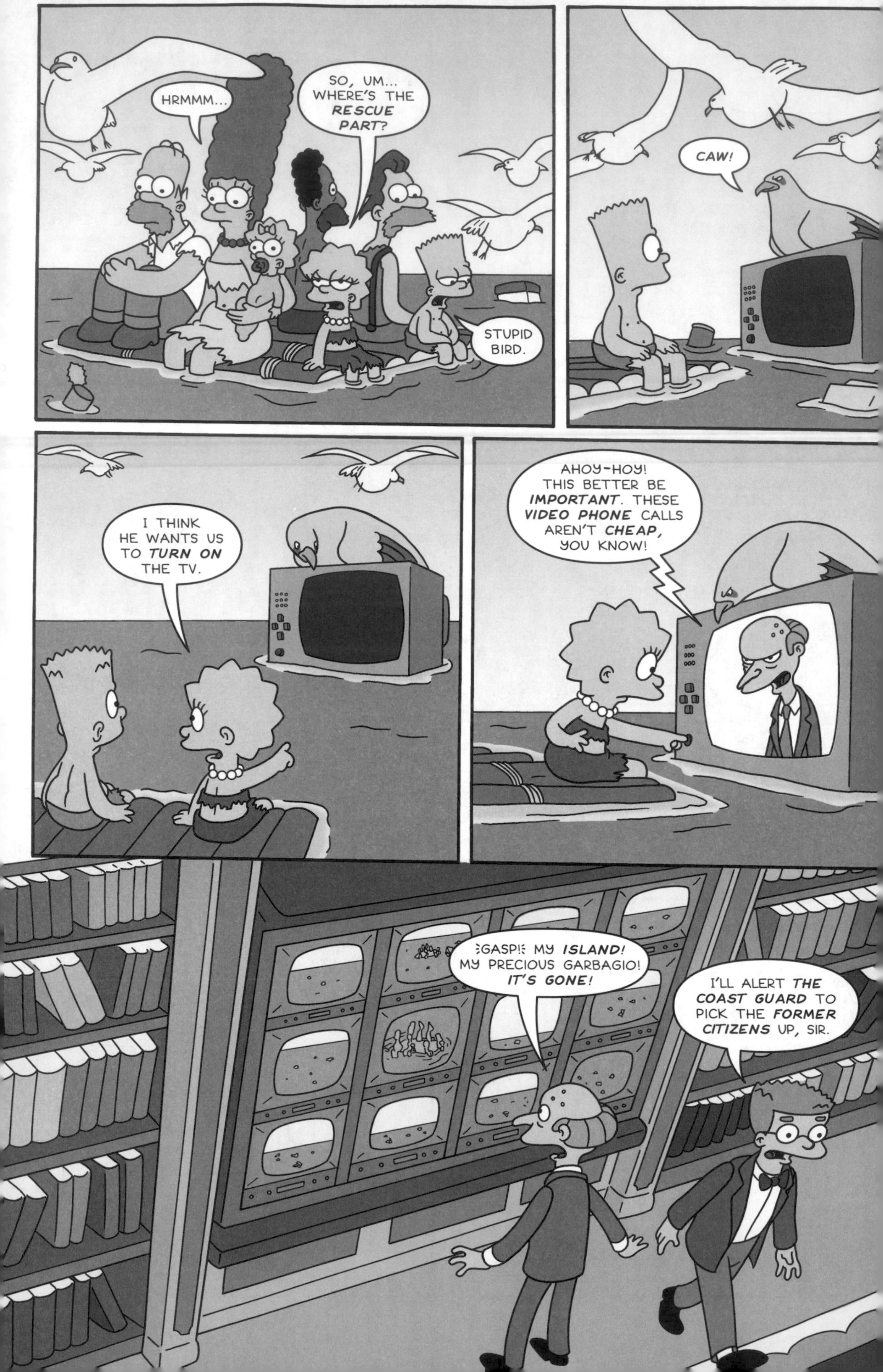
HRMMM...
SO, UM... WHERE'S THE RESCUE PART?
STUPID BIRD.
CAW!
I THINK HE WANTS US TO TURN ON THE TV.
AHOY-HOY! THIS BETTER BE IMPORTANT. THESE VIDEO PHONE CALLS AREN'T CHEAP, YOU KNOW!
GASP! MY ISLAND! MY PRECIOUS GARBAGIO! IT'S GONE!
I'LL ALERT THE COAST GUARD TO PICK THE FORMER CITIZENS UP, SIR.

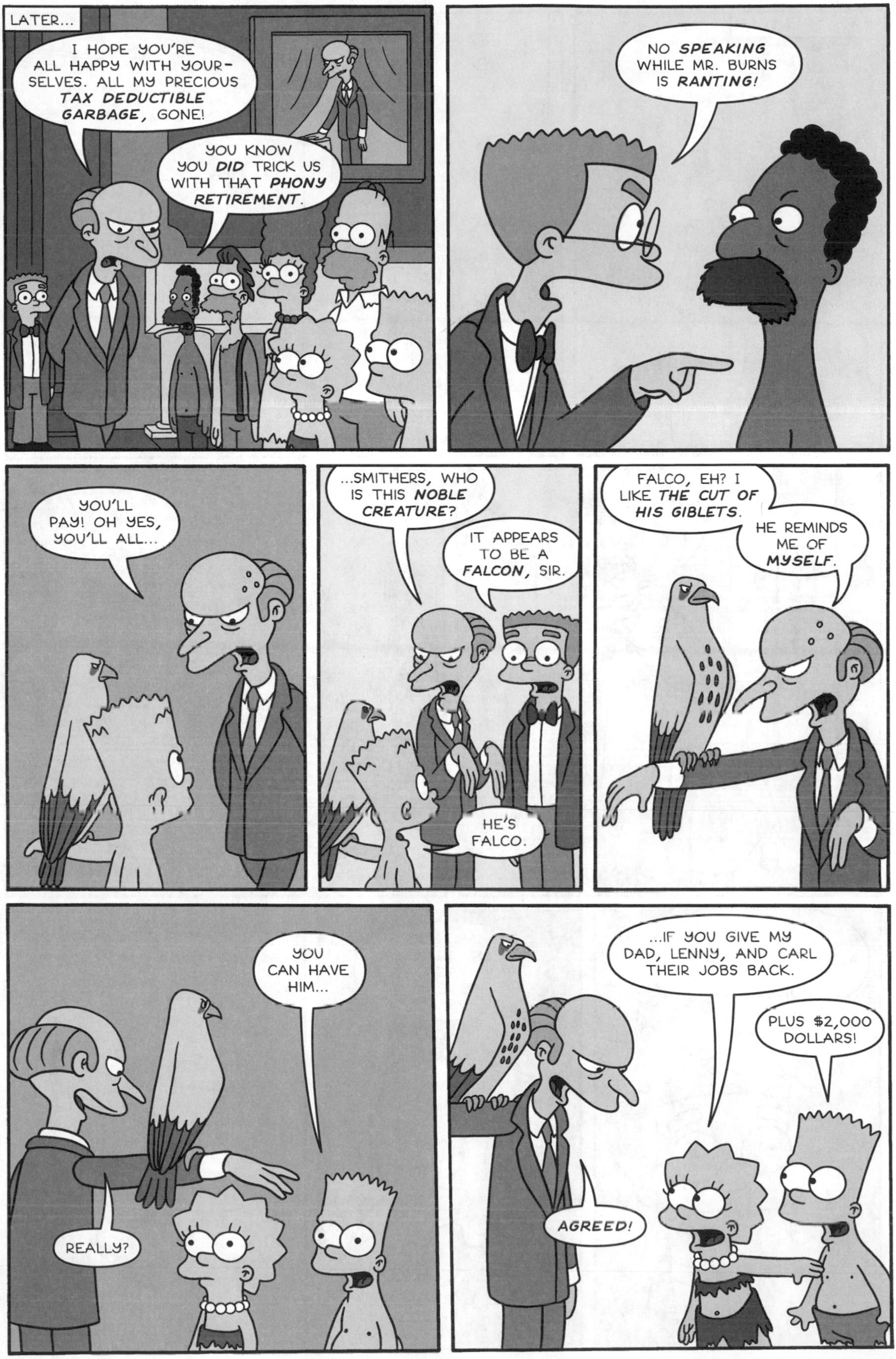

LATER...
I HOPE YOU'RE ALL HAPPY WITH YOURSELVES. ALL MY PRECIOUS **TAX DEDUCTIBLE GARBAGE**, GONE!
YOU KNOW YOU **DID** TRICK US WITH THAT **PHONY RETIREMENT**.
NO **SPEAKING** WHILE MR. BURNS IS **RANTING!**
YOU'LL PAY! OH YES, YOU'LL ALL...
...SMITHERS, WHO IS THIS **NOBLE CREATURE**?
IT APPEARS TO BE A **FALCON**, SIR.
HE'S FALCO.
FALCO, EH? I LIKE **THE CUT OF HIS GIBLETS**.
HE REMINDS ME OF **MYSELF**.
YOU CAN HAVE HIM...
REALLY?
...IF YOU GIVE MY DAD, LENNY, AND CARL THEIR JOBS BACK.
PLUS $2,000 DOLLARS!
AGREED!

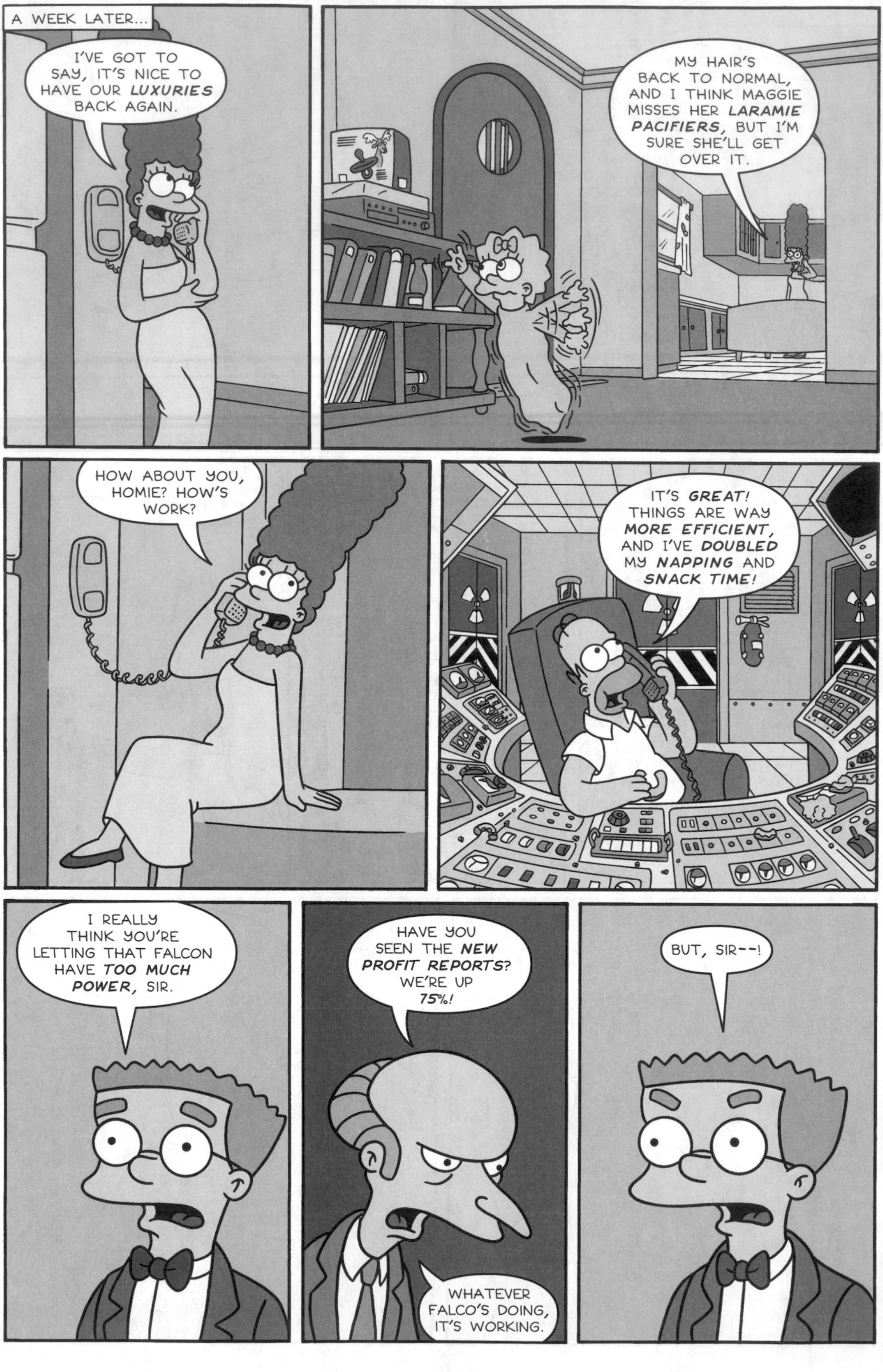
A WEEK LATER...
I'VE GOT TO SAY, IT'S NICE TO HAVE OUR **LUXURIES** BACK AGAIN.
MY HAIR'S BACK TO NORMAL, AND I THINK MAGGIE MISSES HER **LARAMIE PACIFIERS,** BUT I'M SURE SHE'LL GET OVER IT.
HOW ABOUT YOU, HOMIE? HOW'S WORK?
IT'S **GREAT!** THINGS ARE WAY **MORE EFFICIENT,** AND I'VE **DOUBLED** MY **NAPPING** AND **SNACK TIME!**
I REALLY THINK YOU'RE LETTING THAT FALCON HAVE **TOO MUCH POWER,** SIR.
HAVE YOU SEEN THE **NEW PROFIT REPORTS?** WE'RE UP **75%!**
WHATEVER FALCO'S DOING, IT'S WORKING.
BUT, SIR--!

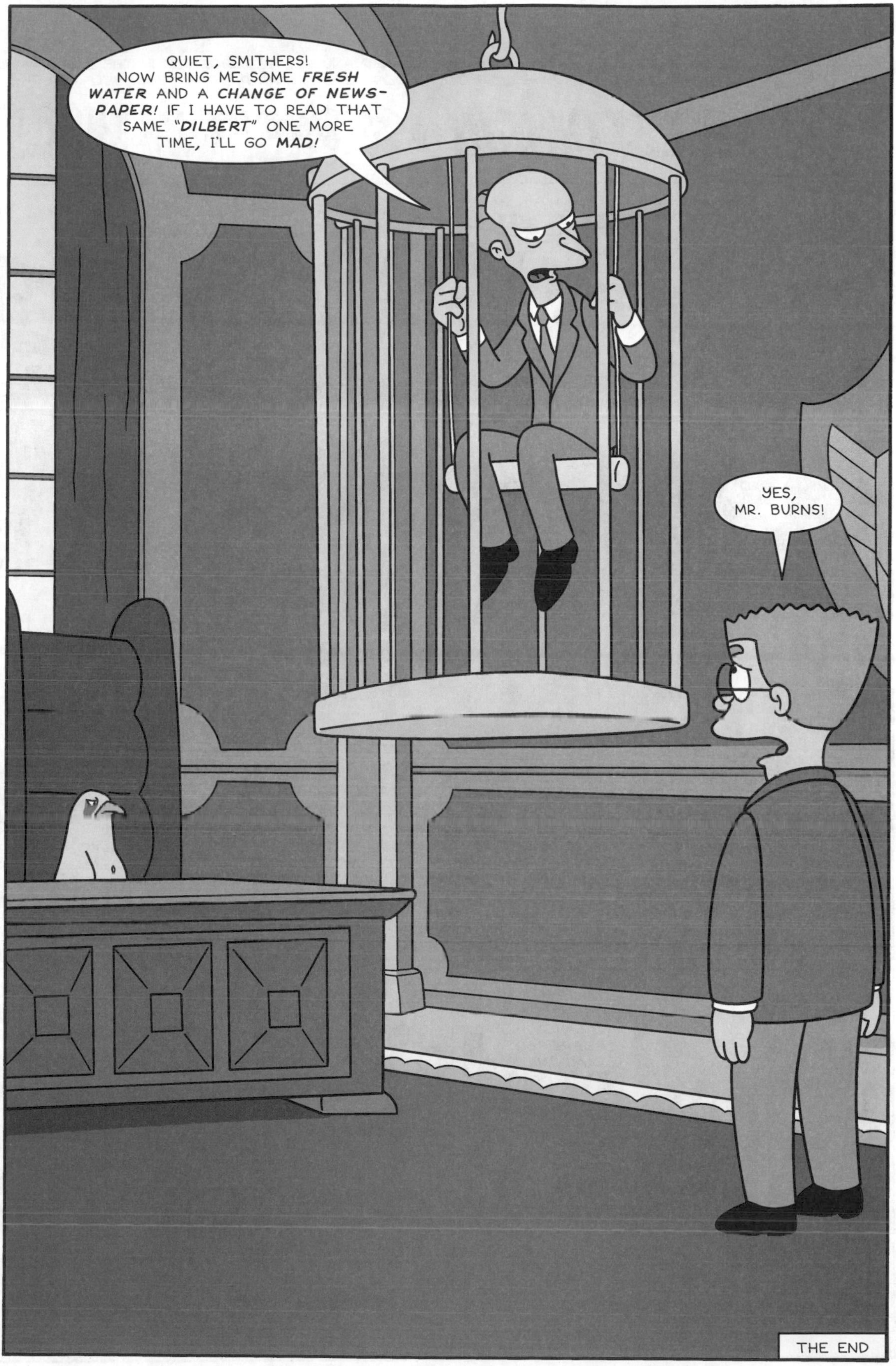
QUIET, SMITHERS! NOW BRING ME SOME **FRESH WATER** AND A **CHANGE OF NEWS-PAPER!** IF I HAVE TO READ THAT SAME "**DILBERT**" ONE MORE TIME, I'LL GO **MAD!**
YES, MR. BURNS!
THE END

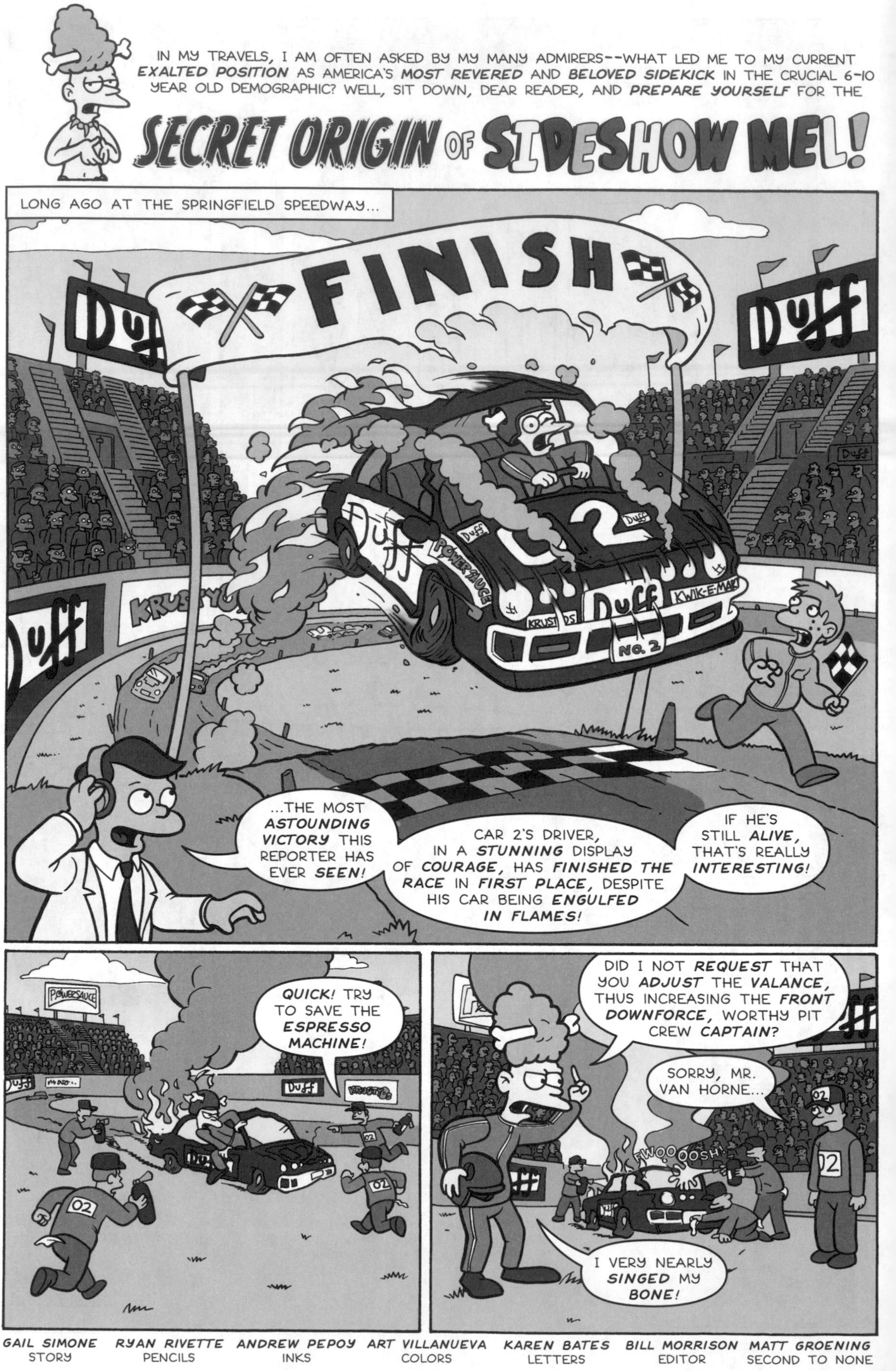
IN MY TRAVELS, I AM OFTEN ASKED BY MY MANY ADMIRERS--WHAT LED ME TO MY CURRENT *EXALTED POSITION* AS AMERICA'S *MOST REVERED* AND *BELOVED SIDEKICK* IN THE CRUCIAL 6-10 YEAR OLD DEMOGRAPHIC? WELL, SIT DOWN, DEAR READER, AND *PREPARE YOURSELF* FOR THE
SECRET ORIGIN OF SIDESHOW MEL!
LONG AGO AT THE SPRINGFIELD SPEEDWAY...
FINISH
...THE MOST *ASTOUNDING VICTORY* THIS REPORTER HAS EVER *SEEN*!
CAR 2'S DRIVER, IN A *STUNNING* DISPLAY OF *COURAGE*, HAS *FINISHED THE RACE* IN *FIRST PLACE*, DESPITE HIS CAR BEING *ENGULFED IN FLAMES*!
IF HE'S STILL *ALIVE*, THAT'S REALLY *INTERESTING*!
QUICK! TRY TO SAVE THE *ESPRESSO MACHINE*!
DID I NOT *REQUEST* THAT YOU *ADJUST* THE *VALANCE*, THUS INCREASING THE *FRONT DOWNFORCE*, WORTHY PIT CREW *CAPTAIN*?
SORRY, MR. VAN HORNE...
FWOOOOSH!
I VERY NEARLY *SINGED* MY *BONE*!

GAIL SIMONE STORY · *RYAN RIVETTE* PENCILS · *ANDREW PEPOY* INKS · *ART VILLANUEVA* COLORS · *KAREN BATES* LETTERS · *BILL MORRISON* EDITOR · *MATT GROENING* SECOND TO NONE

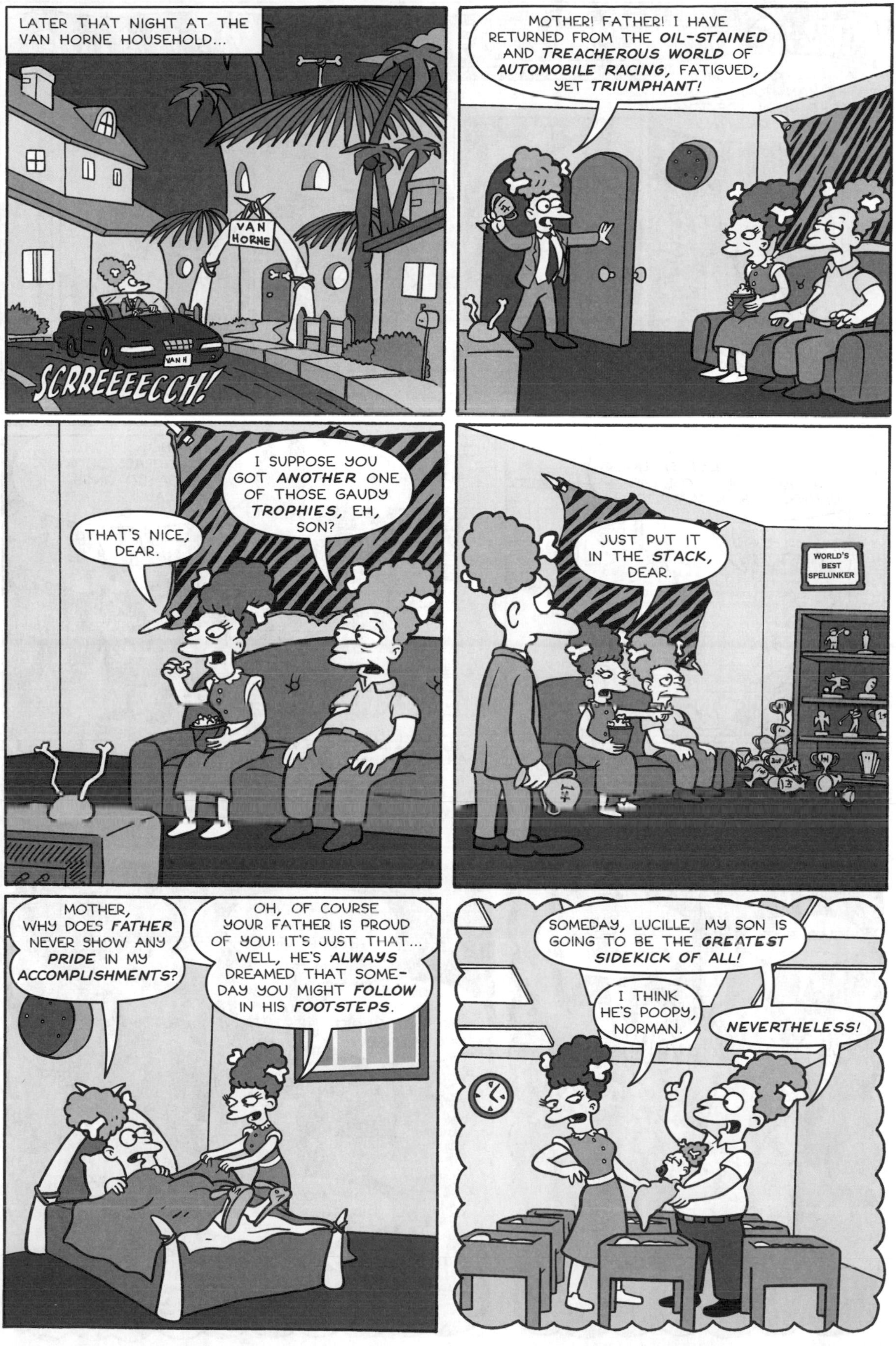
LATER THAT NIGHT AT THE VAN HORNE HOUSEHOLD...
VAN HORNE
VAN H
SCRREEEEECCH!
MOTHER! FATHER! I HAVE RETURNED FROM THE OIL-STAINED AND TREACHEROUS WORLD OF AUTOMOBILE RACING, FATIGUED, YET TRIUMPHANT!
THAT'S NICE, DEAR.
I SUPPOSE YOU GOT ANOTHER ONE OF THOSE GAUDY TROPHIES, EH, SON?
JUST PUT IT IN THE STACK, DEAR.
WORLD'S BEST SPELUNKER
MOTHER, WHY DOES FATHER NEVER SHOW ANY PRIDE IN MY ACCOMPLISHMENTS?
OH, OF COURSE YOUR FATHER IS PROUD OF YOU! IT'S JUST THAT... WELL, HE'S ALWAYS DREAMED THAT SOMEDAY YOU MIGHT FOLLOW IN HIS FOOTSTEPS.
SOMEDAY, LUCILLE, MY SON IS GOING TO BE THE GREATEST SIDEKICK OF ALL!
I THINK HE'S POOPY, NORMAN.
NEVERTHELESS!

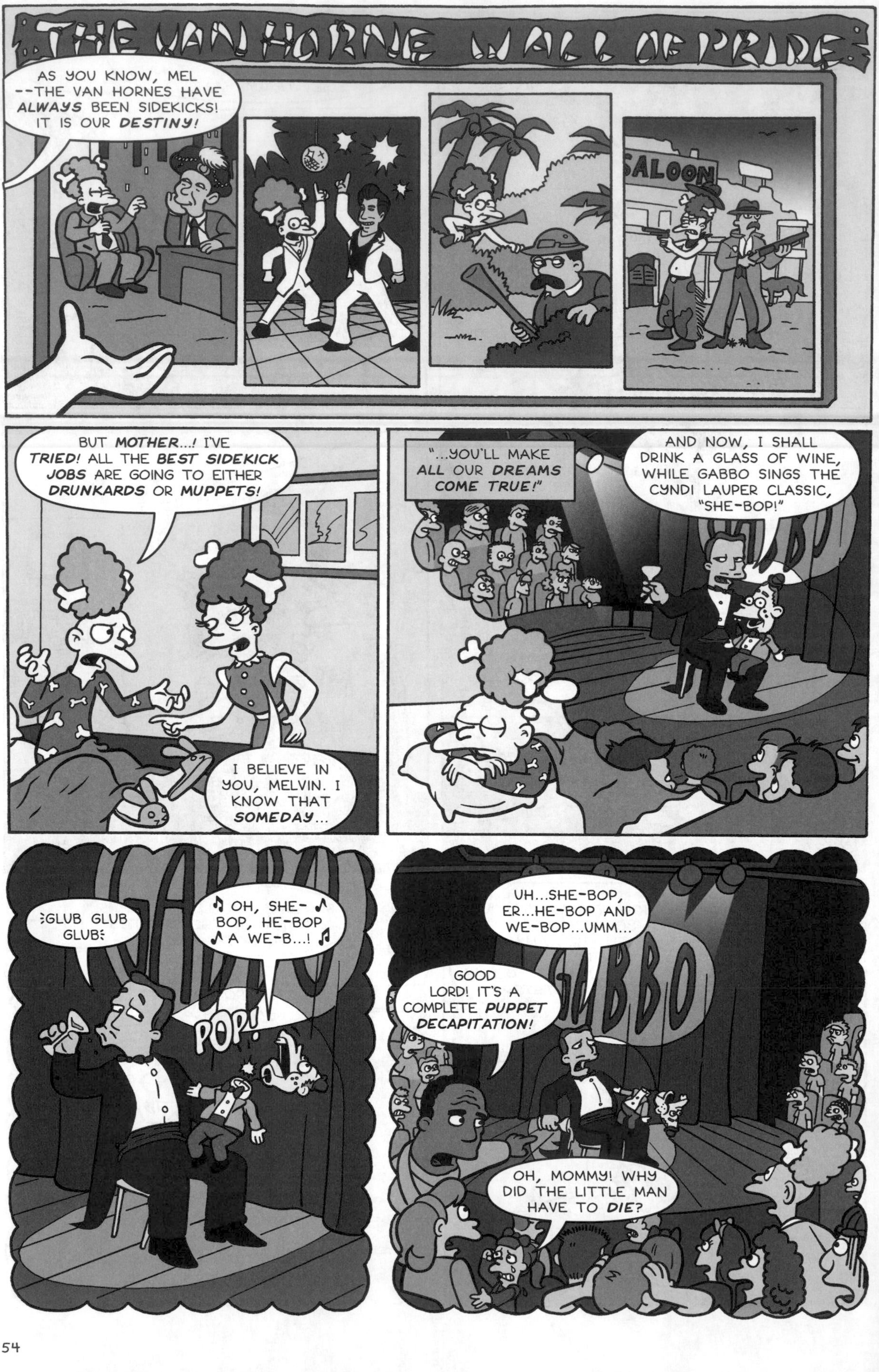
THE VAN HORNE WALL OF PRIDE
AS YOU KNOW, MEL --THE VAN HORNES HAVE ALWAYS BEEN SIDEKICKS! IT IS OUR DESTINY!
SALOON
BUT MOTHER...! I'VE TRIED! ALL THE BEST SIDEKICK JOBS ARE GOING TO EITHER DRUNKARDS OR MUPPETS!
I BELIEVE IN YOU, MELVIN. I KNOW THAT SOMEDAY...
"...YOU'LL MAKE ALL OUR DREAMS COME TRUE!"
AND NOW, I SHALL DRINK A GLASS OF WINE, WHILE GABBO SINGS THE CYNDI LAUPER CLASSIC, "SHE-BOP!"
GLUB GLUB GLUB
♪ OH, SHE-BOP, HE-BOP ♪ A WE-B...! ♪
POP!
UH...SHE-BOP, ER...HE-BOP AND WE-BOP...UMM...
GABBO
GOOD LORD! IT'S A COMPLETE PUPPET DECAPITATION!
OH, MOMMY! WHY DID THE LITTLE MAN HAVE TO DIE?

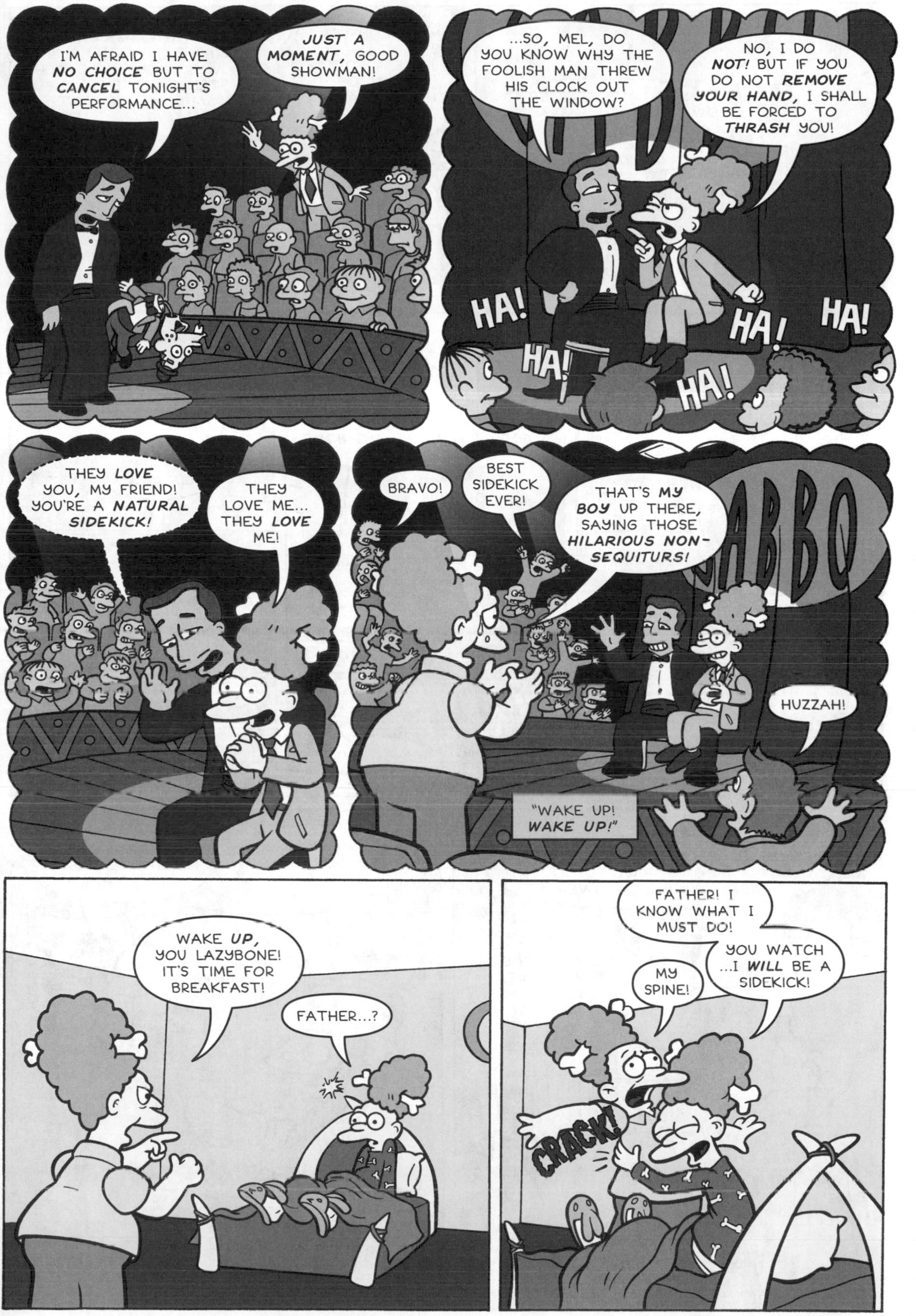

I'M AFRAID I HAVE NO CHOICE BUT TO CANCEL TONIGHT'S PERFORMANCE...
JUST A MOMENT, GOOD SHOWMAN!
...SO, MEL, DO YOU KNOW WHY THE FOOLISH MAN THREW HIS CLOCK OUT THE WINDOW?
NO, I DO NOT! BUT IF YOU DO NOT REMOVE YOUR HAND, I SHALL BE FORCED TO THRASH YOU!
HA! HA! HA! HA! HA!
THEY LOVE YOU, MY FRIEND! YOU'RE A NATURAL SIDEKICK!
THEY LOVE ME... THEY LOVE ME!
BRAVO!
BEST SIDEKICK EVER!
THAT'S MY BOY UP THERE, SAYING THOSE HILARIOUS NON-SEQUITURS!
HUZZAH!
"WAKE UP! WAKE UP!"
WAKE UP, YOU LAZYBONE! IT'S TIME FOR BREAKFAST!
FATHER...?
FATHER! I KNOW WHAT I MUST DO!
YOU WATCH ...I WILL BE A SIDEKICK!
MY SPINE!
CRACK!

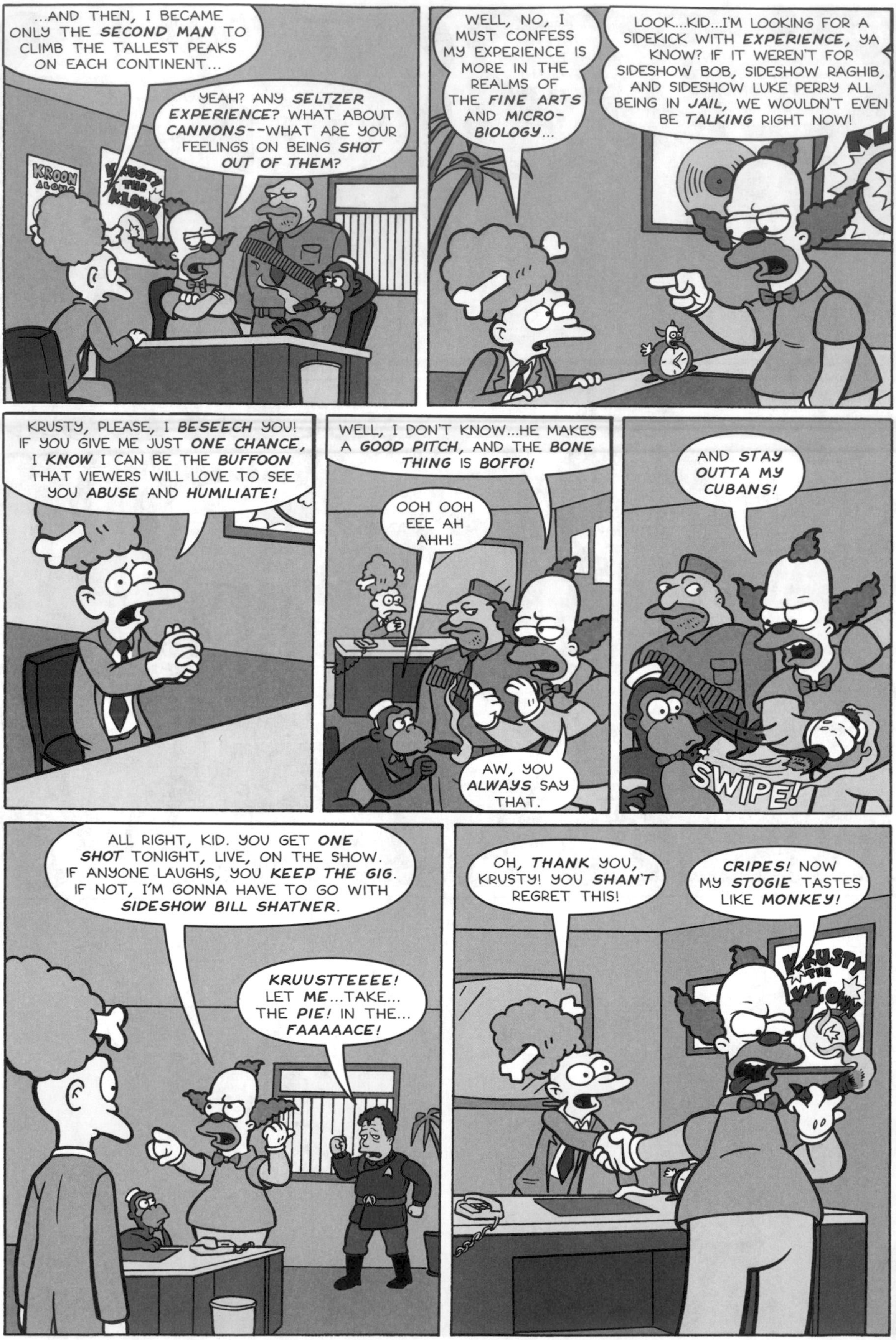
...AND THEN, I BECAME ONLY THE SECOND MAN TO CLIMB THE TALLEST PEAKS ON EACH CONTINENT...
YEAH? ANY SELTZER EXPERIENCE? WHAT ABOUT CANNONS--WHAT ARE YOUR FEELINGS ON BEING SHOT OUT OF THEM?
KROON ALONG
KRUSTY THE KLOWN
WELL, NO, I MUST CONFESS MY EXPERIENCE IS MORE IN THE REALMS OF THE FINE ARTS AND MICRO-BIOLOGY...
LOOK...KID...I'M LOOKING FOR A SIDEKICK WITH EXPERIENCE, YA KNOW? IF IT WEREN'T FOR SIDESHOW BOB, SIDESHOW RAGHIB, AND SIDESHOW LUKE PERRY ALL BEING IN JAIL, WE WOULDN'T EVEN BE TALKING RIGHT NOW!
KRUSTY, PLEASE, I BESEECH YOU! IF YOU GIVE ME JUST ONE CHANCE, I KNOW I CAN BE THE BUFFOON THAT VIEWERS WILL LOVE TO SEE YOU ABUSE AND HUMILIATE!
WELL, I DON'T KNOW...HE MAKES A GOOD PITCH, AND THE BONE THING IS BOFFO!
OOH OOH EEE AH AHH!
AW, YOU ALWAYS SAY THAT.
AND STAY OUTTA MY CUBANS!
SWIPE!
ALL RIGHT, KID. YOU GET ONE SHOT TONIGHT, LIVE, ON THE SHOW. IF ANYONE LAUGHS, YOU KEEP THE GIG. IF NOT, I'M GONNA HAVE TO GO WITH SIDESHOW BILL SHATNER.
KRUUSTTEEEE! LET ME...TAKE... THE PIE! IN THE... FAAAAACE!
OH, THANK YOU, KRUSTY! YOU SHAN'T REGRET THIS!
CRIPES! NOW MY STOGIE TASTES LIKE MONKEY!
KRUSTY THE KLOWN

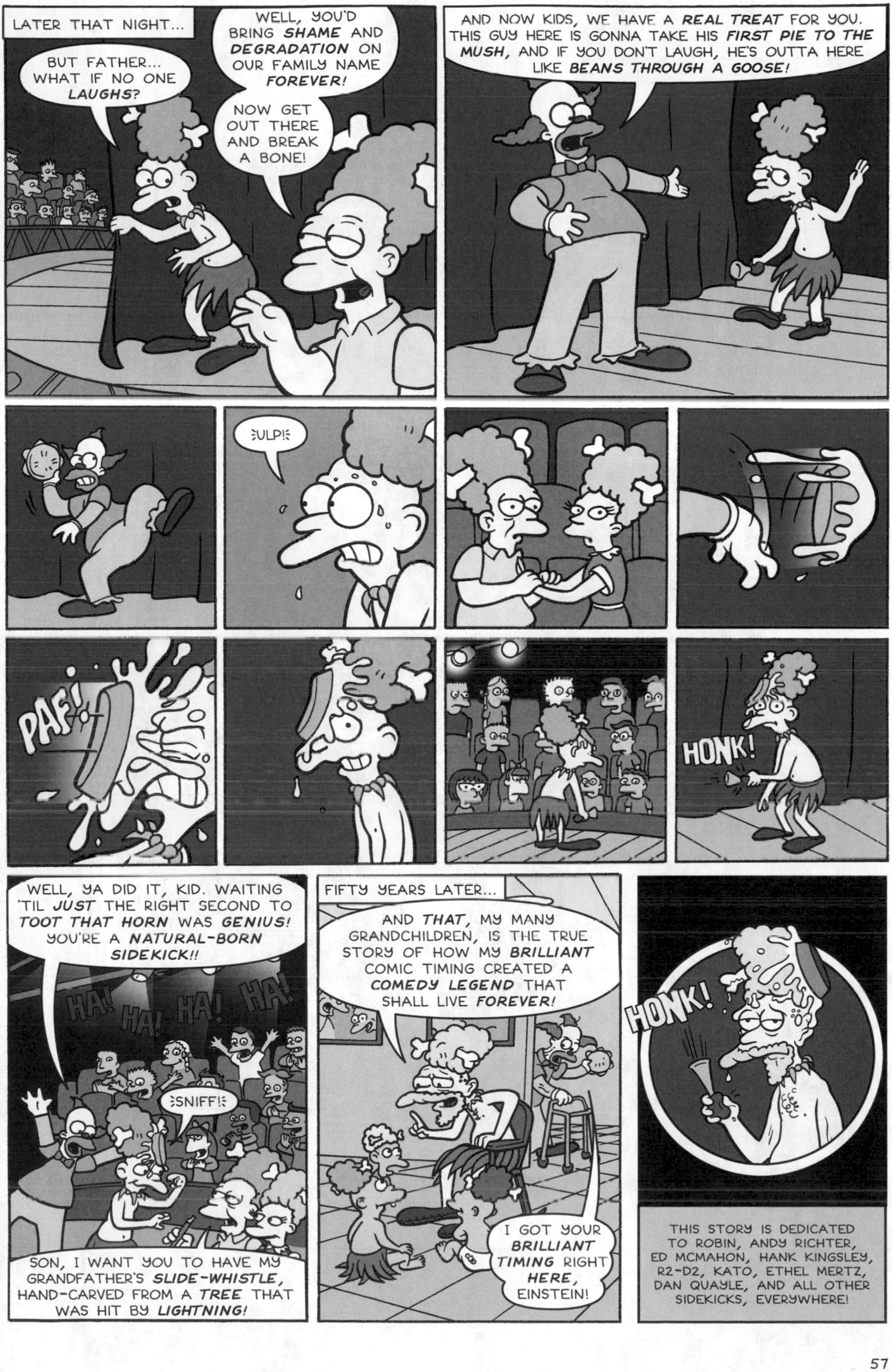
LATER THAT NIGHT...
BUT FATHER... WHAT IF NO ONE LAUGHS?
WELL, YOU'D BRING SHAME AND DEGRADATION ON OUR FAMILY NAME FOREVER!
NOW GET OUT THERE AND BREAK A BONE!
AND NOW KIDS, WE HAVE A REAL TREAT FOR YOU. THIS GUY HERE IS GONNA TAKE HIS FIRST PIE TO THE MUSH, AND IF YOU DON'T LAUGH, HE'S OUTTA HERE LIKE BEANS THROUGH A GOOSE!
ULP!
PAF!
HONK!
WELL, YA DID IT, KID. WAITING 'TIL JUST THE RIGHT SECOND TO TOOT THAT HORN WAS GENIUS! YOU'RE A NATURAL-BORN SIDEKICK!!
HA! HA! HA! HA!
SNIFF!
SON, I WANT YOU TO HAVE MY GRANDFATHER'S SLIDE-WHISTLE, HAND-CARVED FROM A TREE THAT WAS HIT BY LIGHTNING!
FIFTY YEARS LATER...
AND THAT, MY MANY GRANDCHILDREN, IS THE TRUE STORY OF HOW MY BRILLIANT COMIC TIMING CREATED A COMEDY LEGEND THAT SHALL LIVE FOREVER!
I GOT YOUR BRILLIANT TIMING RIGHT HERE, EINSTEIN!
HONK!
THIS STORY IS DEDICATED TO ROBIN, ANDY RICHTER, ED MCMAHON, HANK KINGSLEY, R2-D2, KATO, ETHEL MERTZ, DAN QUAYLE, AND ALL OTHER SIDEKICKS, EVERYWHERE!

WORST COVER EVER!
BONGO COMICS GROUP
#73
SIMPSONS COMICS
APPROVED BY THE COMICS CODE AUTHORITY
WHO WILL BE CROWNED
KING OF THE NERDS?

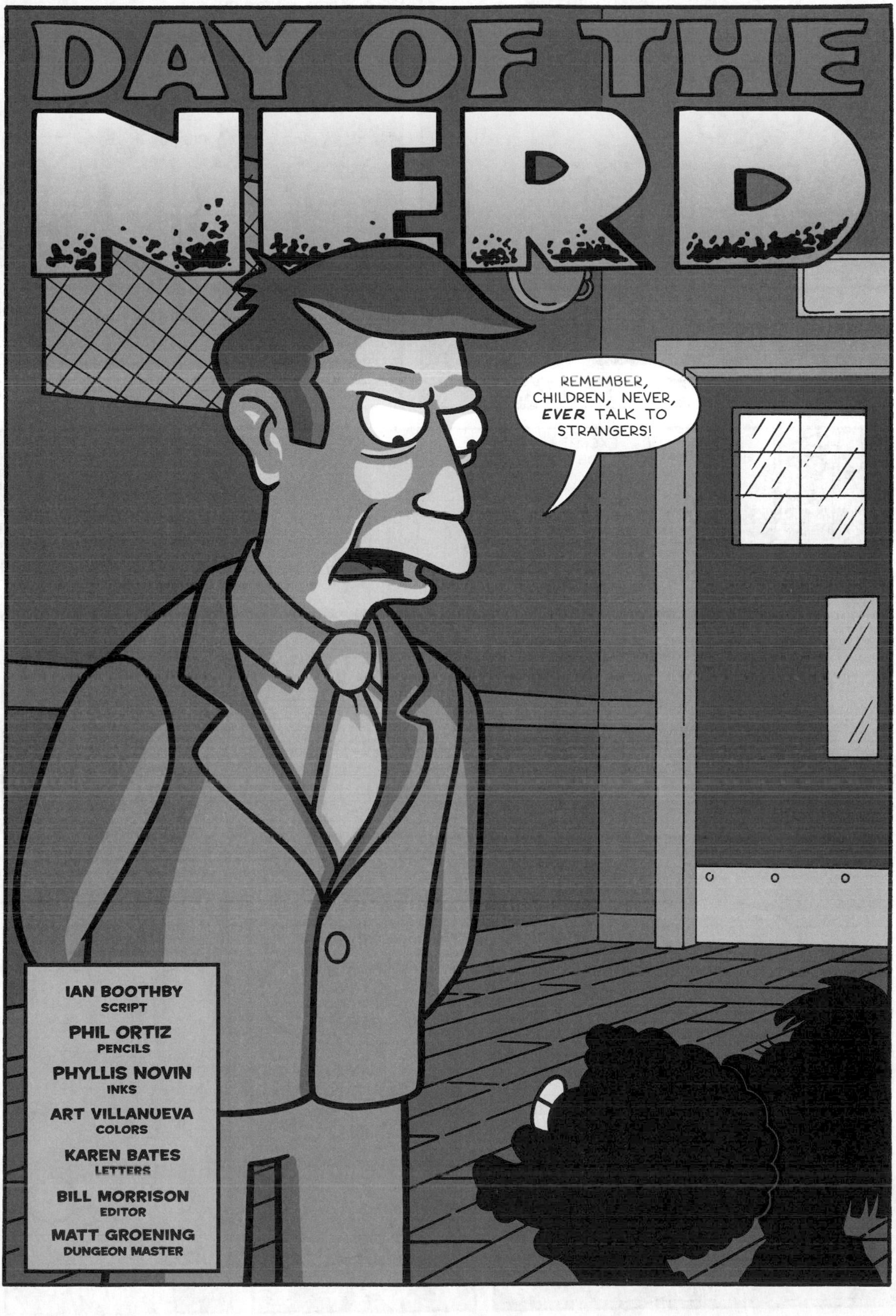
DAY OF THE NERD
REMEMBER, CHILDREN, NEVER, EVER TALK TO STRANGERS!
IAN BOOTHBY SCRIPT
PHIL ORTIZ PENCILS
PHYLLIS NOVIN INKS
ART VILLANUEVA COLORS
KAREN BATES LETTERS
BILL MORRISON EDITOR
MATT GROENING DUNGEON MASTER

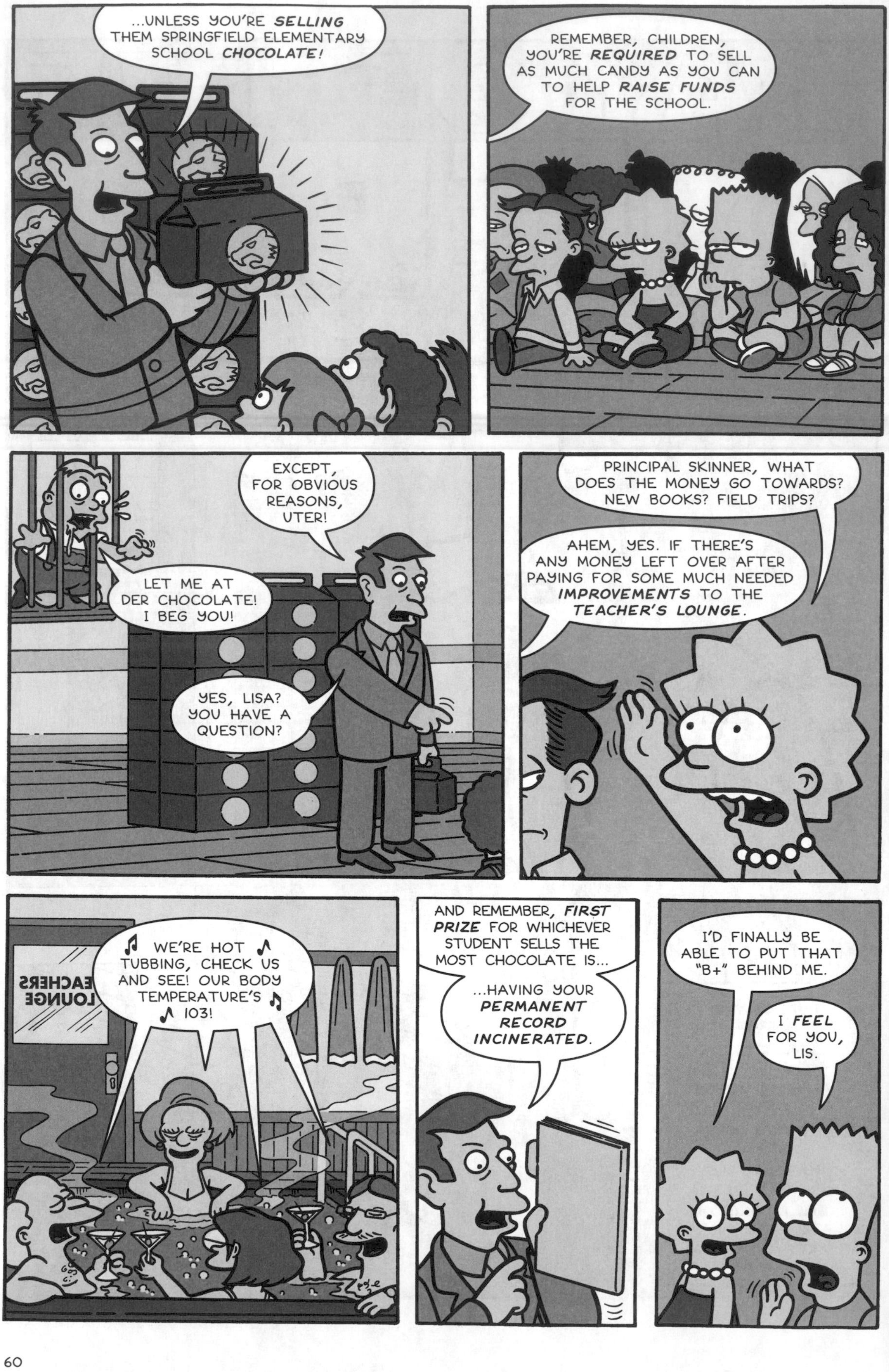

...UNLESS YOU'RE SELLING THEM SPRINGFIELD ELEMENTARY SCHOOL CHOCOLATE!
REMEMBER, CHILDREN, YOU'RE REQUIRED TO SELL AS MUCH CANDY AS YOU CAN TO HELP RAISE FUNDS FOR THE SCHOOL.
EXCEPT, FOR OBVIOUS REASONS, UTER!
LET ME AT DER CHOCOLATE! I BEG YOU!
YES, LISA? YOU HAVE A QUESTION?
PRINCIPAL SKINNER, WHAT DOES THE MONEY GO TOWARDS? NEW BOOKS? FIELD TRIPS?
AHEM, YES. IF THERE'S ANY MONEY LEFT OVER AFTER PAYING FOR SOME MUCH NEEDED IMPROVEMENTS TO THE TEACHER'S LOUNGE.
EACHERS LOUNGE
♪ WE'RE HOT ♪ TUBBING, CHECK US AND SEE! OUR BODY TEMPERATURE'S ♪ ♪ 103!
AND REMEMBER, FIRST PRIZE FOR WHICHEVER STUDENT SELLS THE MOST CHOCOLATE IS...
...HAVING YOUR PERMANENT RECORD INCINERATED.
I'D FINALLY BE ABLE TO PUT THAT "B+" BEHIND ME.
I FEEL FOR YOU, LIS.

LATER...

I THINK I'LL START IN RICHDALE AND WORK MY WAY TO JUNKIEVILLE AND BUMTOWN.

I'M GOING HOME FIRST.

WHAT? WHY?

A *NEW PROBE* HAS LANDED ON *MARS*, AND I WANT TO WATCH THE *LIVE FOOTAGE*.

GIVE ME A HEADS UP IF THE *MARTIANS* ARE PLANNING TO *INVADE*!

YOU GOT IT!

WILLIE! UTER'S FREE! CODE RED! *CODE RED!*

I'LL GET THE *TASER GUN!*

AND SO YOU SEE, MARS' SURFACE IS PRETTY DUSTY. WE'RE READING AN ATMOSPHERE OF 95% CARBON DIOXIDE AND 2% ARGON.

FASCINATING.

BUT I WANTED TO SEE THAT SHOW WHERE GOOD-LOOKING PEOPLE GET COVERED IN RATS.

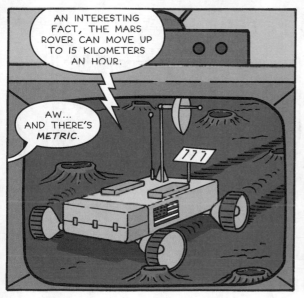

AN INTERESTING FACT, THE MARS ROVER CAN MOVE UP TO 15 KILOMETERS AN HOUR.

AW... AND THERE'S *METRIC*.

DO YOU THINK *I* COULD EVER GO INTO SPACE, DAD?

WHY NOT? *I DID.* YOU SHOULD HAVE SAID SOME-THING. I WOULD HAVE *SMUGGLED* YOU ON BOARD.

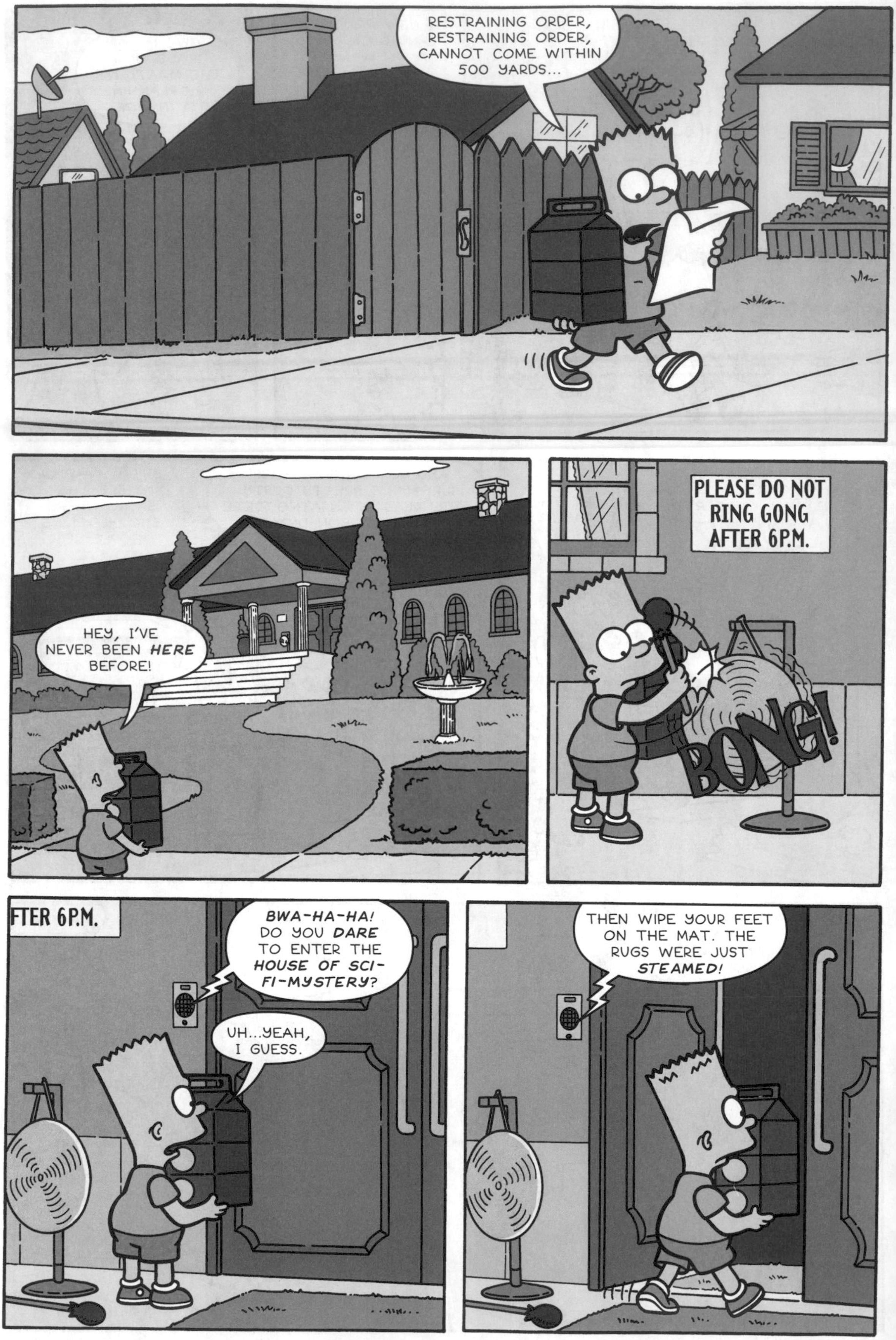
RESTRAINING ORDER, RESTRAINING ORDER, CANNOT COME WITHIN 500 YARDS...
HEY, I'VE NEVER BEEN *HERE* BEFORE!
PLEASE DO NOT RING GONG AFTER 6P.M.
BONG!
FTER 6P.M.
BWA-HA-HA! DO YOU *DARE* TO ENTER THE *HOUSE OF SCI-FI-MYSTERY*?
UH...YEAH, I GUESS.
THEN WIPE YOUR FEET ON THE MAT. THE RUGS WERE JUST *STEAMED!*

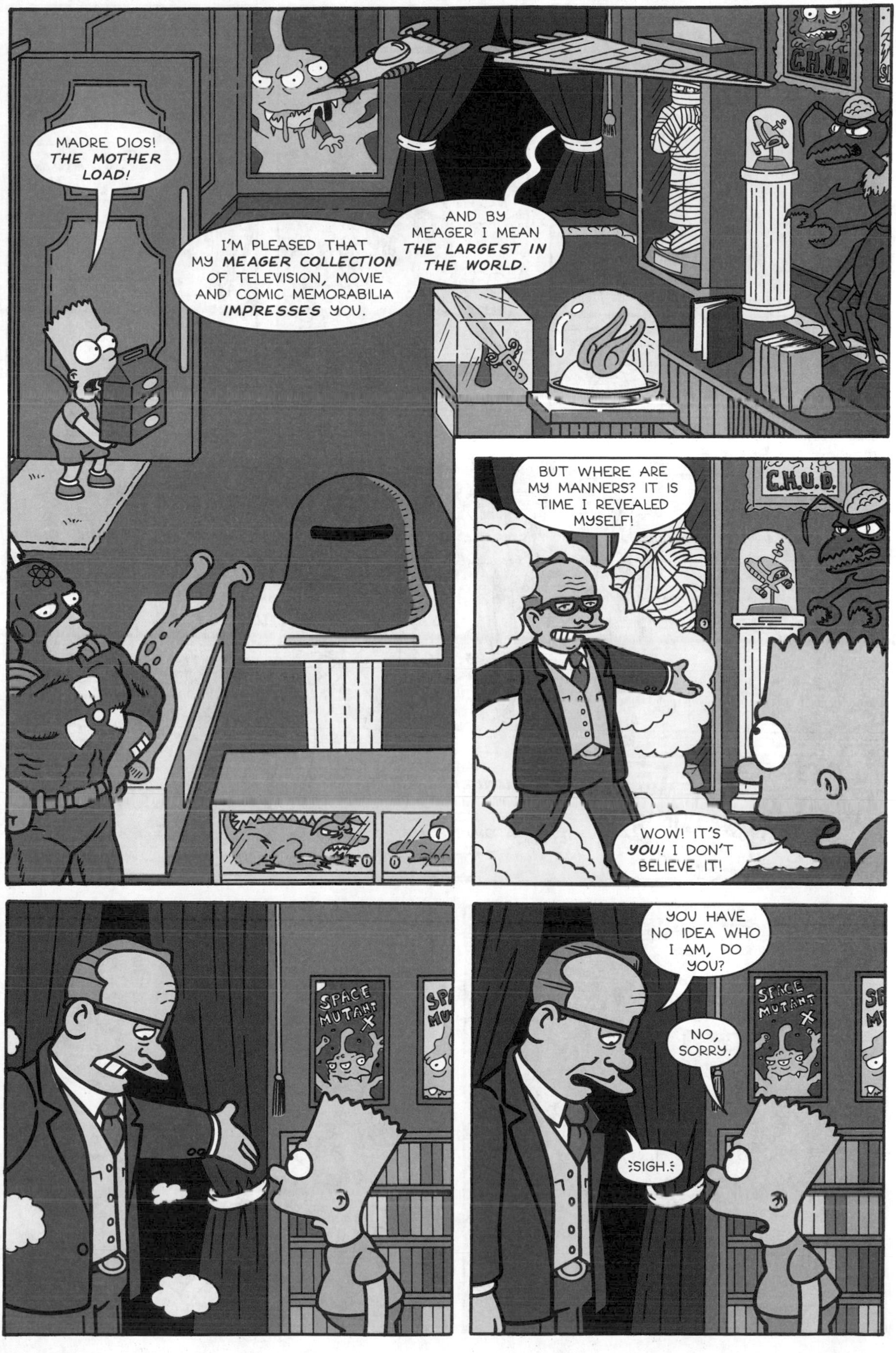
MADRE DIOS! THE MOTHER LOAD!
I'M PLEASED THAT MY MEAGER COLLECTION OF TELEVISION, MOVIE AND COMIC MEMORABILIA IMPRESSES YOU.
AND BY MEAGER I MEAN THE LARGEST IN THE WORLD.
C.H.U.D.
BUT WHERE ARE MY MANNERS? IT IS TIME I REVEALED MYSELF!
WOW! IT'S YOU! I DON'T BELIEVE IT!
SPACE MUTANT X
YOU HAVE NO IDEA WHO I AM, DO YOU?
NO, SORRY.
SIGH.

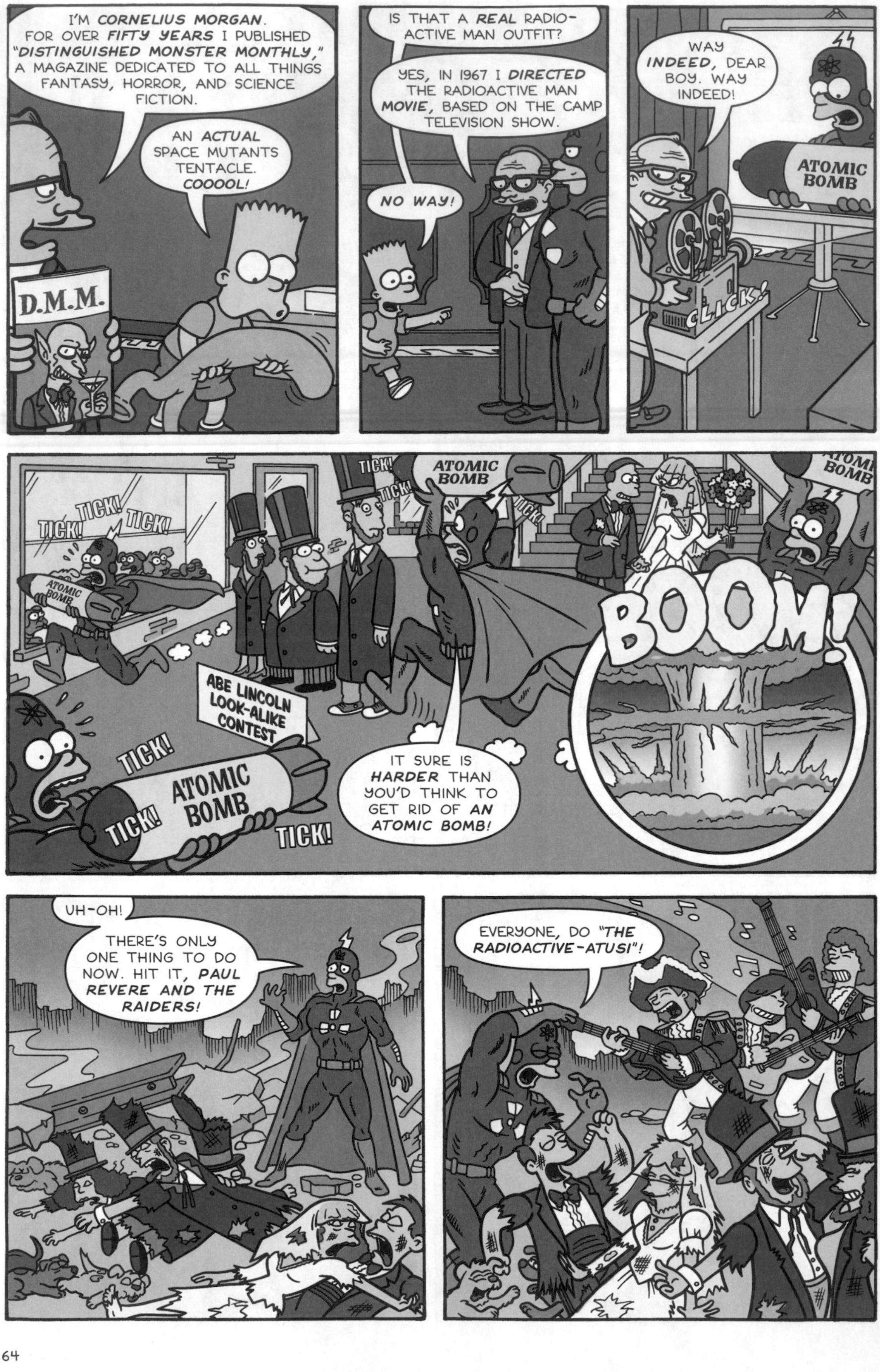

I'M CORNELIUS MORGAN. FOR OVER FIFTY YEARS I PUBLISHED "DISTINGUISHED MONSTER MONTHLY," A MAGAZINE DEDICATED TO ALL THINGS FANTASY, HORROR, AND SCIENCE FICTION.
AN ACTUAL SPACE MUTANTS TENTACLE. COOOOL!
D.M.M.
IS THAT A REAL RADIO-ACTIVE MAN OUTFIT?
YES, IN 1967 I DIRECTED THE RADIOACTIVE MAN MOVIE, BASED ON THE CAMP TELEVISION SHOW.
NO WAY!
WAY INDEED, DEAR BOY. WAY INDEED!
ATOMIC BOMB
CLICK!
TICK!
TICK!
TICK!
ATOMIC BOMB
TICK!
TICK!
ATOMIC BOMB
TICK!
ATOMIC BOMB
ABE LINCOLN LOOK-ALIKE CONTEST
TICK!
ATOMIC BOMB
TICK!
TICK!
IT SURE IS HARDER THAN YOU'D THINK TO GET RID OF AN ATOMIC BOMB!
BOOM!
UH-OH!
THERE'S ONLY ONE THING TO DO NOW. HIT IT, PAUL REVERE AND THE RAIDERS!
EVERYONE, DO "THE RADIOACTIVE-ATUSI"!

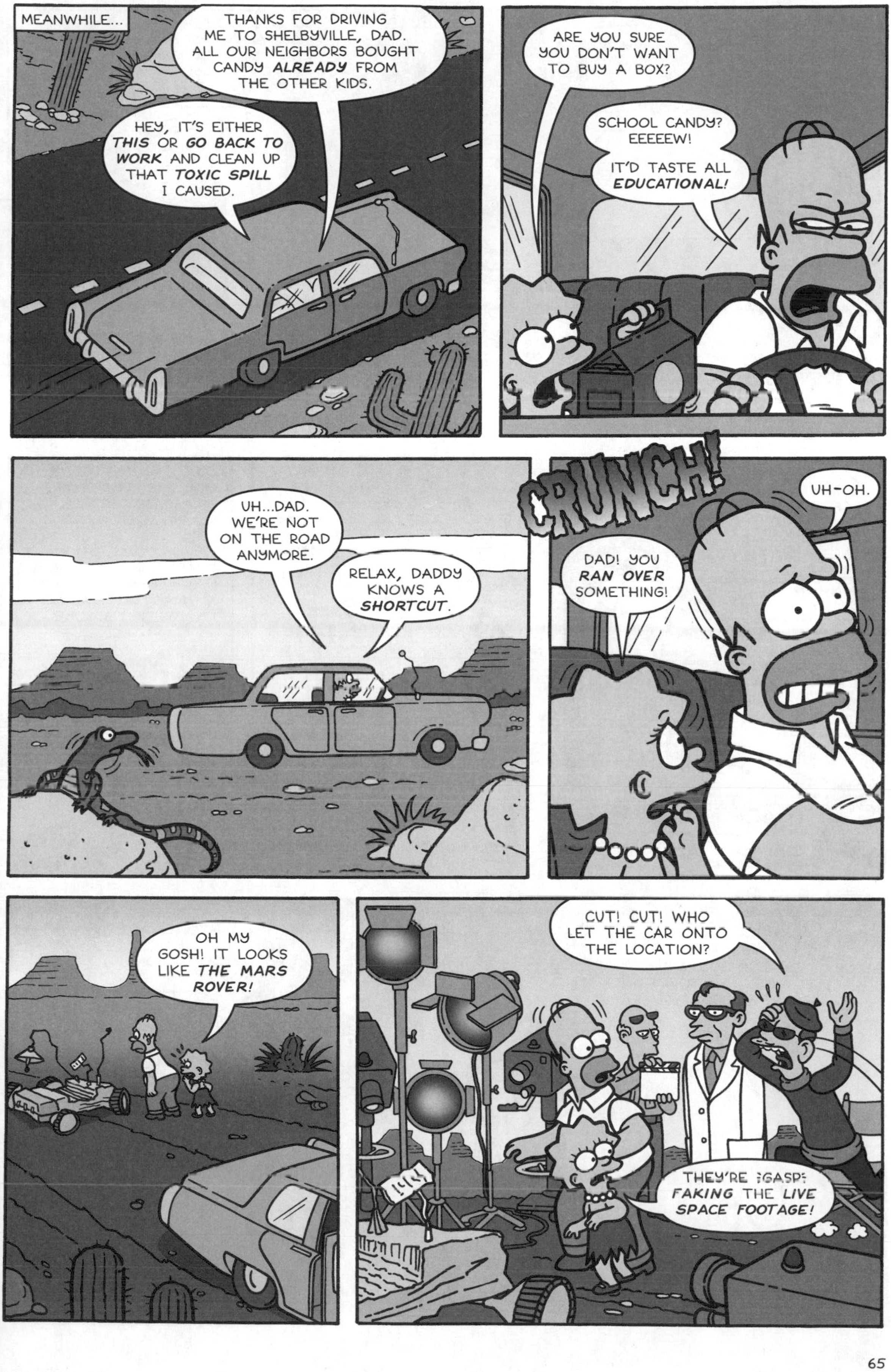
MEANWHILE...
THANKS FOR DRIVING ME TO SHELBYVILLE, DAD. ALL OUR NEIGHBORS BOUGHT CANDY ALREADY FROM THE OTHER KIDS.
HEY, IT'S EITHER THIS OR GO BACK TO WORK AND CLEAN UP THAT TOXIC SPILL I CAUSED.
ARE YOU SURE YOU DON'T WANT TO BUY A BOX?
SCHOOL CANDY? EEEEEW!
IT'D TASTE ALL EDUCATIONAL!
UH...DAD. WE'RE NOT ON THE ROAD ANYMORE.
RELAX, DADDY KNOWS A SHORTCUT.
CRUNCH!
UH-OH.
DAD! YOU RAN OVER SOMETHING!
OH MY GOSH! IT LOOKS LIKE THE MARS ROVER!
CUT! CUT! WHO LET THE CAR ONTO THE LOCATION?
THEY'RE :GASP: FAKING THE LIVE SPACE FOOTAGE!

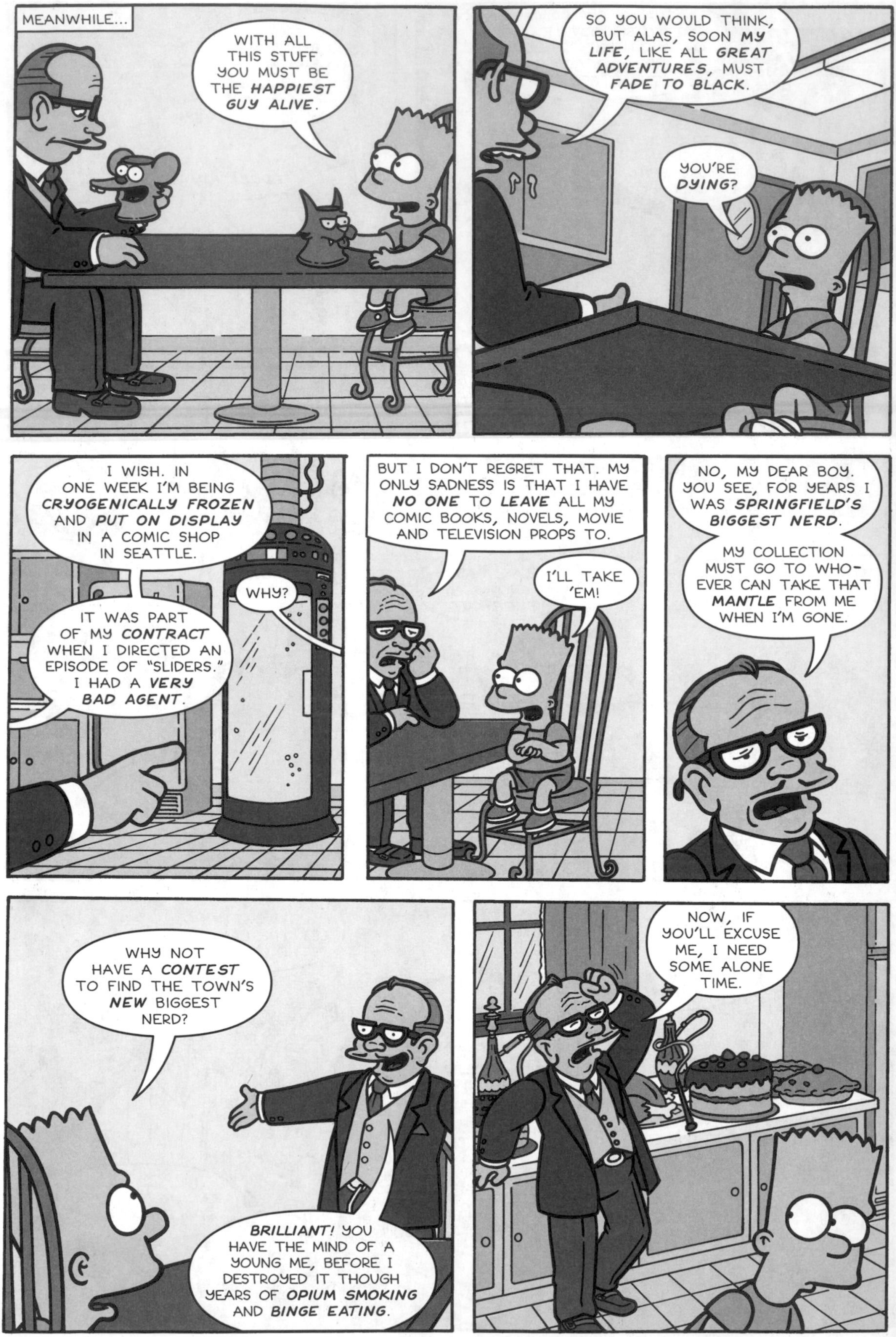
MEANWHILE...
WITH ALL THIS STUFF YOU MUST BE THE **HAPPIEST GUY ALIVE**.
SO YOU WOULD THINK, BUT ALAS, SOON **MY LIFE**, LIKE ALL **GREAT ADVENTURES**, MUST **FADE TO BLACK**.
YOU'RE **DYING**?
I WISH. IN ONE WEEK I'M BEING **CRYOGENICALLY FROZEN** AND **PUT ON DISPLAY** IN A COMIC SHOP IN SEATTLE.
WHY?
IT WAS PART OF MY **CONTRACT** WHEN I DIRECTED AN EPISODE OF "SLIDERS." I HAD A **VERY BAD AGENT**.
BUT I DON'T REGRET THAT. MY ONLY SADNESS IS THAT I HAVE **NO ONE** TO **LEAVE** ALL MY COMIC BOOKS, NOVELS, MOVIE AND TELEVISION PROPS TO.
I'LL TAKE 'EM!
NO, MY DEAR BOY. YOU SEE, FOR YEARS I WAS **SPRINGFIELD'S BIGGEST NERD**.
MY COLLECTION MUST GO TO WHO-EVER CAN TAKE THAT **MANTLE** FROM ME WHEN I'M GONE.
WHY NOT HAVE A **CONTEST** TO FIND THE TOWN'S **NEW** BIGGEST NERD?
BRILLIANT! YOU HAVE THE MIND OF A YOUNG ME, BEFORE I DESTROYED IT THOUGH YEARS OF **OPIUM SMOKING** AND **BINGE EATING**.
NOW, IF YOU'LL EXCUSE ME, I NEED SOME ALONE TIME.

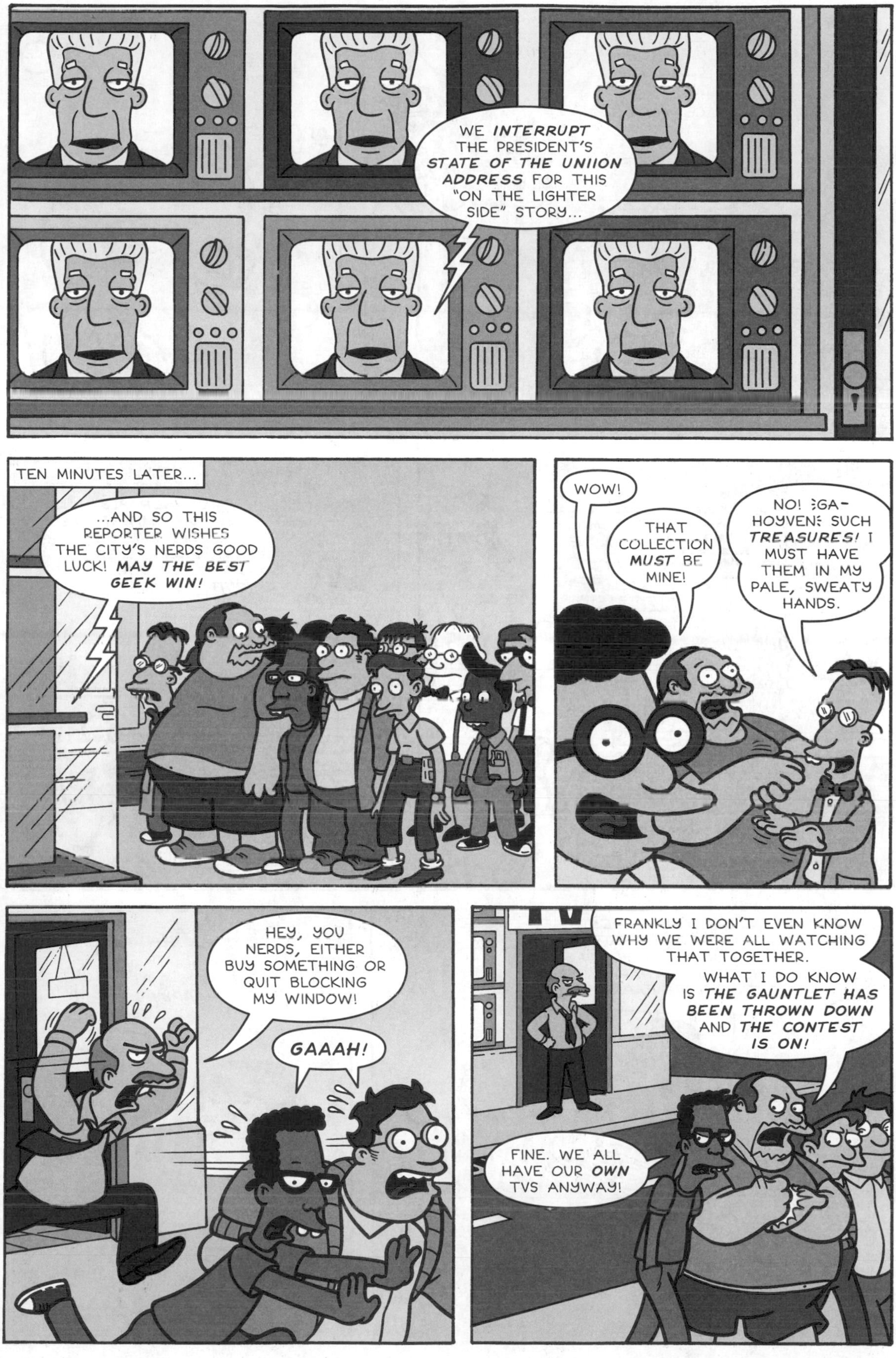
WE INTERRUPT THE PRESIDENT'S STATE OF THE UNIION ADDRESS FOR THIS "ON THE LIGHTER SIDE" STORY...
TEN MINUTES LATER...
...AND SO THIS REPORTER WISHES THE CITY'S NERDS GOOD LUCK! MAY THE BEST GEEK WIN!
WOW!
THAT COLLECTION MUST BE MINE!
NO! GA-HOYVEN! SUCH TREASURES! I MUST HAVE THEM IN MY PALE, SWEATY HANDS.
HEY, YOU NERDS, EITHER BUY SOMETHING OR QUIT BLOCKING MY WINDOW!
GAAAH!
FRANKLY I DON'T EVEN KNOW WHY WE WERE ALL WATCHING THAT TOGETHER.
WHAT I DO KNOW IS THE GAUNTLET HAS BEEN THROWN DOWN AND THE CONTEST IS ON!
FINE. WE ALL HAVE OUR OWN TVS ANYWAY!

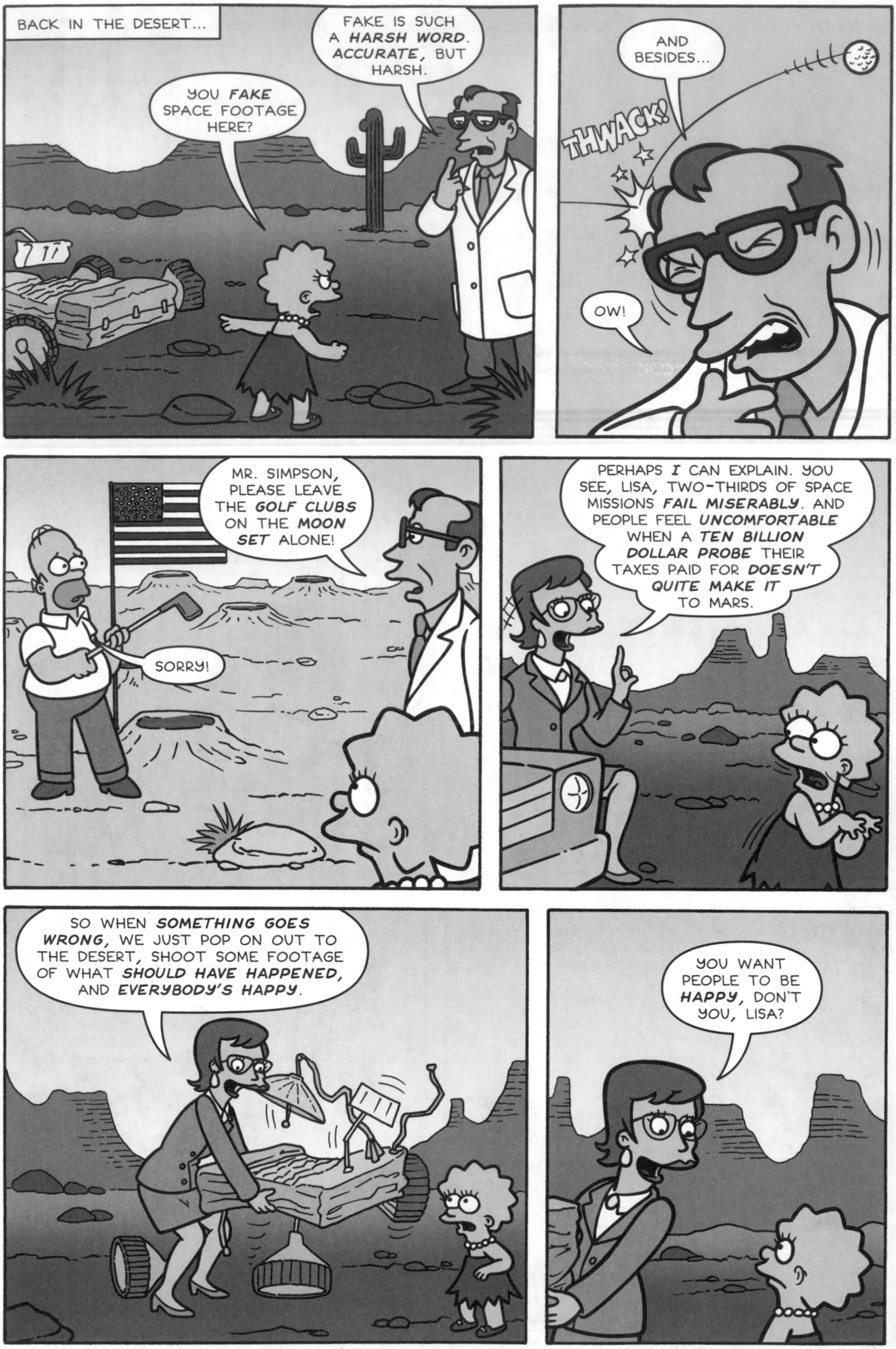
BACK IN THE DESERT...
YOU FAKE SPACE FOOTAGE HERE?
FAKE IS SUCH A HARSH WORD. ACCURATE, BUT HARSH.
AND BESIDES...
THWACK!
OW!
MR. SIMPSON, PLEASE LEAVE THE GOLF CLUBS ON THE MOON SET ALONE!
SORRY!
PERHAPS I CAN EXPLAIN. YOU SEE, LISA, TWO-THIRDS OF SPACE MISSIONS FAIL MISERABLY. AND PEOPLE FEEL UNCOMFORTABLE WHEN A TEN BILLION DOLLAR PROBE THEIR TAXES PAID FOR DOESN'T QUITE MAKE IT TO MARS.
SO WHEN SOMETHING GOES WRONG, WE JUST POP ON OUT TO THE DESERT, SHOOT SOME FOOTAGE OF WHAT SHOULD HAVE HAPPENED, AND EVERYBODY'S HAPPY.
YOU WANT PEOPLE TO BE HAPPY, DON'T YOU, LISA?

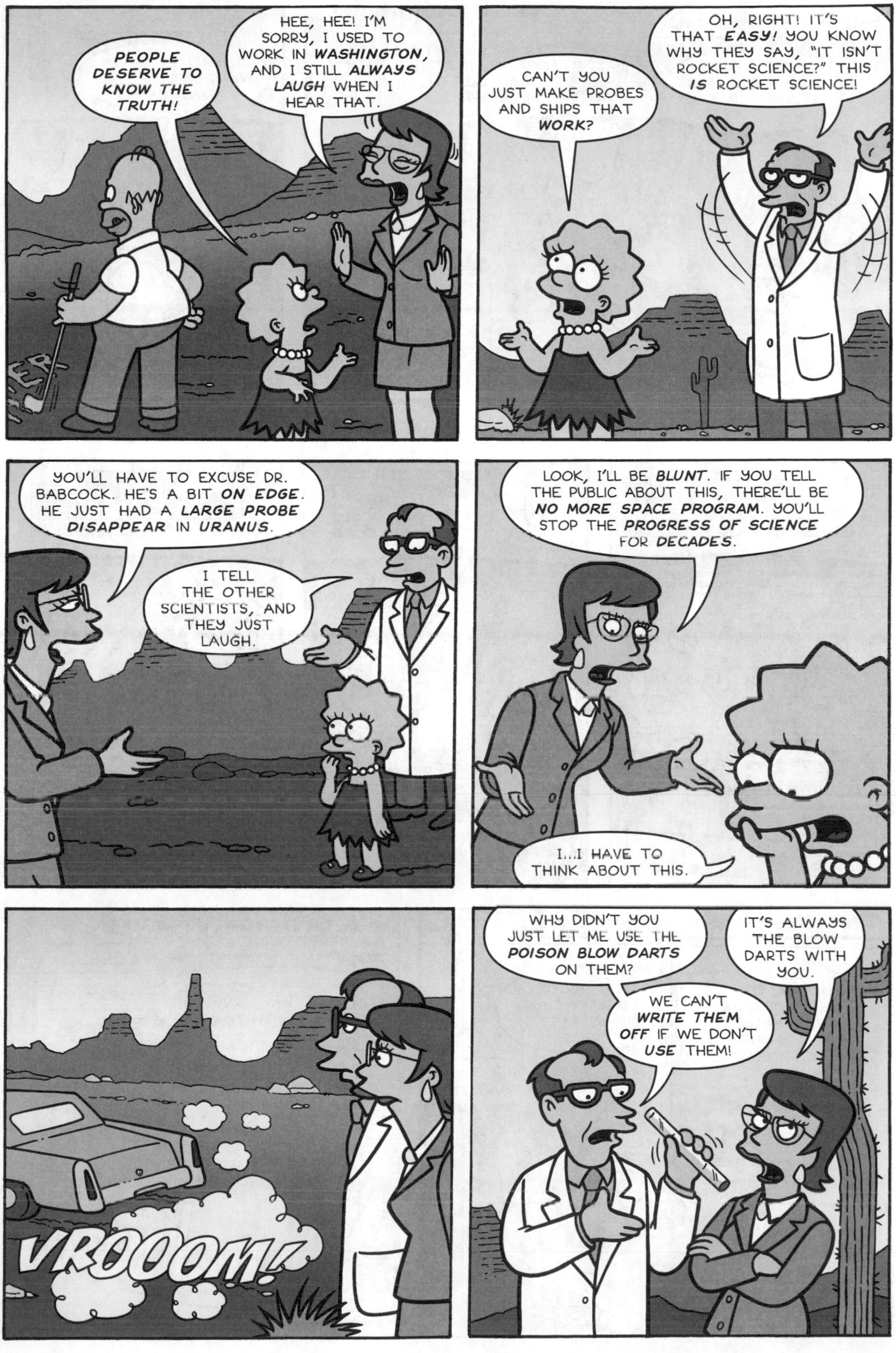
PEOPLE DESERVE TO KNOW THE TRUTH!
HEE, HEE! I'M SORRY, I USED TO WORK IN WASHINGTON, AND I STILL ALWAYS LAUGH WHEN I HEAR THAT.
CAN'T YOU JUST MAKE PROBES AND SHIPS THAT WORK?
OH, RIGHT! IT'S THAT EASY! YOU KNOW WHY THEY SAY, "IT ISN'T ROCKET SCIENCE?" THIS IS ROCKET SCIENCE!
YOU'LL HAVE TO EXCUSE DR. BABCOCK. HE'S A BIT ON EDGE. HE JUST HAD A LARGE PROBE DISAPPEAR IN URANUS.
I TELL THE OTHER SCIENTISTS, AND THEY JUST LAUGH.
LOOK, I'LL BE BLUNT. IF YOU TELL THE PUBLIC ABOUT THIS, THERE'LL BE NO MORE SPACE PROGRAM. YOU'LL STOP THE PROGRESS OF SCIENCE FOR DECADES.
I...I HAVE TO THINK ABOUT THIS.
VROOOM!
WHY DIDN'T YOU JUST LET ME USE THE POISON BLOW DARTS ON THEM?
IT'S ALWAYS THE BLOW DARTS WITH YOU.
WE CAN'T WRITE THEM OFF IF WE DON'T USE THEM!

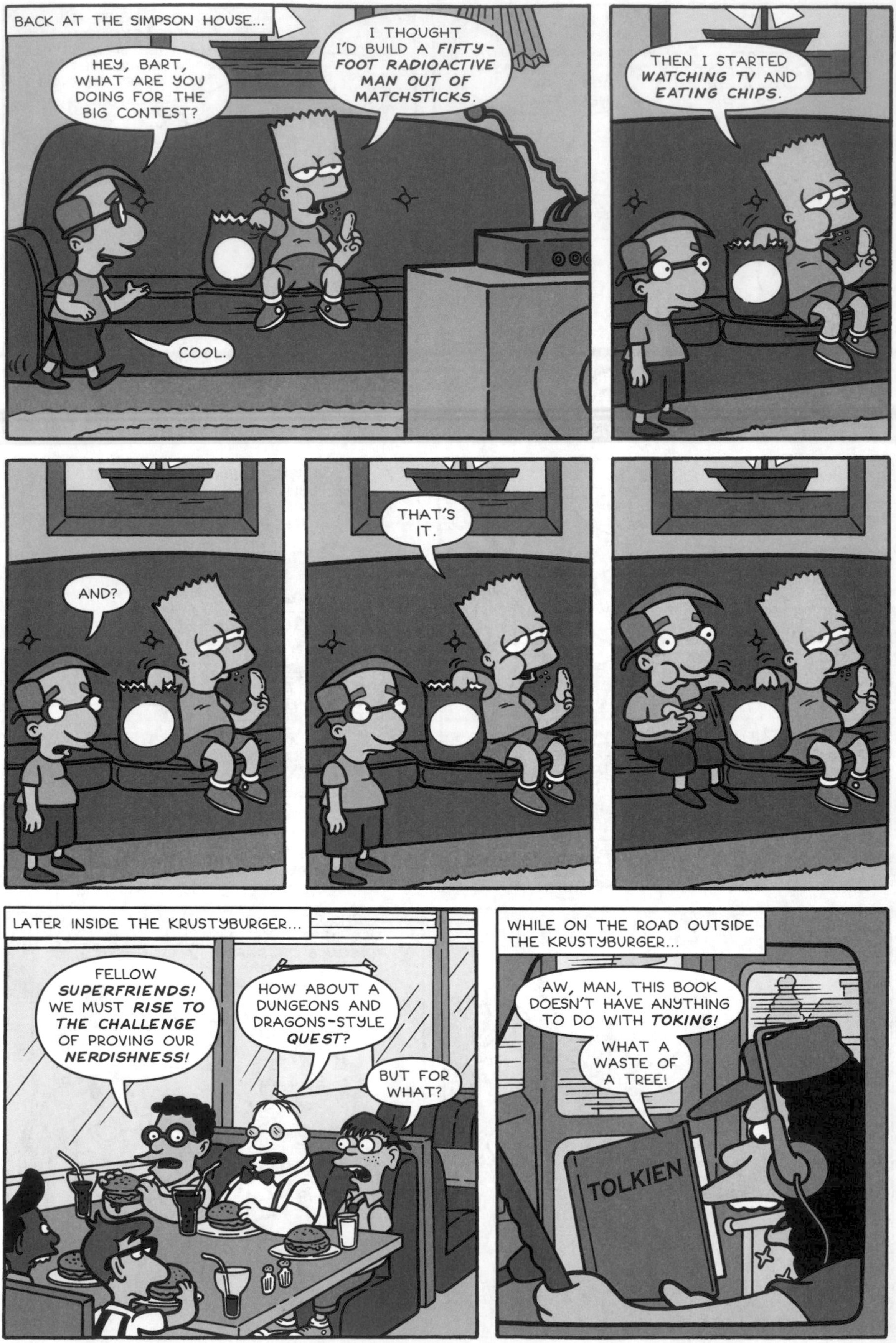
BACK AT THE SIMPSON HOUSE...
HEY, BART, WHAT ARE YOU DOING FOR THE BIG CONTEST?
I THOUGHT I'D BUILD A *FIFTY-FOOT RADIOACTIVE MAN OUT OF MATCHSTICKS*.
COOL.
THEN I STARTED *WATCHING TV* AND *EATING CHIPS*.
AND?
THAT'S IT.
LATER INSIDE THE KRUSTYBURGER...
FELLOW *SUPERFRIENDS!* WE MUST *RISE TO THE CHALLENGE* OF PROVING OUR *NERDISHNESS!*
HOW ABOUT A DUNGEONS AND DRAGONS-STYLE *QUEST?*
BUT FOR WHAT?
WHILE ON THE ROAD OUTSIDE THE KRUSTYBURGER...
AW, MAN, THIS BOOK DOESN'T HAVE ANYTHING TO DO WITH *TOKING!*
WHAT A WASTE OF A TREE!
TOLKIEN

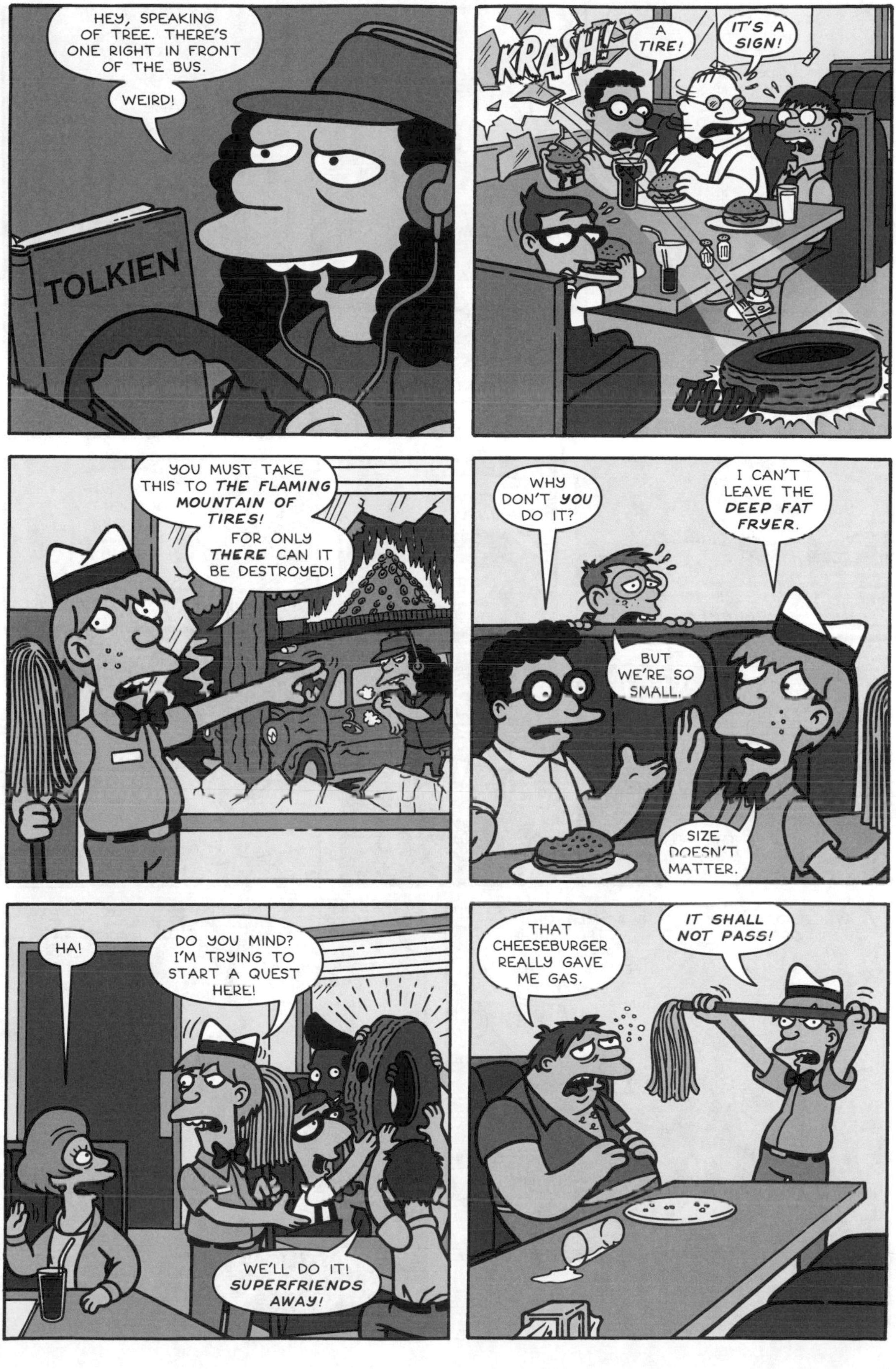
HEY, SPEAKING OF TREE. THERE'S ONE RIGHT IN FRONT OF THE BUS.
WEIRD!
TOLKIEN
KRASH!
A TIRE!
IT'S A SIGN!
THUD!
YOU MUST TAKE THIS TO THE FLAMING MOUNTAIN OF TIRES!
FOR ONLY THERE CAN IT BE DESTROYED!
WHY DON'T YOU DO IT?
I CAN'T LEAVE THE DEEP FAT FRYER.
BUT WE'RE SO SMALL.
SIZE DOESN'T MATTER.
HA!
DO YOU MIND? I'M TRYING TO START A QUEST HERE!
WE'LL DO IT! SUPERFRIENDS AWAY!
THAT CHEESEBURGER REALLY GAVE ME GAS.
IT SHALL NOT PASS!

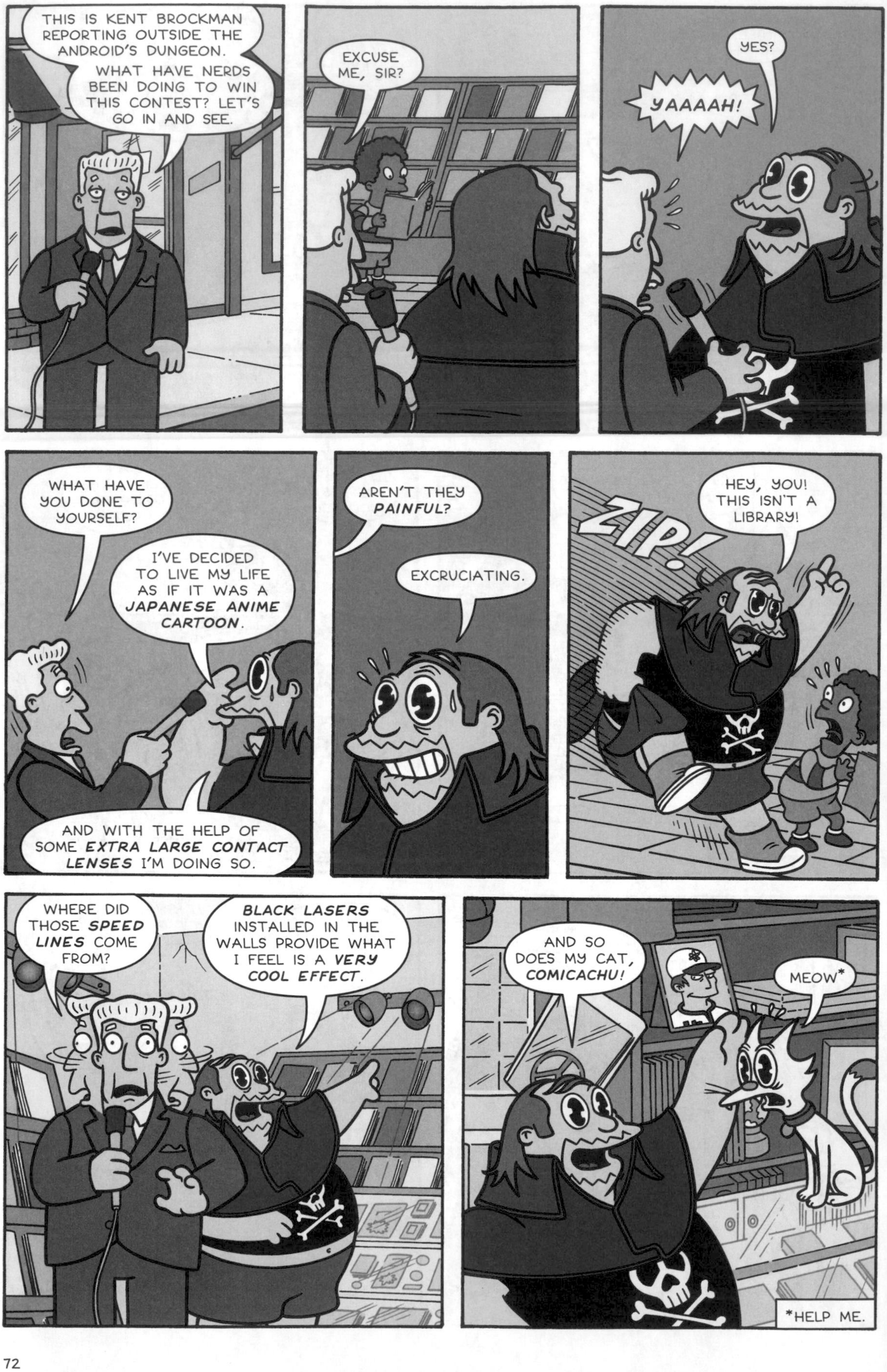

THIS IS KENT BROCKMAN REPORTING OUTSIDE THE ANDROID'S DUNGEON.
WHAT HAVE NERDS BEEN DOING TO WIN THIS CONTEST? LET'S GO IN AND SEE.
EXCUSE ME, SIR?
YES?
YAAAAH!
WHAT HAVE YOU DONE TO YOURSELF?
I'VE DECIDED TO LIVE MY LIFE AS IF IT WAS A JAPANESE ANIME CARTOON.
AND WITH THE HELP OF SOME EXTRA LARGE CONTACT LENSES I'M DOING SO.
AREN'T THEY PAINFUL?
EXCRUCIATING.
ZIP!
HEY, YOU! THIS ISN'T A LIBRARY!
WHERE DID THOSE SPEED LINES COME FROM?
BLACK LASERS INSTALLED IN THE WALLS PROVIDE WHAT I FEEL IS A VERY COOL EFFECT.
AND SO DOES MY CAT, COMICACHU!
MEOW*
*HELP ME.

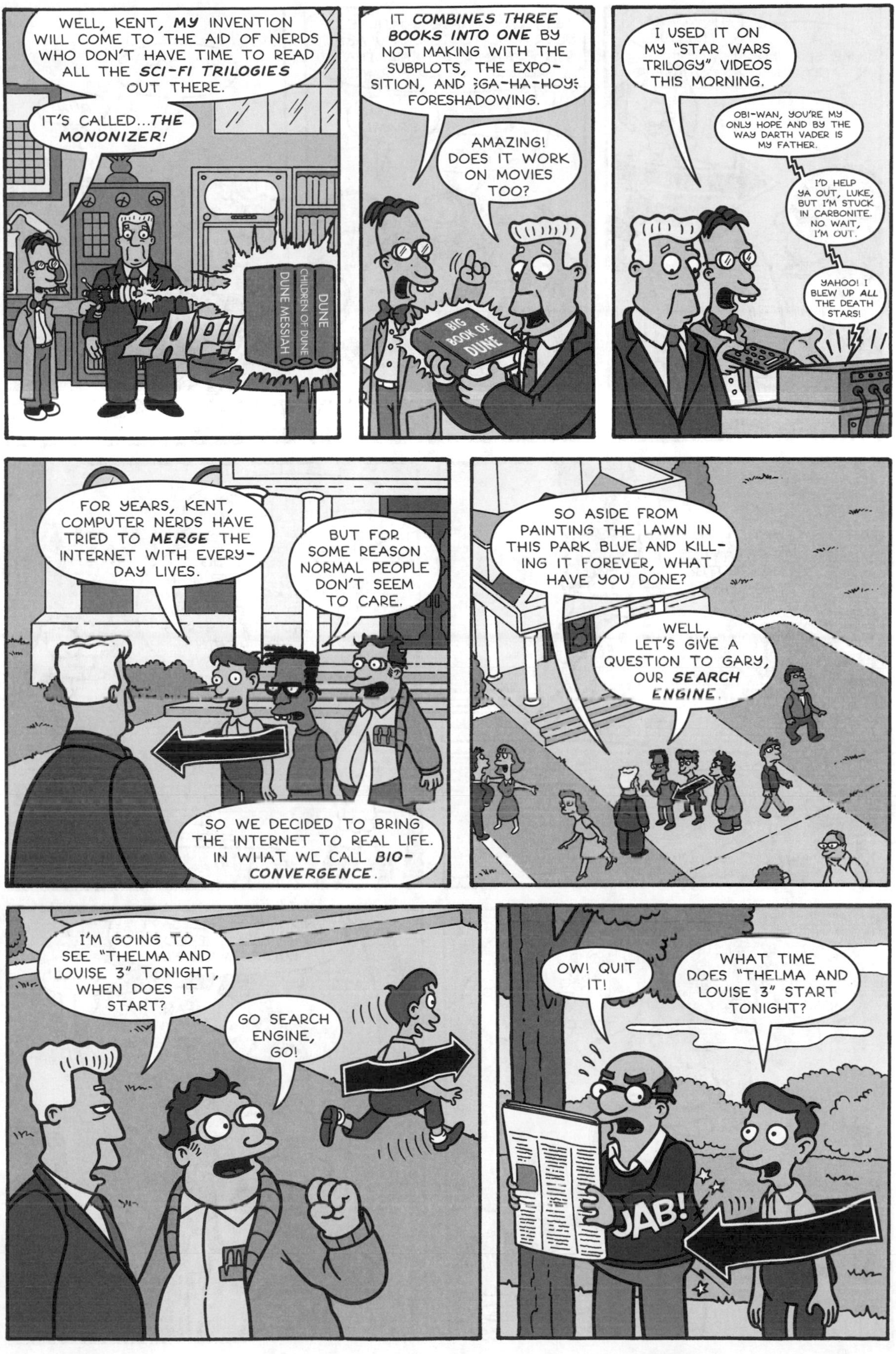
WELL, KENT, MY INVENTION WILL COME TO THE AID OF NERDS WHO DON'T HAVE TIME TO READ ALL THE SCI-FI TRILOGIES OUT THERE.
IT'S CALLED...THE MONONIZER!
DUNE
CHILDREN OF DUNE
DUNE MESSIAH
ZAP!
IT COMBINES THREE BOOKS INTO ONE BY NOT MAKING WITH THE SUBPLOTS, THE EXPOSITION, AND "GA-HA-HOY" FORESHADOWING.
AMAZING! DOES IT WORK ON MOVIES TOO?
BIG BOOK OF DUNE
I USED IT ON MY "STAR WARS TRILOGY" VIDEOS THIS MORNING.
OBI-WAN, YOU'RE MY ONLY HOPE AND BY THE WAY DARTH VADER IS MY FATHER.
I'D HELP YA OUT, LUKE, BUT I'M STUCK IN CARBONITE. NO WAIT, I'M OUT.
YAHOO! I BLEW UP ALL THE DEATH STARS!
FOR YEARS, KENT, COMPUTER NERDS HAVE TRIED TO MERGE THE INTERNET WITH EVERYDAY LIVES.
BUT FOR SOME REASON NORMAL PEOPLE DON'T SEEM TO CARE.
SO WE DECIDED TO BRING THE INTERNET TO REAL LIFE. IN WHAT WE CALL BIO-CONVERGENCE.
SO ASIDE FROM PAINTING THE LAWN IN THIS PARK BLUE AND KILLING IT FOREVER, WHAT HAVE YOU DONE?
WELL, LET'S GIVE A QUESTION TO GARY, OUR SEARCH ENGINE.
I'M GOING TO SEE "THELMA AND LOUISE 3" TONIGHT, WHEN DOES IT START?
GO SEARCH ENGINE, GO!
OW! QUIT IT!
WHAT TIME DOES "THELMA AND LOUISE 3" START TONIGHT?
JAB!

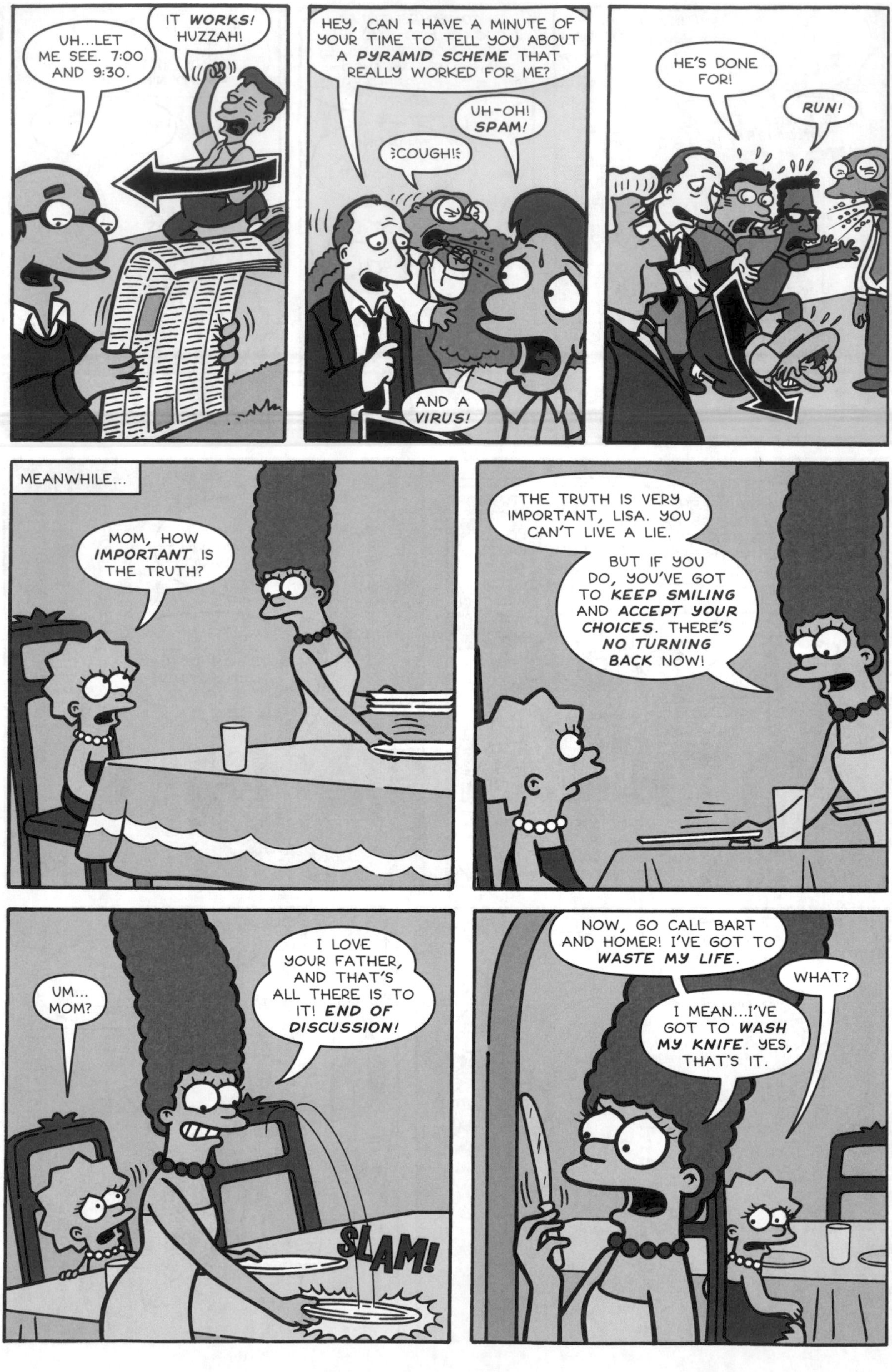
UH...LET ME SEE. 7:00 AND 9:30.
IT WORKS! HUZZAH!
HEY, CAN I HAVE A MINUTE OF YOUR TIME TO TELL YOU ABOUT A PYRAMID SCHEME THAT REALLY WORKED FOR ME?
COUGH!
UH-OH! SPAM!
AND A VIRUS!
HE'S DONE FOR!
RUN!
MEANWHILE...
MOM, HOW IMPORTANT IS THE TRUTH?
THE TRUTH IS VERY IMPORTANT, LISA. YOU CAN'T LIVE A LIE.
BUT IF YOU DO, YOU'VE GOT TO KEEP SMILING AND ACCEPT YOUR CHOICES. THERE'S NO TURNING BACK NOW!
UM... MOM?
I LOVE YOUR FATHER, AND THAT'S ALL THERE IS TO IT! END OF DISCUSSION!
SLAM!
NOW, GO CALL BART AND HOMER! I'VE GOT TO WASTE MY LIFE.
WHAT?
I MEAN...I'VE GOT TO WASH MY KNIFE. YES, THAT'S IT.

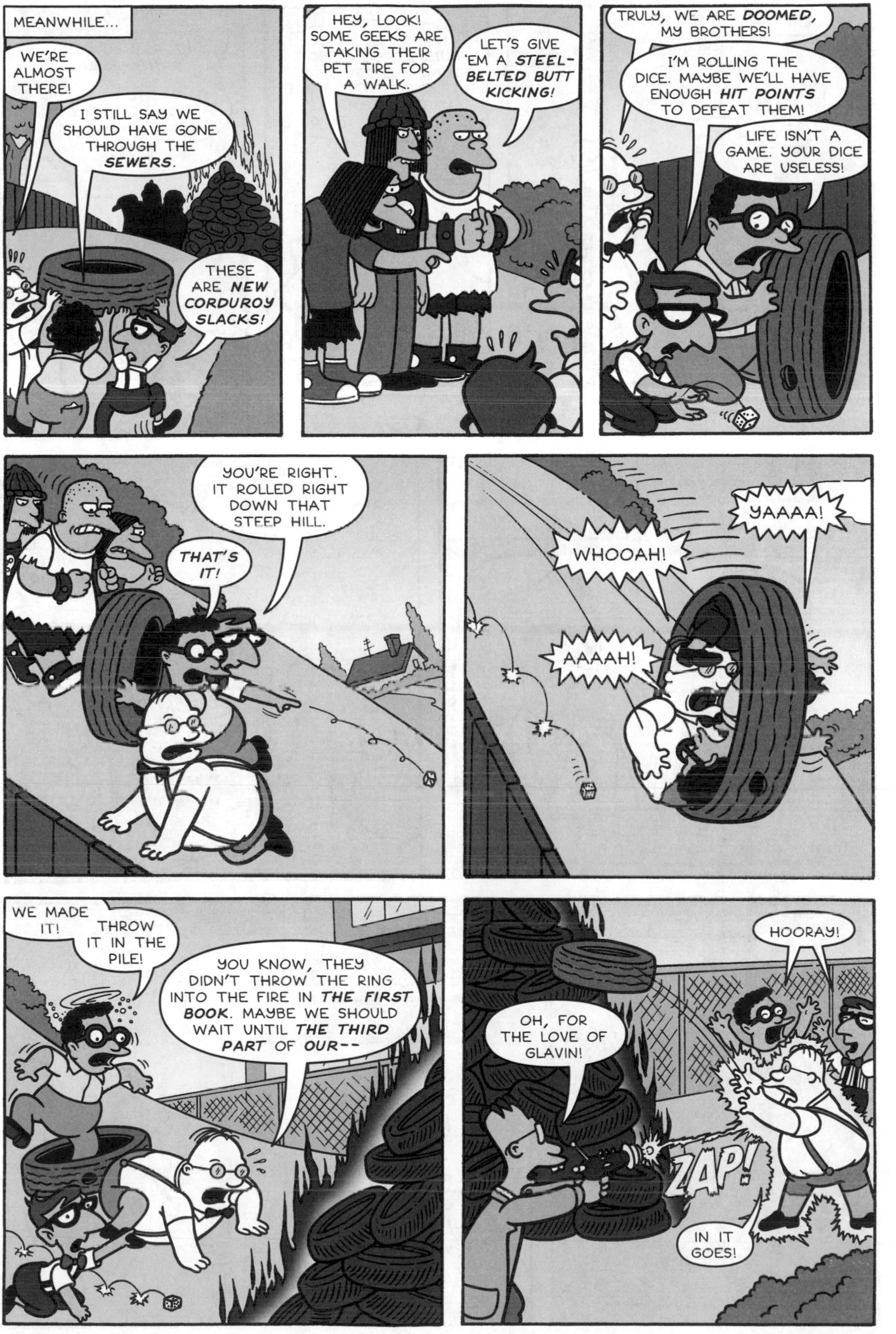
MEANWHILE...
WE'RE ALMOST THERE!
I STILL SAY WE SHOULD HAVE GONE THROUGH THE SEWERS.
THESE ARE NEW CORDUROY SLACKS!
HEY, LOOK! SOME GEEKS ARE TAKING THEIR PET TIRE FOR A WALK.
LET'S GIVE 'EM A STEEL-BELTED BUTT KICKING!
TRULY, WE ARE DOOMED, MY BROTHERS!
I'M ROLLING THE DICE. MAYBE WE'LL HAVE ENOUGH HIT POINTS TO DEFEAT THEM!
LIFE ISN'T A GAME. YOUR DICE ARE USELESS!
YOU'RE RIGHT. IT ROLLED RIGHT DOWN THAT STEEP HILL.
THAT'S IT!
YAAAA!
WHOOAH!
AAAAH!
WE MADE IT!
THROW IT IN THE PILE!
YOU KNOW, THEY DIDN'T THROW THE RING INTO THE FIRE IN THE FIRST BOOK. MAYBE WE SHOULD WAIT UNTIL THE THIRD PART OF OUR--
HOORAY!
OH, FOR THE LOVE OF GLAVIN!
ZAP!
IN IT GOES!

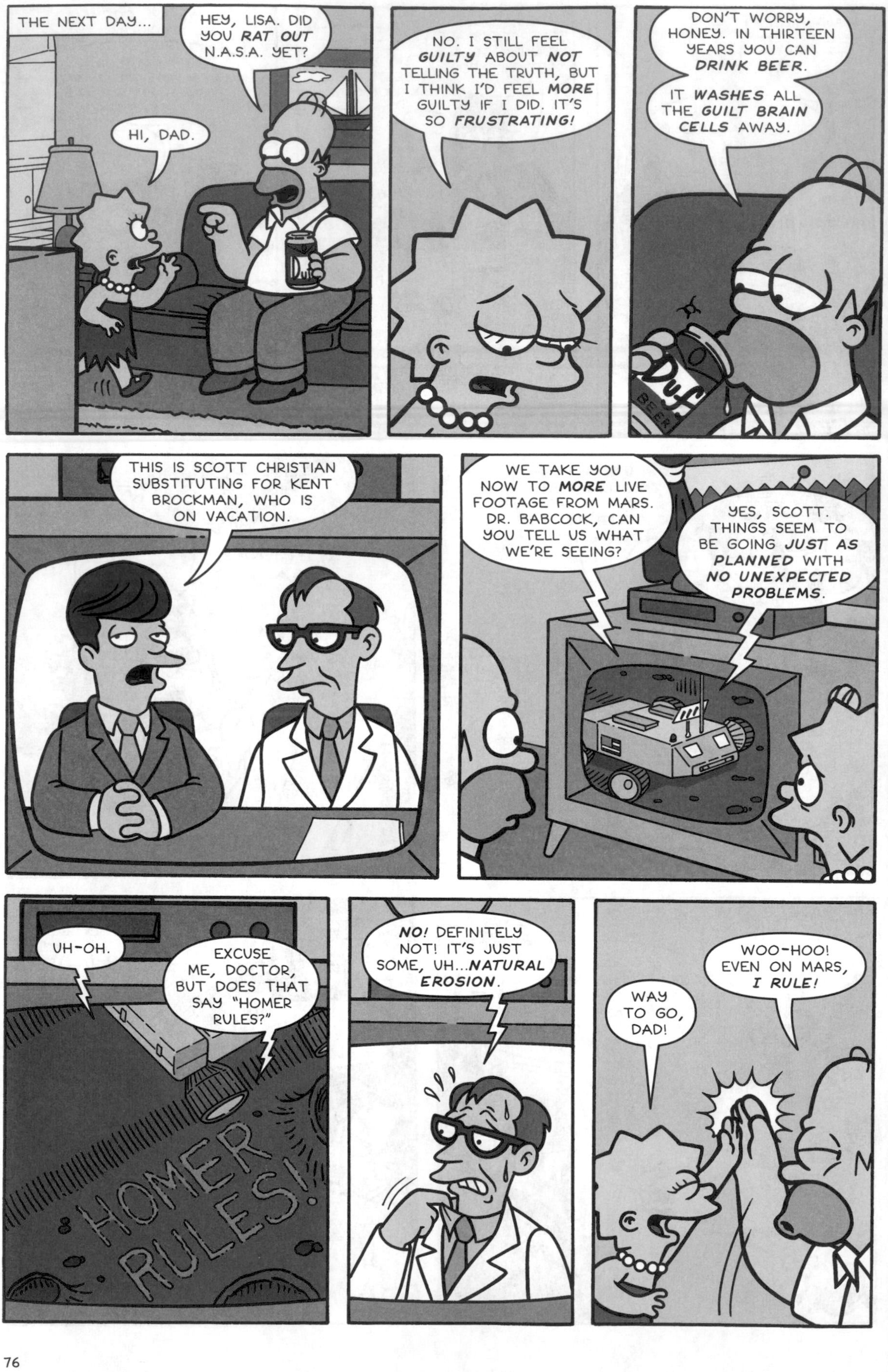

THE NEXT DAY...
HEY, LISA. DID YOU RAT OUT N.A.S.A. YET?
HI, DAD.
NO. I STILL FEEL GUILTY ABOUT NOT TELLING THE TRUTH, BUT I THINK I'D FEEL MORE GUILTY IF I DID. IT'S SO FRUSTRATING!
DON'T WORRY, HONEY. IN THIRTEEN YEARS YOU CAN DRINK BEER.
IT WASHES ALL THE GUILT BRAIN CELLS AWAY.
DUFF BEER
THIS IS SCOTT CHRISTIAN SUBSTITUTING FOR KENT BROCKMAN, WHO IS ON VACATION.
WE TAKE YOU NOW TO MORE LIVE FOOTAGE FROM MARS. DR. BABCOCK, CAN YOU TELL US WHAT WE'RE SEEING?
YES, SCOTT. THINGS SEEM TO BE GOING JUST AS PLANNED WITH NO UNEXPECTED PROBLEMS.
UH-OH.
EXCUSE ME, DOCTOR, BUT DOES THAT SAY "HOMER RULES?"
HOMER RULES!
NO! DEFINITELY NOT! IT'S JUST SOME, UH...NATURAL EROSION.
WAY TO GO, DAD!
WOO-HOO! EVEN ON MARS, I RULE!

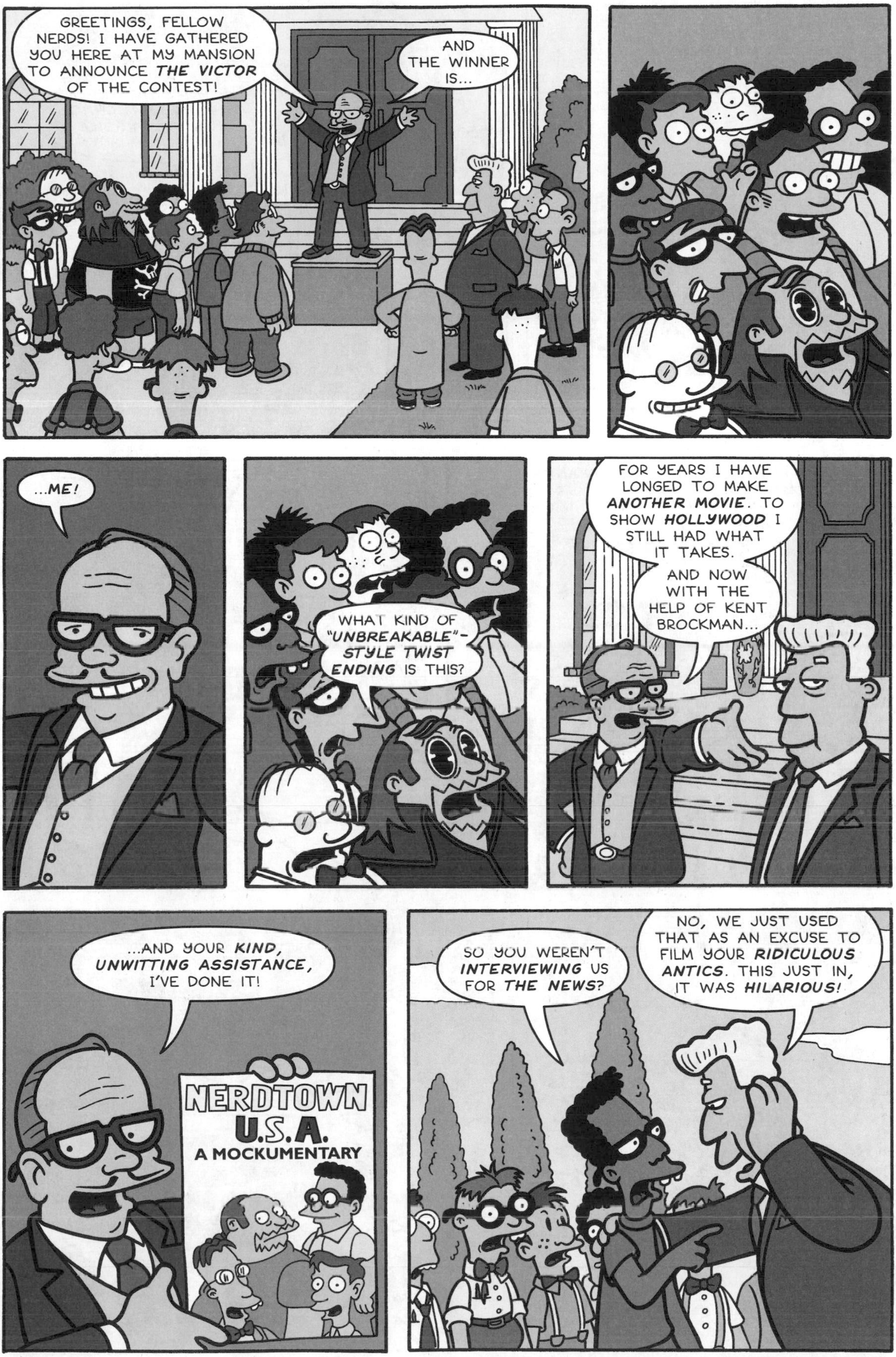
GREETINGS, FELLOW NERDS! I HAVE GATHERED YOU HERE AT MY MANSION TO ANNOUNCE THE VICTOR OF THE CONTEST!
AND THE WINNER IS...
...ME!
WHAT KIND OF "UNBREAKABLE"-STYLE TWIST ENDING IS THIS?
FOR YEARS I HAVE LONGED TO MAKE ANOTHER MOVIE. TO SHOW HOLLYWOOD I STILL HAD WHAT IT TAKES.
AND NOW WITH THE HELP OF KENT BROCKMAN...
...AND YOUR KIND, UNWITTING ASSISTANCE, I'VE DONE IT!
NERDTOWN U.S.A. A MOCKUMENTARY
SO YOU WEREN'T INTERVIEWING US FOR THE NEWS?
NO, WE JUST USED THAT AS AN EXCUSE TO FILM YOUR RIDICULOUS ANTICS. THIS JUST IN, IT WAS HILARIOUS!

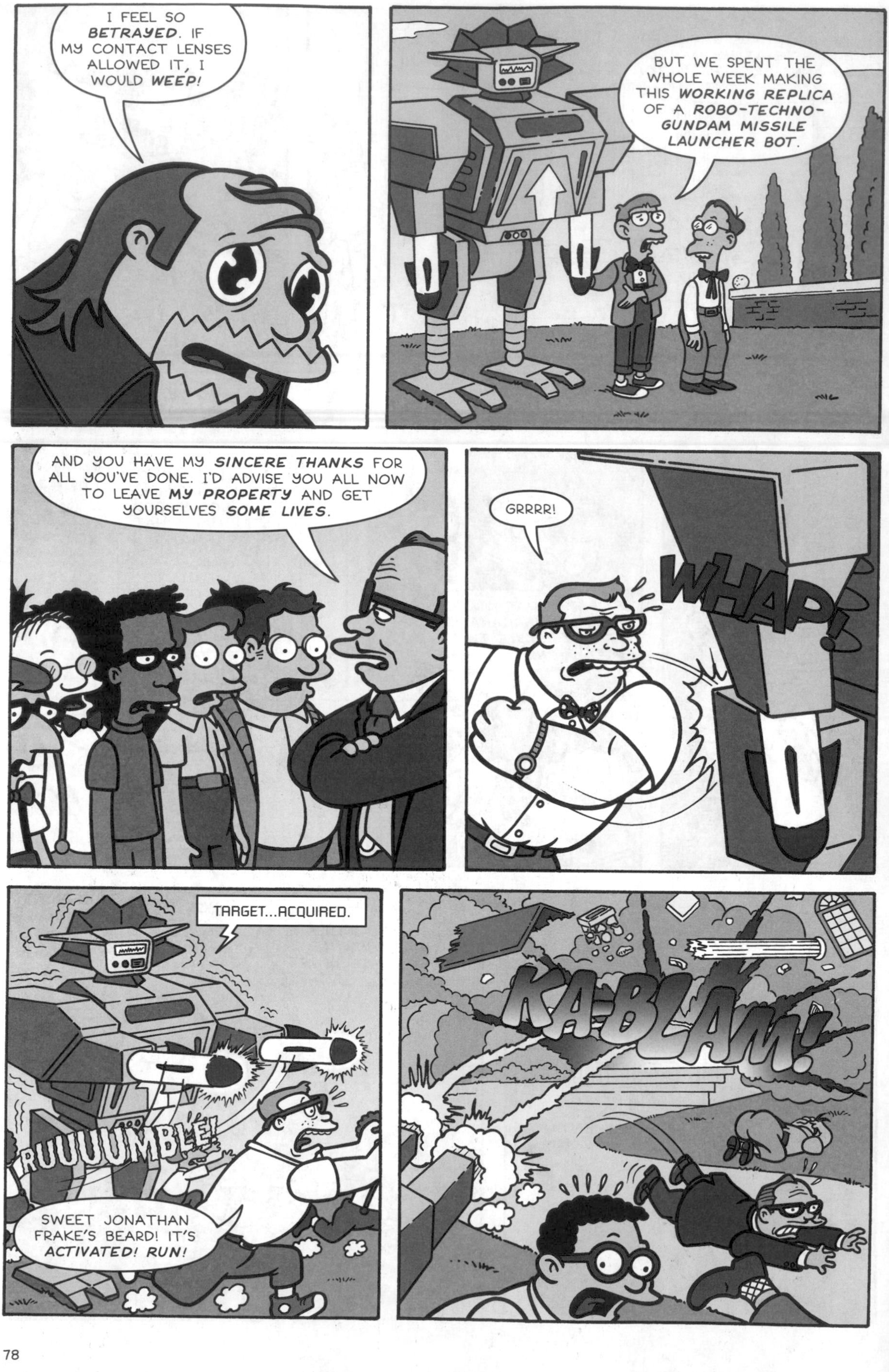

I FEEL SO BETRAYED. IF MY CONTACT LENSES ALLOWED IT, I WOULD WEEP!
BUT WE SPENT THE WHOLE WEEK MAKING THIS WORKING REPLICA OF A ROBO-TECHNO-GUNDAM MISSILE LAUNCHER BOT.
AND YOU HAVE MY SINCERE THANKS FOR ALL YOU'VE DONE. I'D ADVISE YOU ALL NOW TO LEAVE MY PROPERTY AND GET YOURSELVES SOME LIVES.
GRRRR!
WHAP!
TARGET...ACQUIRED.
RUUUUMBLE!
SWEET JONATHAN FRAKE'S BEARD! IT'S ACTIVATED! RUN!
KA-BLAM!

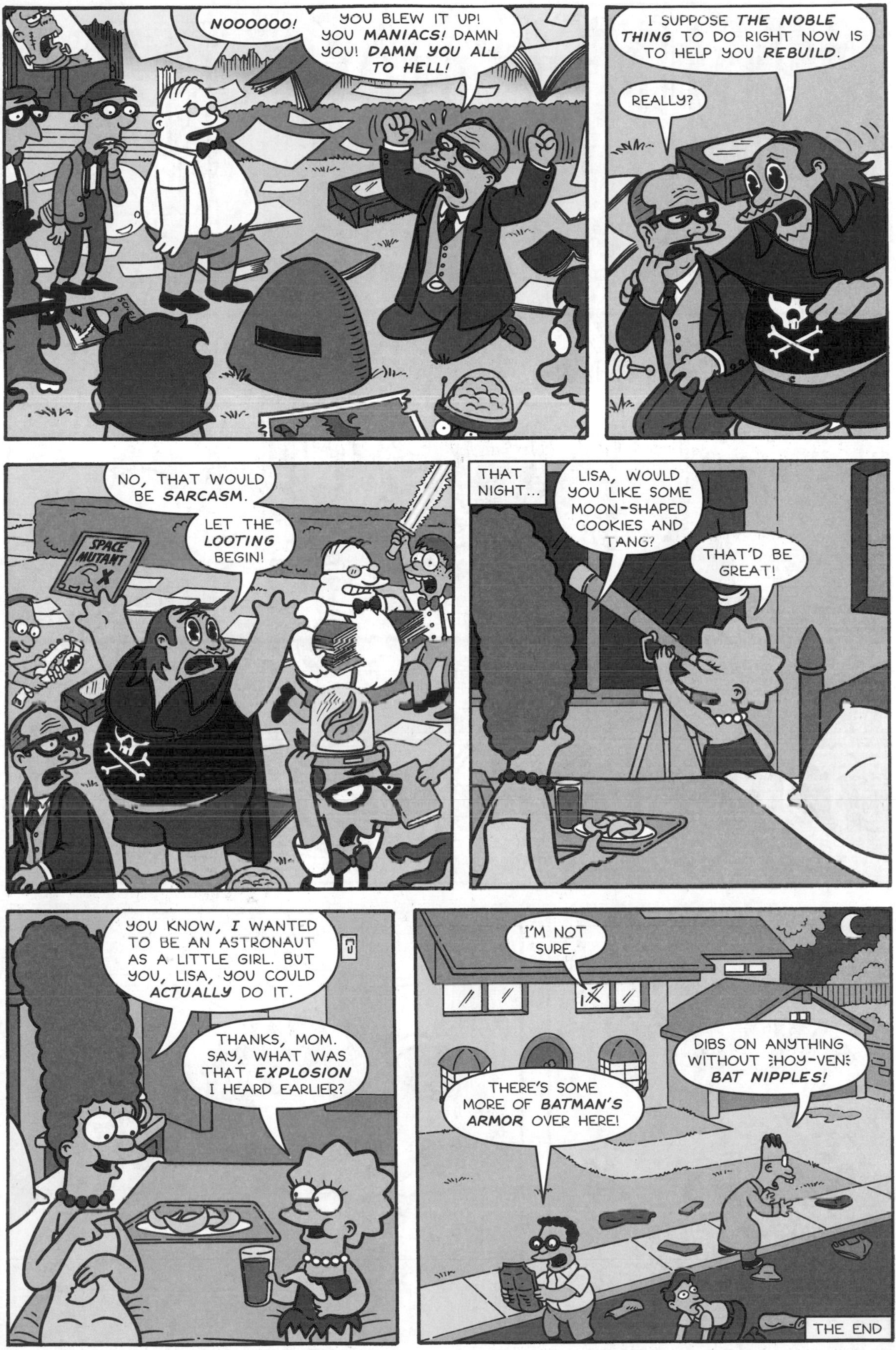
NOOOOOO!
YOU BLEW IT UP! YOU **MANIACS!** DAMN YOU! **DAMN YOU ALL TO HELL!**
I SUPPOSE ***THE NOBLE THING*** TO DO RIGHT NOW IS TO HELP YOU ***REBUILD.***
REALLY?
NO, THAT WOULD BE ***SARCASM.***
LET THE ***LOOTING*** BEGIN!
SPACE MUTANT X
THAT NIGHT...
LISA, WOULD YOU LIKE SOME MOON-SHAPED COOKIES AND TANG?
THAT'D BE GREAT!
YOU KNOW, ***I*** WANTED TO BE AN ASTRONAUT AS A LITTLE GIRL. BUT YOU, LISA, YOU COULD ***ACTUALLY*** DO IT.
THANKS, MOM. SAY, WHAT WAS THAT ***EXPLOSION*** I HEARD EARLIER?
I'M NOT SURE.
THERE'S SOME MORE OF ***BATMAN'S ARMOR*** OVER HERE!
DIBS ON ANYTHING WITHOUT :HOY-VEN: ***BAT NIPPLES!***
THE END

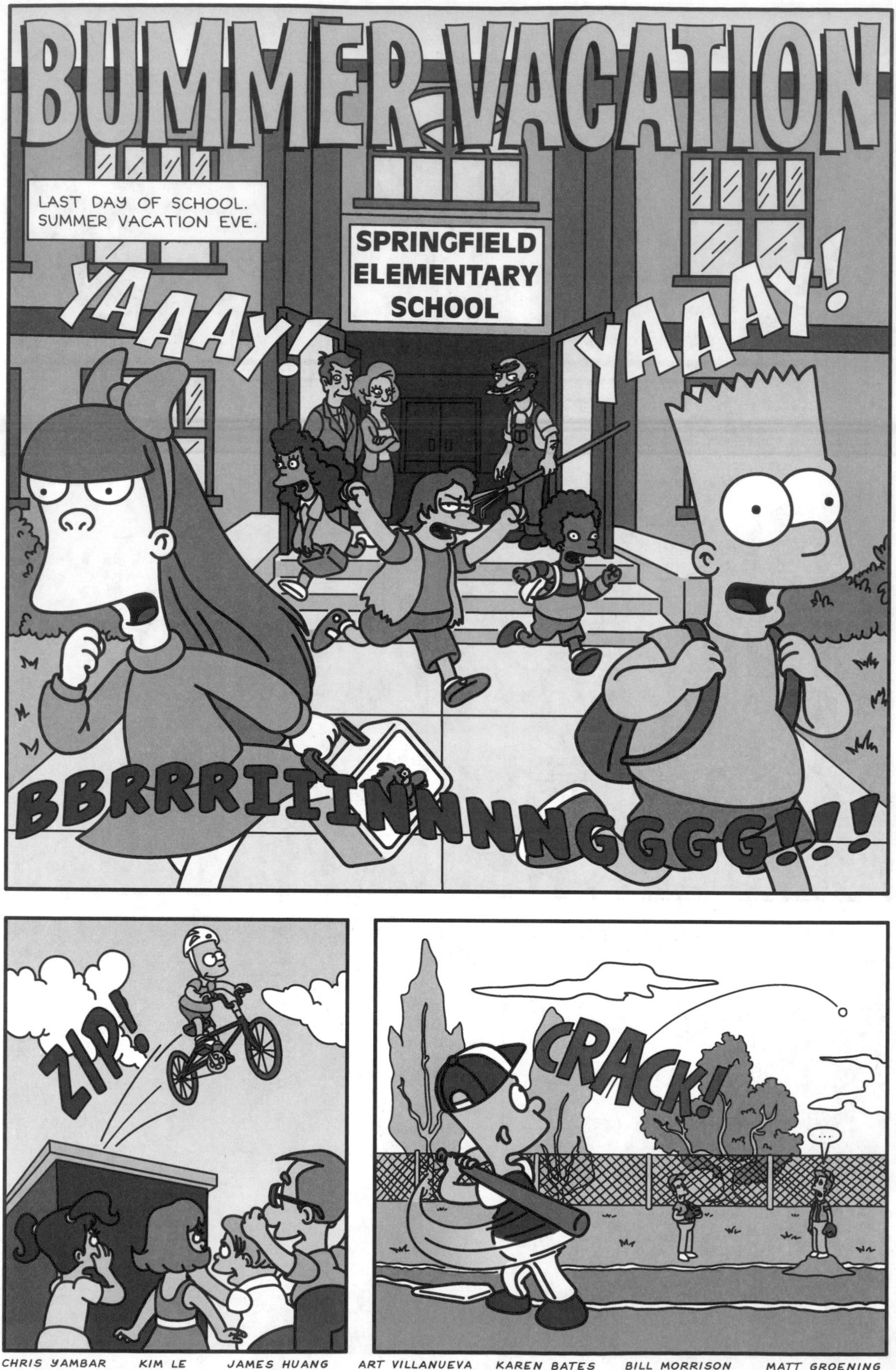
BUMMER VACATION
LAST DAY OF SCHOOL. SUMMER VACATION EVE.
SPRINGFIELD ELEMENTARY SCHOOL
YAAAY!
YAAAY!
BBRRRRIIINNNNGGGG!!!
ZIP!
CRACK!
...

CHRIS YAMBAR STORY · KIM LE PENCILS · JAMES HUANG INKS · ART VILLANUEVA COLORS · KAREN BATES LETTERS · BILL MORRISON EDITOR · MATT GROENING BIKINI INSPECTOR

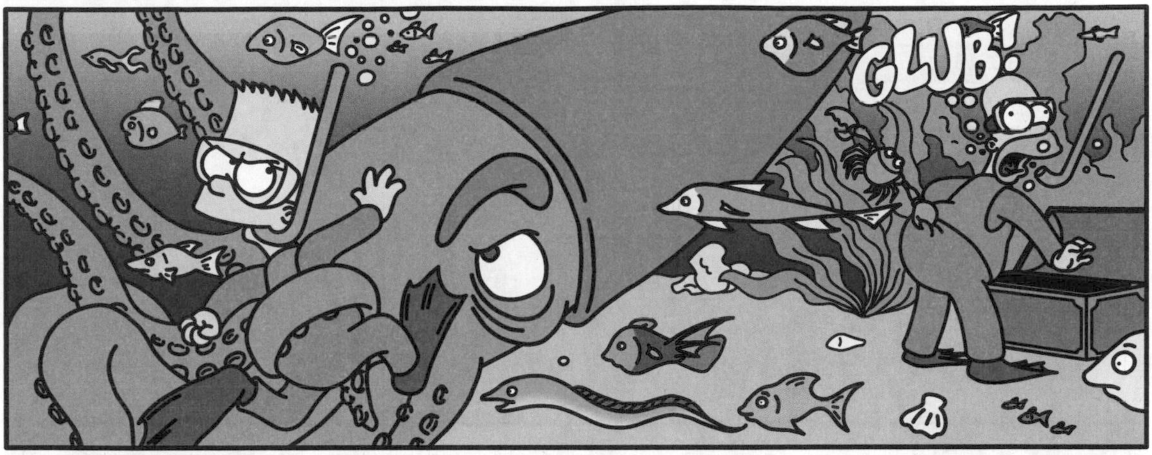
GLUB!
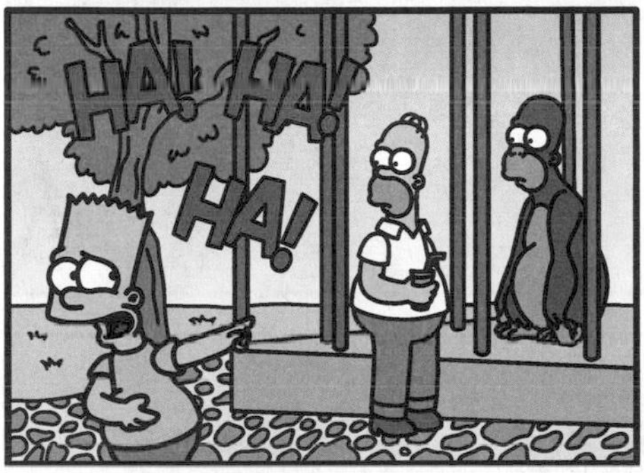
HA! HA!
HA!
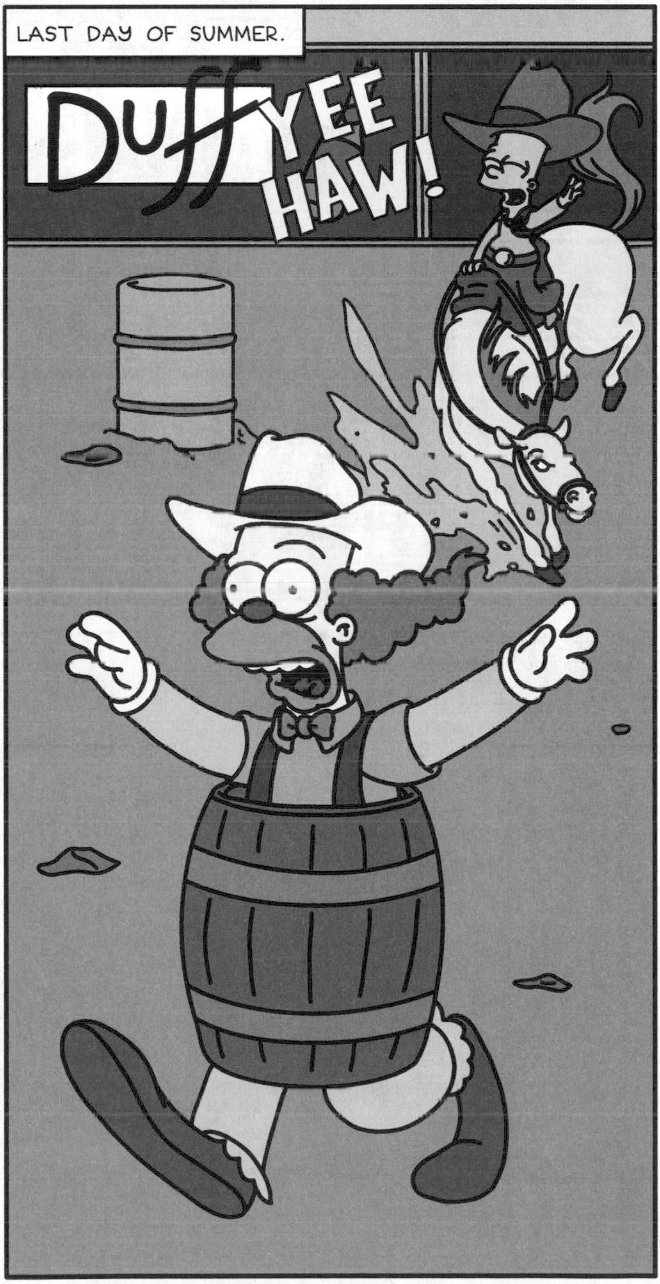
LAST DAY OF SUMMER.
DUFF
YEE HAW!
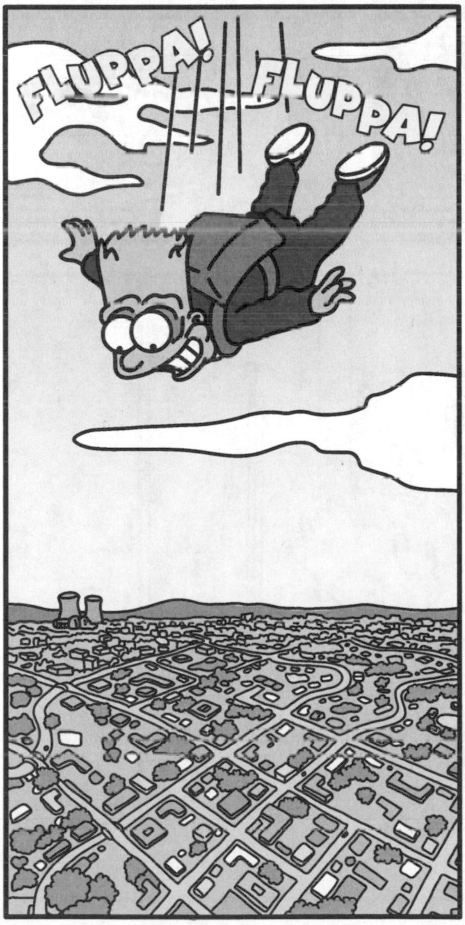
FLUPPA! FLUPPA!

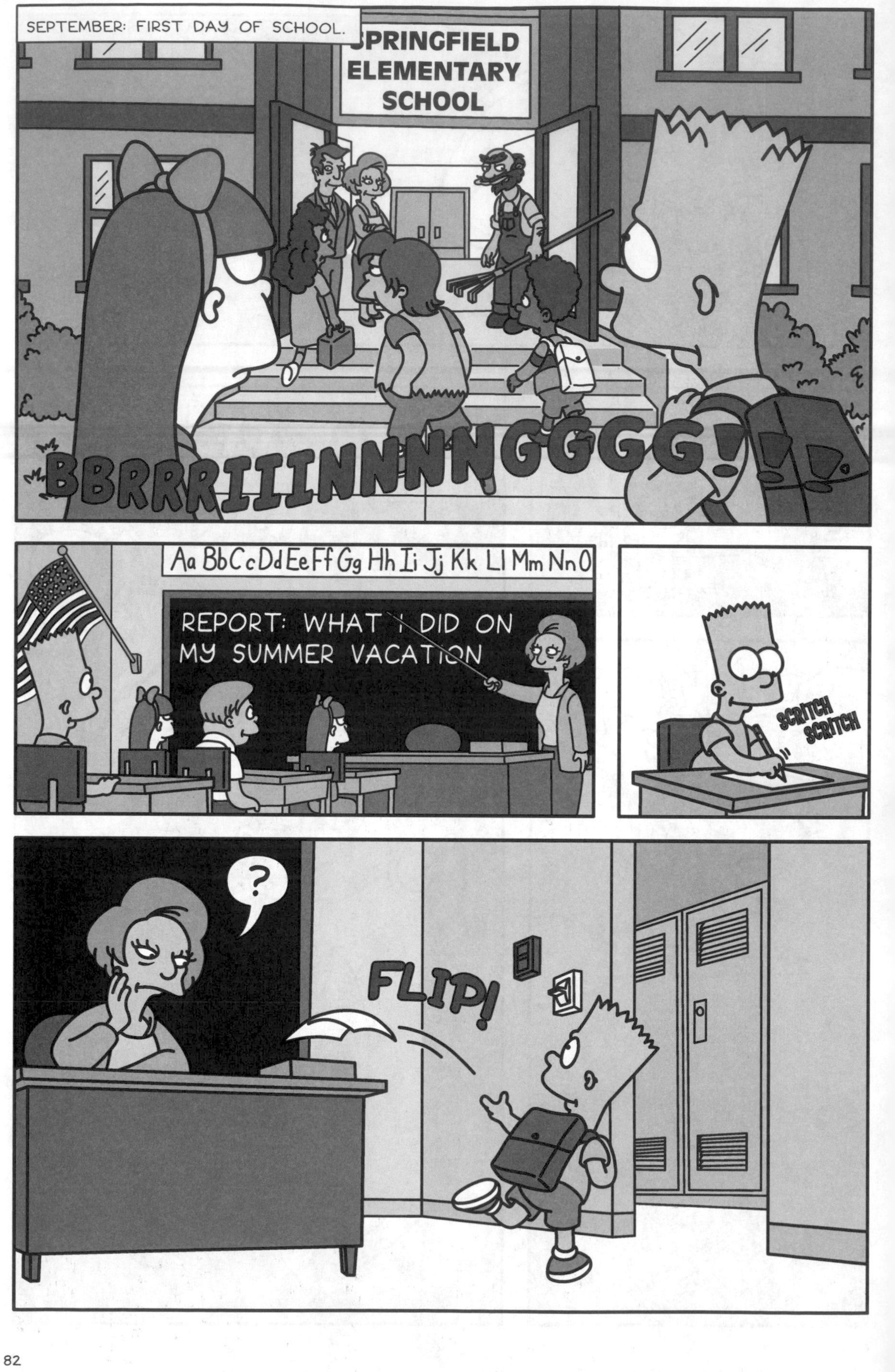
SEPTEMBER: FIRST DAY OF SCHOOL.
PRINGFIELD ELEMENTARY SCHOOL
BBRRRIIINNNNGGGG!!!
Aa Bb Cc Dd Ee Ff Gg Hh Ii Jj Kk Ll Mm Nn O
REPORT: WHAT I DID ON MY SUMMER VACATION
SCRITCH SCRITCH
?
FLIP!

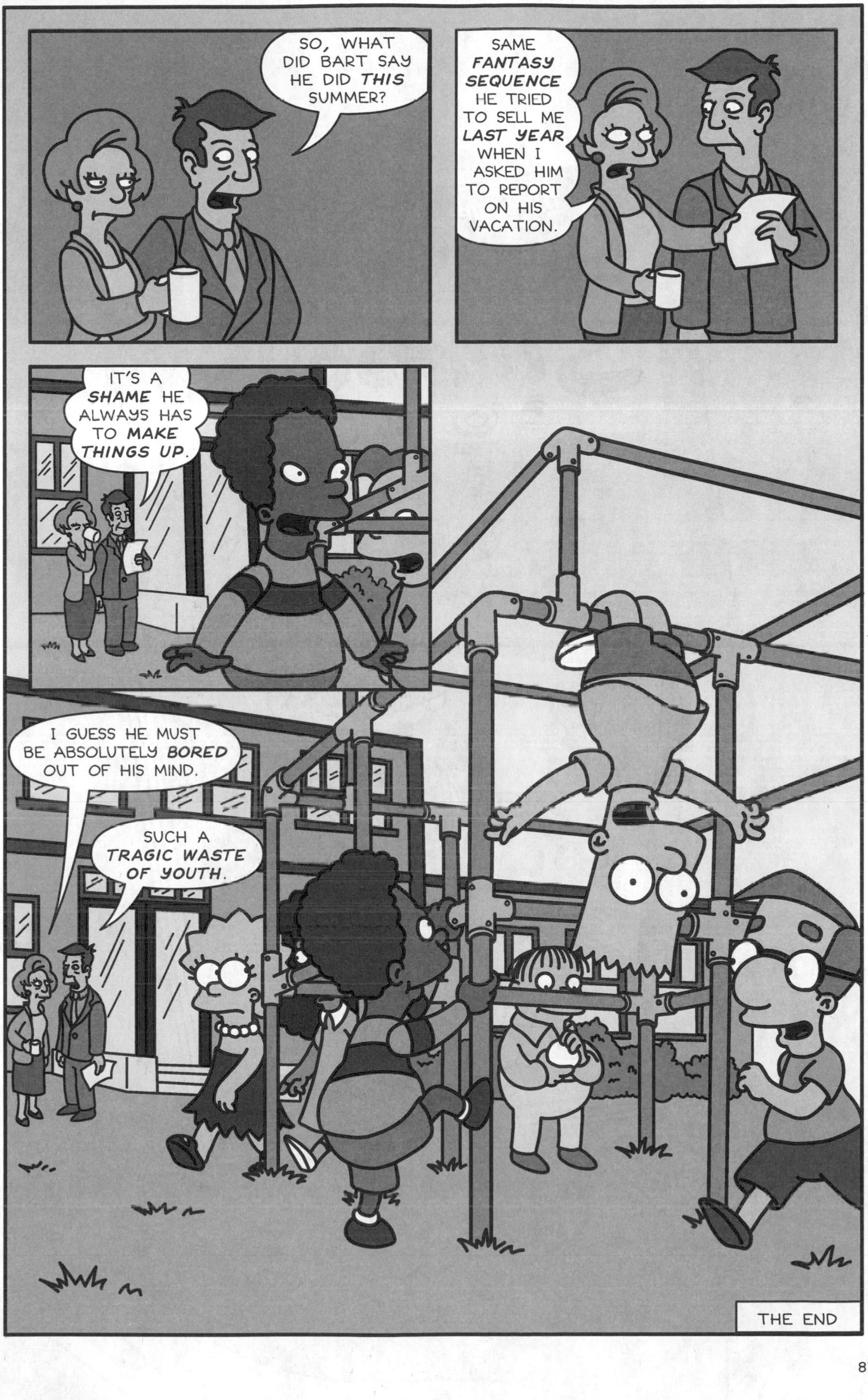
SO, WHAT DID BART SAY HE DID THIS SUMMER?
SAME FANTASY SEQUENCE HE TRIED TO SELL ME LAST YEAR WHEN I ASKED HIM TO REPORT ON HIS VACATION.
IT'S A SHAME HE ALWAYS HAS TO MAKE THINGS UP.
I GUESS HE MUST BE ABSOLUTELY BORED OUT OF HIS MIND.
SUCH A TRAGIC WASTE OF YOUTH.
THE END

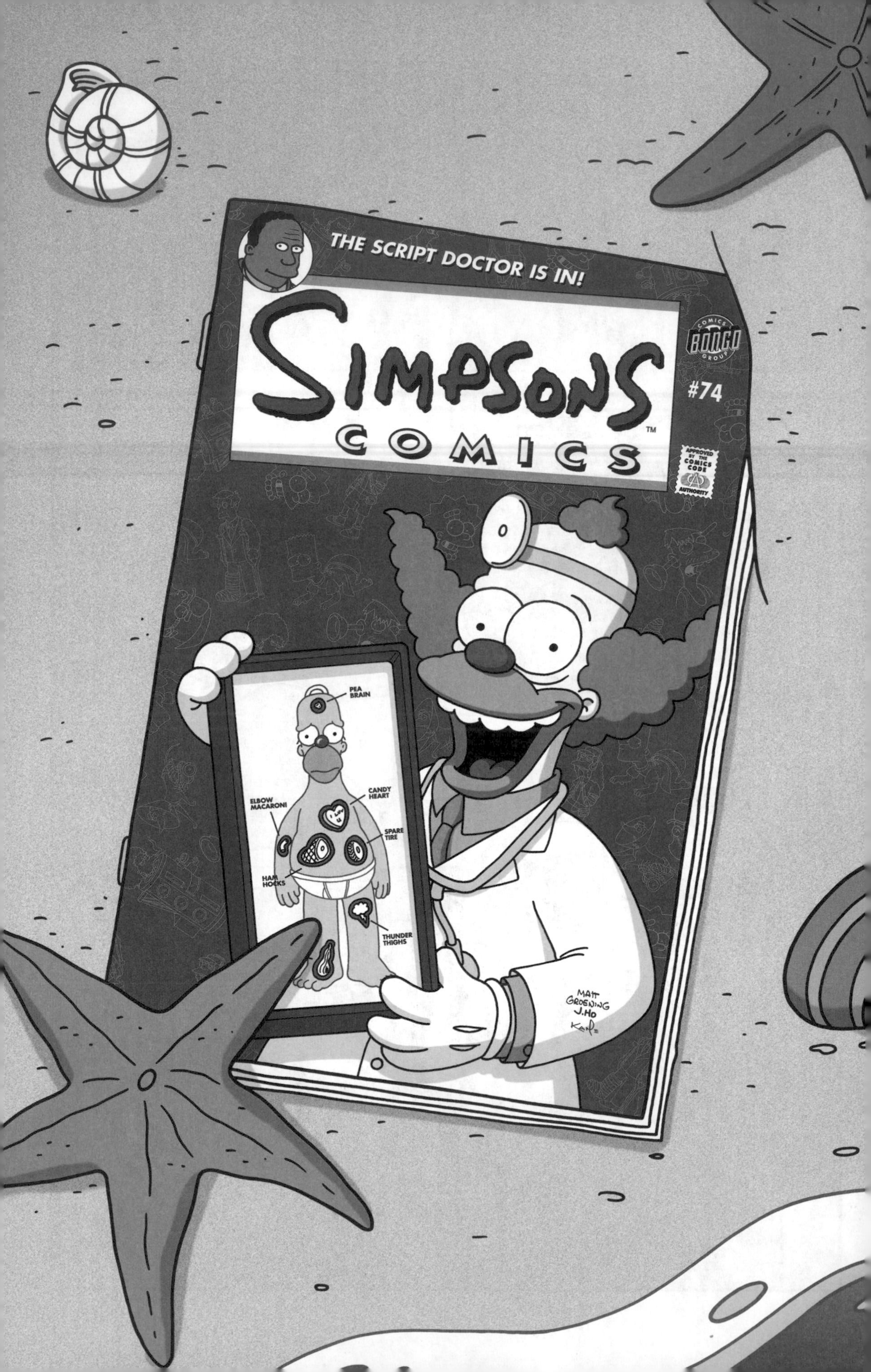

THE SCRIPT DOCTOR IS IN!
SIMPSONS COMICS™
#74
APPROVED BY THE COMICS CODE AUTHORITY
PEA BRAIN
ELBOW MACARONI
CANDY HEART
SPARE TIRE
HAM HOCKS
THUNDER THIGHS
MATT GROENING J.HO

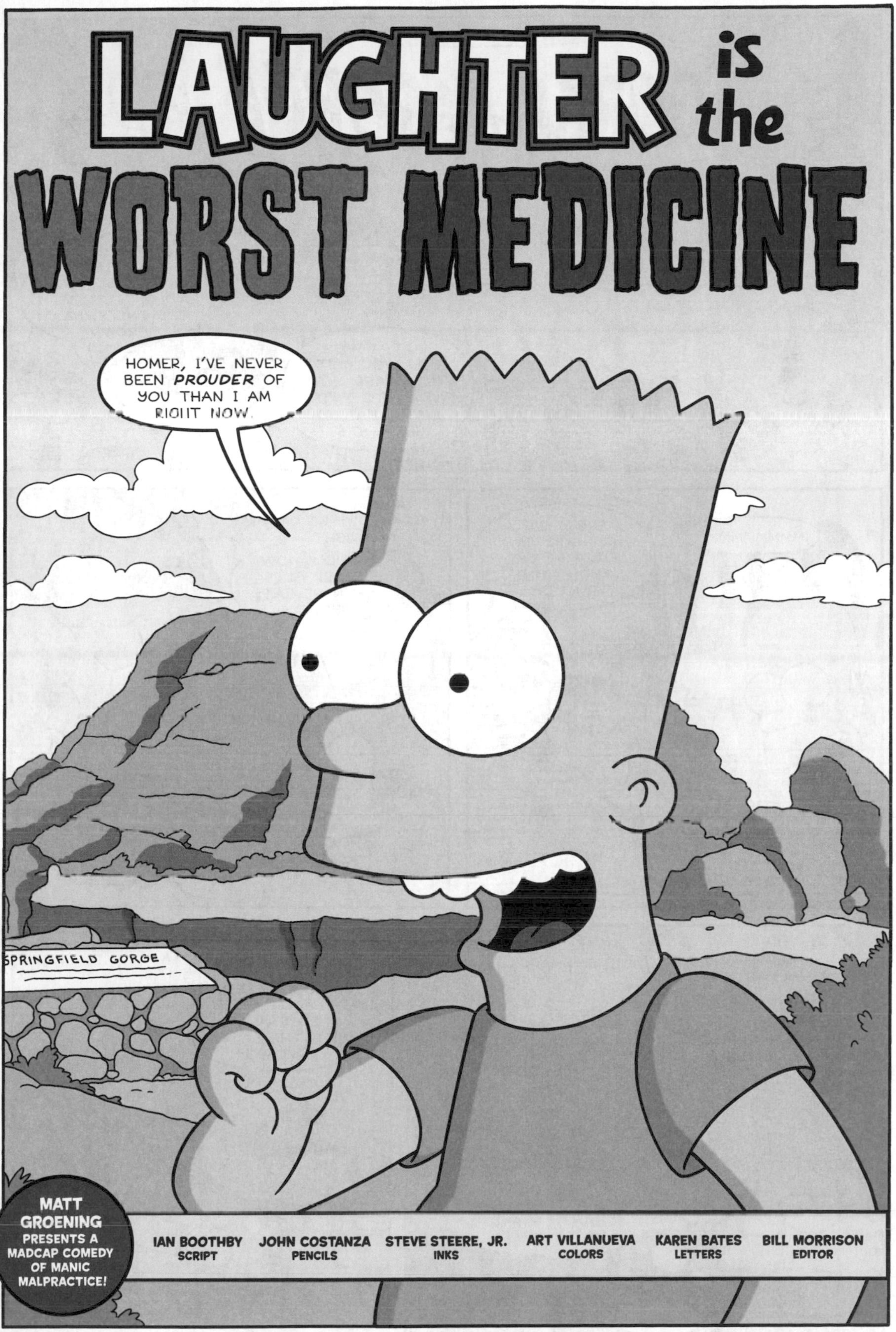
LAUGHTER is the WORST MEDICINE
HOMER, I'VE NEVER BEEN PROUDER OF YOU THAN I AM RIGHT NOW.
SPRINGFIELD GORGE
MATT GROENING PRESENTS A MADCAP COMEDY OF MANIC MALPRACTICE!
IAN BOOTHBY SCRIPT
JOHN COSTANZA PENCILS
STEVE STEERE, JR. INKS
ART VILLANUEVA COLORS
KAREN BATES LETTERS
BILL MORRISON EDITOR

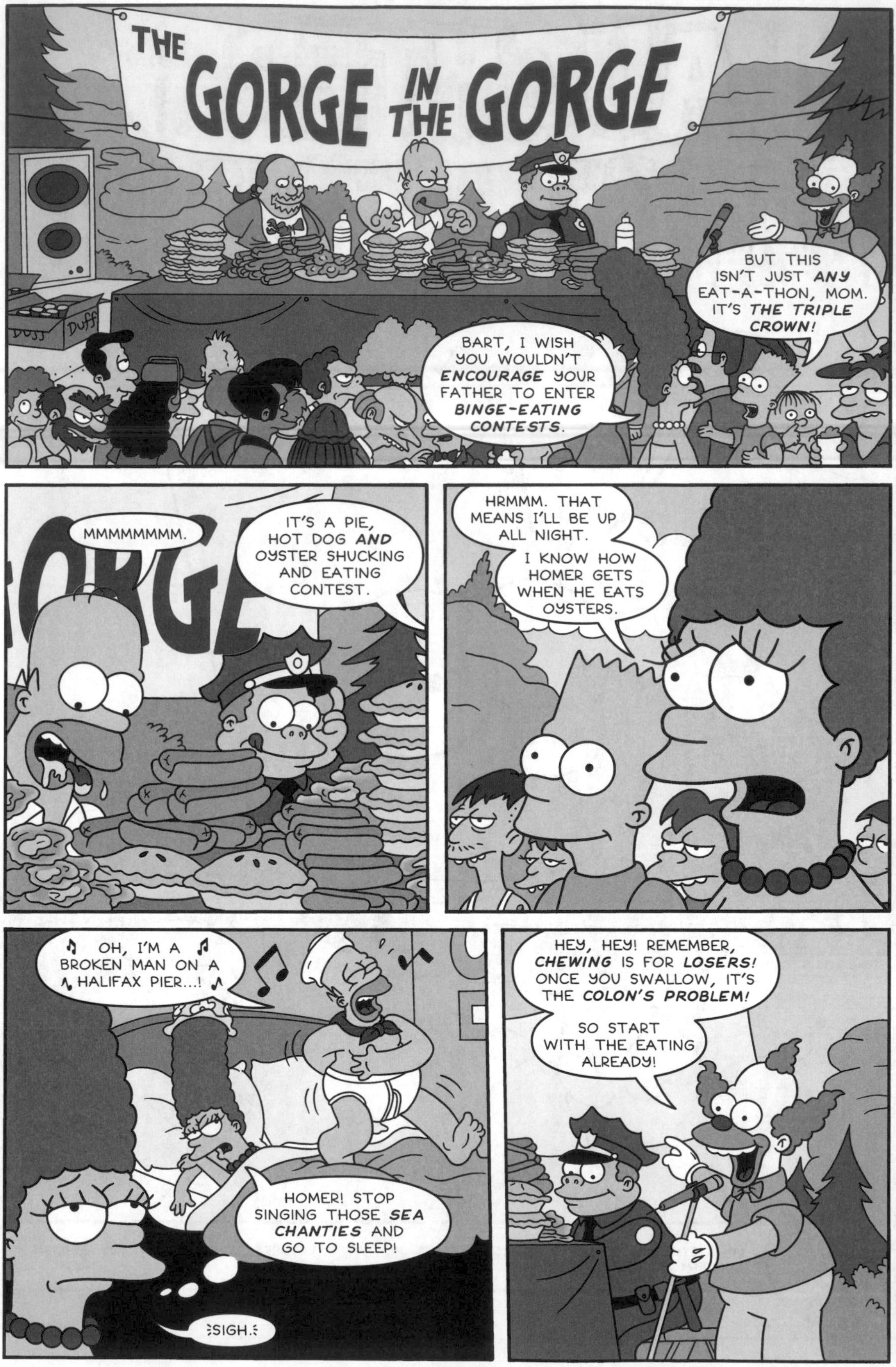
THE GORGE IN THE GORGE
BART, I WISH YOU WOULDN'T ENCOURAGE YOUR FATHER TO ENTER BINGE-EATING CONTESTS.
BUT THIS ISN'T JUST ANY EAT-A-THON, MOM. IT'S THE TRIPLE CROWN!
MMMMMMMM.
IT'S A PIE, HOT DOG AND OYSTER SHUCKING AND EATING CONTEST.
HRMMM. THAT MEANS I'LL BE UP ALL NIGHT.
I KNOW HOW HOMER GETS WHEN HE EATS OYSTERS.
OH, I'M A BROKEN MAN ON A HALIFAX PIER...!
HOMER! STOP SINGING THOSE SEA CHANTIES AND GO TO SLEEP!
SIGH.
HEY, HEY! REMEMBER, CHEWING IS FOR LOSERS! ONCE YOU SWALLOW, IT'S THE COLON'S PROBLEM!
SO START WITH THE EATING ALREADY!

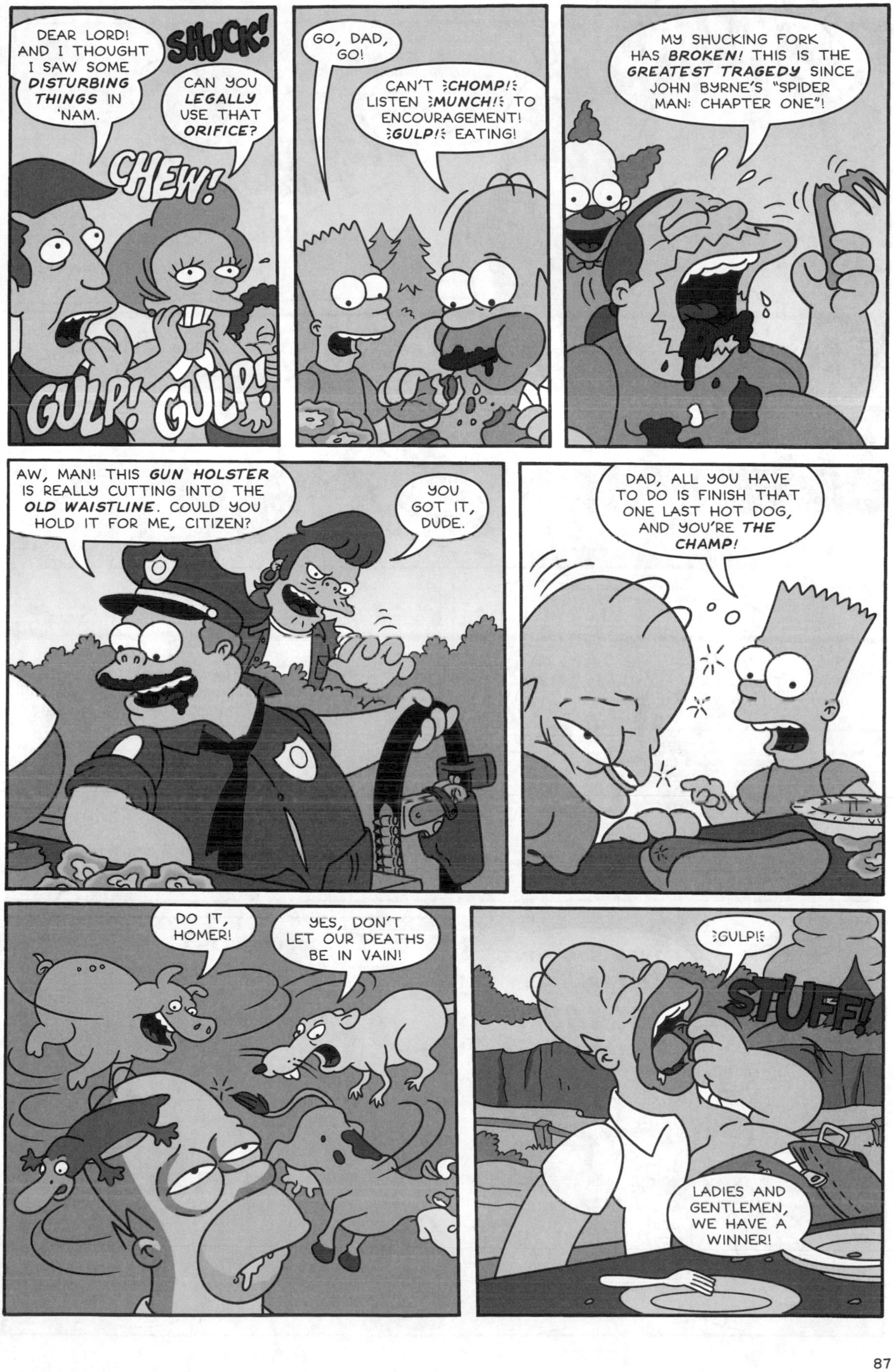

DEAR LORD! AND I THOUGHT I SAW SOME DISTURBING THINGS IN 'NAM.
SHUCK!
CAN YOU LEGALLY USE THAT ORIFICE?
CHEW!
GULP! GULP!
GO, DAD, GO!
CAN'T CHOMP! LISTEN MUNCH! TO ENCOURAGEMENT! GULP! EATING!
MY SHUCKING FORK HAS BROKEN! THIS IS THE GREATEST TRAGEDY SINCE JOHN BYRNE'S "SPIDER MAN: CHAPTER ONE"!
AW, MAN! THIS GUN HOLSTER IS REALLY CUTTING INTO THE OLD WAISTLINE. COULD YOU HOLD IT FOR ME, CITIZEN?
YOU GOT IT, DUDE.
DAD, ALL YOU HAVE TO DO IS FINISH THAT ONE LAST HOT DOG, AND YOU'RE THE CHAMP!
DO IT, HOMER!
YES, DON'T LET OUR DEATHS BE IN VAIN!
GULP!
STUFF!
LADIES AND GENTLEMEN, WE HAVE A WINNER!

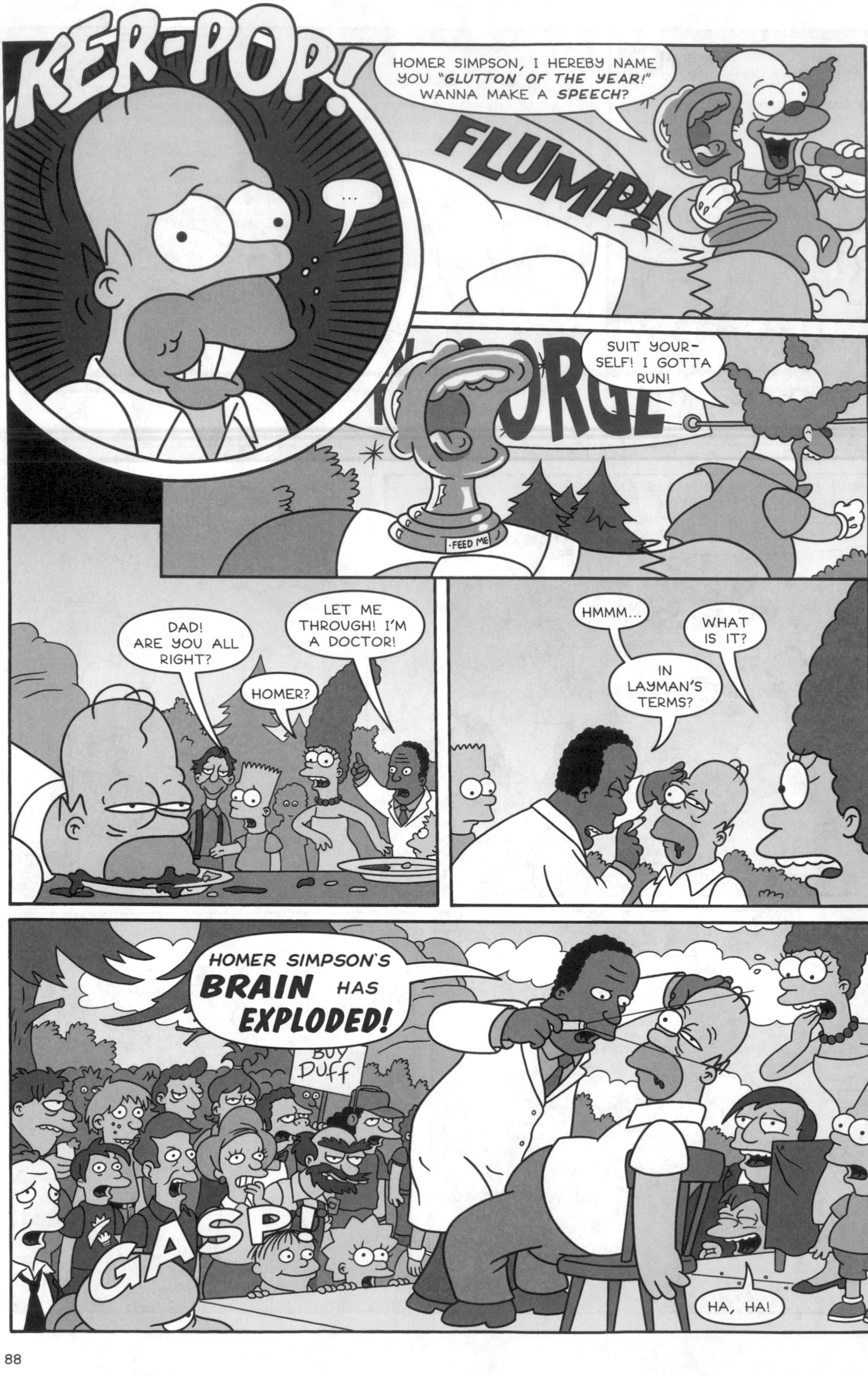

KER-POP!
...
HOMER SIMPSON, I HEREBY NAME YOU "GLUTTON OF THE YEAR!" WANNA MAKE A SPEECH?
FLUMP!
SUIT YOURSELF! I GOTTA RUN!
ORGE
FEED ME
DAD! ARE YOU ALL RIGHT?
HOMER?
LET ME THROUGH! I'M A DOCTOR!
HMMM...
WHAT IS IT?
IN LAYMAN'S TERMS?
HOMER SIMPSON'S BRAIN HAS EXPLODED!
BUY Duff
GASP!
HA, HA!

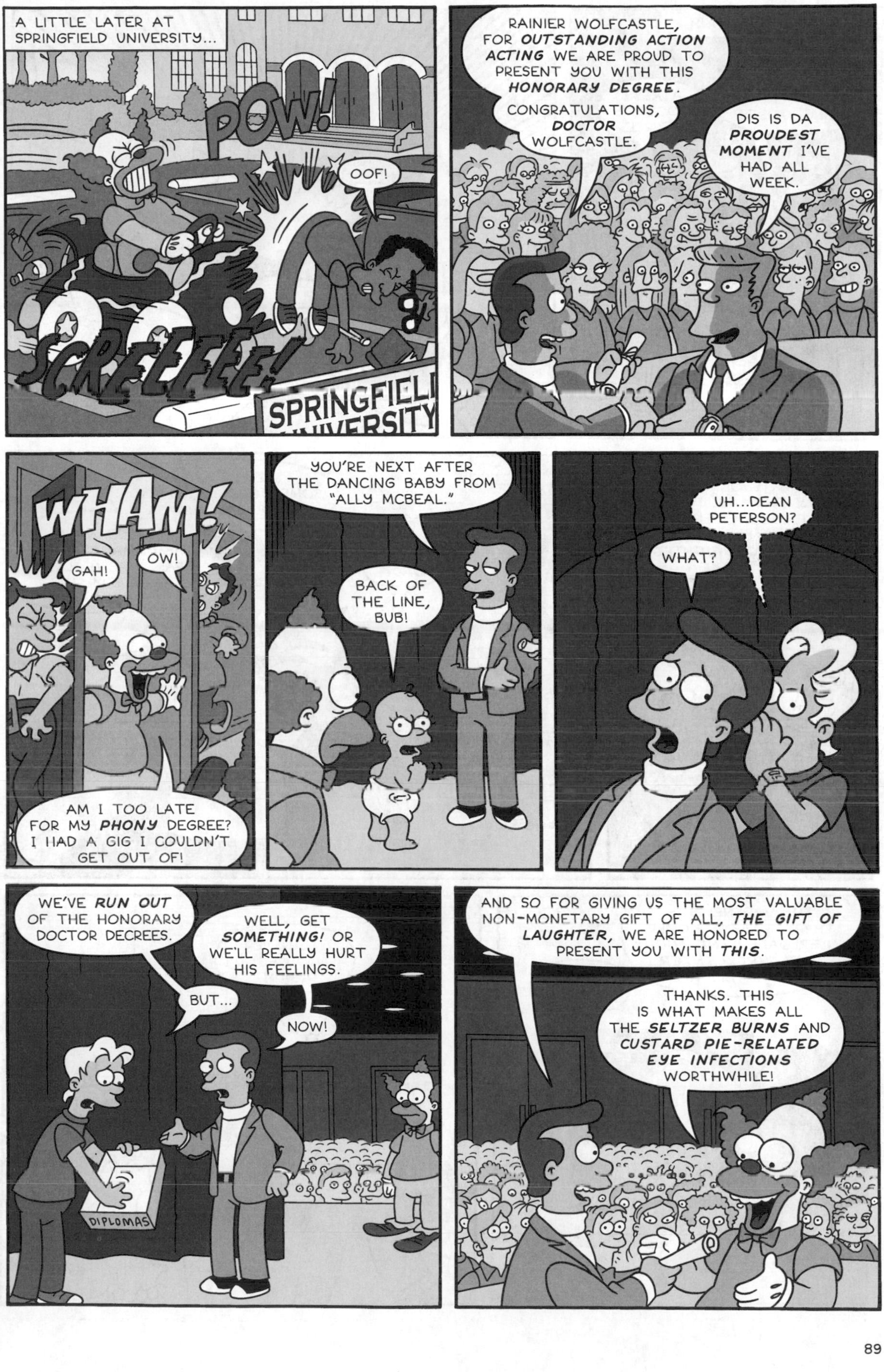
A LITTLE LATER AT SPRINGFIELD UNIVERSITY...
POW!
OOF!
SCREEEEE!
SPRINGFIELD UNIVERSITY
RAINIER WOLFCASTLE, FOR *OUTSTANDING ACTION ACTING* WE ARE PROUD TO PRESENT YOU WITH THIS *HONORARY DEGREE*.
CONGRATULATIONS, *DOCTOR* WOLFCASTLE.
DIS IS DA *PROUDEST MOMENT* I'VE HAD ALL WEEK.
WHAM!
GAH!
OW!
AM I TOO LATE FOR MY *PHONY* DEGREE? I HAD A GIG I COULDN'T GET OUT OF!
YOU'RE NEXT AFTER THE DANCING BABY FROM "ALLY MCBEAL."
BACK OF THE LINE, BUB!
UH...DEAN PETERSON?
WHAT?
WE'VE *RUN OUT* OF THE HONORARY DOCTOR DECREES.
WELL, GET *SOMETHING!* OR WE'LL REALLY HURT HIS FEELINGS.
BUT...
NOW!
DIPLOMAS
AND SO FOR GIVING US THE MOST VALUABLE NON-MONETARY GIFT OF ALL, *THE GIFT OF LAUGHTER,* WE ARE HONORED TO PRESENT YOU WITH *THIS*.
THANKS. THIS IS WHAT MAKES ALL THE *SELTZER BURNS* AND *CUSTARD PIE-RELATED EYE INFECTIONS* WORTHWHILE!

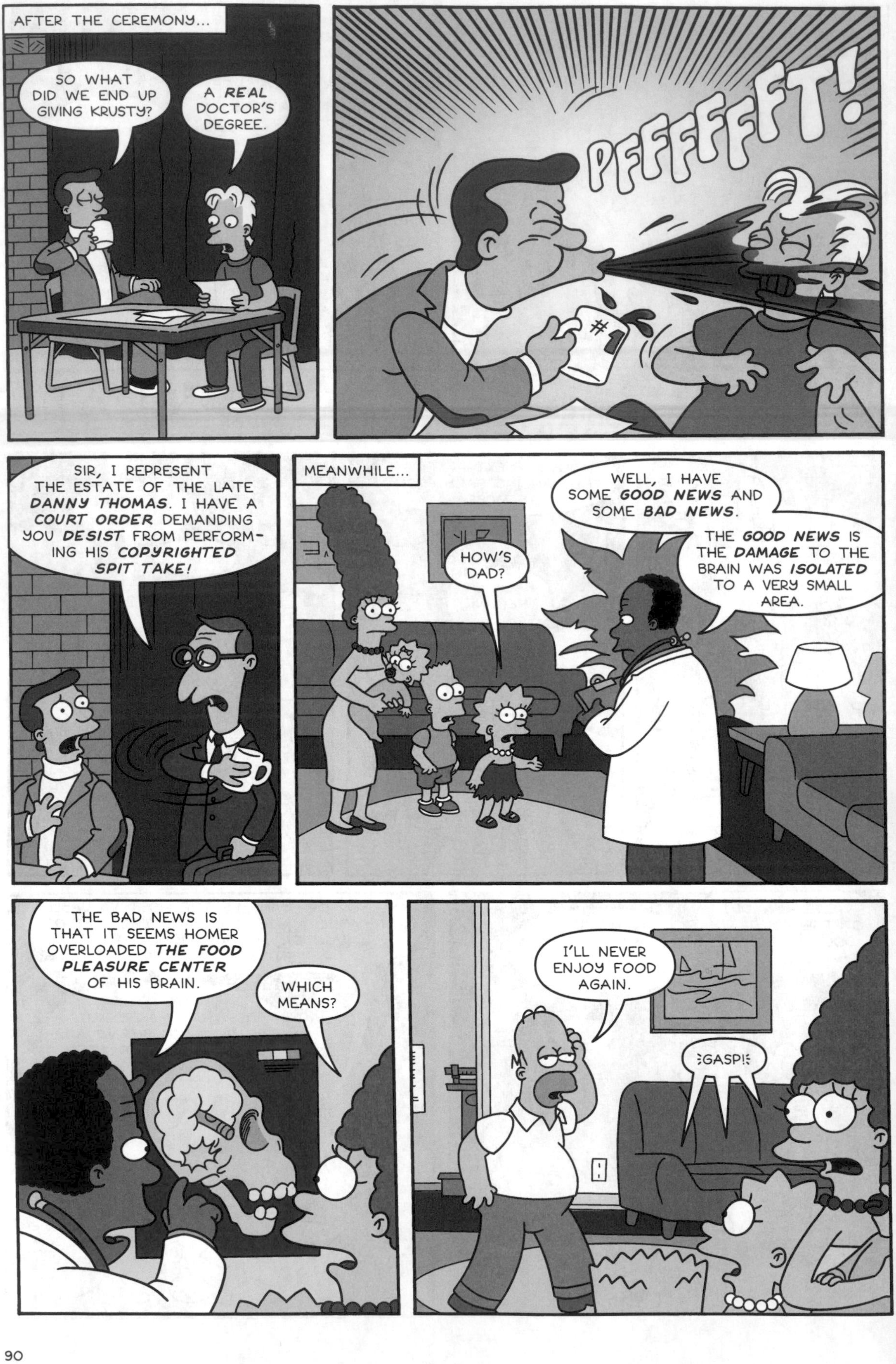
AFTER THE CEREMONY...
SO WHAT DID WE END UP GIVING KRUSTY?
A REAL DOCTOR'S DEGREE.
PFFFFFFT!
#1
SIR, I REPRESENT THE ESTATE OF THE LATE DANNY THOMAS. I HAVE A COURT ORDER DEMANDING YOU DESIST FROM PERFORMING HIS COPYRIGHTED SPIT TAKE!
MEANWHILE...
HOW'S DAD?
WELL, I HAVE SOME GOOD NEWS AND SOME BAD NEWS.
THE GOOD NEWS IS THE DAMAGE TO THE BRAIN WAS ISOLATED TO A VERY SMALL AREA.
THE BAD NEWS IS THAT IT SEEMS HOMER OVERLOADED THE FOOD PLEASURE CENTER OF HIS BRAIN.
WHICH MEANS?
I'LL NEVER ENJOY FOOD AGAIN.
GASP!

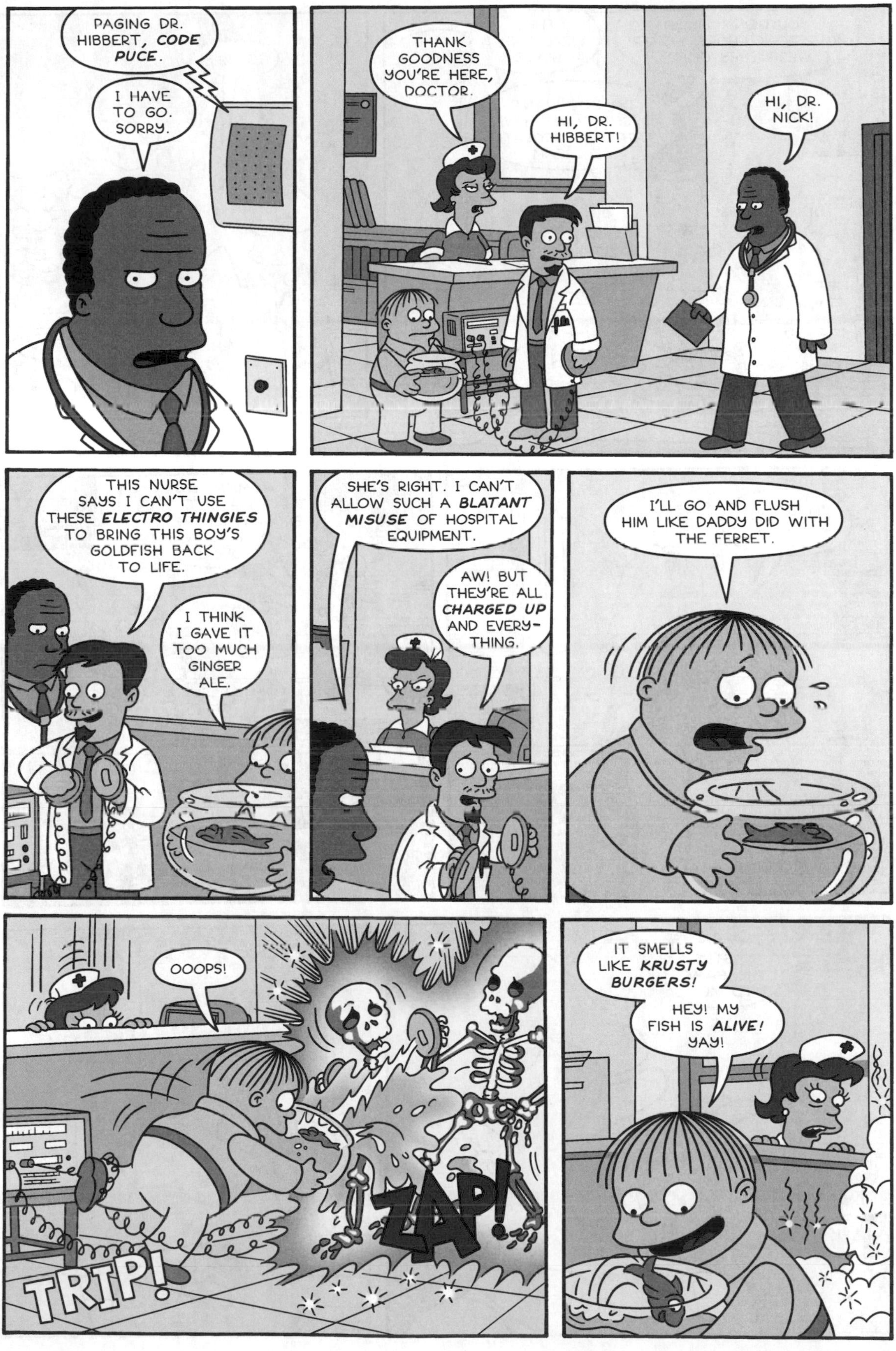
PAGING DR. HIBBERT, CODE PUCE.
I HAVE TO GO. SORRY.
THANK GOODNESS YOU'RE HERE, DOCTOR.
HI, DR. HIBBERT!
HI, DR. NICK!
THIS NURSE SAYS I CAN'T USE THESE ELECTRO THINGIES TO BRING THIS BOY'S GOLDFISH BACK TO LIFE.
I THINK I GAVE IT TOO MUCH GINGER ALE.
SHE'S RIGHT. I CAN'T ALLOW SUCH A BLATANT MISUSE OF HOSPITAL EQUIPMENT.
AW! BUT THEY'RE ALL CHARGED UP AND EVERY-THING.
I'LL GO AND FLUSH HIM LIKE DADDY DID WITH THE FERRET.
OOOPS!
ZAP!
TRIP!
IT SMELLS LIKE KRUSTY BURGERS!
HEY! MY FISH IS ALIVE! YAY!

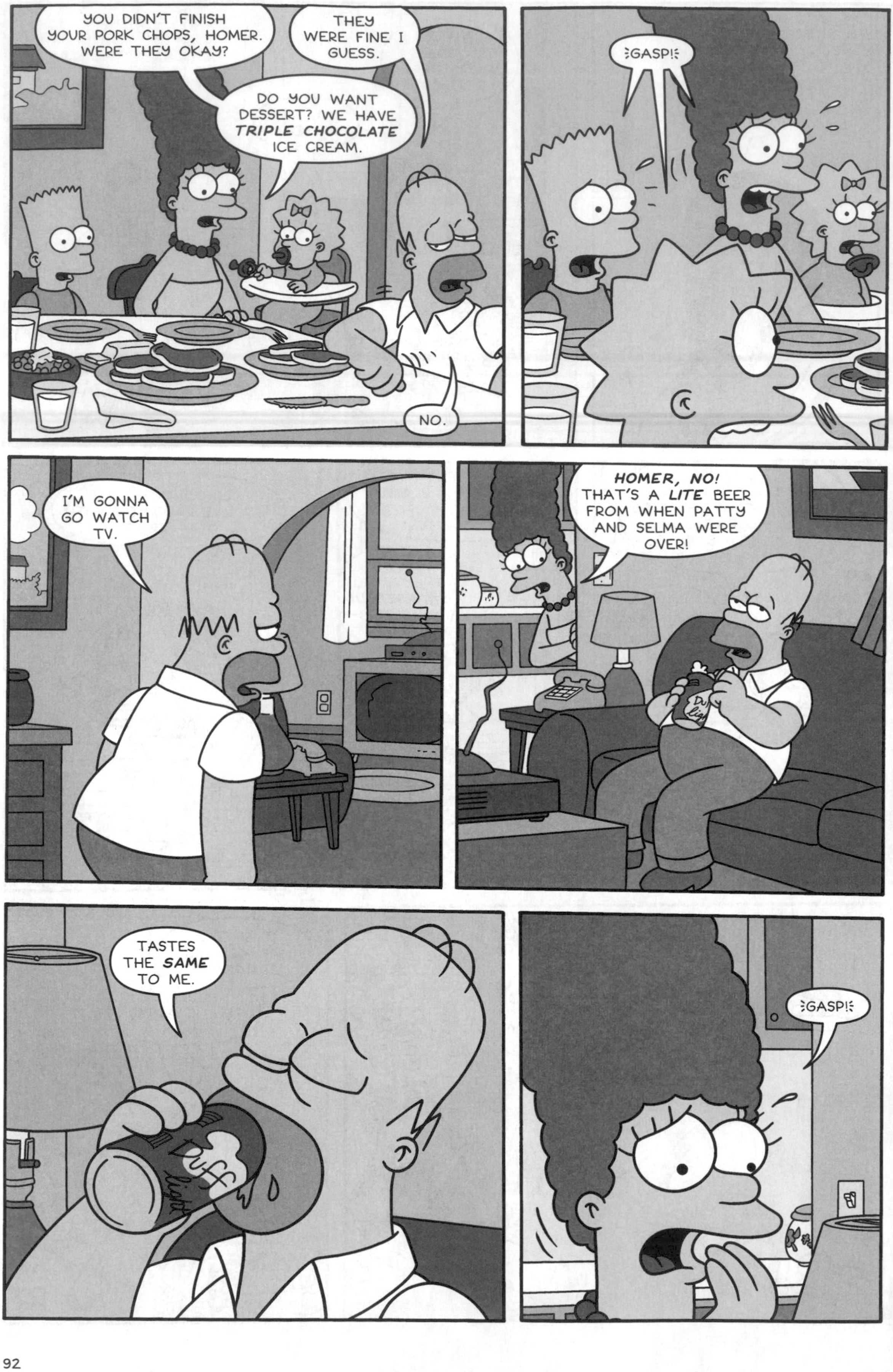

YOU DIDN'T FINISH YOUR PORK CHOPS, HOMER. WERE THEY OKAY?
THEY WERE FINE I GUESS.
DO YOU WANT DESSERT? WE HAVE TRIPLE CHOCOLATE ICE CREAM.
NO.
GASP!
I'M GONNA GO WATCH TV.
HOMER, NO! THAT'S A LITE BEER FROM WHEN PATTY AND SELMA WERE OVER!
TASTES THE SAME TO ME.
GASP!

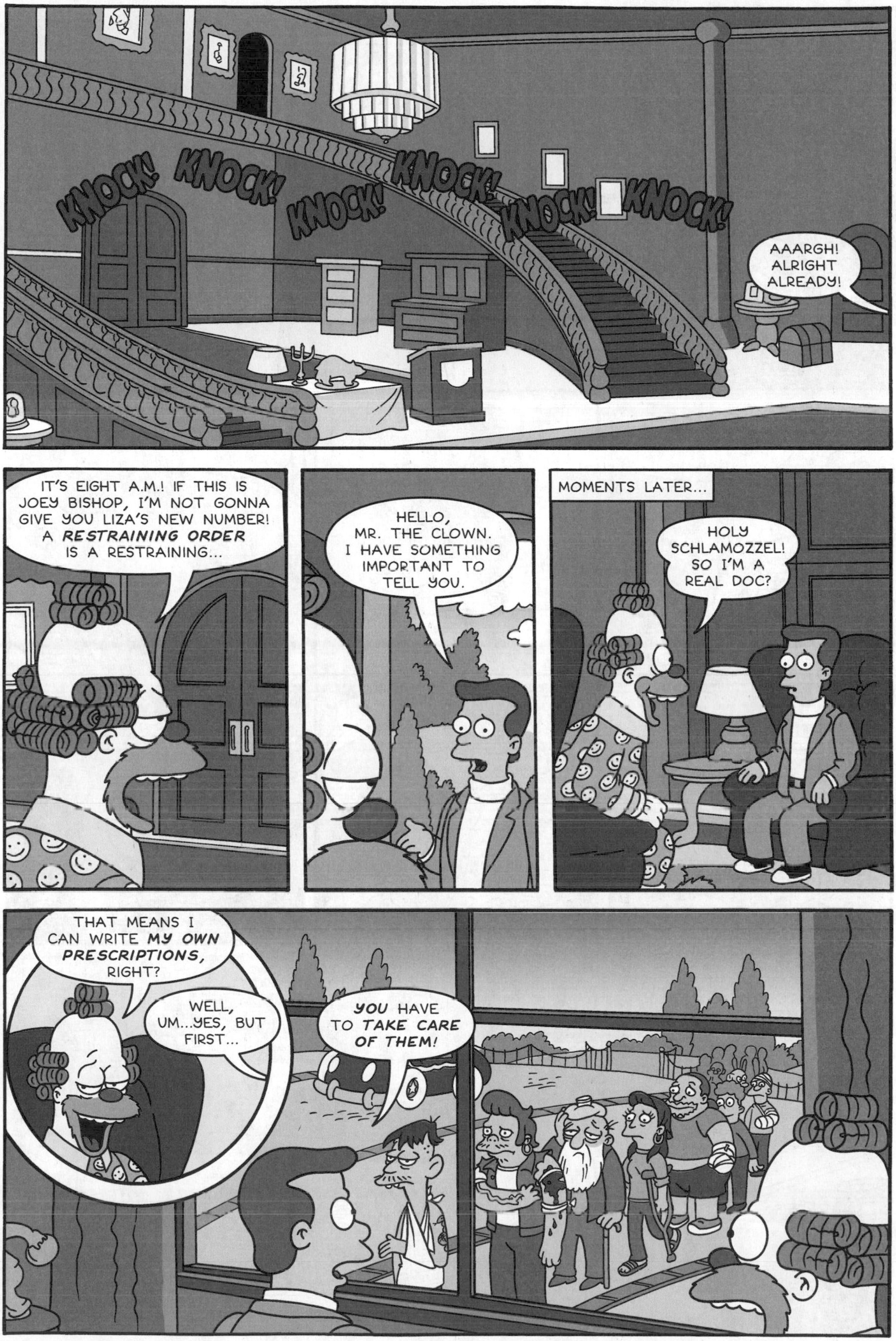
KNOCK! KNOCK! KNOCK! KNOCK! KNOCK! KNOCK!
AAARGH! ALRIGHT ALREADY!
IT'S EIGHT A.M.! IF THIS IS JOEY BISHOP, I'M NOT GONNA GIVE YOU LIZA'S NEW NUMBER! A RESTRAINING ORDER IS A RESTRAINING...
HELLO, MR. THE CLOWN. I HAVE SOMETHING IMPORTANT TO TELL YOU.
MOMENTS LATER...
HOLY SCHLAMOZZEL! SO I'M A REAL DOC?
THAT MEANS I CAN WRITE MY OWN PRESCRIPTIONS, RIGHT?
WELL, UM...YES, BUT FIRST...
YOU HAVE TO TAKE CARE OF THEM!

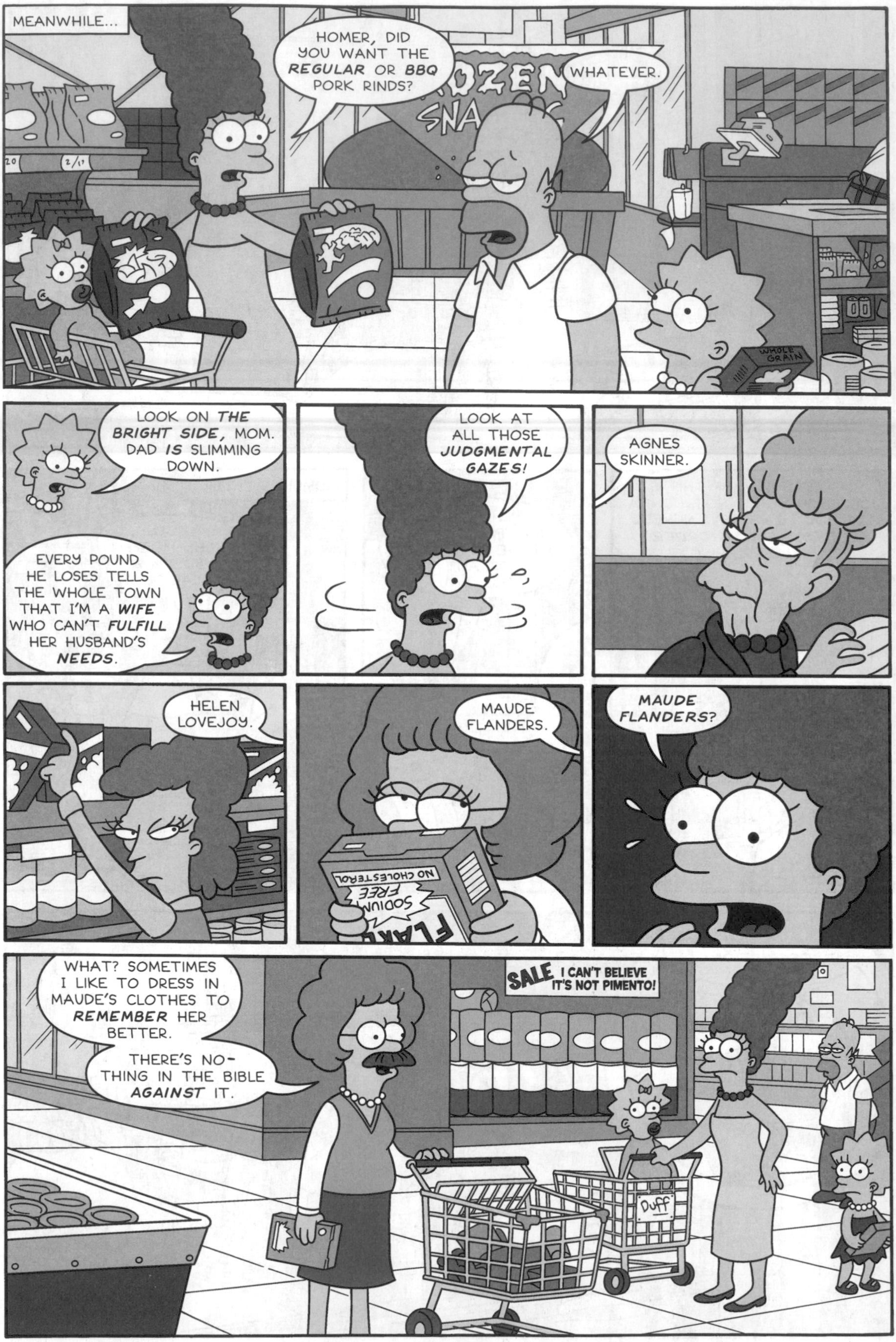
MEANWHILE...
HOMER, DID YOU WANT THE REGULAR OR BBQ PORK RINDS?
WHATEVER.
WHOLE GRAIN
LOOK ON THE BRIGHT SIDE, MOM. DAD IS SLIMMING DOWN.
EVERY POUND HE LOSES TELLS THE WHOLE TOWN THAT I'M A WIFE WHO CAN'T FULFILL HER HUSBAND'S NEEDS.
LOOK AT ALL THOSE JUDGMENTAL GAZES!
AGNES SKINNER.
HELEN LOVEJOY.
MAUDE FLANDERS.
NO CHOLESTEROL
SODIUM FREE
MAUDE FLANDERS?
WHAT? SOMETIMES I LIKE TO DRESS IN MAUDE'S CLOTHES TO REMEMBER HER BETTER.
THERE'S NOTHING IN THE BIBLE AGAINST IT.
SALE I CAN'T BELIEVE IT'S NOT PIMENTO!
Duff

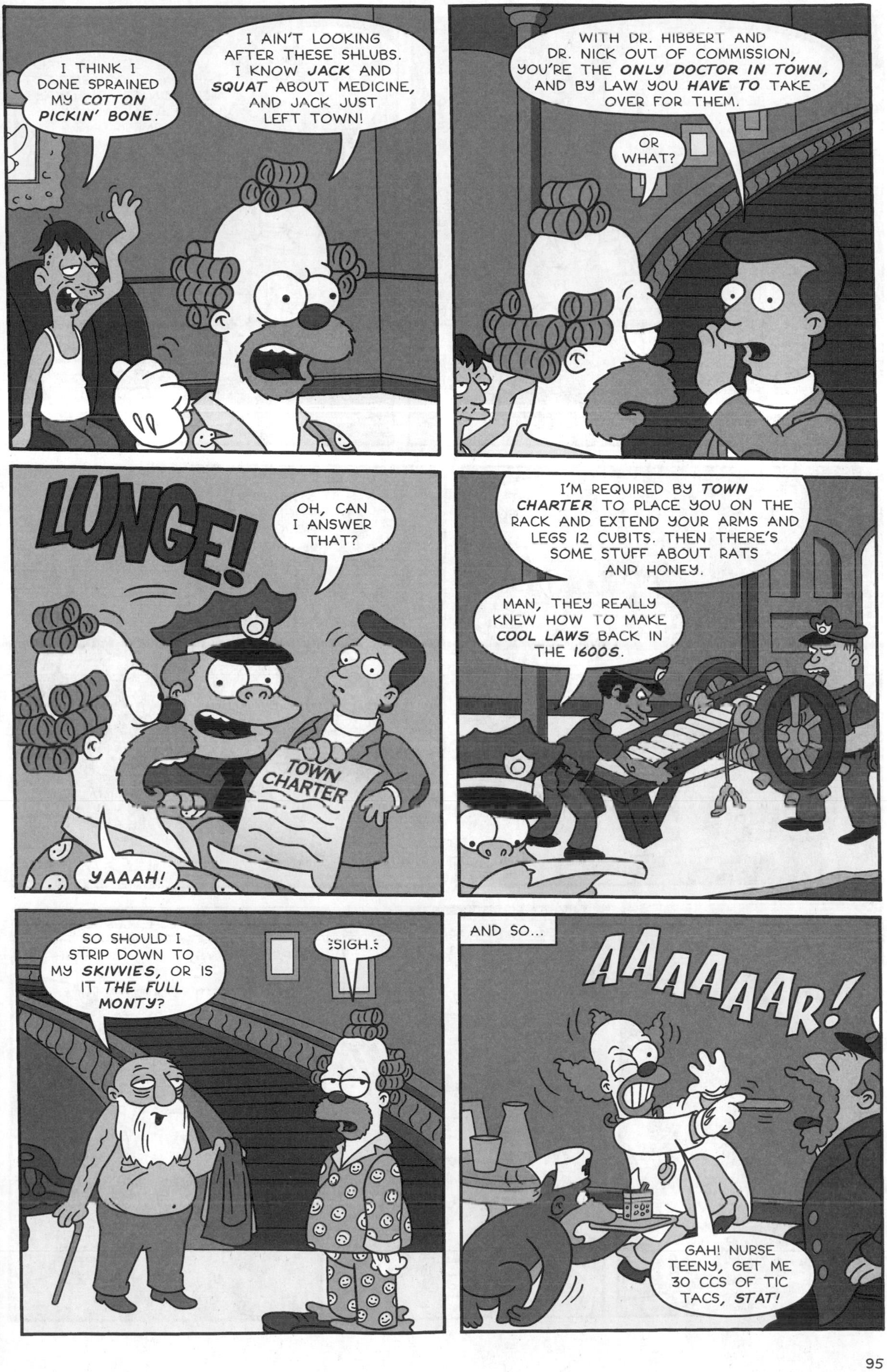
I THINK I DONE SPRAINED MY COTTON PICKIN' BONE.
I AIN'T LOOKING AFTER THESE SHLUBS. I KNOW JACK AND SQUAT ABOUT MEDICINE, AND JACK JUST LEFT TOWN!
WITH DR. HIBBERT AND DR. NICK OUT OF COMMISSION, YOU'RE THE ONLY DOCTOR IN TOWN, AND BY LAW YOU HAVE TO TAKE OVER FOR THEM.
OR WHAT?
LUNGE!
OH, CAN I ANSWER THAT?
TOWN CHARTER
YAAAH!
I'M REQUIRED BY TOWN CHARTER TO PLACE YOU ON THE RACK AND EXTEND YOUR ARMS AND LEGS 12 CUBITS. THEN THERE'S SOME STUFF ABOUT RATS AND HONEY.
MAN, THEY REALLY KNEW HOW TO MAKE COOL LAWS BACK IN THE 1600S.
SO SHOULD I STRIP DOWN TO MY SKIVVIES, OR IS IT THE FULL MONTY?
SIGH.
AND SO...
AAAAAAAR!
GAH! NURSE TEENY, GET ME 30 CCS OF TIC TACS, STAT!

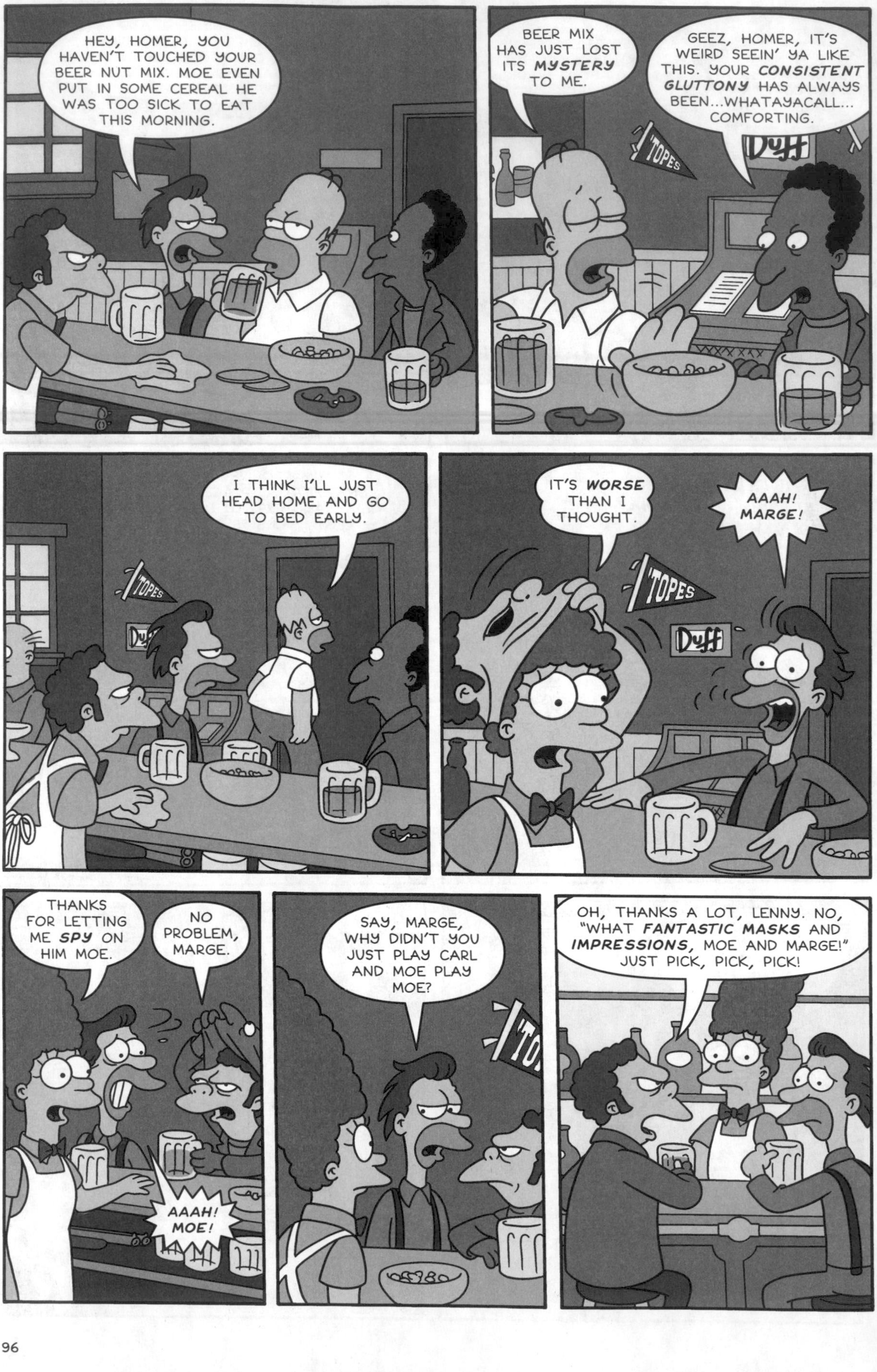
HEY, HOMER, YOU HAVEN'T TOUCHED YOUR BEER NUT MIX. MOE EVEN PUT IN SOME CEREAL HE WAS TOO SICK TO EAT THIS MORNING.
BEER MIX HAS JUST LOST ITS MYSTERY TO ME.
GEEZ, HOMER, IT'S WEIRD SEEIN' YA LIKE THIS. YOUR CONSISTENT GLUTTONY HAS ALWAYS BEEN...WHATAYACALL... COMFORTING.
'TOPES
Duff
I THINK I'LL JUST HEAD HOME AND GO TO BED EARLY.
'TOPES
IT'S WORSE THAN I THOUGHT.
AAAH! MARGE!
'TOPES
Duff
THANKS FOR LETTING ME SPY ON HIM MOE.
NO PROBLEM, MARGE.
AAAH! MOE!
SAY, MARGE, WHY DIDN'T YOU JUST PLAY CARL AND MOE PLAY MOE?
OH, THANKS A LOT, LENNY. NO, "WHAT FANTASTIC MASKS AND IMPRESSIONS, MOE AND MARGE!" JUST PICK, PICK, PICK!

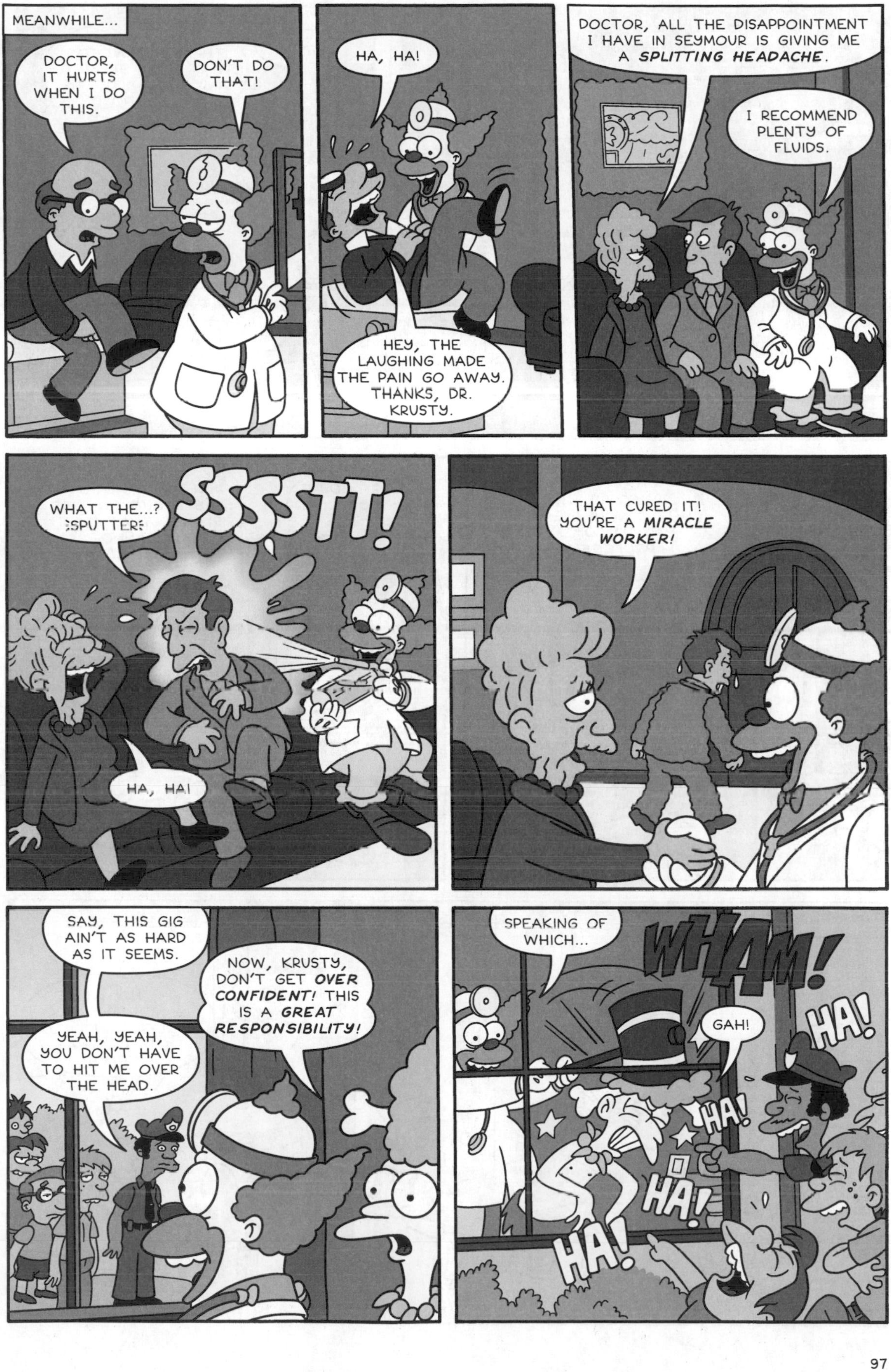
MEANWHILE...
DOCTOR, IT HURTS WHEN I DO THIS.
DON'T DO THAT!
HA, HA!
HEY, THE LAUGHING MADE THE PAIN GO AWAY. THANKS, DR. KRUSTY.
DOCTOR, ALL THE DISAPPOINTMENT I HAVE IN SEYMOUR IS GIVING ME A SPLITTING HEADACHE.
I RECOMMEND PLENTY OF FLUIDS.
SSSSTT!
WHAT THE...? SPUTTER
HA, HA!
THAT CURED IT! YOU'RE A MIRACLE WORKER!
SAY, THIS GIG AIN'T AS HARD AS IT SEEMS.
NOW, KRUSTY, DON'T GET OVER CONFIDENT! THIS IS A GREAT RESPONSIBILITY!
YEAH, YEAH, YOU DON'T HAVE TO HIT ME OVER THE HEAD.
SPEAKING OF WHICH...
WHAM!
GAH!
HA!
HA!
HA!
HA!

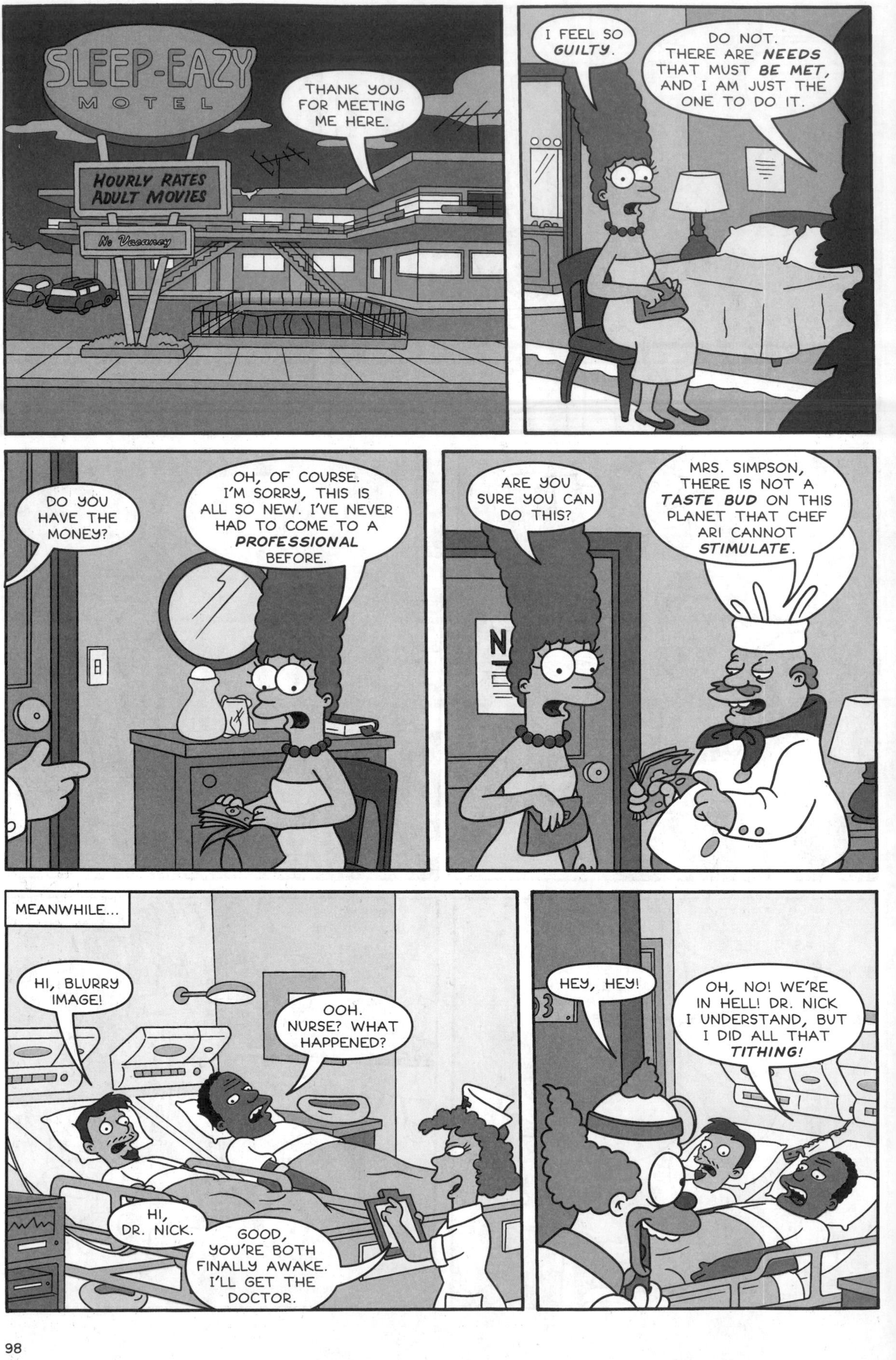
SLEEP-EAZY MOTEL
HOURLY RATES ADULT MOVIES
No Vacancy
THANK YOU FOR MEETING ME HERE.
I FEEL SO GUILTY.
DO NOT. THERE ARE NEEDS THAT MUST BE MET, AND I AM JUST THE ONE TO DO IT.
DO YOU HAVE THE MONEY?
OH, OF COURSE. I'M SORRY, THIS IS ALL SO NEW. I'VE NEVER HAD TO COME TO A PROFESSIONAL BEFORE.
ARE YOU SURE YOU CAN DO THIS?
MRS. SIMPSON, THERE IS NOT A TASTE BUD ON THIS PLANET THAT CHEF ARI CANNOT STIMULATE.
MEANWHILE...
HI, BLURRY IMAGE!
OOH. NURSE? WHAT HAPPENED?
HI, DR. NICK.
GOOD, YOU'RE BOTH FINALLY AWAKE. I'LL GET THE DOCTOR.
HEY, HEY!
OH, NO! WE'RE IN HELL! DR. NICK I UNDERSTAND, BUT I DID ALL THAT TITHING!

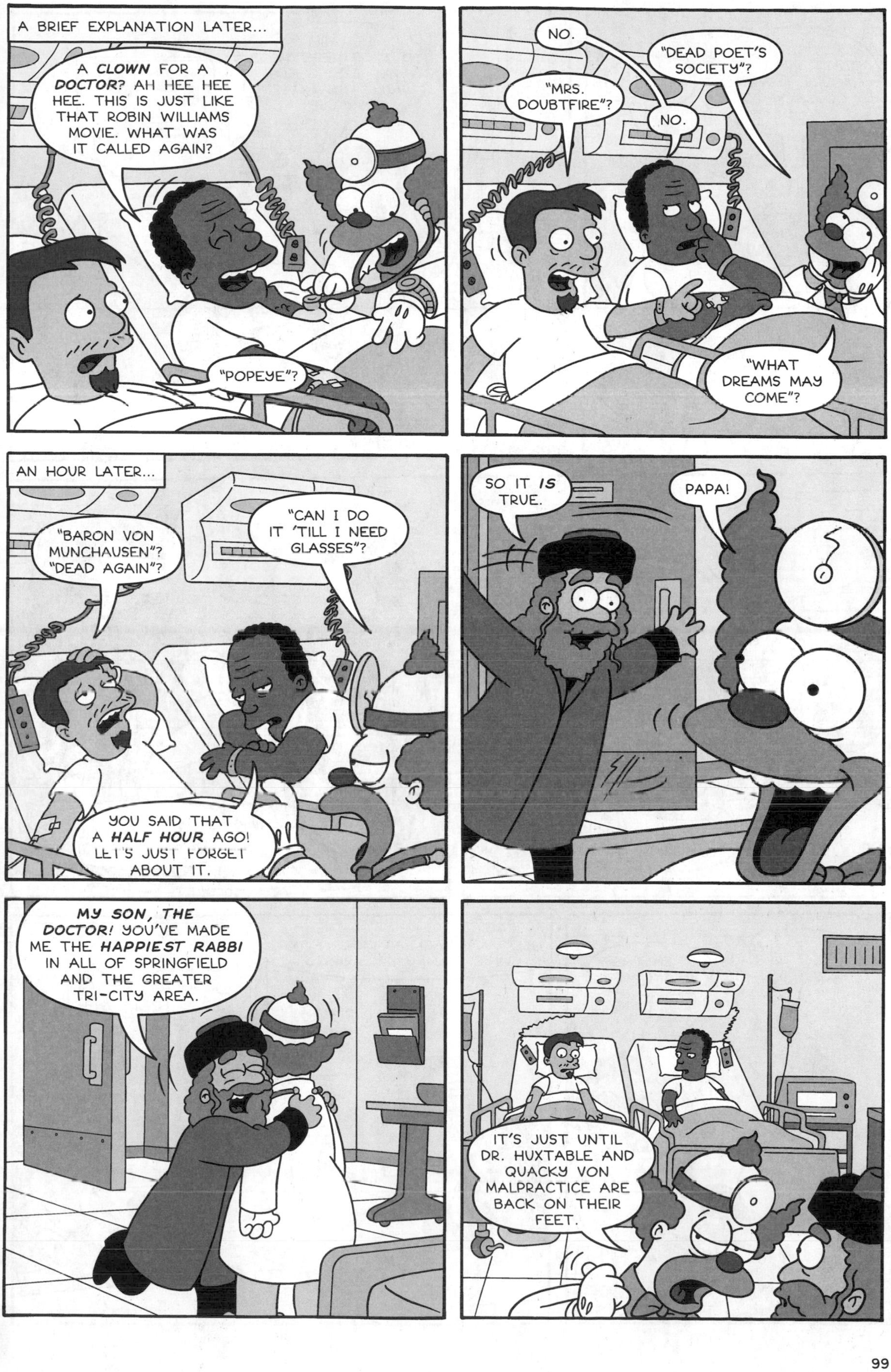

A BRIEF EXPLANATION LATER...
A CLOWN FOR A DOCTOR? AH HEE HEE HEE. THIS IS JUST LIKE THAT ROBIN WILLIAMS MOVIE. WHAT WAS IT CALLED AGAIN?
"POPEYE"?
NO.
"DEAD POET'S SOCIETY"?
"MRS. DOUBTFIRE"?
NO.
"WHAT DREAMS MAY COME"?
AN HOUR LATER...
"BARON VON MUNCHAUSEN"? "DEAD AGAIN"?
"CAN I DO IT 'TILL I NEED GLASSES"?
YOU SAID THAT A HALF HOUR AGO! LET'S JUST FORGET ABOUT IT.
SO IT IS TRUE.
PAPA!
MY SON, THE DOCTOR! YOU'VE MADE ME THE HAPPIEST RABBI IN ALL OF SPRINGFIELD AND THE GREATER TRI-CITY AREA.
IT'S JUST UNTIL DR. HUXTABLE AND QUACKY VON MALPRACTICE ARE BACK ON THEIR FEET.

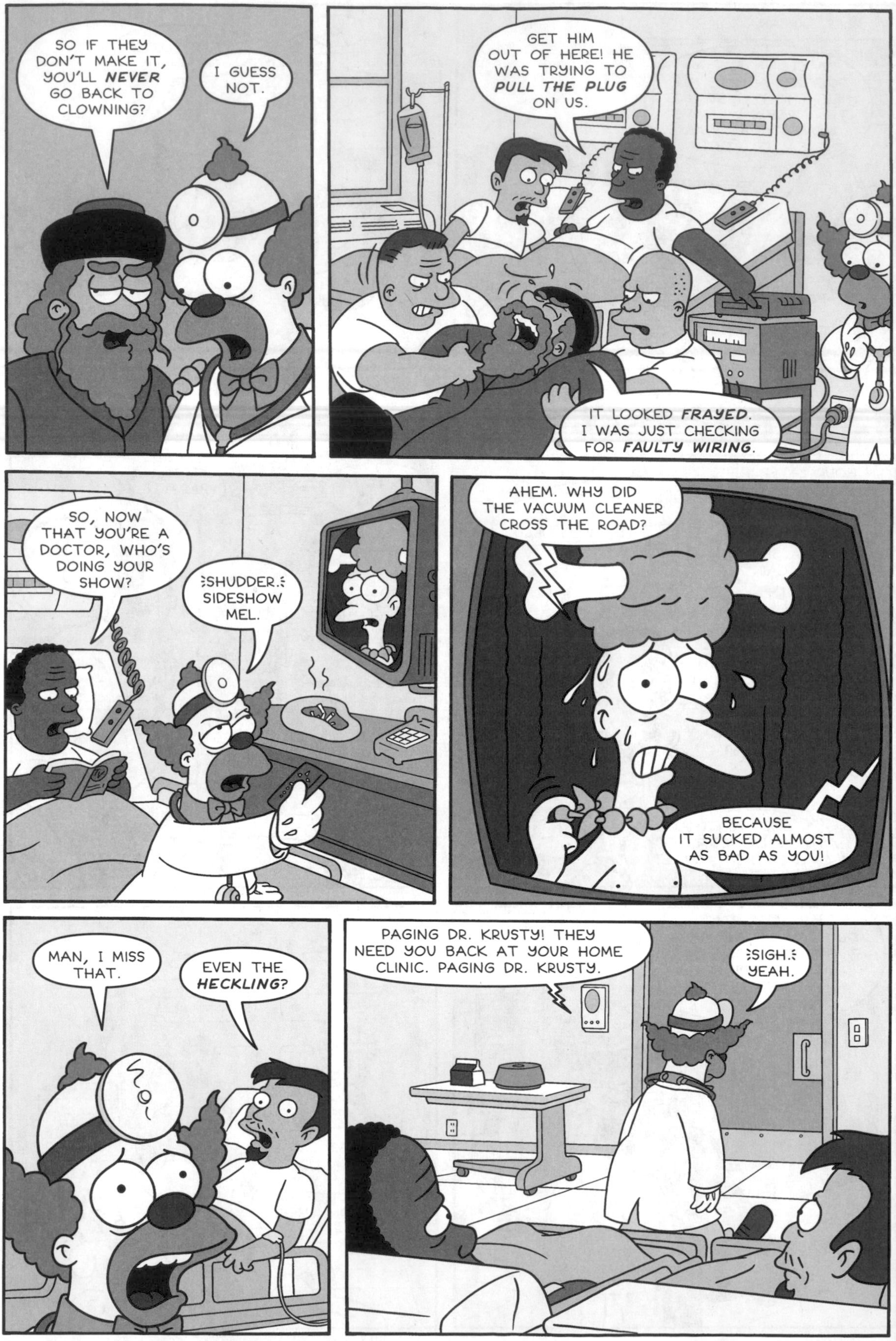
SO IF THEY DON'T MAKE IT, YOU'LL NEVER GO BACK TO CLOWNING?
I GUESS NOT.
GET HIM OUT OF HERE! HE WAS TRYING TO PULL THE PLUG ON US.
IT LOOKED FRAYED. I WAS JUST CHECKING FOR FAULTY WIRING.
SO, NOW THAT YOU'RE A DOCTOR, WHO'S DOING YOUR SHOW?
SHUDDER. SIDESHOW MEL.
AHEM. WHY DID THE VACUUM CLEANER CROSS THE ROAD?
BECAUSE IT SUCKED ALMOST AS BAD AS YOU!
MAN, I MISS THAT.
EVEN THE HECKLING?
PAGING DR. KRUSTY! THEY NEED YOU BACK AT YOUR HOME CLINIC. PAGING DR. KRUSTY.
SIGH. YEAH.

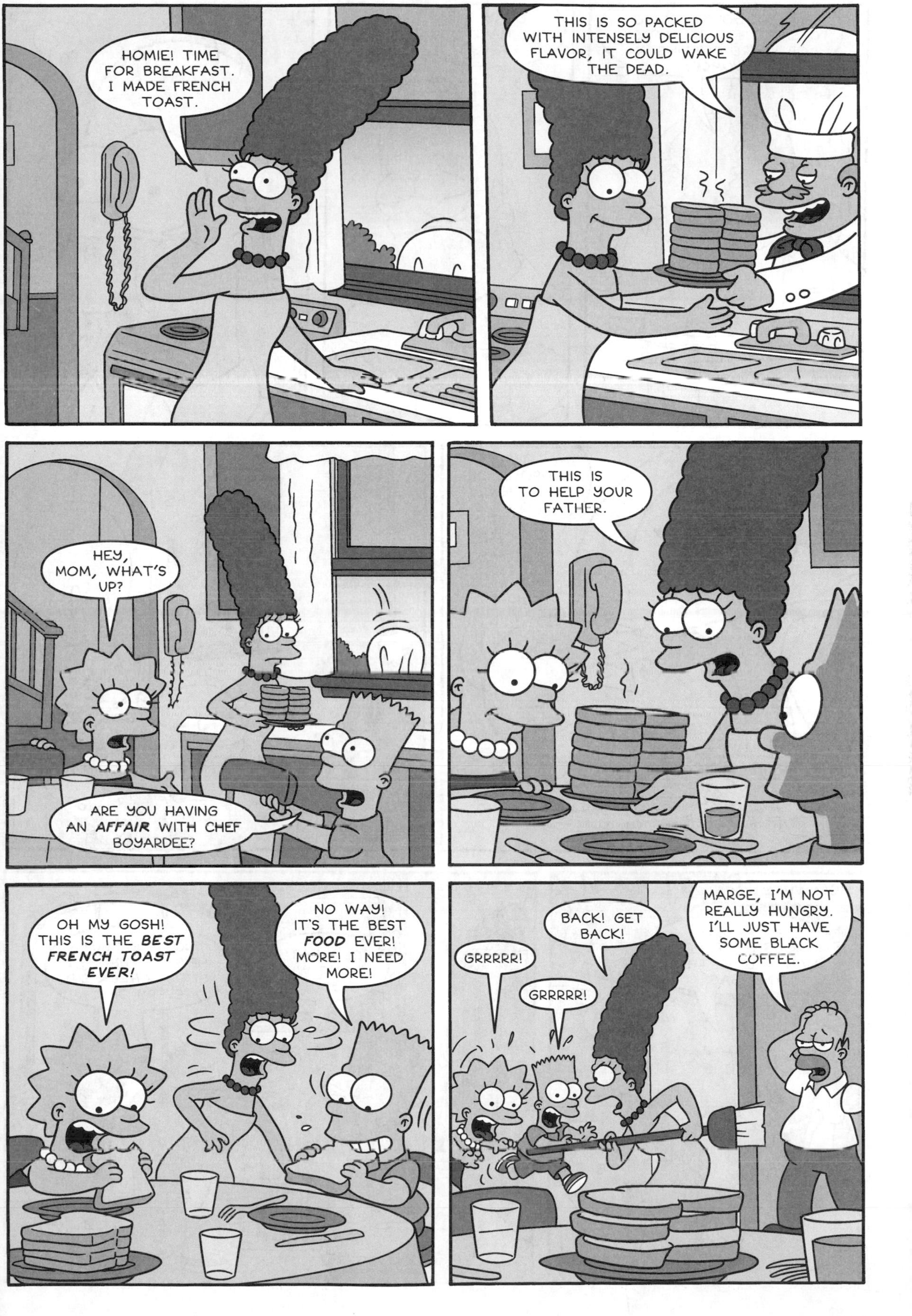
HOMIE! TIME FOR BREAKFAST. I MADE FRENCH TOAST.
THIS IS SO PACKED WITH INTENSELY DELICIOUS FLAVOR, IT COULD WAKE THE DEAD.
HEY, MOM, WHAT'S UP?
ARE YOU HAVING AN AFFAIR WITH CHEF BOYARDEE?
THIS IS TO HELP YOUR FATHER.
OH MY GOSH! THIS IS THE BEST FRENCH TOAST EVER!
NO WAY! IT'S THE BEST FOOD EVER! MORE! I NEED MORE!
GRRRRR!
GRRRRR!
BACK! GET BACK!
MARGE, I'M NOT REALLY HUNGRY. I'LL JUST HAVE SOME BLACK COFFEE.

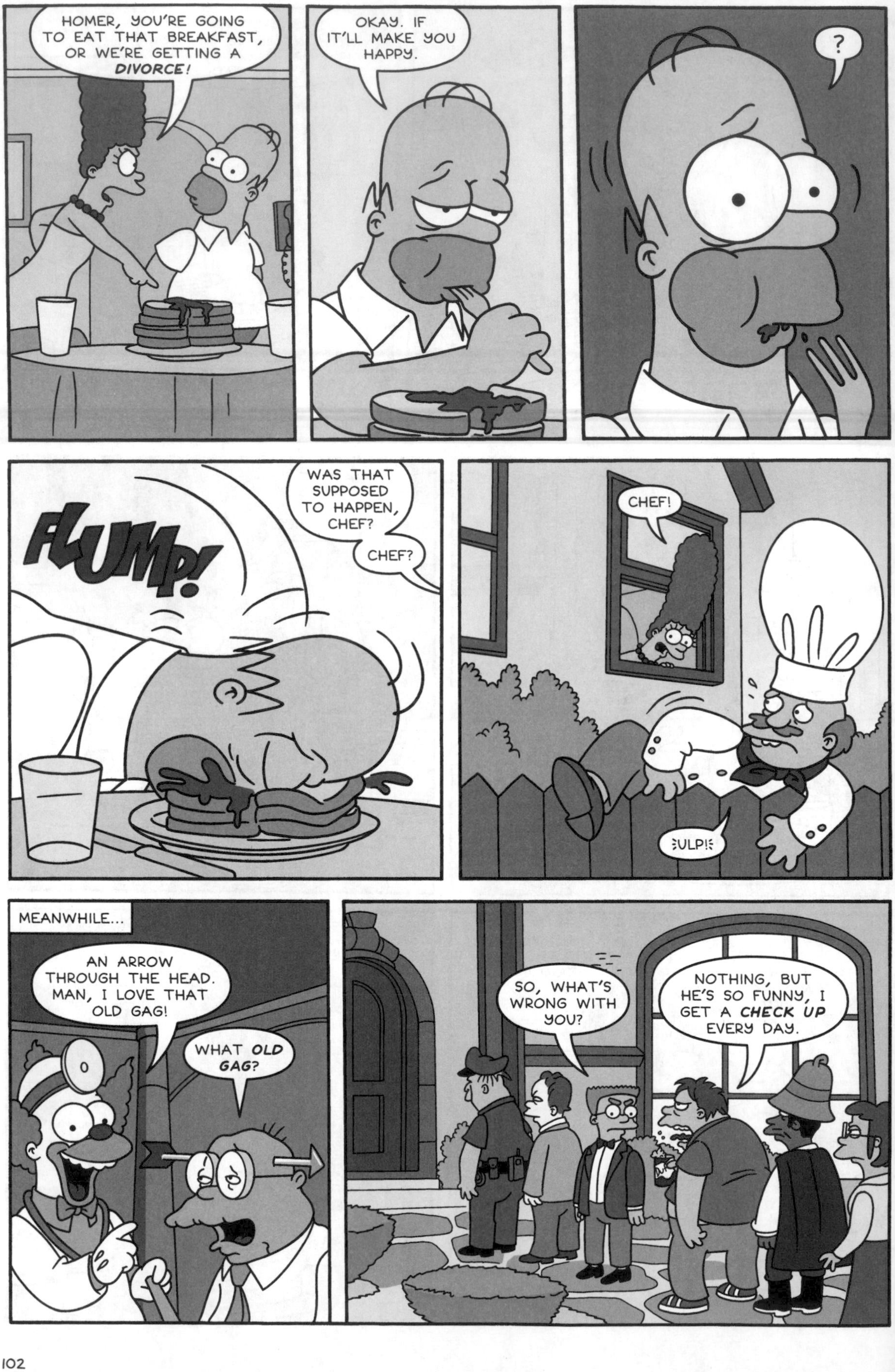
HOMER, YOU'RE GOING TO EAT THAT BREAKFAST, OR WE'RE GETTING A **DIVORCE**!
OKAY. IF IT'LL MAKE YOU HAPPY.
?
FLUMP!
WAS THAT SUPPOSED TO HAPPEN, CHEF?
CHEF?
CHEF!
ULP!
MEANWHILE...
AN ARROW THROUGH THE HEAD. MAN, I LOVE THAT OLD GAG!
WHAT **OLD GAG**?
SO, WHAT'S WRONG WITH YOU?
NOTHING, BUT HE'S SO FUNNY, I GET A **CHECK UP** EVERY DAY.

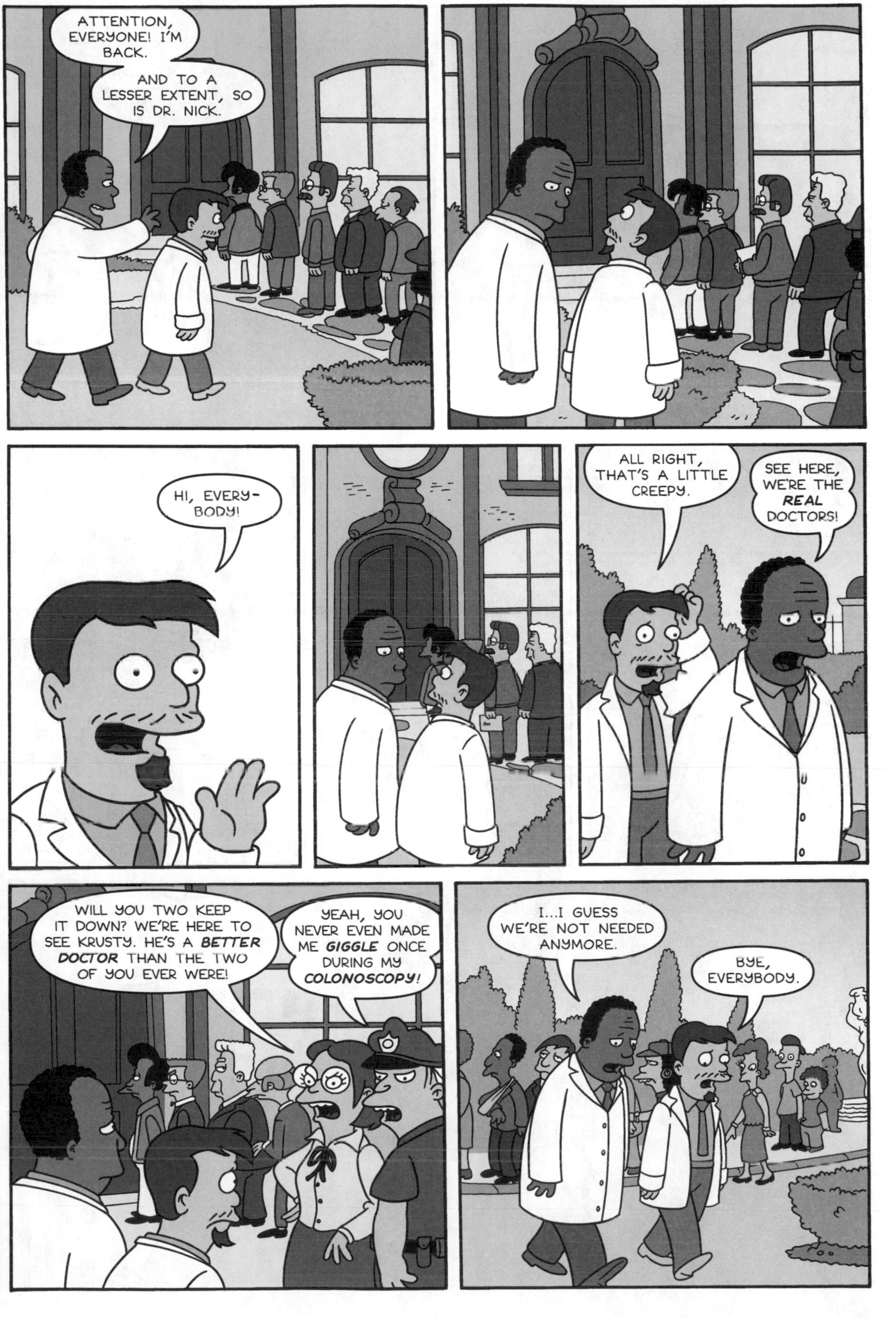
ATTENTION, EVERYONE! I'M BACK.
AND TO A LESSER EXTENT, SO IS DR. NICK.
HI, EVERY-BODY!
ALL RIGHT, THAT'S A LITTLE CREEPY.
SEE HERE, WE'RE THE *REAL* DOCTORS!
WILL YOU TWO KEEP IT DOWN? WE'RE HERE TO SEE KRUSTY. HE'S A ***BETTER DOCTOR*** THAN THE TWO OF YOU EVER WERE!
YEAH, YOU NEVER EVEN MADE ME ***GIGGLE*** ONCE DURING MY ***COLONOSCOPY!***
I...I GUESS WE'RE NOT NEEDED ANYMORE.
BYE, EVERYBODY.

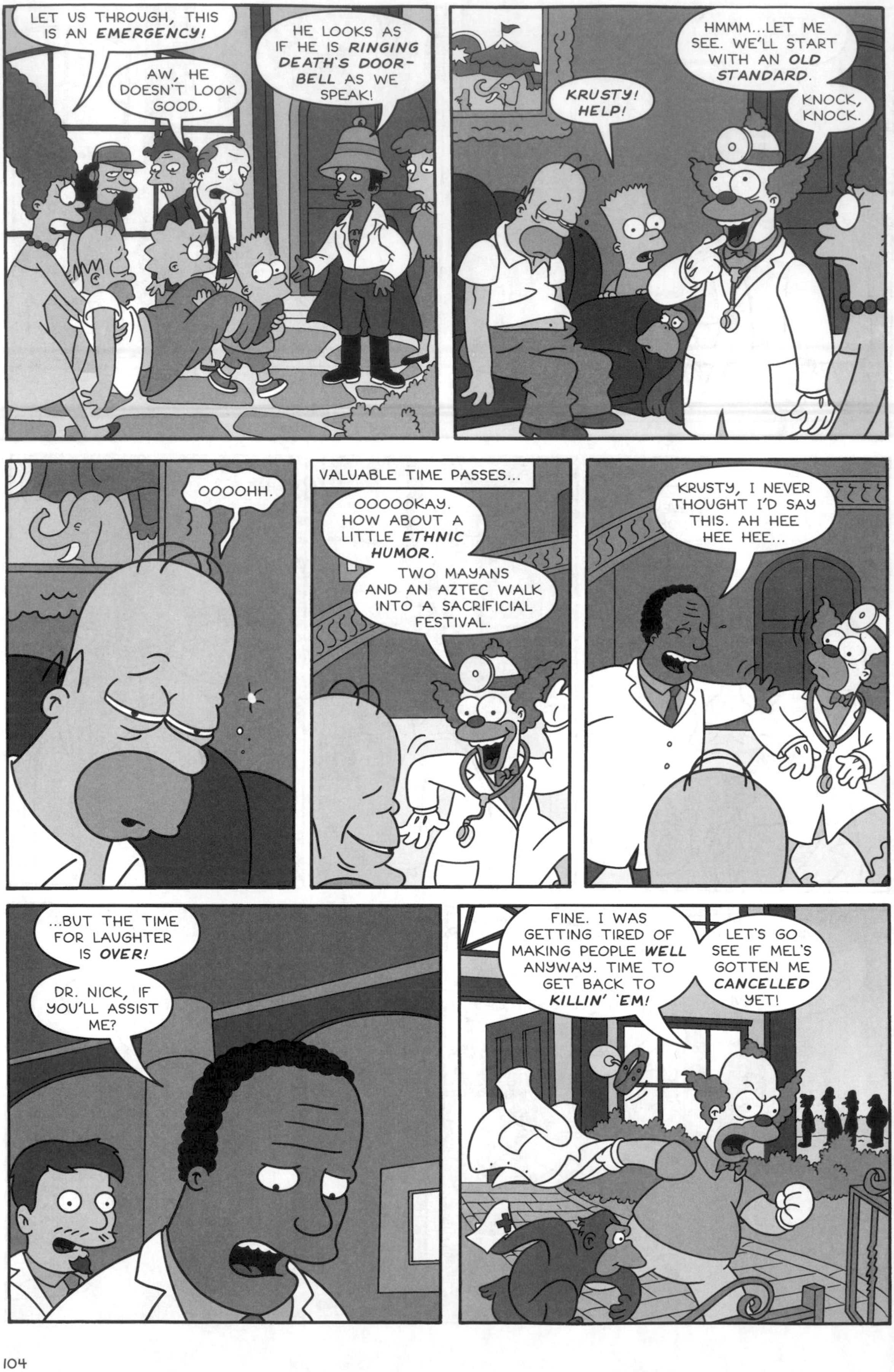
LET US THROUGH, THIS IS AN **EMERGENCY**!
AW, HE DOESN'T LOOK GOOD.
HE LOOKS AS IF HE IS **RINGING DEATH'S DOOR-BELL** AS WE SPEAK!
KRUSTY! HELP!
HMMM...LET ME SEE. WE'LL START WITH AN **OLD STANDARD**.
KNOCK, KNOCK.
OOOOHH.
VALUABLE TIME PASSES...
OOOOOKAY. HOW ABOUT A LITTLE **ETHNIC HUMOR**.
TWO MAYANS AND AN AZTEC WALK INTO A SACRIFICIAL FESTIVAL.
KRUSTY, I NEVER THOUGHT I'D SAY THIS. AH HEE HEE HEE...
...BUT THE TIME FOR LAUGHTER IS **OVER**!
DR. NICK, IF YOU'LL ASSIST ME?
FINE. I WAS GETTING TIRED OF MAKING PEOPLE **WELL** ANYWAY. TIME TO GET BACK TO **KILLIN' 'EM**!
LET'S GO SEE IF MEL'S GOTTEN ME **CANCELLED** YET!

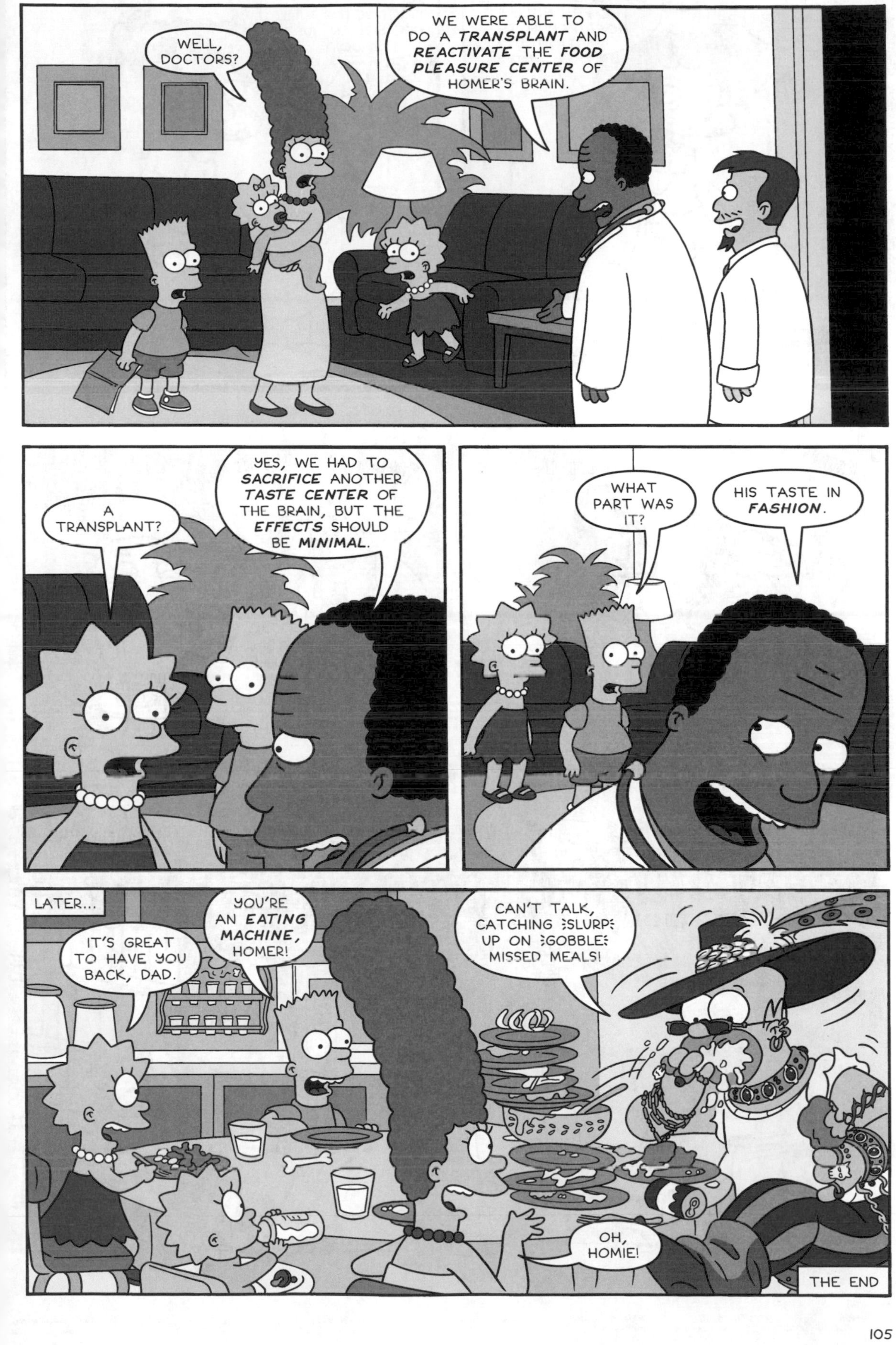
WELL, DOCTORS?
WE WERE ABLE TO DO A **TRANSPLANT** AND **REACTIVATE** THE **FOOD PLEASURE CENTER** OF HOMER'S BRAIN.
A TRANSPLANT?
YES, WE HAD TO **SACRIFICE** ANOTHER **TASTE CENTER** OF THE BRAIN, BUT THE **EFFECTS** SHOULD BE **MINIMAL**.
WHAT PART WAS IT?
HIS TASTE IN **FASHION**.
LATER...
IT'S GREAT TO HAVE YOU BACK, DAD.
YOU'RE AN **EATING MACHINE**, HOMER!
CAN'T TALK, CATCHING SLURP UP ON GOBBLE MISSED MEALS!
OH, HOMIE!
THE END

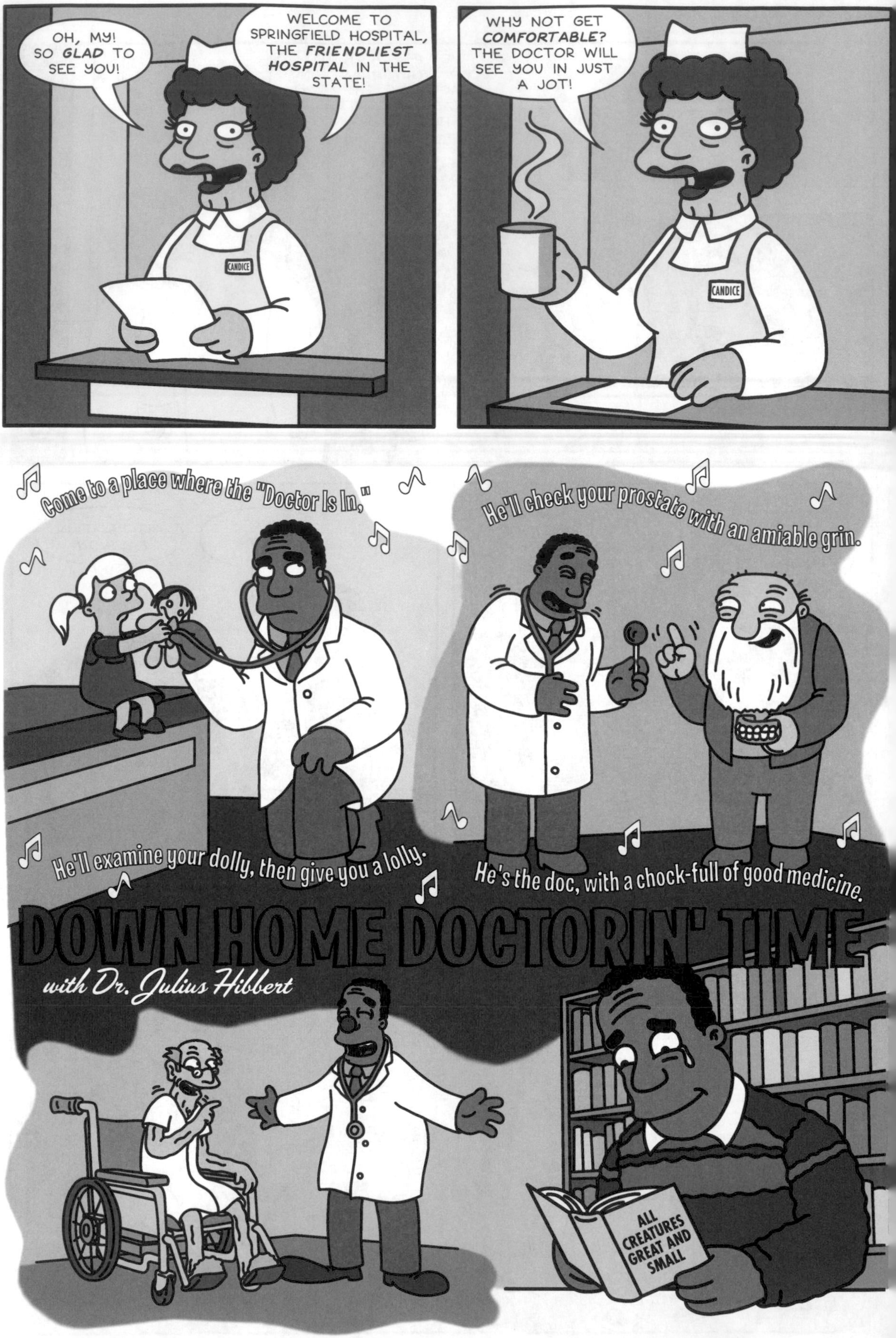
OH, MY! SO GLAD TO SEE YOU!
WELCOME TO SPRINGFIELD HOSPITAL, THE FRIENDLIEST HOSPITAL IN THE STATE!
CANDICE
WHY NOT GET COMFORTABLE? THE DOCTOR WILL SEE YOU IN JUST A JOT!
CANDICE
Come to a place where the "Doctor Is In,"
He'll check your prostate with an amiable grin.
He'll examine your dolly, then give you a lolly.
He's the doc, with a chock-full of good medicine.
DOWN HOME DOCTORIN' TIME
with Dr. Julius Hibbert
ALL CREATURES GREAT AND SMALL

GAIL SIMONE NIGHT NURSE · JOEY NILGES DOCTOR OF PENCILOLOGY · JAMES HUANG INKING ORDERLY · ART VILLANUEVA COLORING CARDIOLOGIST · KAREN BATES LETTERING L.P.N. · BILL MORRISON EDITING ADMINISTRATOR · MATT GROENING MEDICAL CADAVER

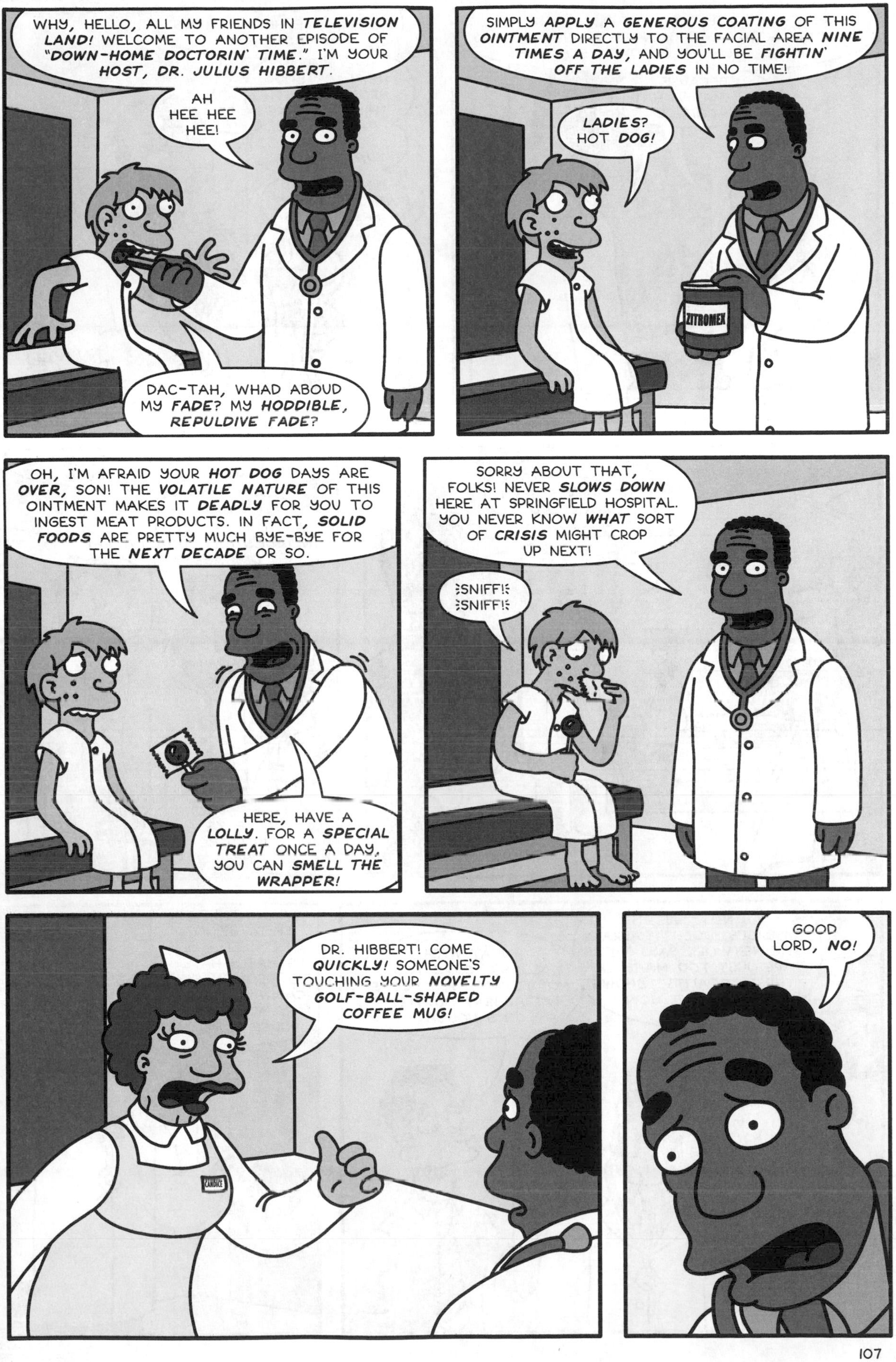
WHY, HELLO, ALL MY FRIENDS IN TELEVISION LAND! WELCOME TO ANOTHER EPISODE OF "DOWN-HOME DOCTORIN' TIME." I'M YOUR HOST, DR. JULIUS HIBBERT.
AH HEE HEE HEE!
DAC-TAH, WHAD ABOUD MY FADE? MY HODDIBLE, REPULDIVE FADE?
SIMPLY APPLY A GENEROUS COATING OF THIS OINTMENT DIRECTLY TO THE FACIAL AREA NINE TIMES A DAY, AND YOU'LL BE FIGHTIN' OFF THE LADIES IN NO TIME!
LADIES? HOT DOG!
ZITROMEX
OH, I'M AFRAID YOUR HOT DOG DAYS ARE OVER, SON! THE VOLATILE NATURE OF THIS OINTMENT MAKES IT DEADLY FOR YOU TO INGEST MEAT PRODUCTS. IN FACT, SOLID FOODS ARE PRETTY MUCH BYE-BYE FOR THE NEXT DECADE OR SO.
HERE, HAVE A LOLLY. FOR A SPECIAL TREAT ONCE A DAY, YOU CAN SMELL THE WRAPPER!
SORRY ABOUT THAT, FOLKS! NEVER SLOWS DOWN HERE AT SPRINGFIELD HOSPITAL. YOU NEVER KNOW WHAT SORT OF CRISIS MIGHT CROP UP NEXT!
SNIFF! SNIFF!
DR. HIBBERT! COME QUICKLY! SOMEONE'S TOUCHING YOUR NOVELTY GOLF-BALL-SHAPED COFFEE MUG!
CANDICE
GOOD LORD, NO!

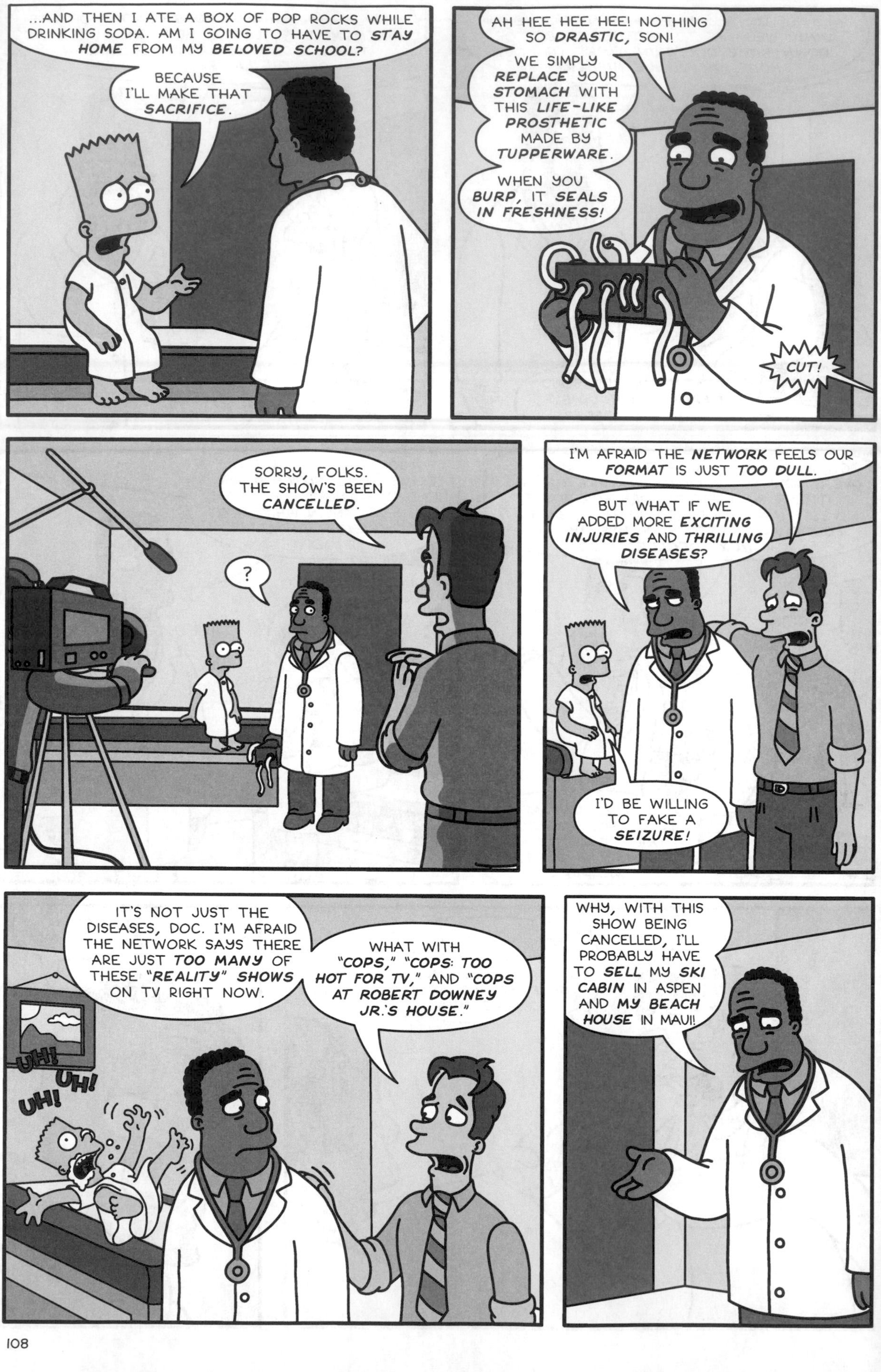
...AND THEN I ATE A BOX OF POP ROCKS WHILE DRINKING SODA. AM I GOING TO HAVE TO STAY HOME FROM MY BELOVED SCHOOL?
BECAUSE I'LL MAKE THAT SACRIFICE.
AH HEE HEE HEE! NOTHING SO DRASTIC, SON!
WE SIMPLY REPLACE YOUR STOMACH WITH THIS LIFE-LIKE PROSTHETIC MADE BY TUPPERWARE.
WHEN YOU BURP, IT SEALS IN FRESHNESS!
CUT!
SORRY, FOLKS. THE SHOW'S BEEN CANCELLED.
?
I'M AFRAID THE NETWORK FEELS OUR FORMAT IS JUST TOO DULL.
BUT WHAT IF WE ADDED MORE EXCITING INJURIES AND THRILLING DISEASES?
I'D BE WILLING TO FAKE A SEIZURE!
IT'S NOT JUST THE DISEASES, DOC. I'M AFRAID THE NETWORK SAYS THERE ARE JUST TOO MANY OF THESE "REALITY" SHOWS ON TV RIGHT NOW.
WHAT WITH "COPS," "COPS: TOO HOT FOR TV," AND "COPS AT ROBERT DOWNEY JR.'S HOUSE."
UH! UH! UH!
WHY, WITH THIS SHOW BEING CANCELLED, I'LL PROBABLY HAVE TO SELL MY SKI CABIN IN ASPEN AND MY BEACH HOUSE IN MAUI!

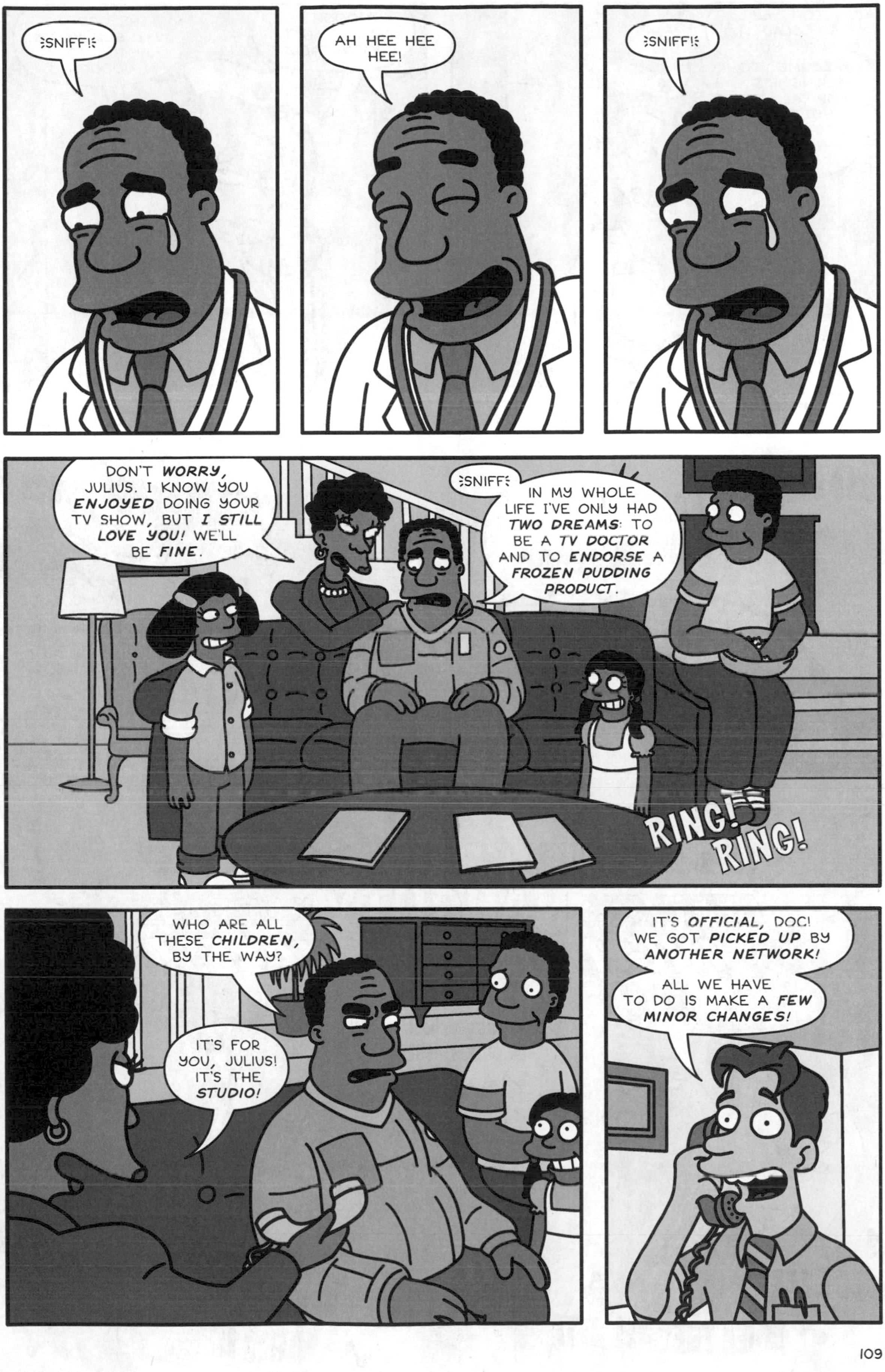
:SNIFF!:
AH HEE HEE HEE!
:SNIFF!:
DON'T WORRY, JULIUS. I KNOW YOU ENJOYED DOING YOUR TV SHOW, BUT I STILL LOVE YOU! WE'LL BE FINE.
:SNIFF:
IN MY WHOLE LIFE I'VE ONLY HAD TWO DREAMS: TO BE A TV DOCTOR AND TO ENDORSE A FROZEN PUDDING PRODUCT.
RING! RING!
WHO ARE ALL THESE CHILDREN, BY THE WAY?
IT'S FOR YOU, JULIUS! IT'S THE STUDIO!
IT'S OFFICIAL, DOC! WE GOT PICKED UP BY ANOTHER NETWORK!
ALL WE HAVE TO DO IS MAKE A FEW MINOR CHANGES!

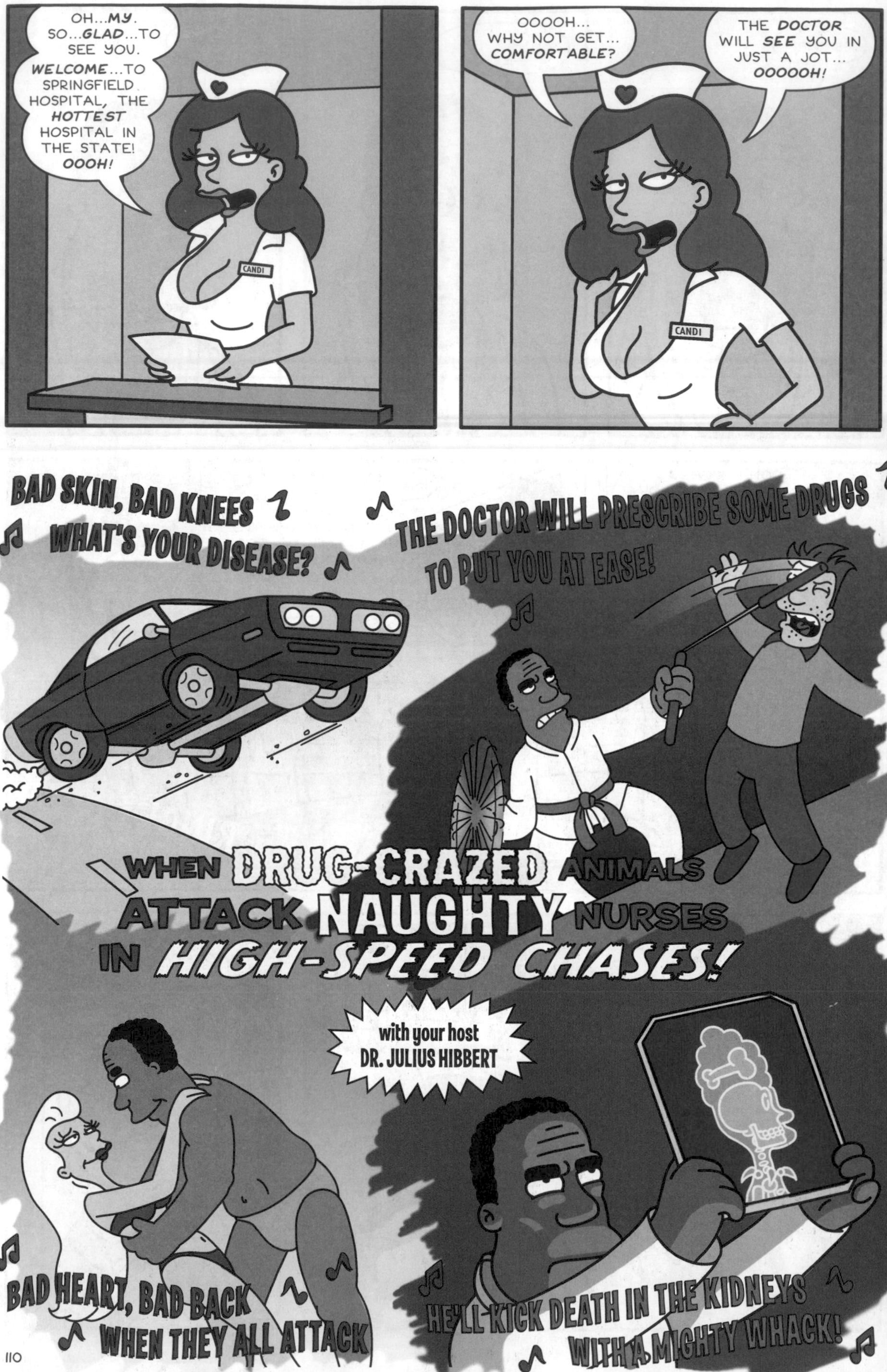
OH...MY. SO...GLAD...TO SEE YOU. WELCOME...TO SPRINGFIELD HOSPITAL, THE HOTTEST HOSPITAL IN THE STATE! OOOH!
CANDI
OOOOH... WHY NOT GET... COMFORTABLE?
THE DOCTOR WILL SEE YOU IN JUST A JOT... OOOOOH!
CANDI
BAD SKIN, BAD KNEES
WHAT'S YOUR DISEASE?
THE DOCTOR WILL PRESCRIBE SOME DRUGS
TO PUT YOU AT EASE!
WHEN DRUG-CRAZED ANIMALS
ATTACK NAUGHTY NURSES
IN HIGH-SPEED CHASES!
with your host
DR. JULIUS HIBBERT
BAD HEART, BAD BACK
WHEN THEY ALL ATTACK
HE'LL KICK DEATH IN THE KIDNEYS
WITH A MIGHTY WHACK!

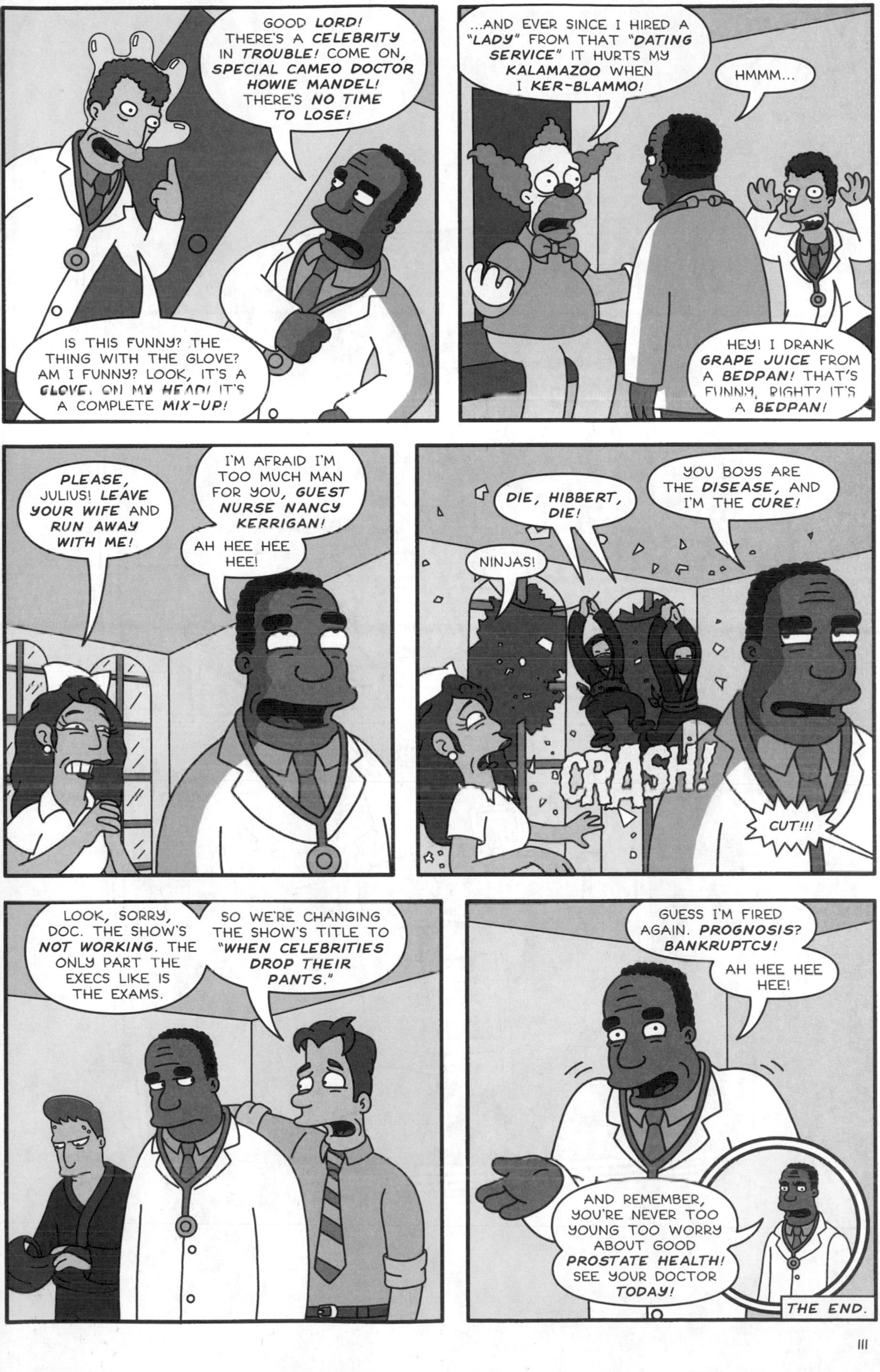
GOOD LORD! THERE'S A CELEBRITY IN TROUBLE! COME ON, SPECIAL CAMEO DOCTOR HOWIE MANDEL! THERE'S NO TIME TO LOSE!
IS THIS FUNNY? THE THING WITH THE GLOVE? AM I FUNNY? LOOK, IT'S A GLOVE, ON MY HEAD! IT'S A COMPLETE MIX-UP!
...AND EVER SINCE I HIRED A "LADY" FROM THAT "DATING SERVICE" IT HURTS MY KALAMAZOO WHEN I KER-BLAMMO!
HMMM...
HEY! I DRANK GRAPE JUICE FROM A BEDPAN! THAT'S FUNNY, RIGHT? IT'S A BEDPAN!
PLEASE, JULIUS! LEAVE YOUR WIFE AND RUN AWAY WITH ME!
I'M AFRAID I'M TOO MUCH MAN FOR YOU, GUEST NURSE NANCY KERRIGAN!
AH HEE HEE HEE!
DIE, HIBBERT, DIE!
YOU BOYS ARE THE DISEASE, AND I'M THE CURE!
NINJAS!
CRASH!
CUT!!!
LOOK, SORRY, DOC. THE SHOW'S NOT WORKING. THE ONLY PART THE EXECS LIKE IS THE EXAMS.
SO WE'RE CHANGING THE SHOW'S TITLE TO "WHEN CELEBRITIES DROP THEIR PANTS."
GUESS I'M FIRED AGAIN. PROGNOSIS? BANKRUPTCY!
AH HEE HEE HEE!
AND REMEMBER, YOU'RE NEVER TOO YOUNG TOO WORRY ABOUT GOOD PROSTATE HEALTH! SEE YOUR DOCTOR TODAY!
THE END.

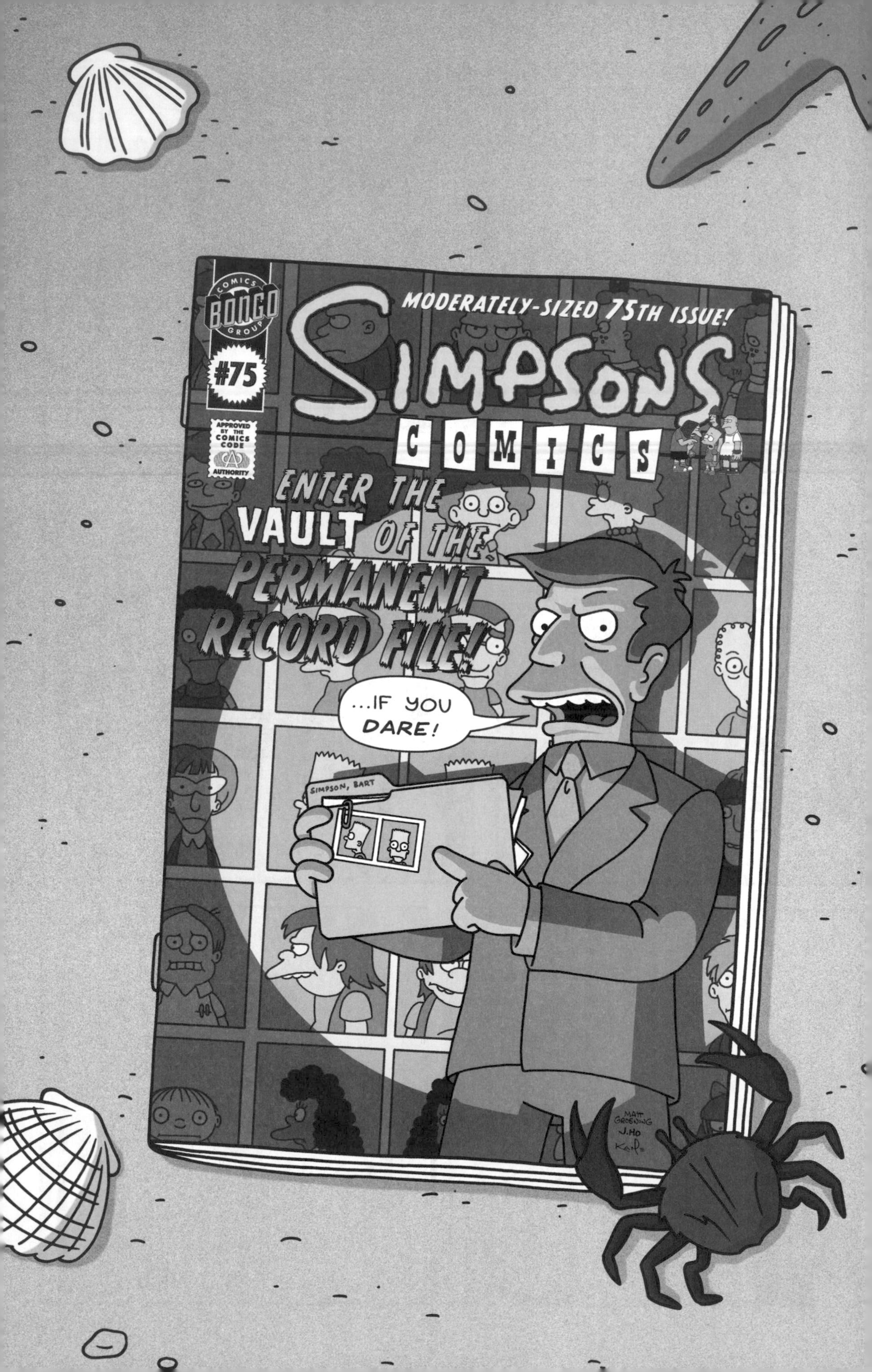
COMICS BONGO GROUP
#75
APPROVED BY THE COMICS CODE AUTHORITY
MODERATELY-SIZED 75TH ISSUE!
SIMPSONS COMICS
ENTER THE VAULT OF THE PERMANENT RECORD FILE!
...IF YOU DARE!
SIMPSON, BART
MATT GROENING
J.HO

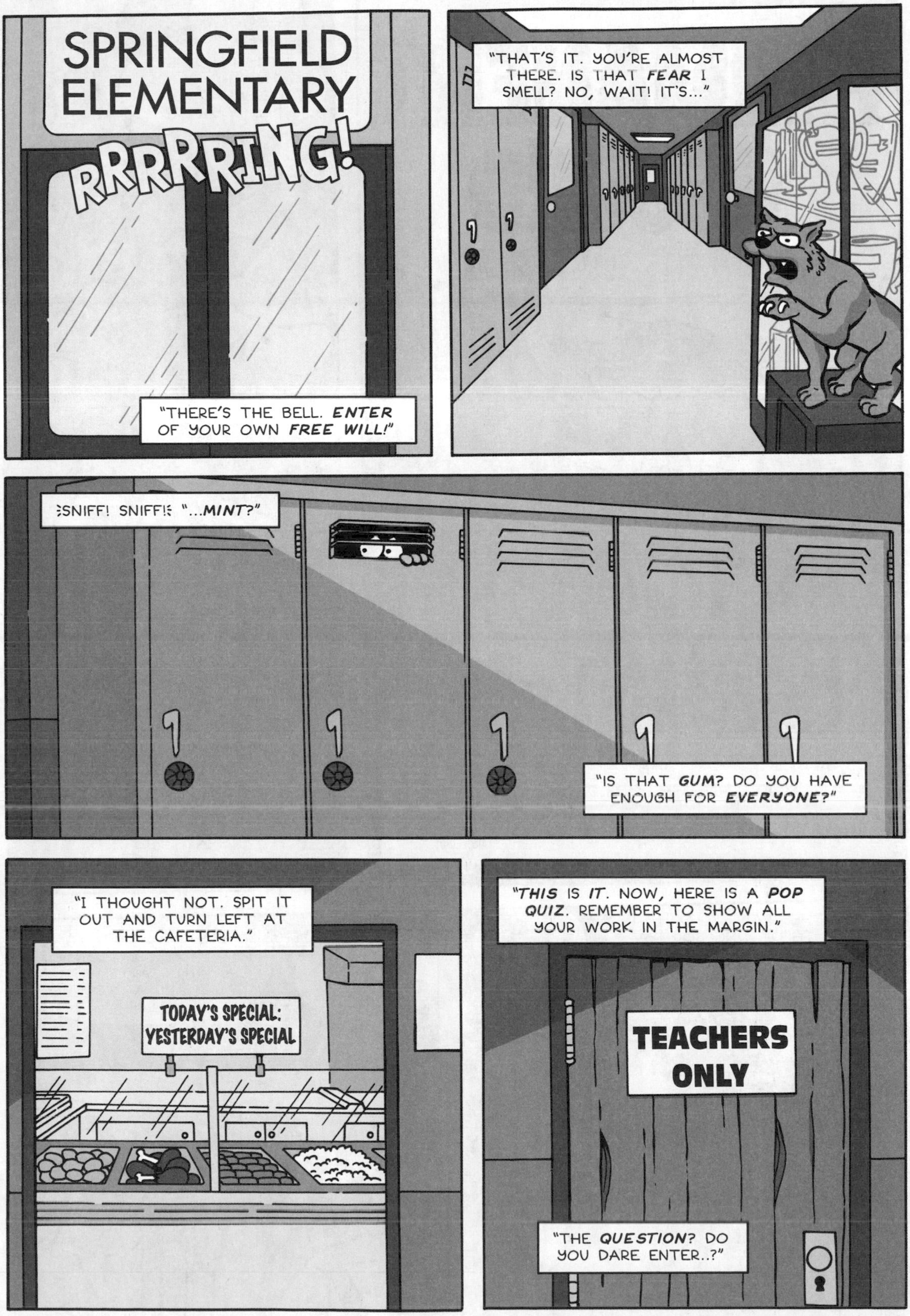
SPRINGFIELD ELEMENTARY
RRRRRING!
"THERE'S THE BELL. ENTER OF YOUR OWN FREE WILL!"
"THAT'S IT. YOU'RE ALMOST THERE. IS THAT FEAR I SMELL? NO, WAIT! IT'S..."
SNIFF! SNIFF! "...MINT?"
"IS THAT GUM? DO YOU HAVE ENOUGH FOR EVERYONE?"
"I THOUGHT NOT. SPIT IT OUT AND TURN LEFT AT THE CAFETERIA."
TODAY'S SPECIAL: YESTERDAY'S SPECIAL
"THIS IS IT. NOW, HERE IS A POP QUIZ. REMEMBER TO SHOW ALL YOUR WORK IN THE MARGIN."
TEACHERS ONLY
"THE QUESTION? DO YOU DARE ENTER..?"

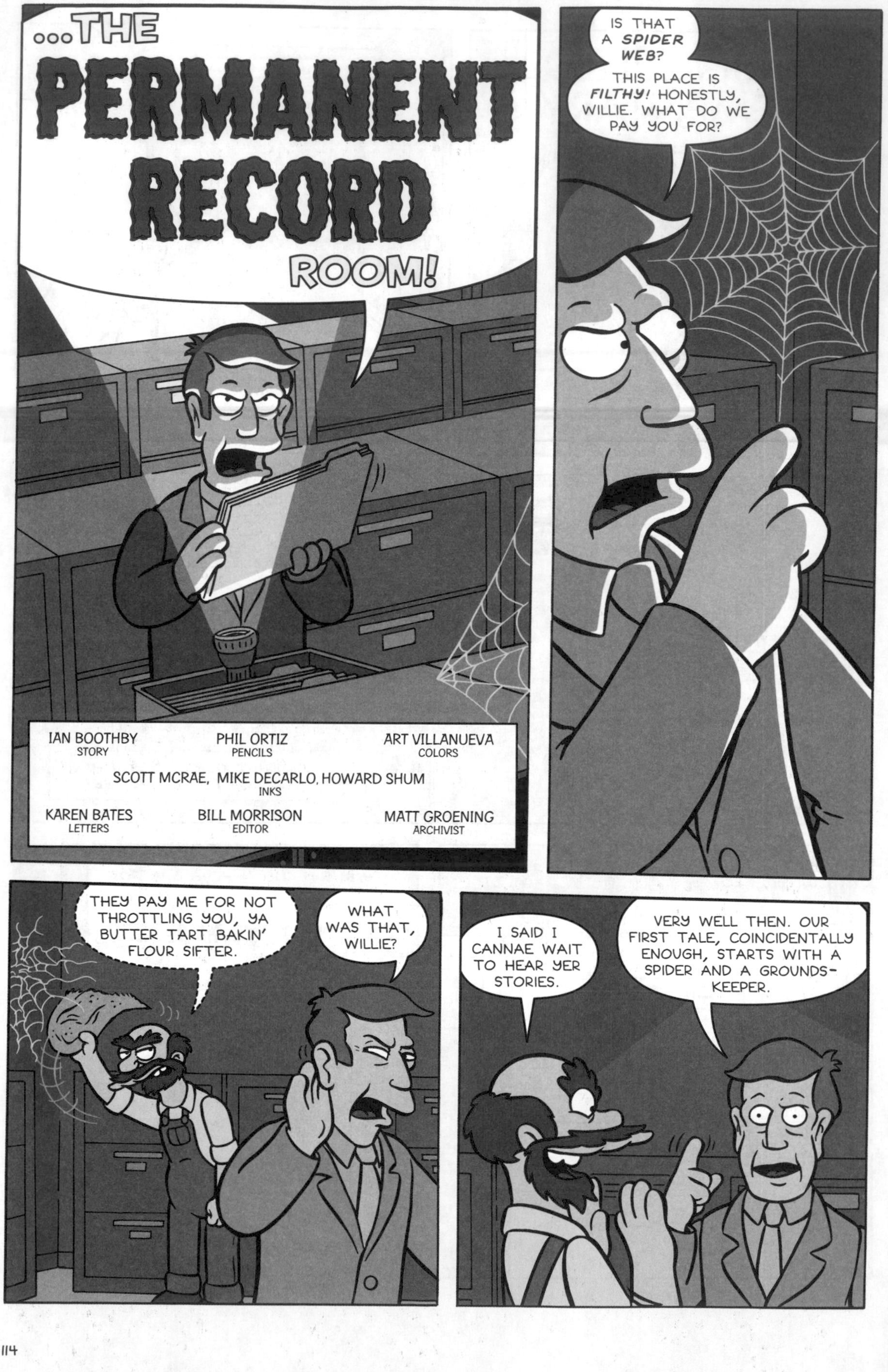

...THE PERMANENT RECORD ROOM!
IAN BOOTHBY STORY
PHIL ORTIZ PENCILS
ART VILLANUEVA COLORS
SCOTT MCRAE, MIKE DECARLO, HOWARD SHUM INKS
KAREN BATES LETTERS
BILL MORRISON EDITOR
MATT GROENING ARCHIVIST
IS THAT A *SPIDER WEB*?
THIS PLACE IS *FILTHY!* HONESTLY, WILLIE. WHAT DO WE PAY YOU FOR?
THEY PAY ME FOR NOT THROTTLING YOU, YA BUTTER TART BAKIN' FLOUR SIFTER.
WHAT WAS THAT, WILLIE?
I SAID I CANNAE WAIT TO HEAR YER STORIES.
VERY WELL THEN. OUR FIRST TALE, COINCIDENTALLY ENOUGH, STARTS WITH A SPIDER AND A GROUNDS-KEEPER.

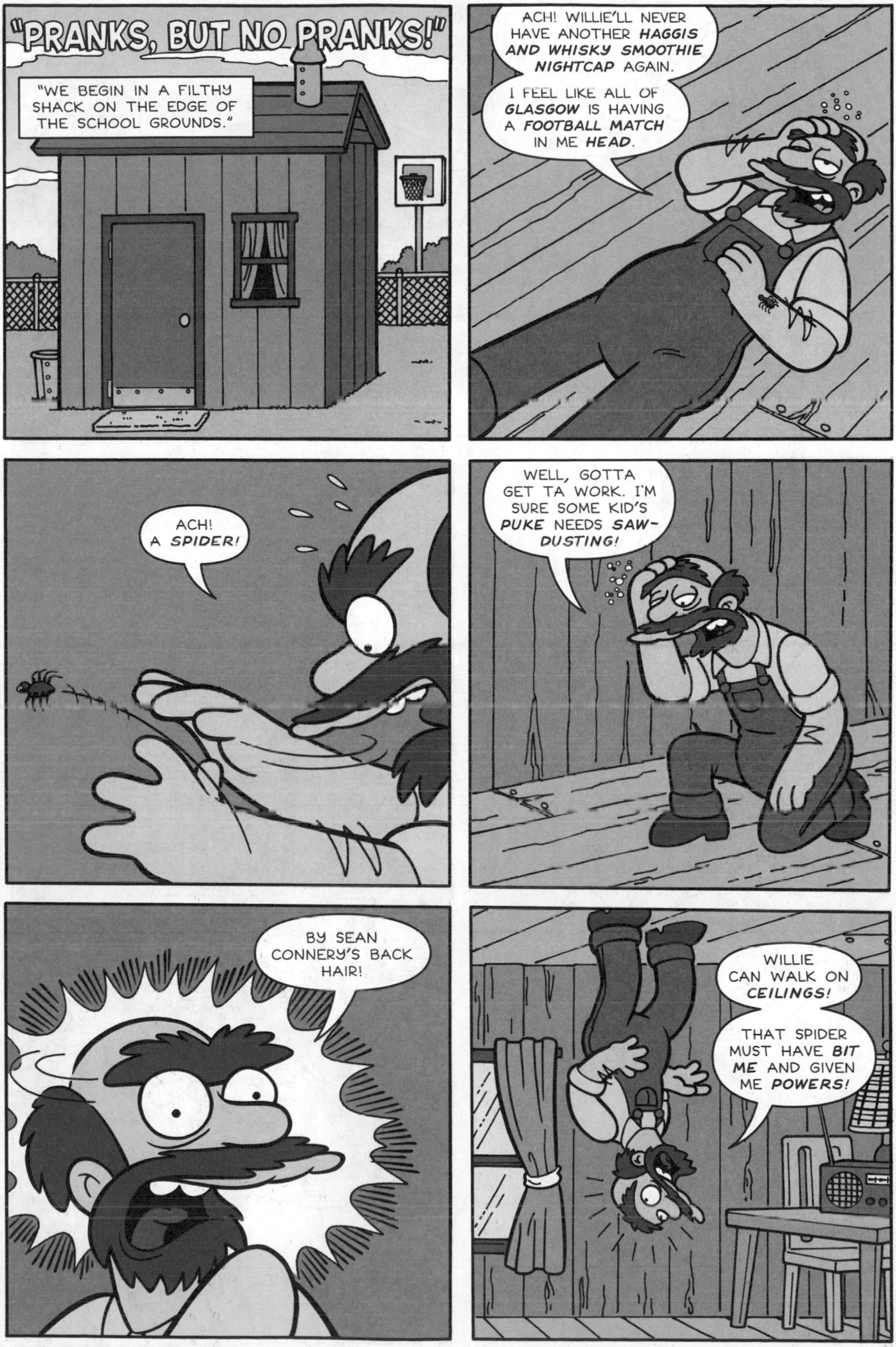
"PRANKS, BUT NO PRANKS!"
"WE BEGIN IN A FILTHY SHACK ON THE EDGE OF THE SCHOOL GROUNDS."
ACH! WILLIE'LL NEVER HAVE ANOTHER HAGGIS AND WHISKY SMOOTHIE NIGHTCAP AGAIN.
I FEEL LIKE ALL OF GLASGOW IS HAVING A FOOTBALL MATCH IN ME HEAD.
ACH! A SPIDER!
WELL, GOTTA GET TA WORK. I'M SURE SOME KID'S PUKE NEEDS SAW-DUSTING!
BY SEAN CONNERY'S BACK HAIR!
WILLIE CAN WALK ON CEILINGS!
THAT SPIDER MUST HAVE BIT ME AND GIVEN ME POWERS!

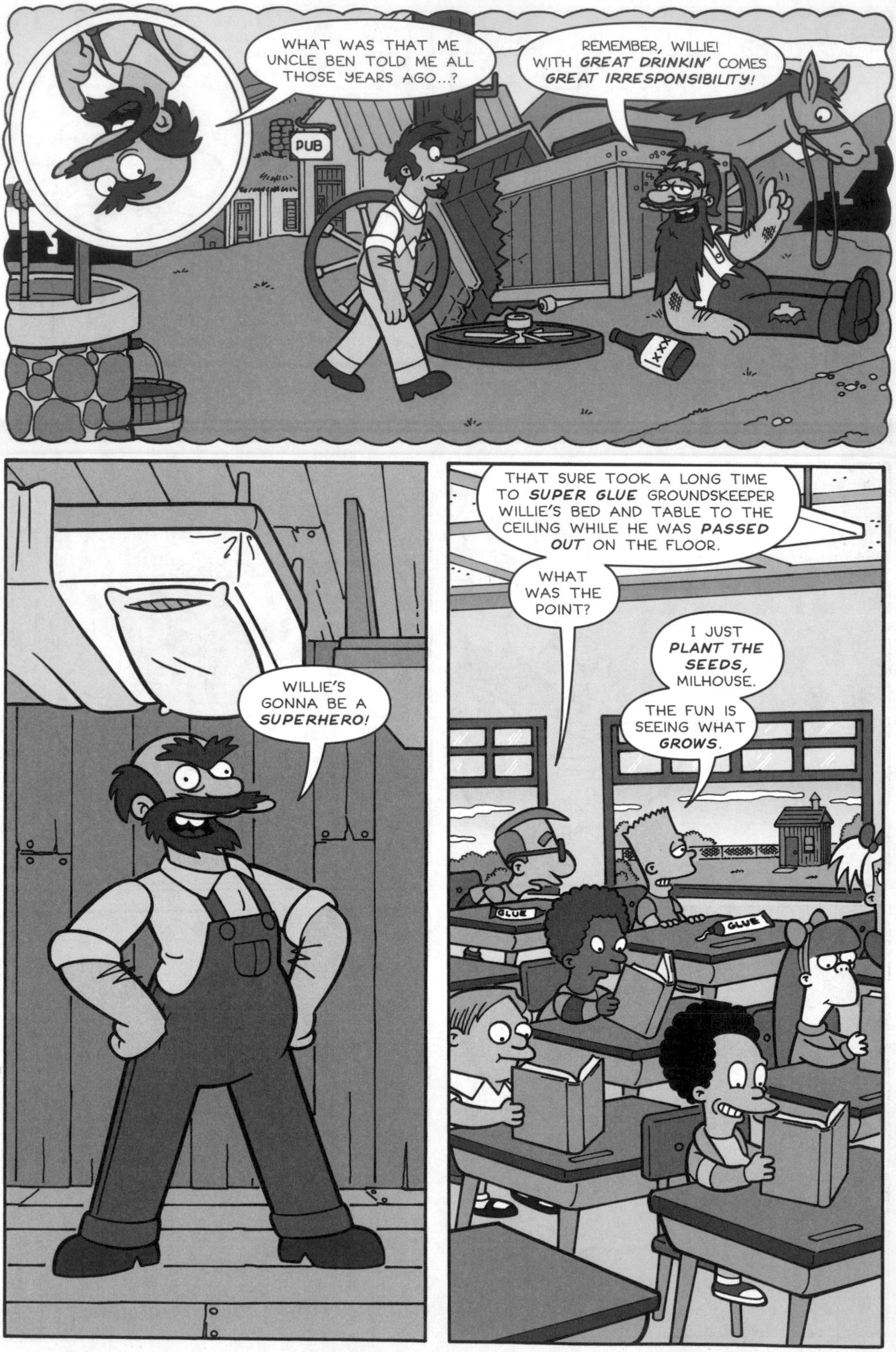
WHAT WAS THAT ME UNCLE BEN TOLD ME ALL THOSE YEARS AGO...?
REMEMBER, WILLIE! WITH GREAT DRINKIN' COMES GREAT IRRESPONSIBILITY!
PUB
XXX
WILLIE'S GONNA BE A SUPERHERO!
THAT SURE TOOK A LONG TIME TO SUPER GLUE GROUNDSKEEPER WILLIE'S BED AND TABLE TO THE CEILING WHILE HE WAS PASSED OUT ON THE FLOOR.
WHAT WAS THE POINT?
I JUST PLANT THE SEEDS, MILHOUSE.
THE FUN IS SEEING WHAT GROWS.
GLUE
GLUE

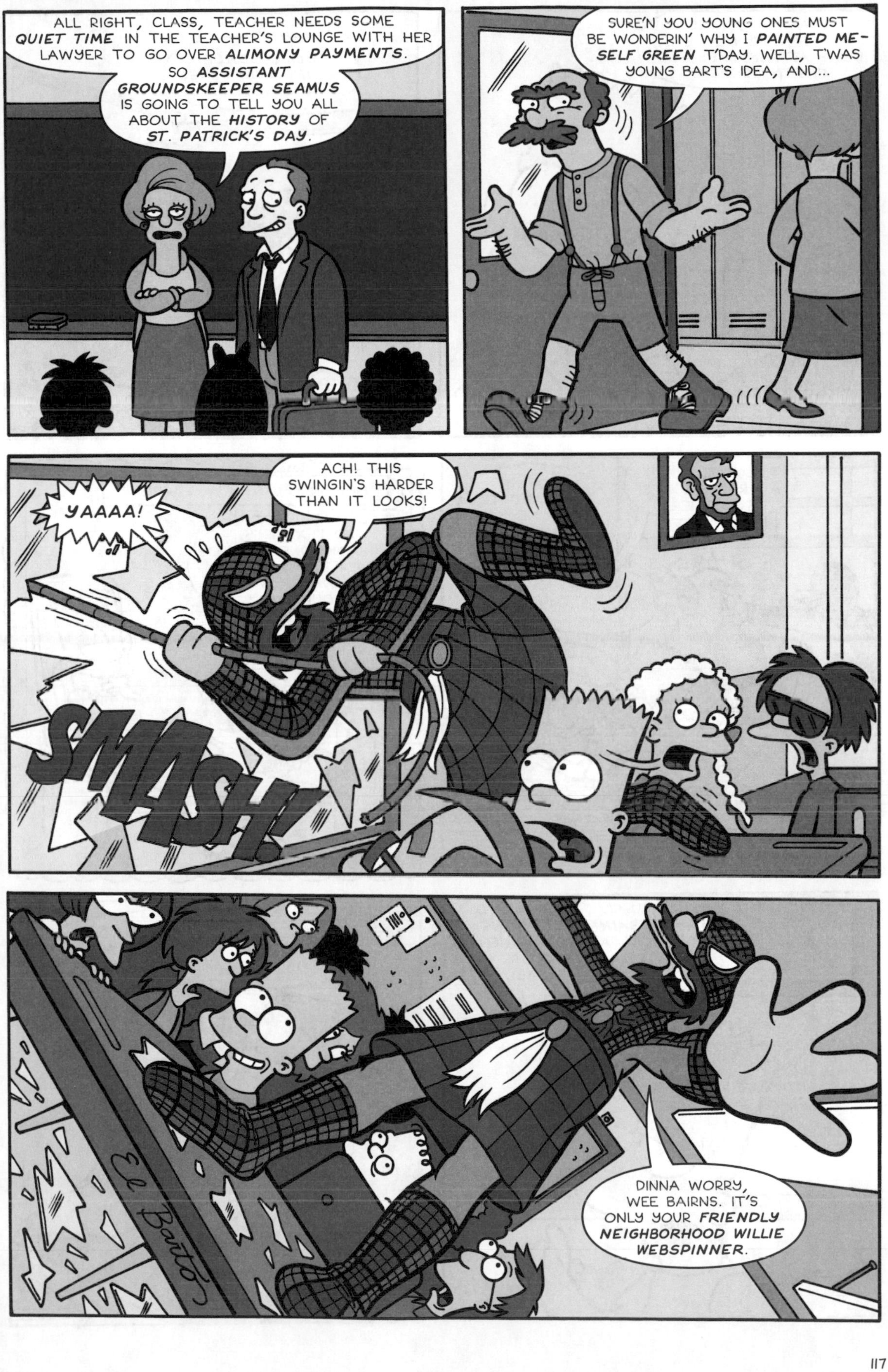
ALL RIGHT, CLASS, TEACHER NEEDS SOME QUIET TIME IN THE TEACHER'S LOUNGE WITH HER LAWYER TO GO OVER ALIMONY PAYMENTS.
SO ASSISTANT GROUNDSKEEPER SEAMUS IS GOING TO TELL YOU ALL ABOUT THE HISTORY OF ST. PATRICK'S DAY.
SURE'N YOU YOUNG ONES MUST BE WONDERIN' WHY I PAINTED ME-SELF GREEN T'DAY. WELL, T'WAS YOUNG BART'S IDEA, AND...
YAAAA!
ACH! THIS SWINGIN'S HARDER THAN IT LOOKS!
SMASH!
DINNA WORRY, WEE BAIRNS. IT'S ONLY YOUR FRIENDLY NEIGHBORHOOD WILLIE WEBSPINNER.

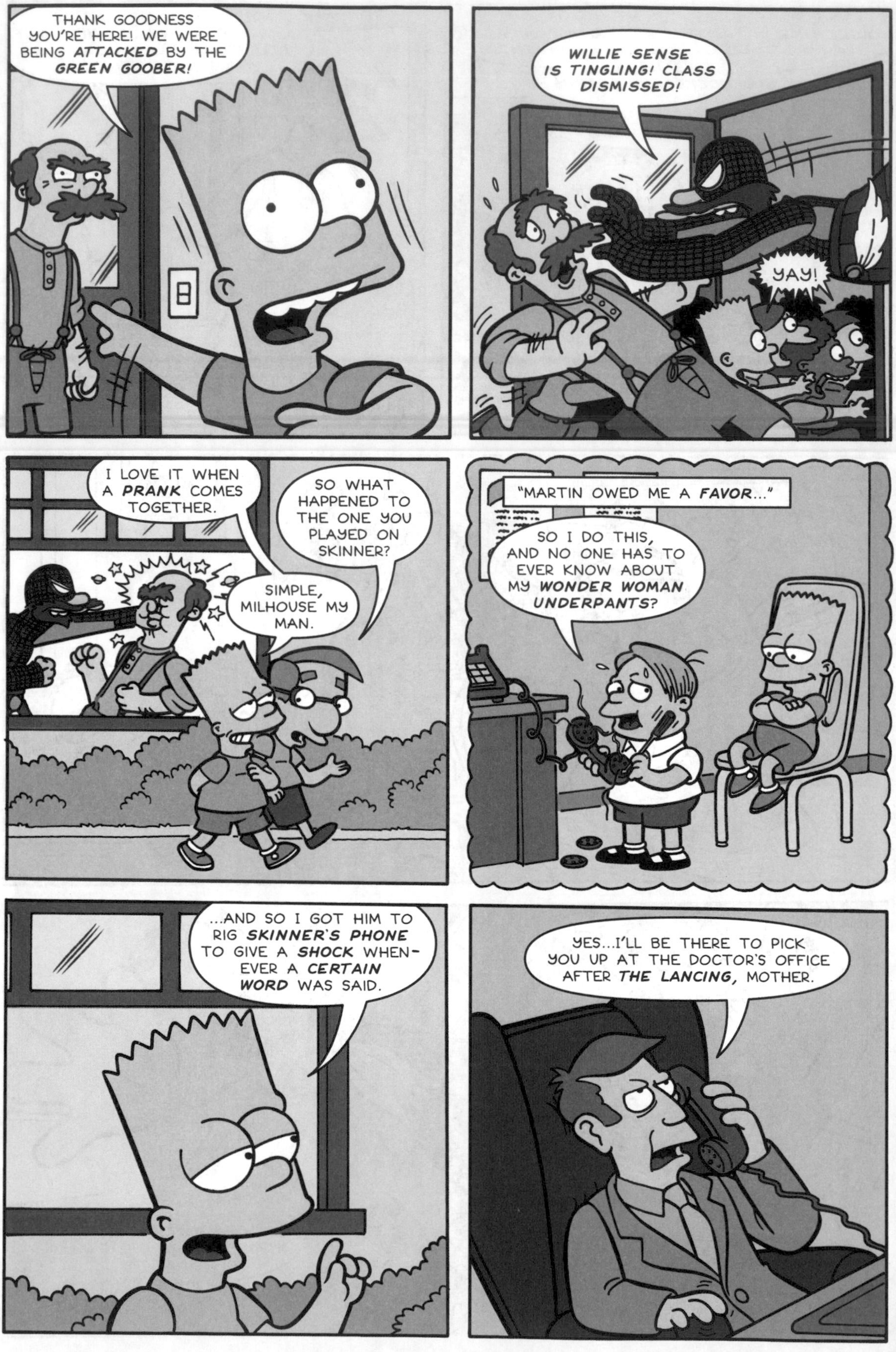
THANK GOODNESS YOU'RE HERE! WE WERE BEING ATTACKED BY THE GREEN GOOBER!
WILLIE SENSE IS TINGLING! CLASS DISMISSED!
YAY!
I LOVE IT WHEN A PRANK COMES TOGETHER.
SO WHAT HAPPENED TO THE ONE YOU PLAYED ON SKINNER?
SIMPLE, MILHOUSE MY MAN.
"MARTIN OWED ME A FAVOR..."
SO I DO THIS, AND NO ONE HAS TO EVER KNOW ABOUT MY WONDER WOMAN UNDERPANTS?
...AND SO I GOT HIM TO RIG SKINNER'S PHONE TO GIVE A SHOCK WHEN-EVER A CERTAIN WORD WAS SAID.
YES...I'LL BE THERE TO PICK YOU UP AT THE DOCTOR'S OFFICE AFTER THE LANCING, MOTHER.

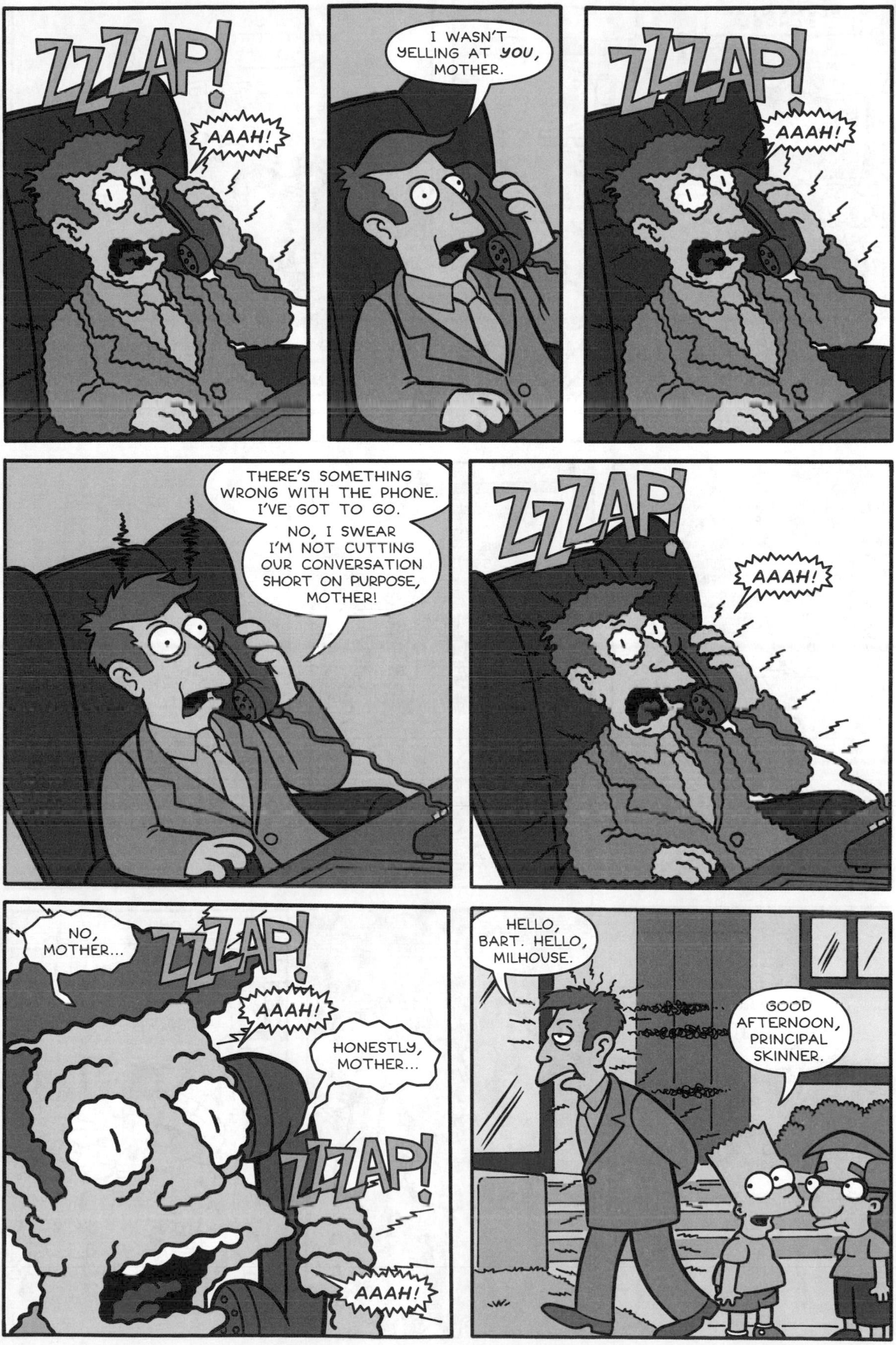
ZZZAP!
AAAH!
I WASN'T YELLING AT *YOU*, MOTHER.
ZZZAP!
AAAH!
THERE'S SOMETHING WRONG WITH THE PHONE. I'VE GOT TO GO.
NO, I SWEAR I'M NOT CUTTING OUR CONVERSATION SHORT ON PURPOSE, MOTHER!
ZZZAP!
AAAH!
NO, MOTHER...
ZZZAP!
AAAH!
HONESTLY, MOTHER...
ZZZAP!
AAAH!
HELLO, BART. HELLO, MILHOUSE.
GOOD AFTERNOON, PRINCIPAL SKINNER.

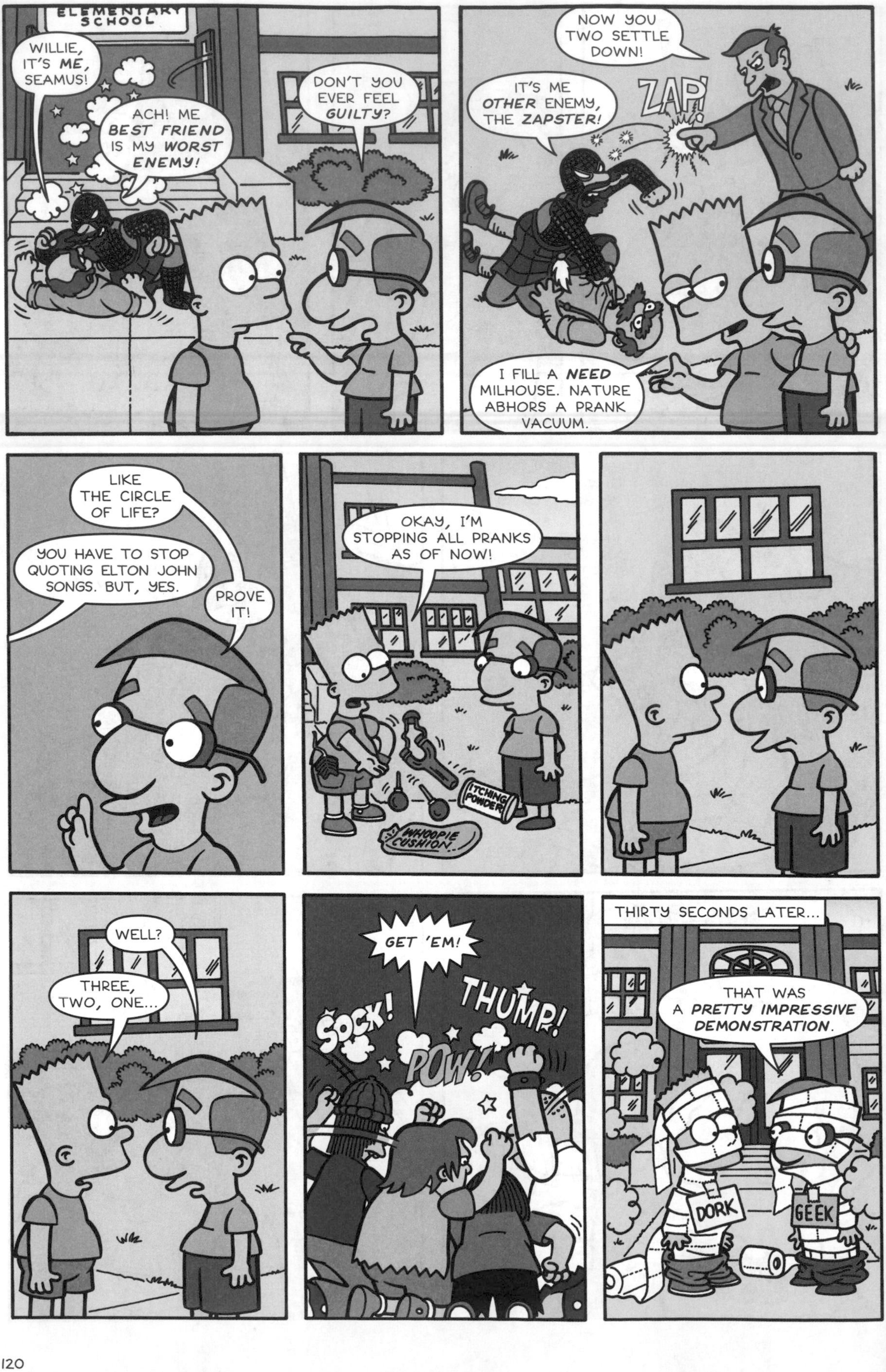
ELEMENTARY SCHOOL
WILLIE, IT'S ME, SEAMUS!
ACH! ME BEST FRIEND IS MY WORST ENEMY!
DON'T YOU EVER FEEL GUILTY?
NOW YOU TWO SETTLE DOWN!
IT'S ME OTHER ENEMY, THE ZAPSTER!
ZAP!
I FILL A NEED MILHOUSE. NATURE ABHORS A PRANK VACUUM.
LIKE THE CIRCLE OF LIFE?
YOU HAVE TO STOP QUOTING ELTON JOHN SONGS. BUT, YES.
PROVE IT!
OKAY, I'M STOPPING ALL PRANKS AS OF NOW!
ITCHING POWDER
WHOOPIE CUSHION
WELL?
THREE, TWO, ONE...
GET 'EM!
SOCK!
THUMP!
POW!
THIRTY SECONDS LATER...
THAT WAS A PRETTY IMPRESSIVE DEMONSTRATION.
DORK
GEEK

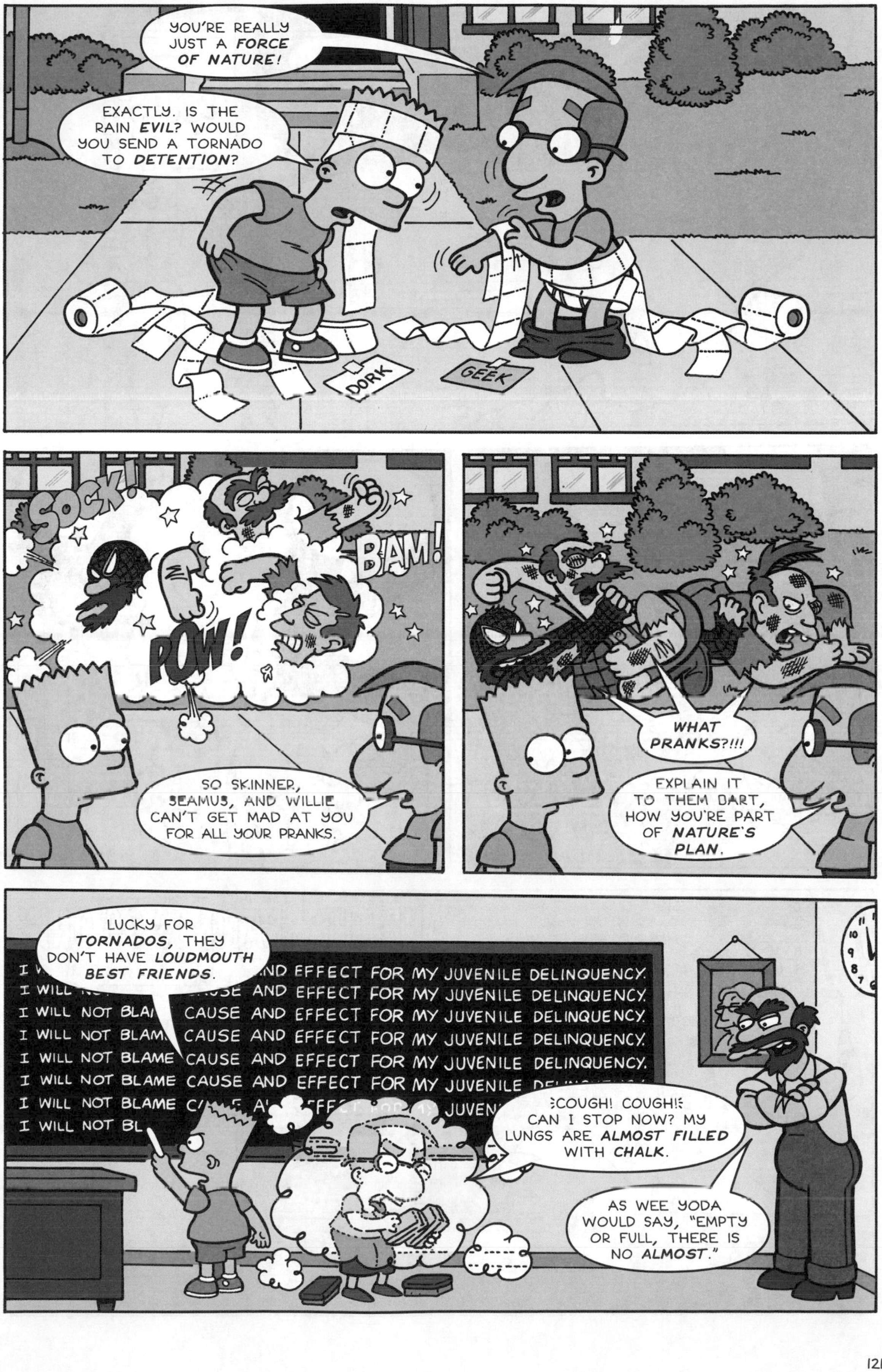
YOU'RE REALLY JUST A FORCE OF NATURE!
EXACTLY. IS THE RAIN EVIL? WOULD YOU SEND A TORNADO TO DETENTION?
DORK
GEEK
SOCK!
BAM!
POW!
SO SKINNER, SEAMUS, AND WILLIE CAN'T GET MAD AT YOU FOR ALL YOUR PRANKS.
WHAT PRANKS?!!!
EXPLAIN IT TO THEM BART, HOW YOU'RE PART OF NATURE'S PLAN.
LUCKY FOR TORNADOS, THEY DON'T HAVE LOUDMOUTH BEST FRIENDS.
I WILL NOT BLAME CAUSE AND EFFECT FOR MY JUVENILE DELINQUENCY.
COUGH! COUGH! CAN I STOP NOW? MY LUNGS ARE ALMOST FILLED WITH CHALK.
AS WEE YODA WOULD SAY, "EMPTY OR FULL, THERE IS NO ALMOST."

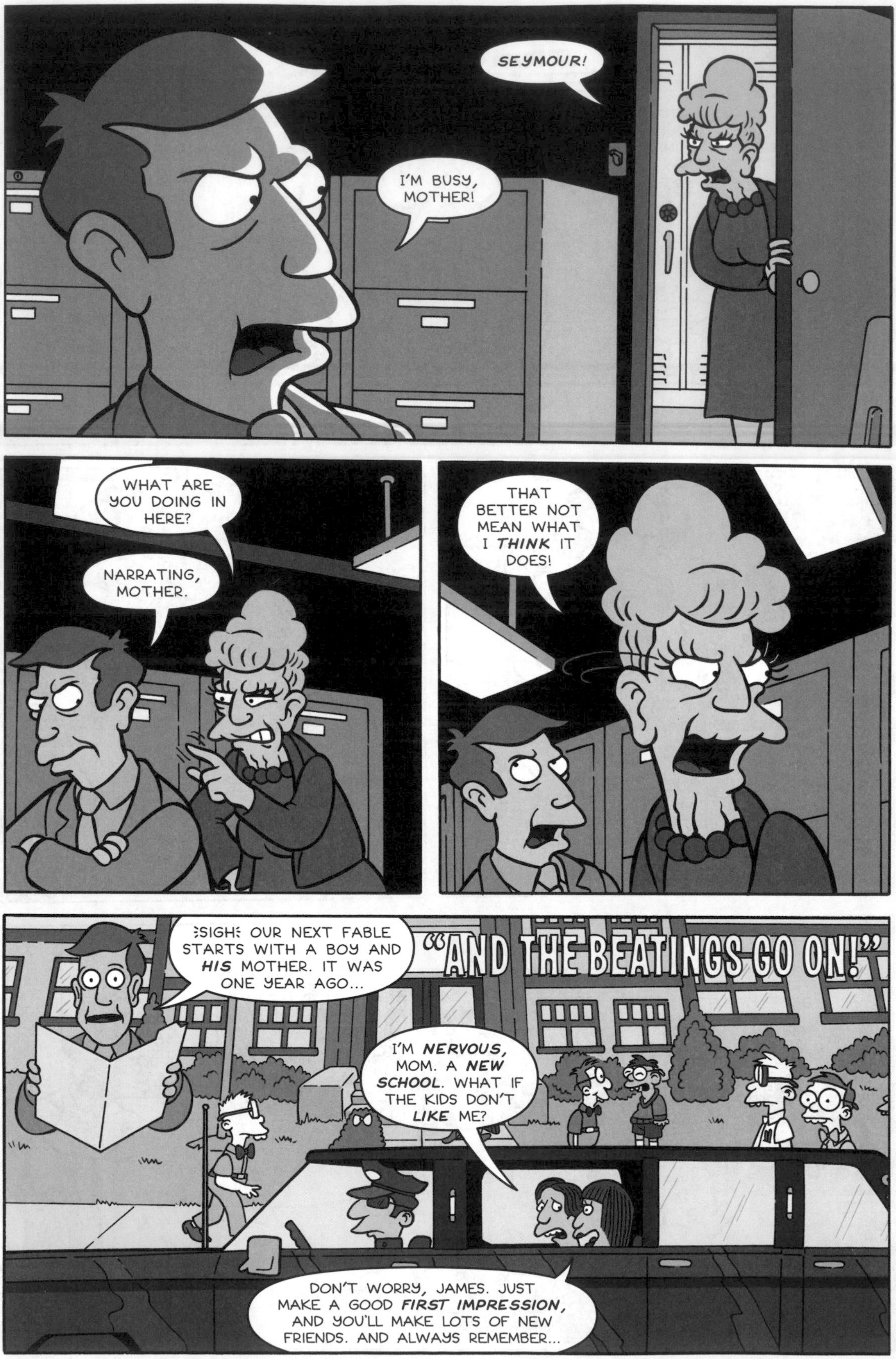

SEYMOUR!
I'M BUSY, MOTHER!
WHAT ARE YOU DOING IN HERE?
NARRATING, MOTHER.
THAT BETTER NOT MEAN WHAT I *THINK* IT DOES!
:SIGH: OUR NEXT FABLE STARTS WITH A BOY AND *HIS* MOTHER. IT WAS ONE YEAR AGO...
"AND THE BEATINGS GO ON!"
I'M *NERVOUS*, MOM. A *NEW SCHOOL*. WHAT IF THE KIDS DON'T *LIKE* ME?
DON'T WORRY, JAMES. JUST MAKE A GOOD *FIRST IMPRESSION*, AND YOU'LL MAKE LOTS OF NEW FRIENDS. AND ALWAYS REMEMBER...

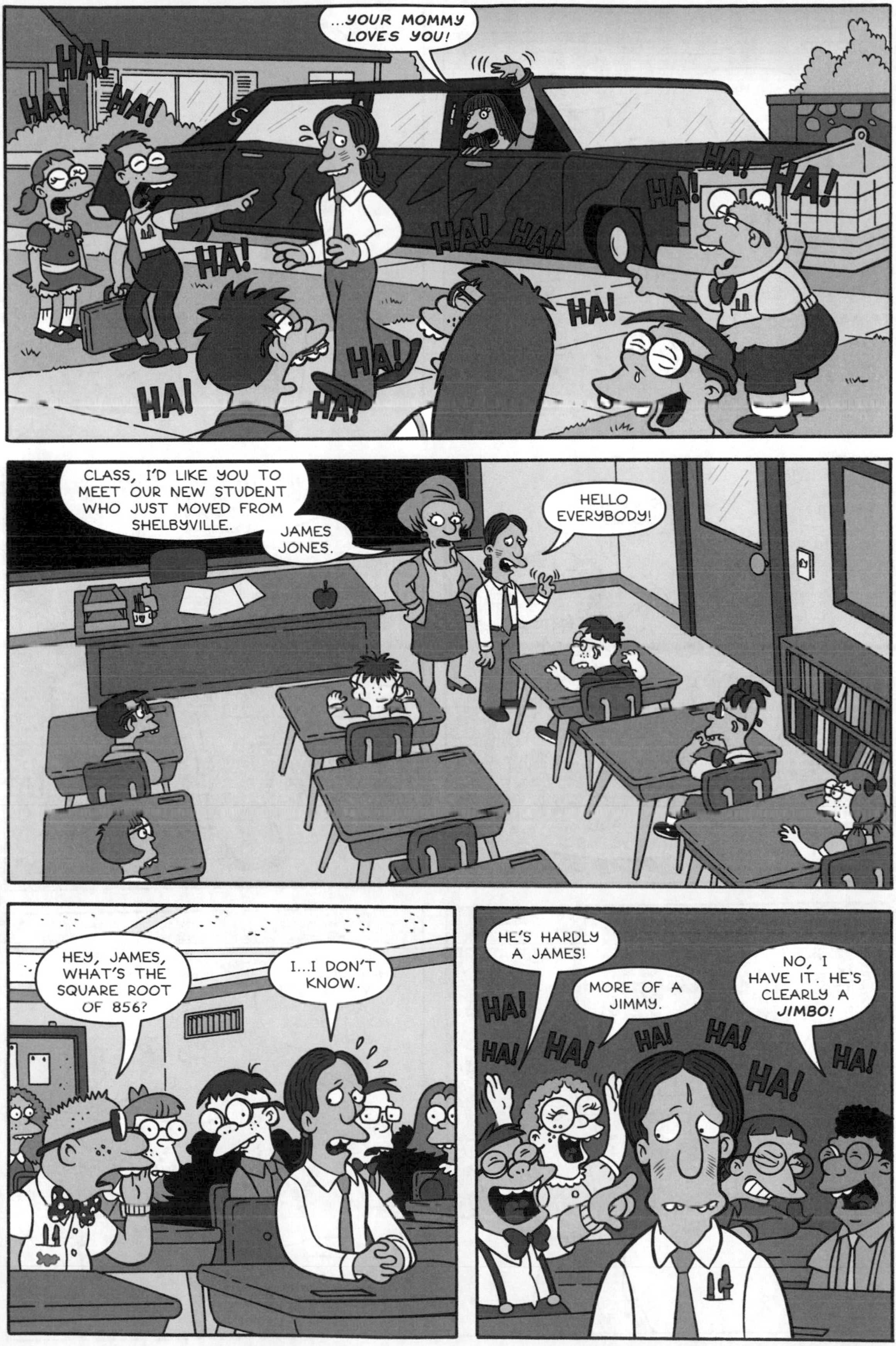
HA!
HA!
HA!
...YOUR MOMMY LOVES YOU!
HA!
HA!
HA!
HA!
HA!
HA!
HA!
HA!
HA!
HA!
CLASS, I'D LIKE YOU TO MEET OUR NEW STUDENT WHO JUST MOVED FROM SHELBYVILLE.
JAMES JONES.
HELLO EVERYBODY!
HEY, JAMES, WHAT'S THE SQUARE ROOT OF 856?
I...I DON'T KNOW.
HE'S HARDLY A JAMES!
MORE OF A JIMMY.
NO, I HAVE IT. HE'S CLEARLY A ***JIMBO!***
HA!
HA!
HA!
HA!
HA!
HA!
HA!

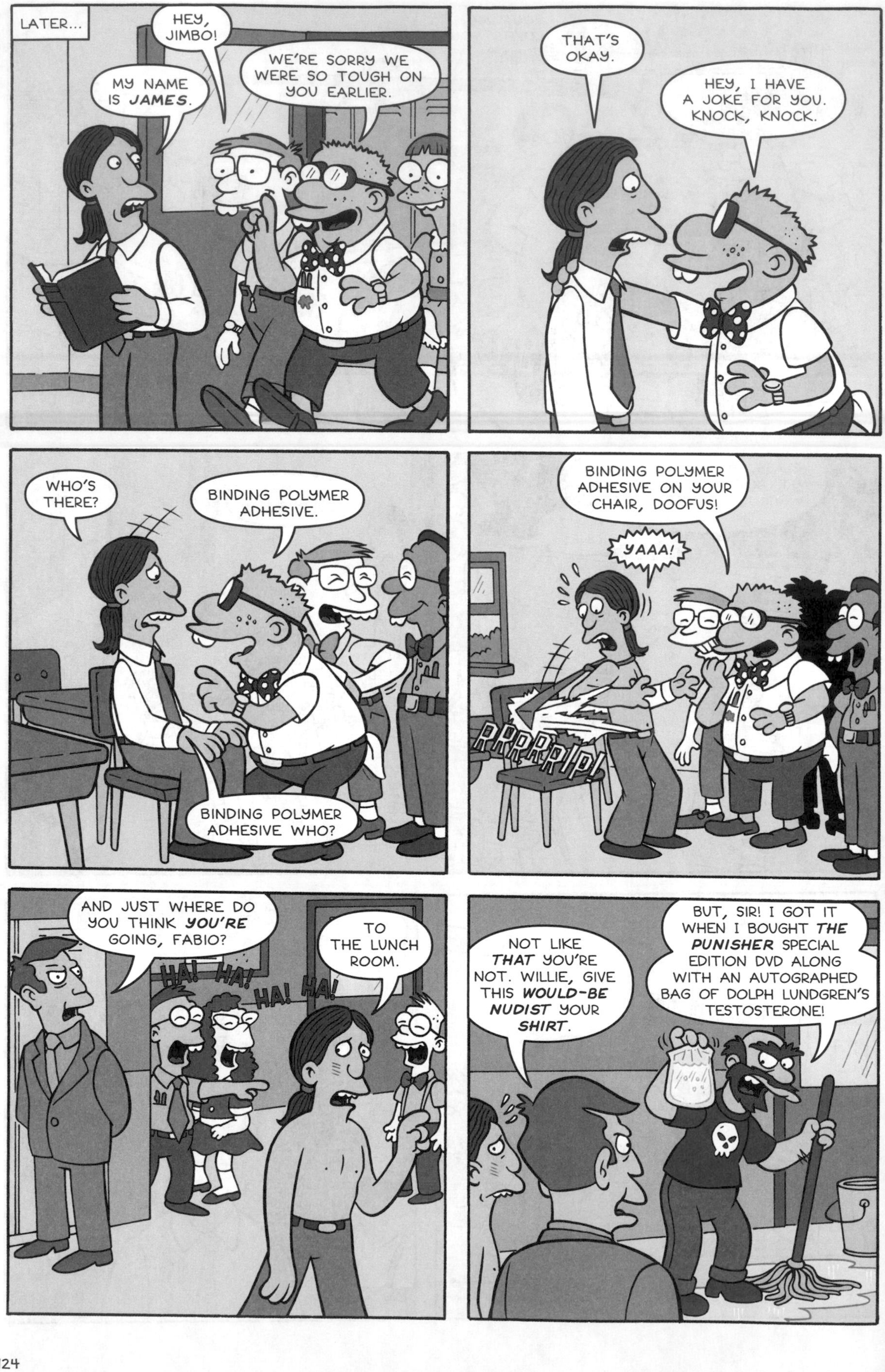
LATER...
HEY, JIMBO!
MY NAME IS JAMES.
WE'RE SORRY WE WERE SO TOUGH ON YOU EARLIER.
THAT'S OKAY.
HEY, I HAVE A JOKE FOR YOU. KNOCK, KNOCK.
WHO'S THERE?
BINDING POLYMER ADHESIVE.
BINDING POLYMER ADHESIVE WHO?
BINDING POLYMER ADHESIVE ON YOUR CHAIR, DOOFUS!
YAAA!
RRRRRRIP!
AND JUST WHERE DO YOU THINK YOU'RE GOING, FABIO?
HA! HA! HA! HA!
TO THE LUNCH ROOM.
NOT LIKE THAT YOU'RE NOT. WILLIE, GIVE THIS WOULD-BE NUDIST YOUR SHIRT.
BUT, SIR! I GOT IT WHEN I BOUGHT THE PUNISHER SPECIAL EDITION DVD ALONG WITH AN AUTOGRAPHED BAG OF DOLPH LUNDGREN'S TESTOSTERONE!

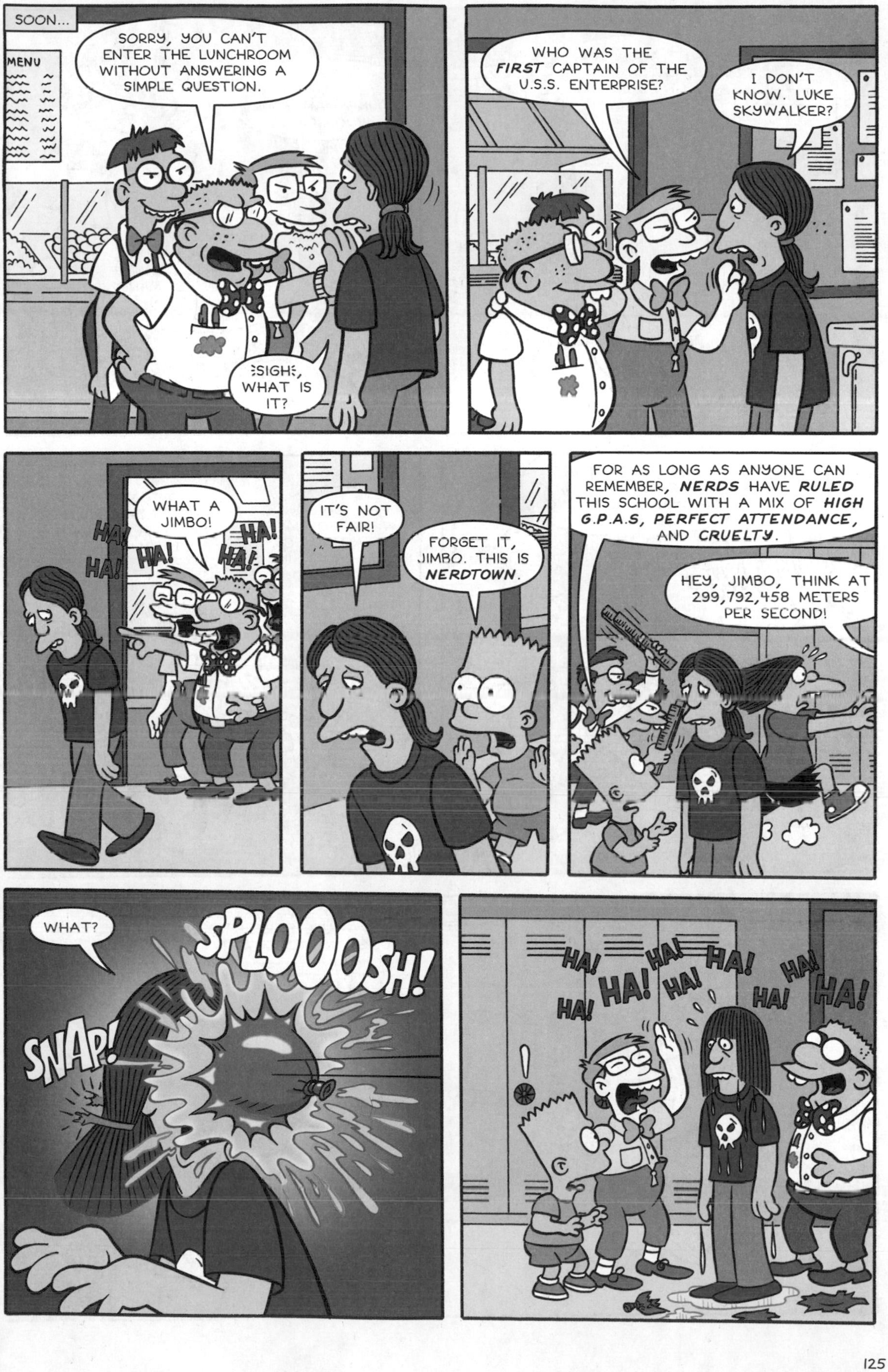
SOON...
SORRY, YOU CAN'T ENTER THE LUNCHROOM WITHOUT ANSWERING A SIMPLE QUESTION.
MENU
SIGH, WHAT IS IT?
WHO WAS THE *FIRST* CAPTAIN OF THE U.S.S. ENTERPRISE?
I DON'T KNOW. LUKE SKYWALKER?
WHAT A JIMBO!
HA! HA! HA! HA! HA!
IT'S NOT FAIR!
FORGET IT, JIMBO. THIS IS *NERDTOWN*.
FOR AS LONG AS ANYONE CAN REMEMBER, ***NERDS*** HAVE ***RULED*** THIS SCHOOL WITH A MIX OF ***HIGH G.P.A.S, PERFECT ATTENDANCE,*** AND ***CRUELTY***.
HEY, JIMBO, THINK AT 299,792,458 METERS PER SECOND!
WHAT?
SPLOOOSH!
SNAP!
HA! HA! HA! HA! HA! HA! HA! HA! HA!
!

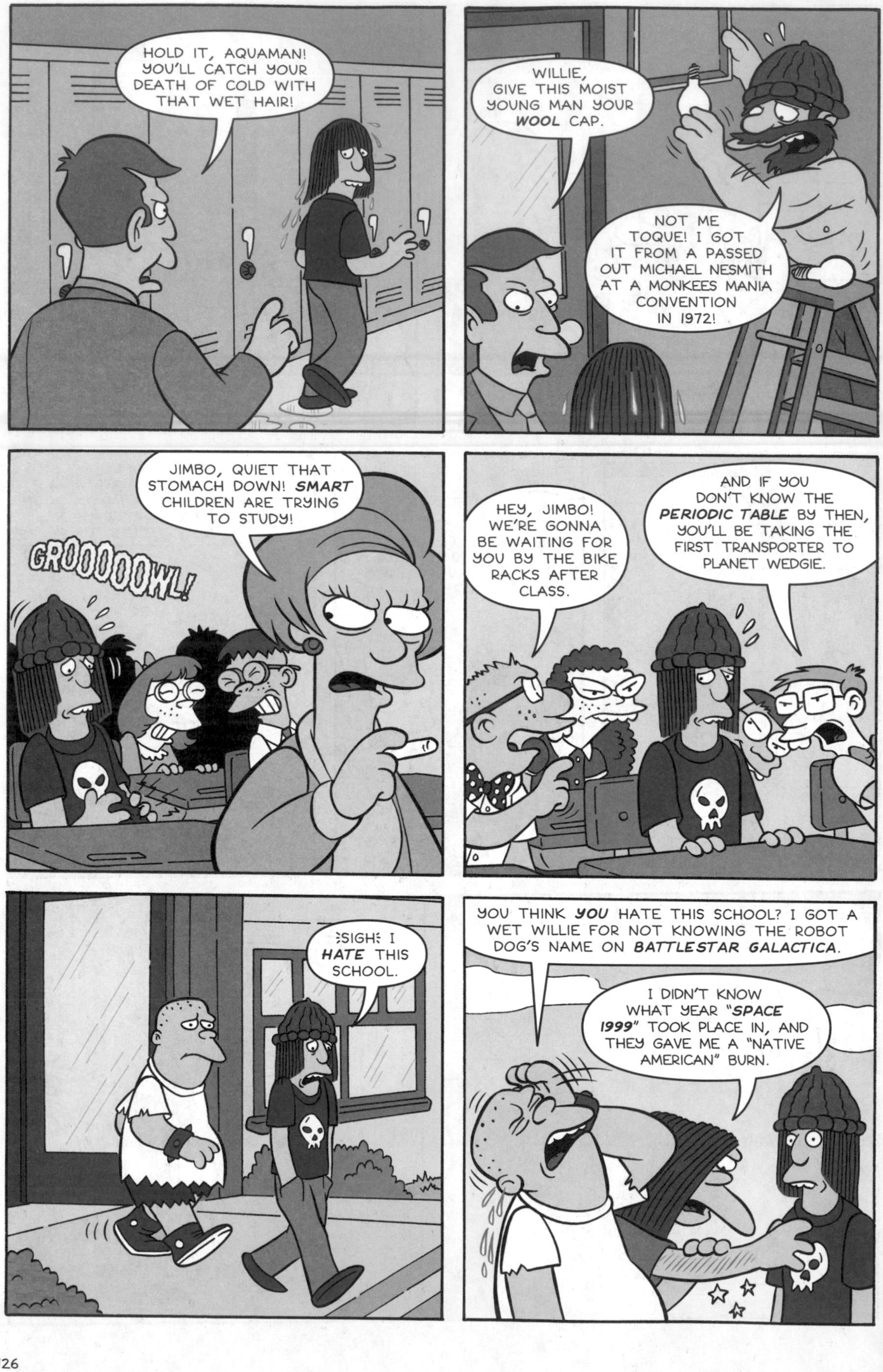
HOLD IT, AQUAMAN! YOU'LL CATCH YOUR DEATH OF COLD WITH THAT WET HAIR!
WILLIE, GIVE THIS MOIST YOUNG MAN YOUR WOOL CAP.
NOT ME TOQUE! I GOT IT FROM A PASSED OUT MICHAEL NESMITH AT A MONKEES MANIA CONVENTION IN 1972!
JIMBO, QUIET THAT STOMACH DOWN! SMART CHILDREN ARE TRYING TO STUDY!
GROOOOOWL!
HEY, JIMBO! WE'RE GONNA BE WAITING FOR YOU BY THE BIKE RACKS AFTER CLASS.
AND IF YOU DON'T KNOW THE PERIODIC TABLE BY THEN, YOU'LL BE TAKING THE FIRST TRANSPORTER TO PLANET WEDGIE.
:SIGH: I HATE THIS SCHOOL.
YOU THINK YOU HATE THIS SCHOOL? I GOT A WET WILLIE FOR NOT KNOWING THE ROBOT DOG'S NAME ON BATTLESTAR GALACTICA.
I DIDN'T KNOW WHAT YEAR "SPACE 1999" TOOK PLACE IN, AND THEY GAVE ME A "NATIVE AMERICAN" BURN.

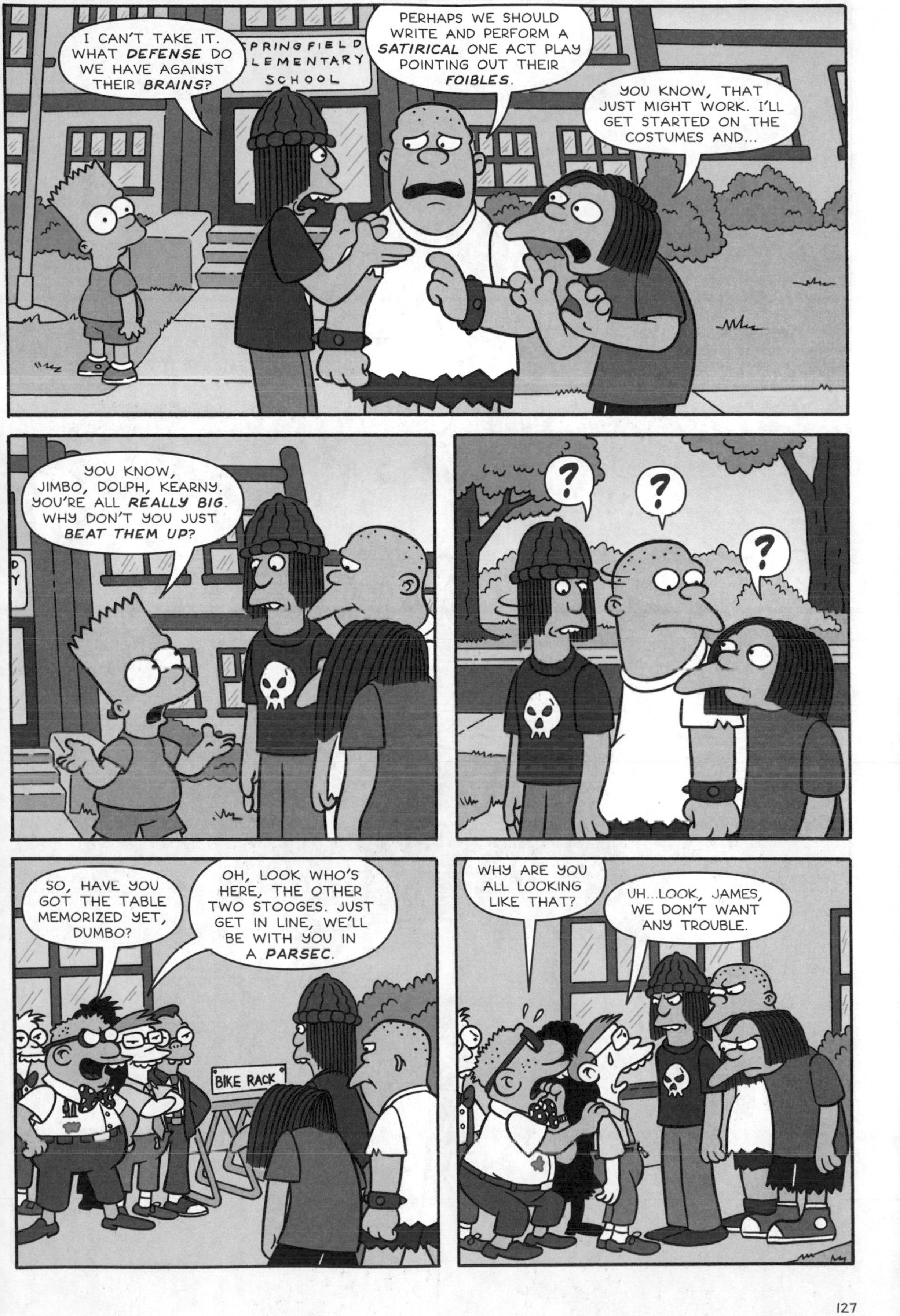
SPRINGFIELD ELEMENTARY SCHOOL
I CAN'T TAKE IT. WHAT DEFENSE DO WE HAVE AGAINST THEIR BRAINS?
PERHAPS WE SHOULD WRITE AND PERFORM A SATIRICAL ONE ACT PLAY POINTING OUT THEIR FOIBLES.
YOU KNOW, THAT JUST MIGHT WORK. I'LL GET STARTED ON THE COSTUMES AND...
YOU KNOW, JIMBO, DOLPH, KEARNY. YOU'RE ALL REALLY BIG. WHY DON'T YOU JUST BEAT THEM UP?
?
?
?
SO, HAVE YOU GOT THE TABLE MEMORIZED YET, DUMBO?
OH, LOOK WHO'S HERE, THE OTHER TWO STOOGES. JUST GET IN LINE, WE'LL BE WITH YOU IN A PARSEC.
BIKE RACK
WHY ARE YOU ALL LOOKING LIKE THAT?
UH...LOOK, JAMES, WE DON'T WANT ANY TROUBLE.

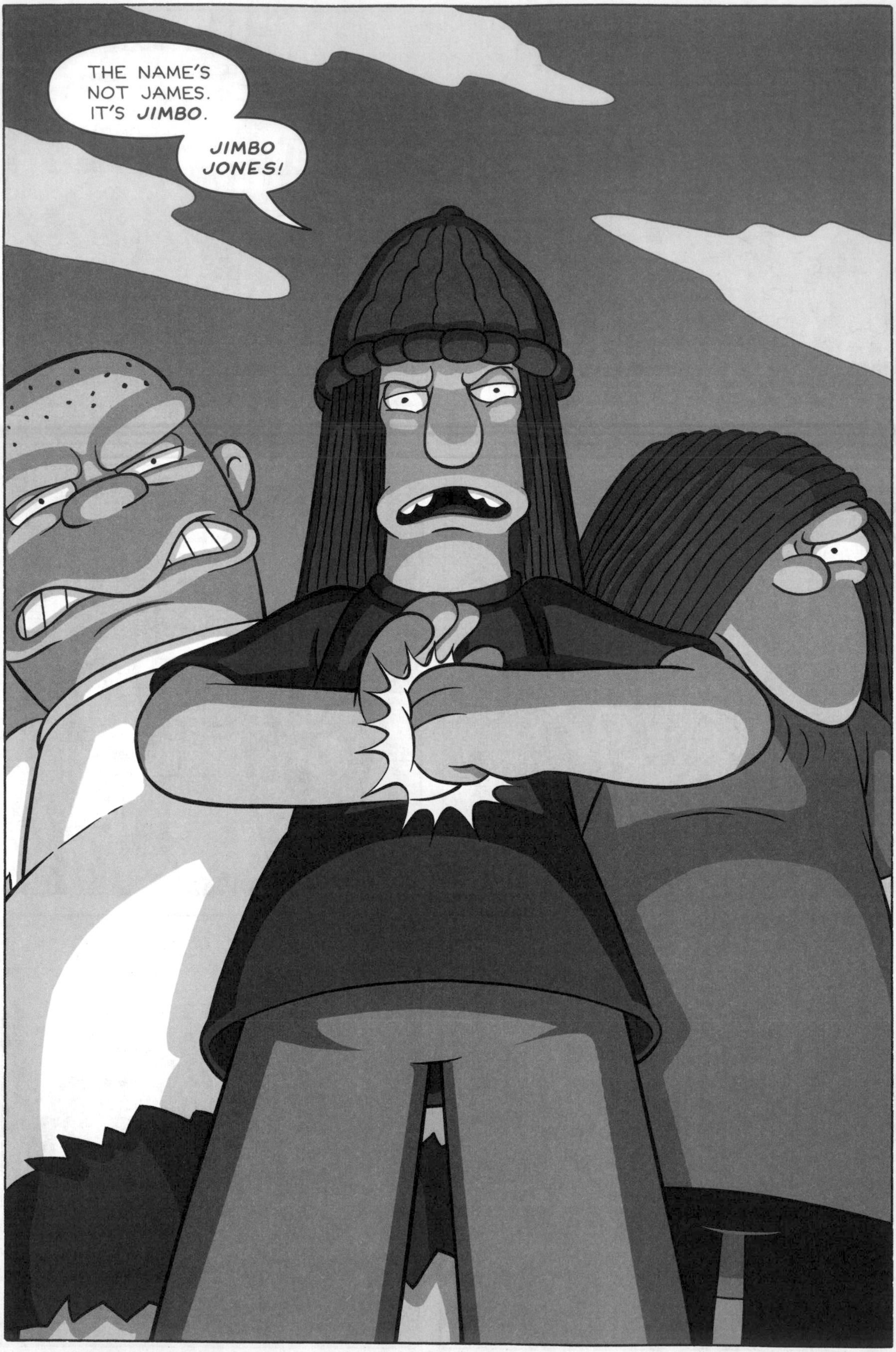
THE NAME'S NOT JAMES. IT'S *JIMBO*.
JIMBO JONES!

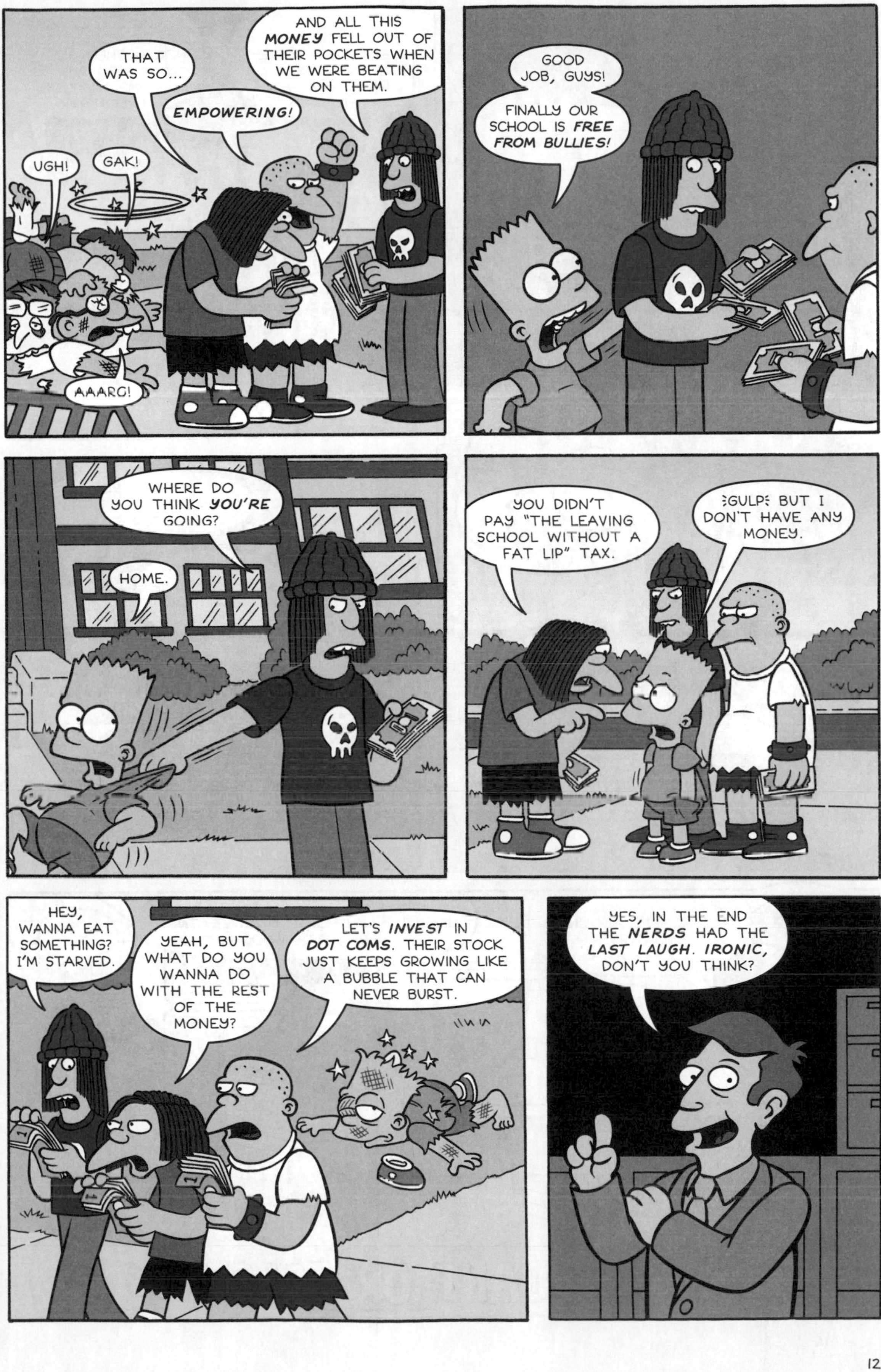
UGH!
GAK!
AAARG!
THAT WAS SO...
EMPOWERING!
AND ALL THIS MONEY FELL OUT OF THEIR POCKETS WHEN WE WERE BEATING ON THEM.
GOOD JOB, GUYS!
FINALLY OUR SCHOOL IS FREE FROM BULLIES!
WHERE DO YOU THINK YOU'RE GOING?
HOME.
YOU DIDN'T PAY "THE LEAVING SCHOOL WITHOUT A FAT LIP" TAX.
:GULP: BUT I DON'T HAVE ANY MONEY.
HEY, WANNA EAT SOMETHING? I'M STARVED.
YEAH, BUT WHAT DO YOU WANNA DO WITH THE REST OF THE MONEY?
LET'S INVEST IN DOT COMS. THEIR STOCK JUST KEEPS GROWING LIKE A BUBBLE THAT CAN NEVER BURST.
YES, IN THE END THE NERDS HAD THE LAST LAUGH. IRONIC, DON'T YOU THINK?

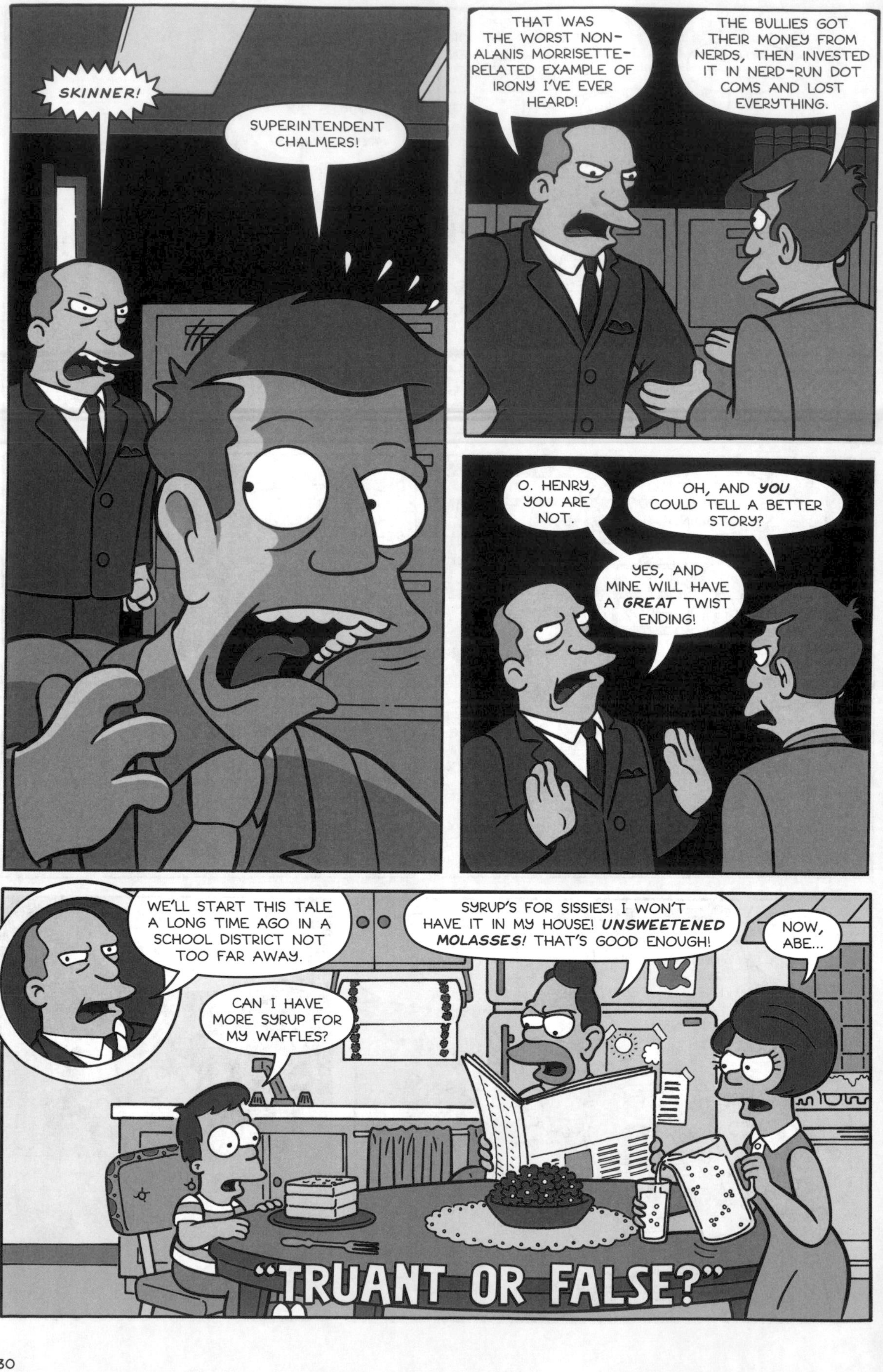
SKINNER!
SUPERINTENDENT CHALMERS!
THAT WAS THE WORST NON-ALANIS MORRISETTE-RELATED EXAMPLE OF IRONY I'VE EVER HEARD!
THE BULLIES GOT THEIR MONEY FROM NERDS, THEN INVESTED IT IN NERD-RUN DOT COMS AND LOST EVERYTHING.
O. HENRY, YOU ARE NOT.
OH, AND YOU COULD TELL A BETTER STORY?
YES, AND MINE WILL HAVE A GREAT TWIST ENDING!
WE'LL START THIS TALE A LONG TIME AGO IN A SCHOOL DISTRICT NOT TOO FAR AWAY.
CAN I HAVE MORE SYRUP FOR MY WAFFLES?
SYRUP'S FOR SISSIES! I WON'T HAVE IT IN MY HOUSE! UNSWEETENED MOLASSES! THAT'S GOOD ENOUGH!
NOW, ABE...
"TRUANT OR FALSE?"

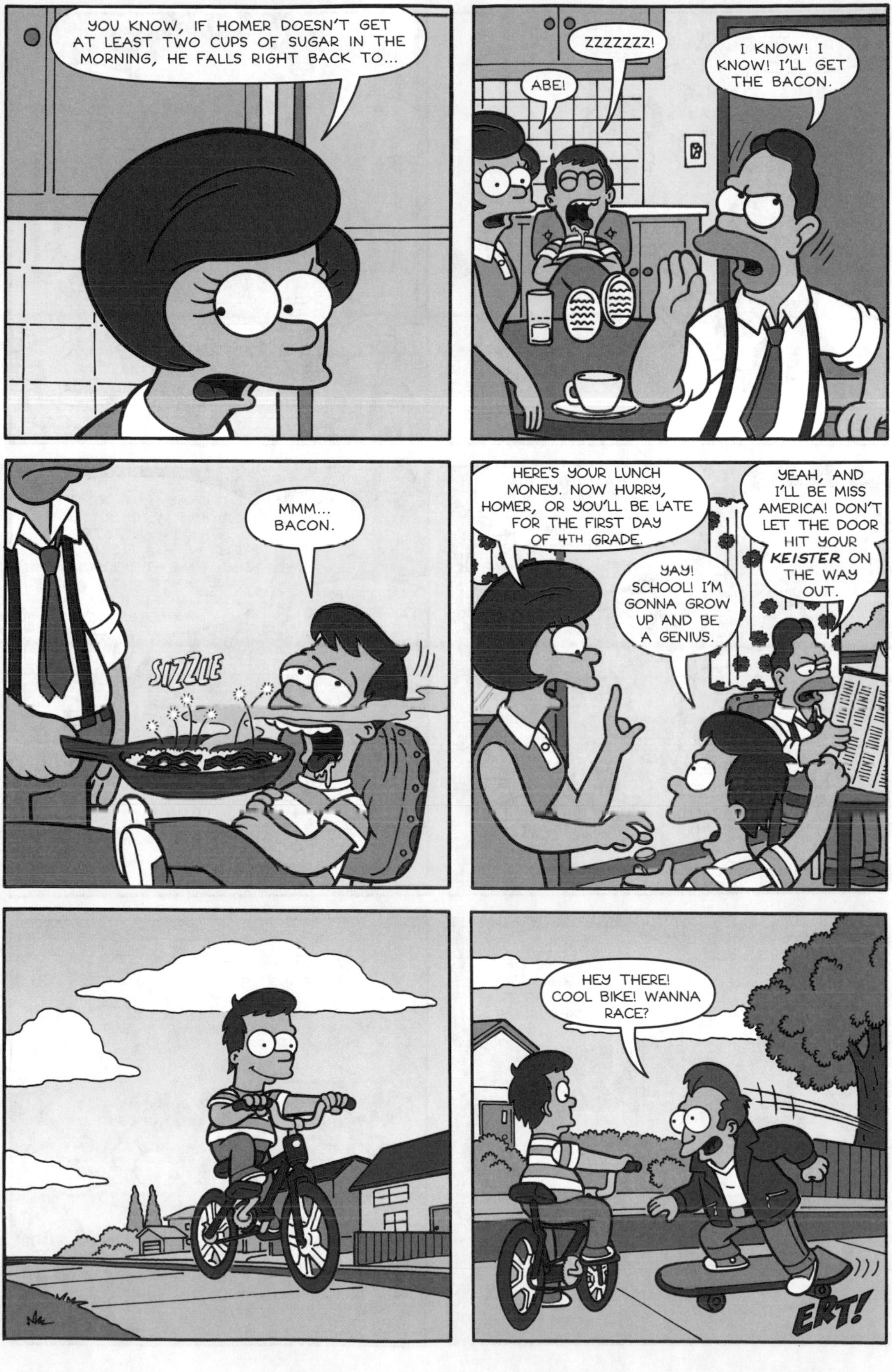
YOU KNOW, IF HOMER DOESN'T GET AT LEAST TWO CUPS OF SUGAR IN THE MORNING, HE FALLS RIGHT BACK TO...
ABE!
ZZZZZZZ!
I KNOW! I KNOW! I'LL GET THE BACON.
MMM... BACON.
SIZZLE
HERE'S YOUR LUNCH MONEY. NOW HURRY, HOMER, OR YOU'LL BE LATE FOR THE FIRST DAY OF 4TH GRADE.
YAY! SCHOOL! I'M GONNA GROW UP AND BE A GENIUS.
YEAH, AND I'LL BE MISS AMERICA! DON'T LET THE DOOR HIT YOUR KEISTER ON THE WAY OUT.
HEY THERE! COOL BIKE! WANNA RACE?
ERT!

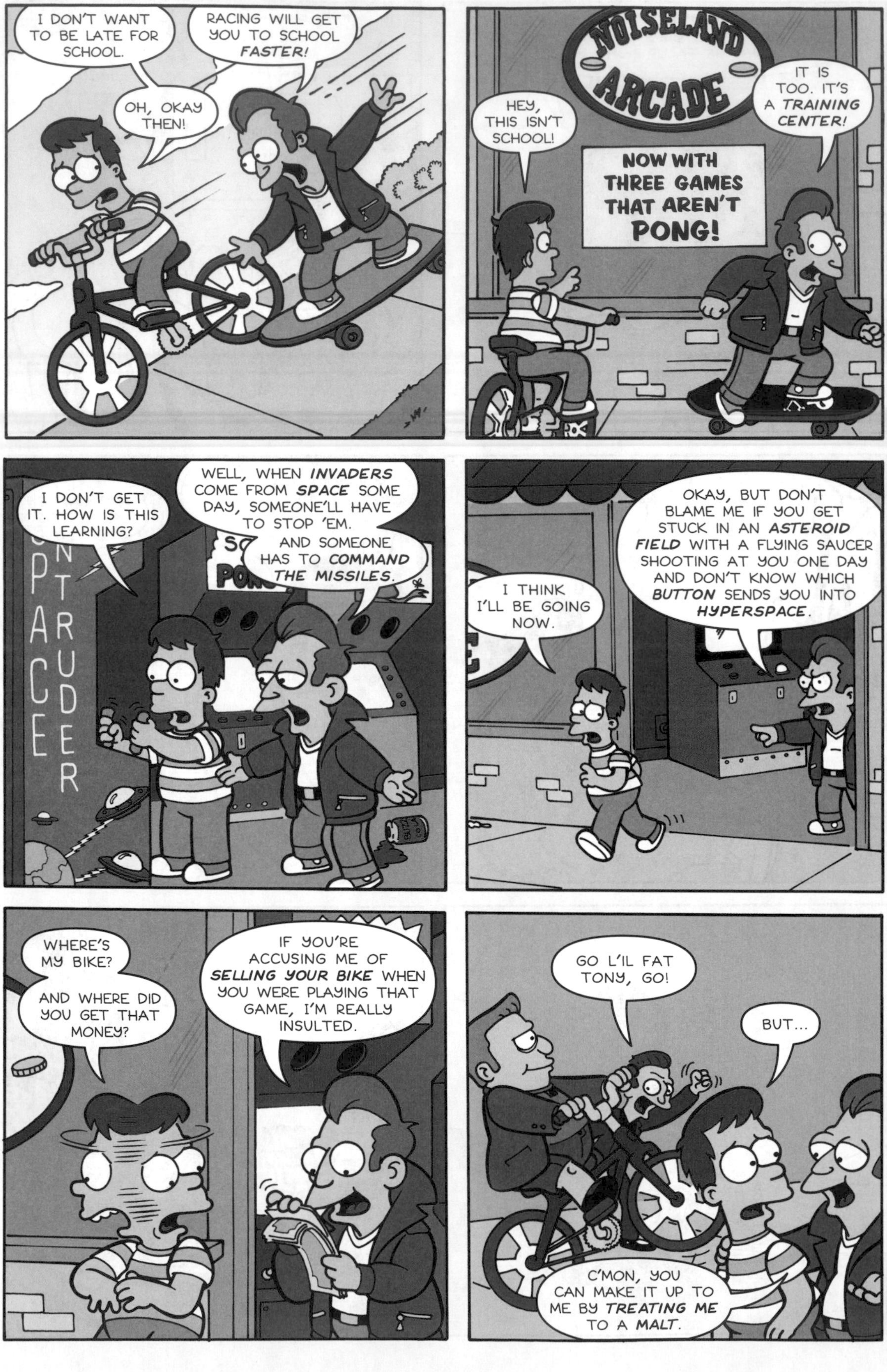

I DON'T WANT TO BE LATE FOR SCHOOL.
RACING WILL GET YOU TO SCHOOL FASTER!
OH, OKAY THEN!
NOISELAND ARCADE
HEY, THIS ISN'T SCHOOL!
IT IS TOO. IT'S A TRAINING CENTER!
NOW WITH THREE GAMES THAT AREN'T PONG!
I DON'T GET IT. HOW IS THIS LEARNING?
WELL, WHEN INVADERS COME FROM SPACE SOME DAY, SOMEONE'LL HAVE TO STOP 'EM.
AND SOMEONE HAS TO COMMAND THE MISSILES.
SPACE INTRUDER
I THINK I'LL BE GOING NOW.
OKAY, BUT DON'T BLAME ME IF YOU GET STUCK IN AN ASTEROID FIELD WITH A FLYING SAUCER SHOOTING AT YOU ONE DAY AND DON'T KNOW WHICH BUTTON SENDS YOU INTO HYPERSPACE.
WHERE'S MY BIKE?
AND WHERE DID YOU GET THAT MONEY?
IF YOU'RE ACCUSING ME OF SELLING YOUR BIKE WHEN YOU WERE PLAYING THAT GAME, I'M REALLY INSULTED.
GO L'IL FAT TONY, GO!
BUT...
C'MON, YOU CAN MAKE IT UP TO ME BY TREATING ME TO A MALT.

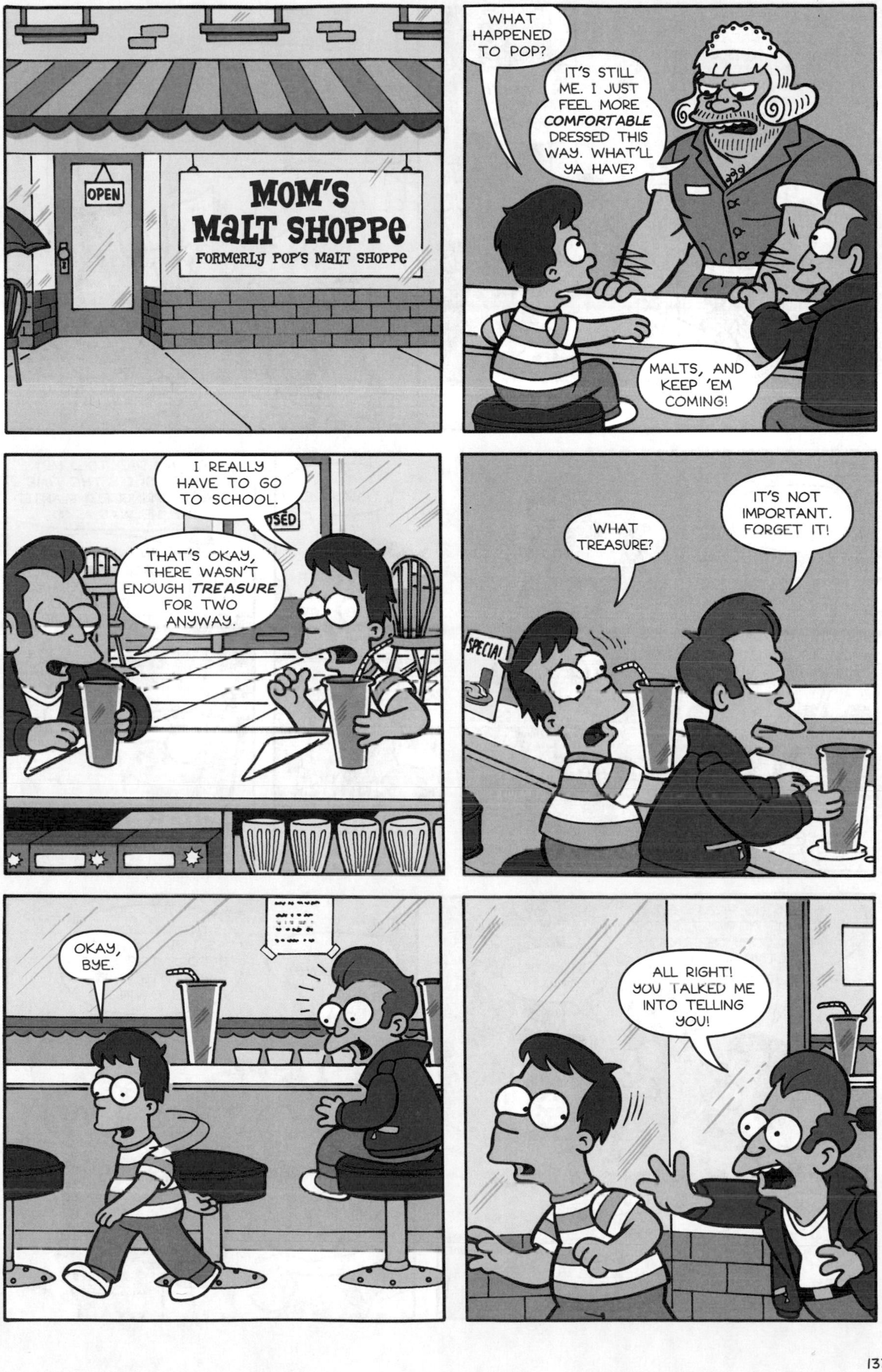
OPEN
MOM'S MALT SHOPPE
FORMERLY POP'S MALT SHOPPE
WHAT HAPPENED TO POP?
IT'S STILL ME. I JUST FEEL MORE COMFORTABLE DRESSED THIS WAY. WHAT'LL YA HAVE?
MALTS, AND KEEP 'EM COMING!
I REALLY HAVE TO GO TO SCHOOL.
THAT'S OKAY, THERE WASN'T ENOUGH TREASURE FOR TWO ANYWAY.
WHAT TREASURE?
IT'S NOT IMPORTANT. FORGET IT!
SPECIAL
OKAY, BYE.
ALL RIGHT! YOU TALKED ME INTO TELLING YOU!

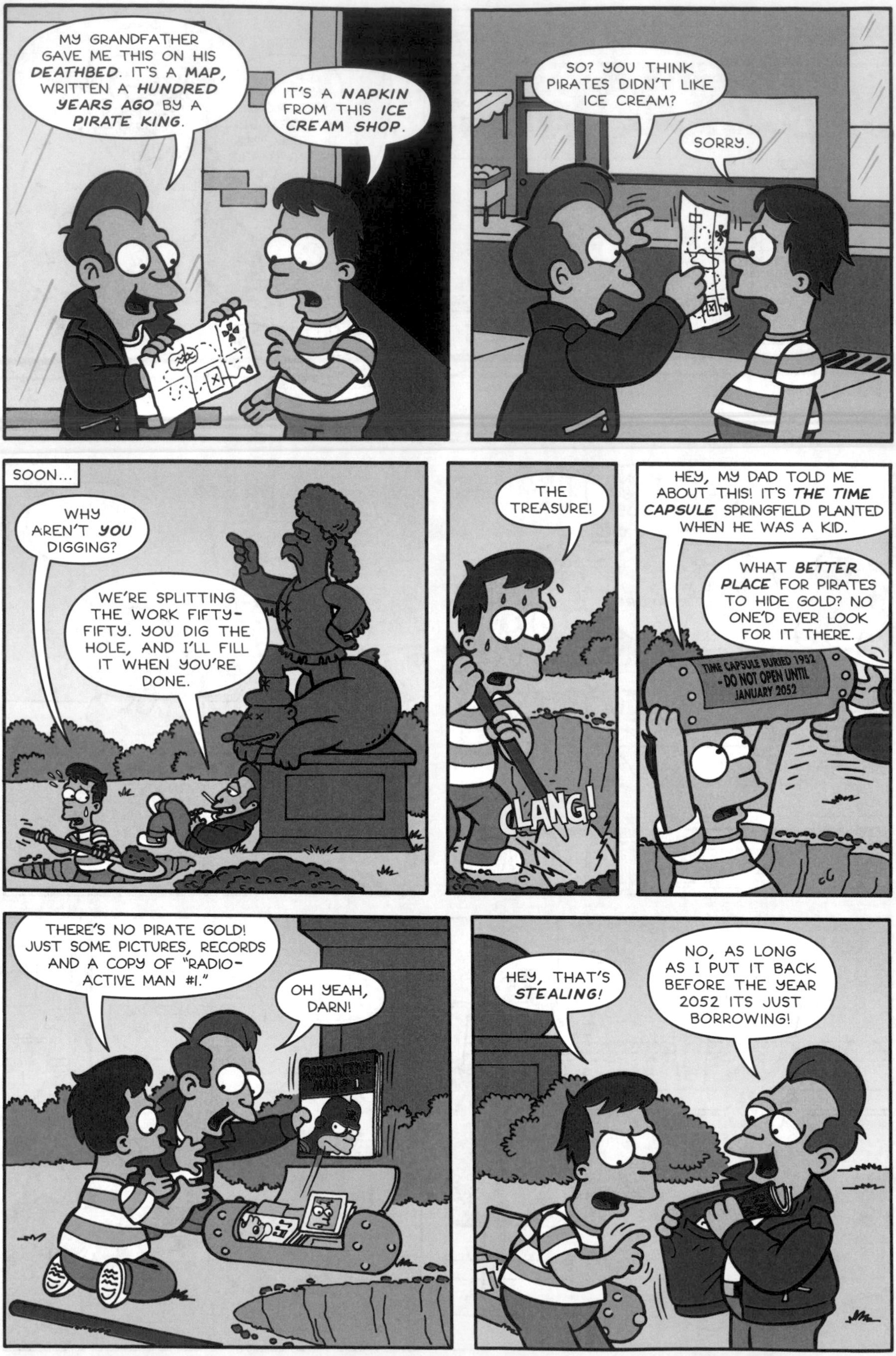

MY GRANDFATHER GAVE ME THIS ON HIS DEATHBED. IT'S A MAP, WRITTEN A HUNDRED YEARS AGO BY A PIRATE KING.
IT'S A NAPKIN FROM THIS ICE CREAM SHOP.
SO? YOU THINK PIRATES DIDN'T LIKE ICE CREAM?
SORRY.
SOON...
WHY AREN'T YOU DIGGING?
WE'RE SPLITTING THE WORK FIFTY-FIFTY. YOU DIG THE HOLE, AND I'LL FILL IT WHEN YOU'RE DONE.
THE TREASURE!
CLANG!
HEY, MY DAD TOLD ME ABOUT THIS! IT'S THE TIME CAPSULE SPRINGFIELD PLANTED WHEN HE WAS A KID.
WHAT BETTER PLACE FOR PIRATES TO HIDE GOLD? NO ONE'D EVER LOOK FOR IT THERE.
TIME CAPSULE BURIED 1952 - DO NOT OPEN UNTIL JANUARY 2052
THERE'S NO PIRATE GOLD! JUST SOME PICTURES, RECORDS AND A COPY OF "RADIO-ACTIVE MAN #1."
OH YEAH, DARN!
RADIOACTIVE MAN 1
HEY, THAT'S STEALING!
NO, AS LONG AS I PUT IT BACK BEFORE THE YEAR 2052 ITS JUST BORROWING!

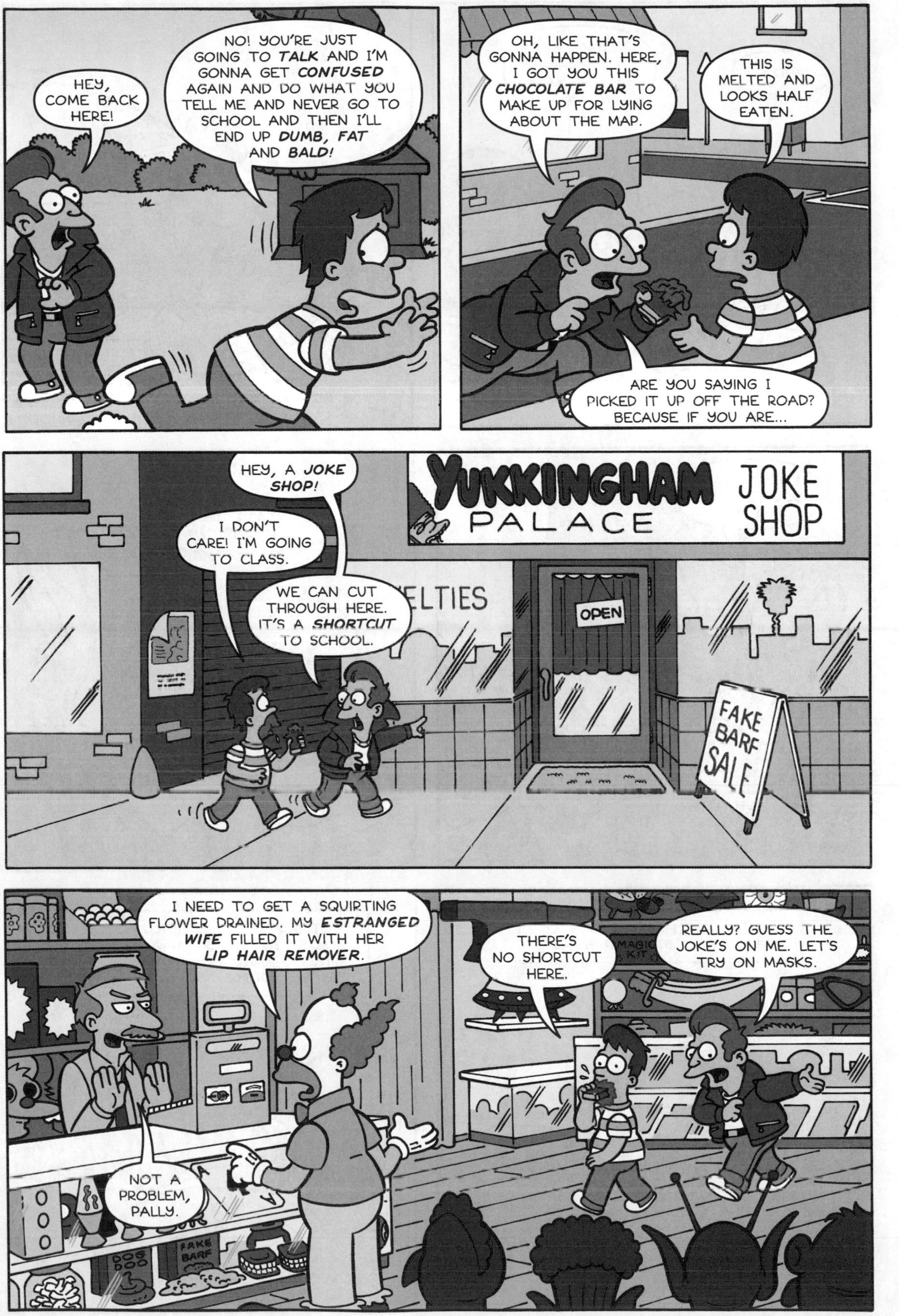
HEY, COME BACK HERE!
NO! YOU'RE JUST GOING TO TALK AND I'M GONNA GET CONFUSED AGAIN AND DO WHAT YOU TELL ME AND NEVER GO TO SCHOOL AND THEN I'LL END UP DUMB, FAT AND BALD!
OH, LIKE THAT'S GONNA HAPPEN. HERE, I GOT YOU THIS CHOCOLATE BAR TO MAKE UP FOR LYING ABOUT THE MAP.
THIS IS MELTED AND LOOKS HALF EATEN.
ARE YOU SAYING I PICKED IT UP OFF THE ROAD? BECAUSE IF YOU ARE...
YUKKINGHAM PALACE JOKE SHOP
HEY, A JOKE SHOP!
I DON'T CARE! I'M GOING TO CLASS.
WE CAN CUT THROUGH HERE. IT'S A SHORTCUT TO SCHOOL.
ELTIES
OPEN
FAKE BARF SALE
I NEED TO GET A SQUIRTING FLOWER DRAINED. MY ESTRANGED WIFE FILLED IT WITH HER LIP HAIR REMOVER.
NOT A PROBLEM, PALLY.
THERE'S NO SHORTCUT HERE.
REALLY? GUESS THE JOKE'S ON ME. LET'S TRY ON MASKS.
DOG DOO
FAKE BARF

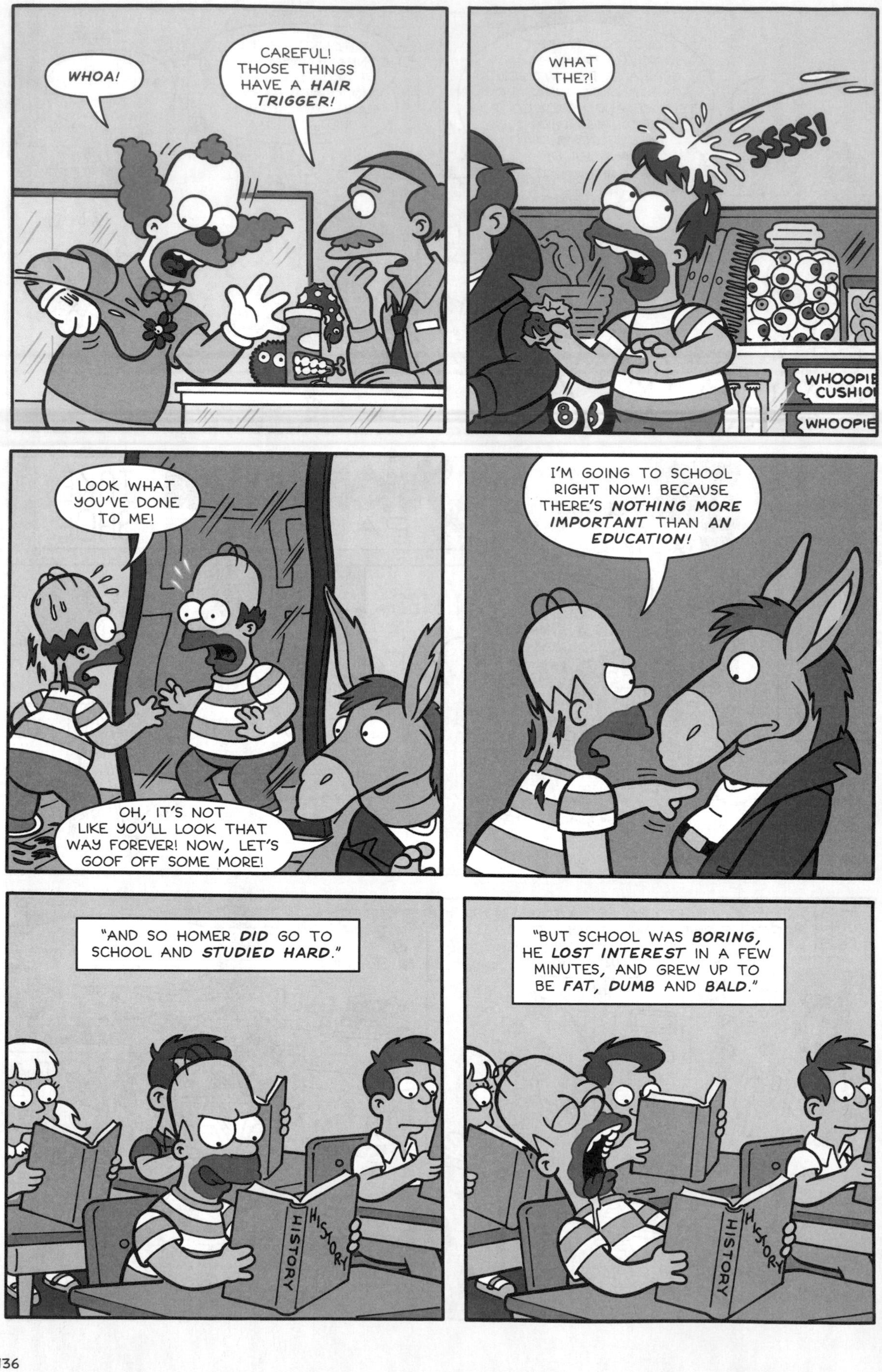
WHOA!
CAREFUL! THOSE THINGS HAVE A **HAIR TRIGGER**!
WHAT THE?!
SSSS!
WHOOPIE CUSHIO
WHOOPIE
LOOK WHAT YOU'VE DONE TO ME!
OH, IT'S NOT LIKE YOU'LL LOOK THAT WAY FOREVER! NOW, LET'S GOOF OFF SOME MORE!
I'M GOING TO SCHOOL RIGHT NOW! BECAUSE THERE'S ***NOTHING MORE IMPORTANT*** THAN ***AN EDUCATION***!
"AND SO HOMER ***DID*** GO TO SCHOOL AND ***STUDIED HARD***."
HISTORY
HISTORY
"BUT SCHOOL WAS ***BORING***, HE ***LOST INTEREST*** IN A FEW MINUTES, AND GREW UP TO BE ***FAT, DUMB*** AND ***BALD***."
HISTORY
HISTORY

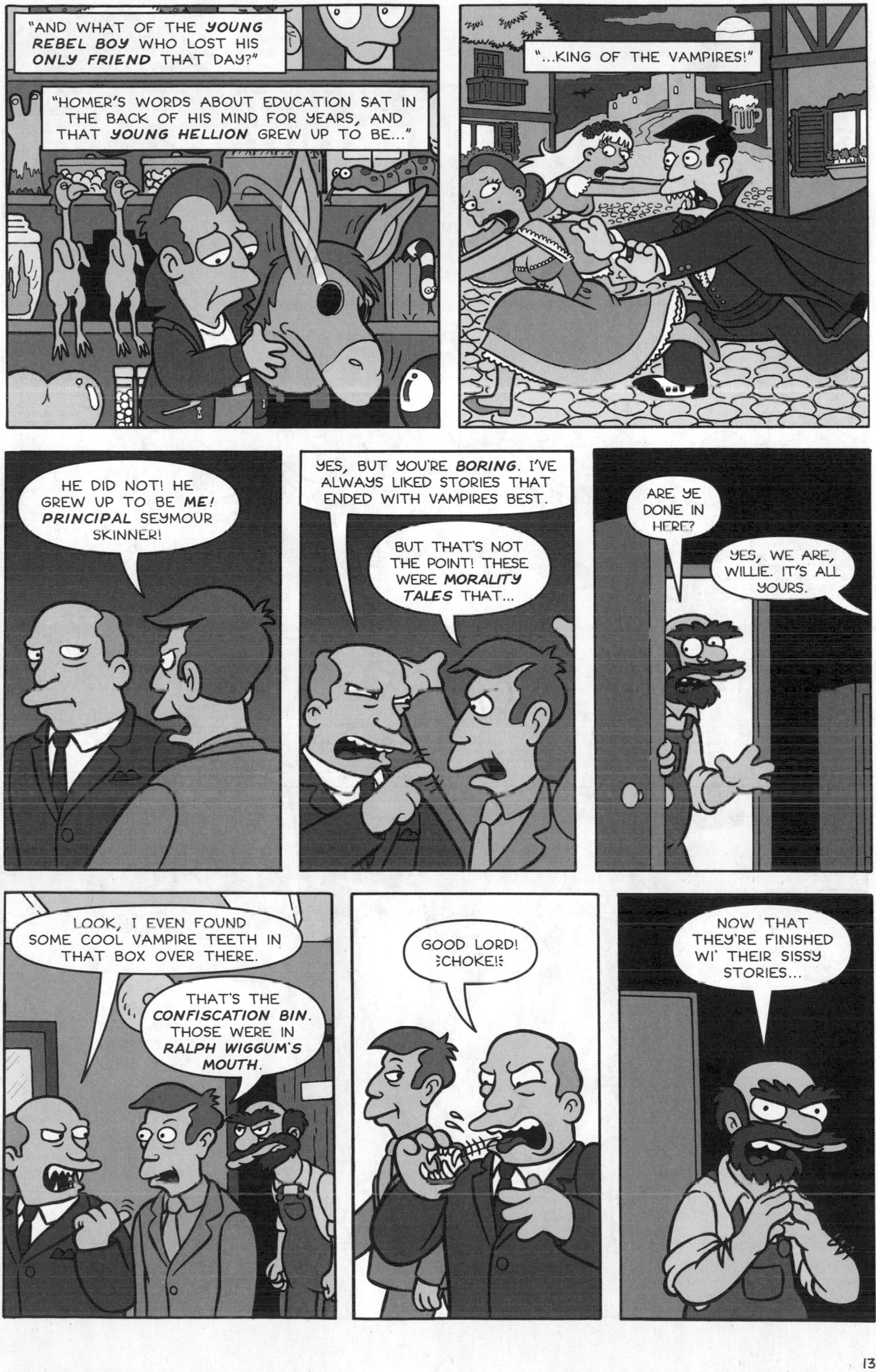
"AND WHAT OF THE YOUNG REBEL BOY WHO LOST HIS ONLY FRIEND THAT DAY?"
"HOMER'S WORDS ABOUT EDUCATION SAT IN THE BACK OF HIS MIND FOR YEARS, AND THAT YOUNG HELLION GREW UP TO BE..."
"...KING OF THE VAMPIRES!"
HE DID NOT! HE GREW UP TO BE ME! PRINCIPAL SEYMOUR SKINNER!
YES, BUT YOU'RE BORING. I'VE ALWAYS LIKED STORIES THAT ENDED WITH VAMPIRES BEST.
BUT THAT'S NOT THE POINT! THESE WERE MORALITY TALES THAT...
ARE YE DONE IN HERE?
YES, WE ARE, WILLIE. IT'S ALL YOURS.
LOOK, I EVEN FOUND SOME COOL VAMPIRE TEETH IN THAT BOX OVER THERE.
THAT'S THE CONFISCATION BIN. THOSE WERE IN RALPH WIGGUM'S MOUTH.
GOOD LORD! ⁝CHOKE!⁝
NOW THAT THEY'RE FINISHED WI' THEIR SISSY STORIES...

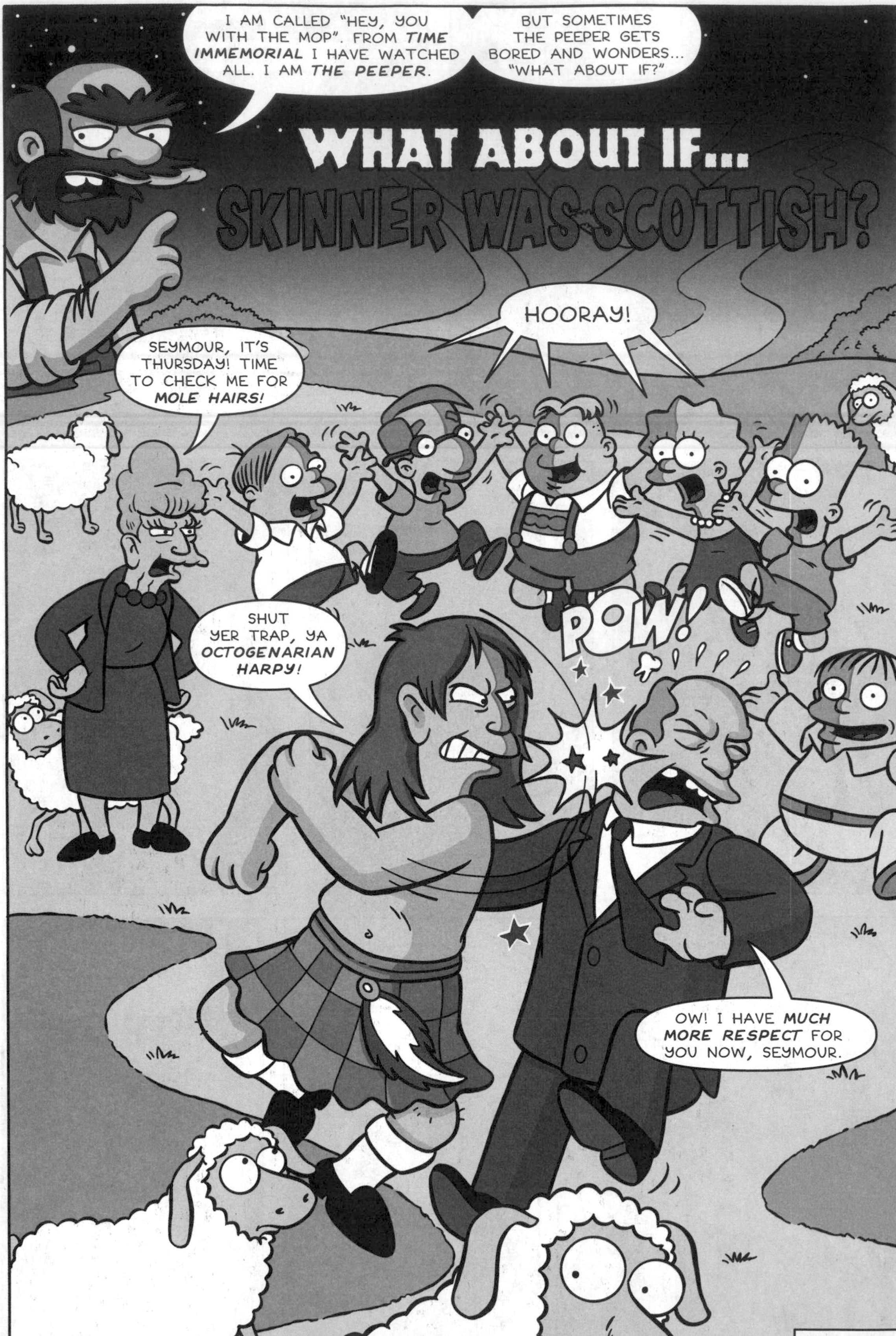
I AM CALLED "HEY, YOU WITH THE MOP". FROM TIME IMMEMORIAL I HAVE WATCHED ALL. I AM THE PEEPER.
BUT SOMETIMES THE PEEPER GETS BORED AND WONDERS... "WHAT ABOUT IF?"
WHAT ABOUT IF...
SKINNER WAS SCOTTISH?
HOORAY!
SEYMOUR, IT'S THURSDAY! TIME TO CHECK ME FOR MOLE HAIRS!
SHUT YER TRAP, YA OCTOGENARIAN HARPY!
POW!
OW! I HAVE MUCH MORE RESPECT FOR YOU NOW, SEYMOUR.
THE END

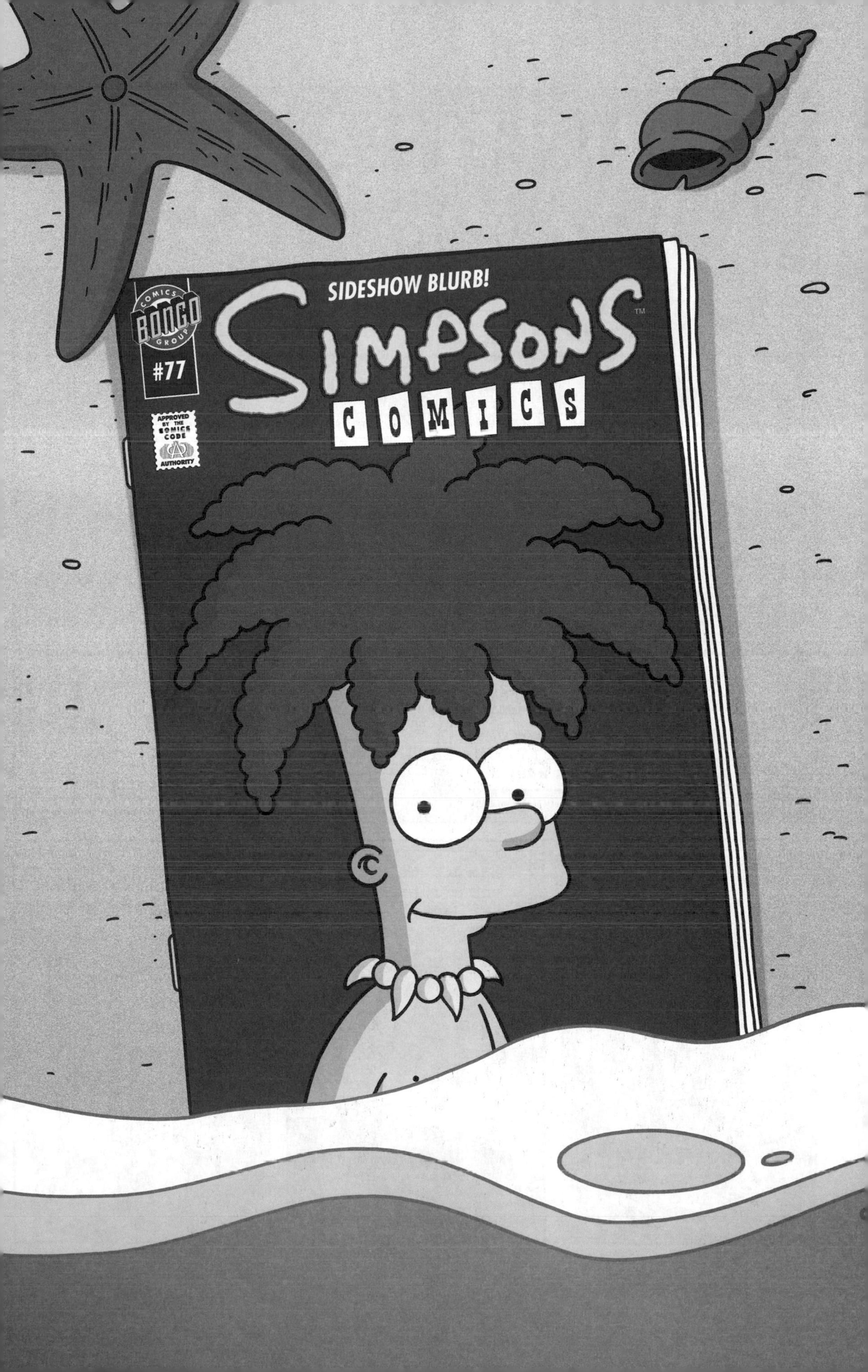
SIDESHOW BLURB!
BONGO COMICS GROUP
#77
SIMPSONS
COMICS
APPROVED BY THE COMICS CODE AUTHORITY

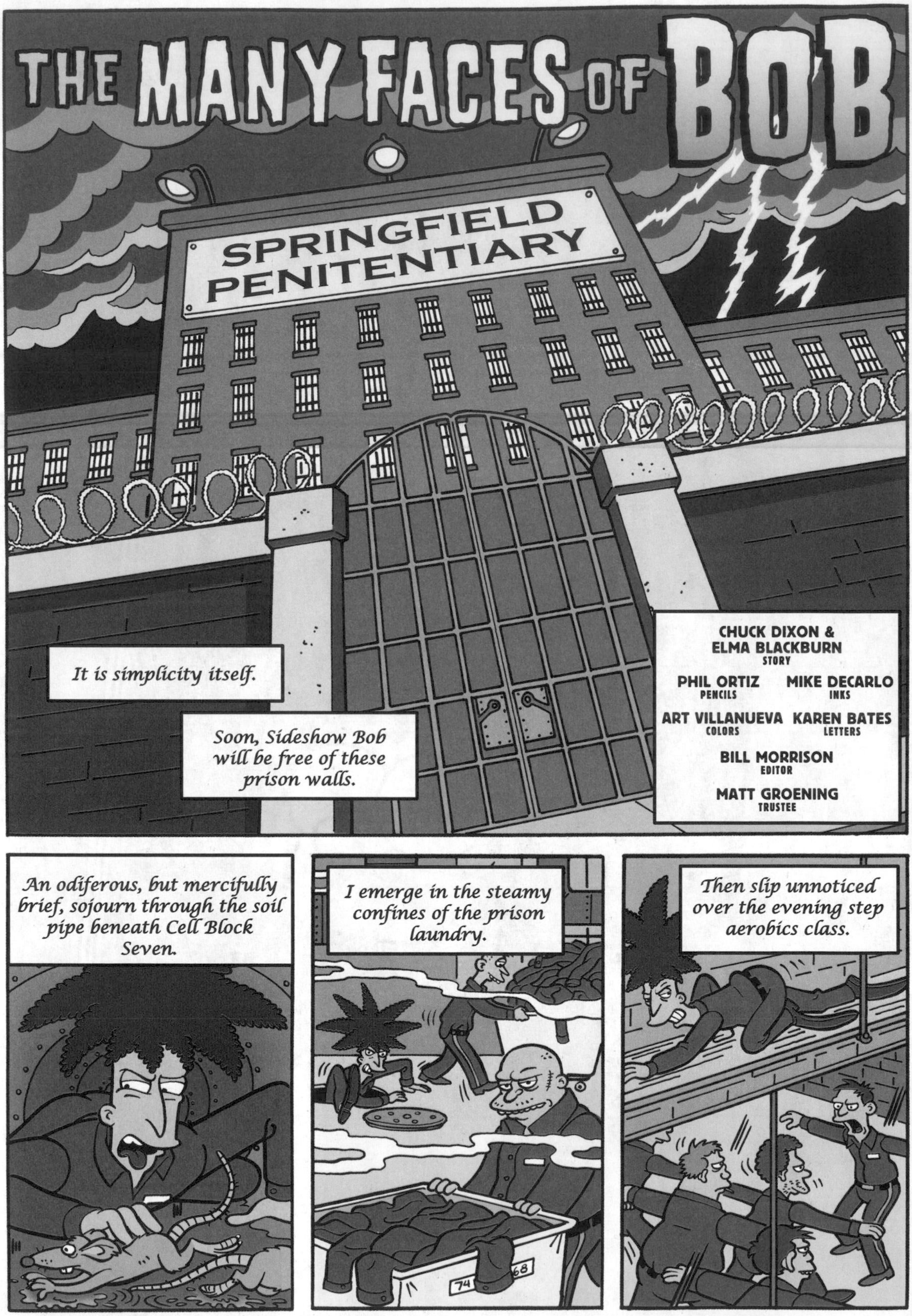
THE MANY FACES OF BOB
SPRINGFIELD PENITENTIARY
It is simplicity itself.
Soon, Sideshow Bob will be free of these prison walls.
CHUCK DIXON & ELMA BLACKBURN
STORY
PHIL ORTIZ
PENCILS
MIKE DECARLO
INKS
ART VILLANUEVA
COLORS
KAREN BATES
LETTERS
BILL MORRISON
EDITOR
MATT GROENING
TRUSTEE
An odiferous, but mercifully brief, sojourn through the soil pipe beneath Cell Block Seven.
I emerge in the steamy confines of the prison laundry.
74
68
Then slip unnoticed over the evening step aerobics class.

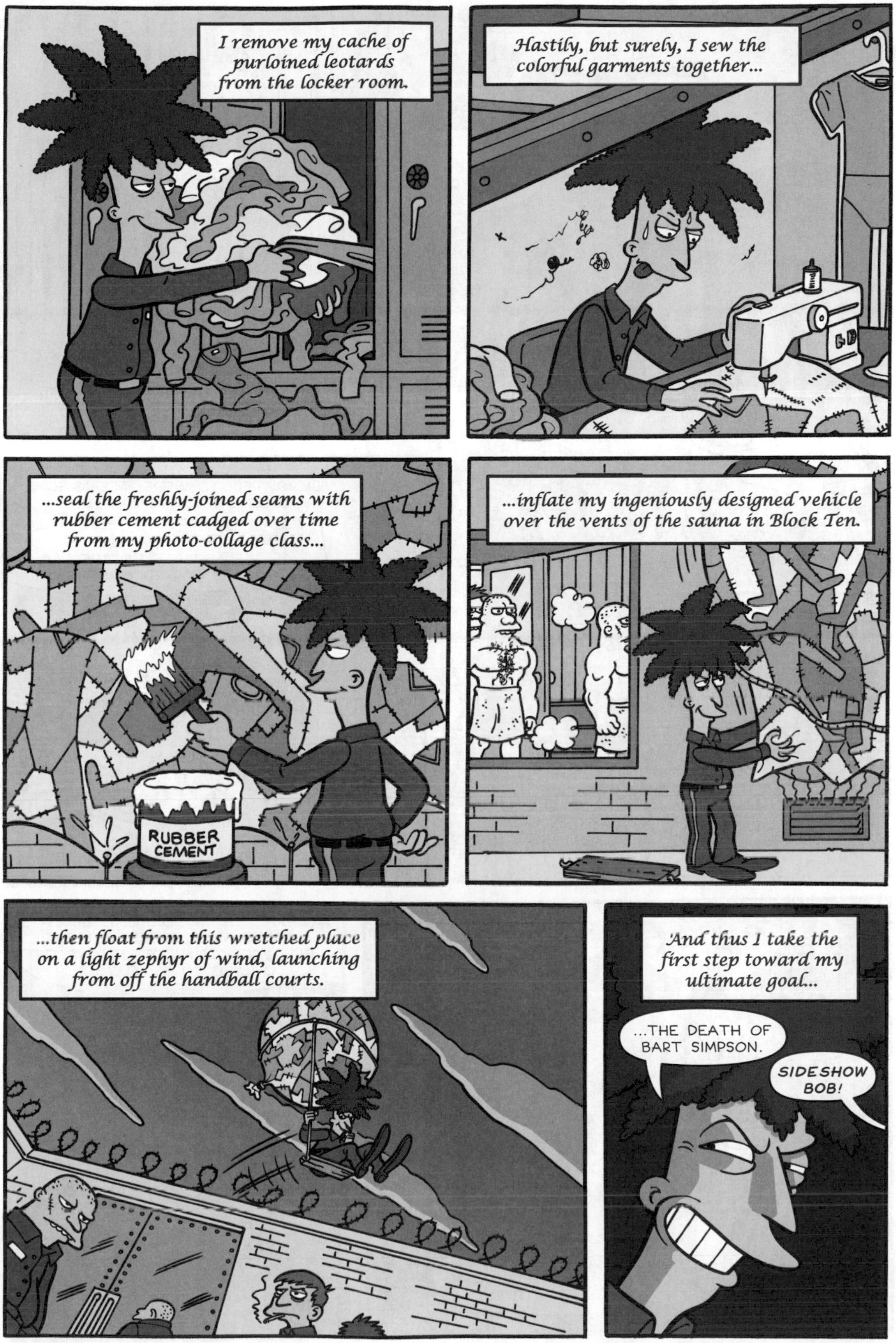
I remove my cache of purloined leotards from the locker room.
Hastily, but surely, I sew the colorful garments together...
...seal the freshly-joined seams with rubber cement cadged over time from my photo-collage class...
RUBBER CEMENT
...inflate my ingeniously designed vehicle over the vents of the sauna in Block Ten.
...then float from this wretched place on a light zephyr of wind, launching from off the handball courts.
And thus I take the first step toward my ultimate goal...
...THE DEATH OF BART SIMPSON.
SIDESHOW BOB!

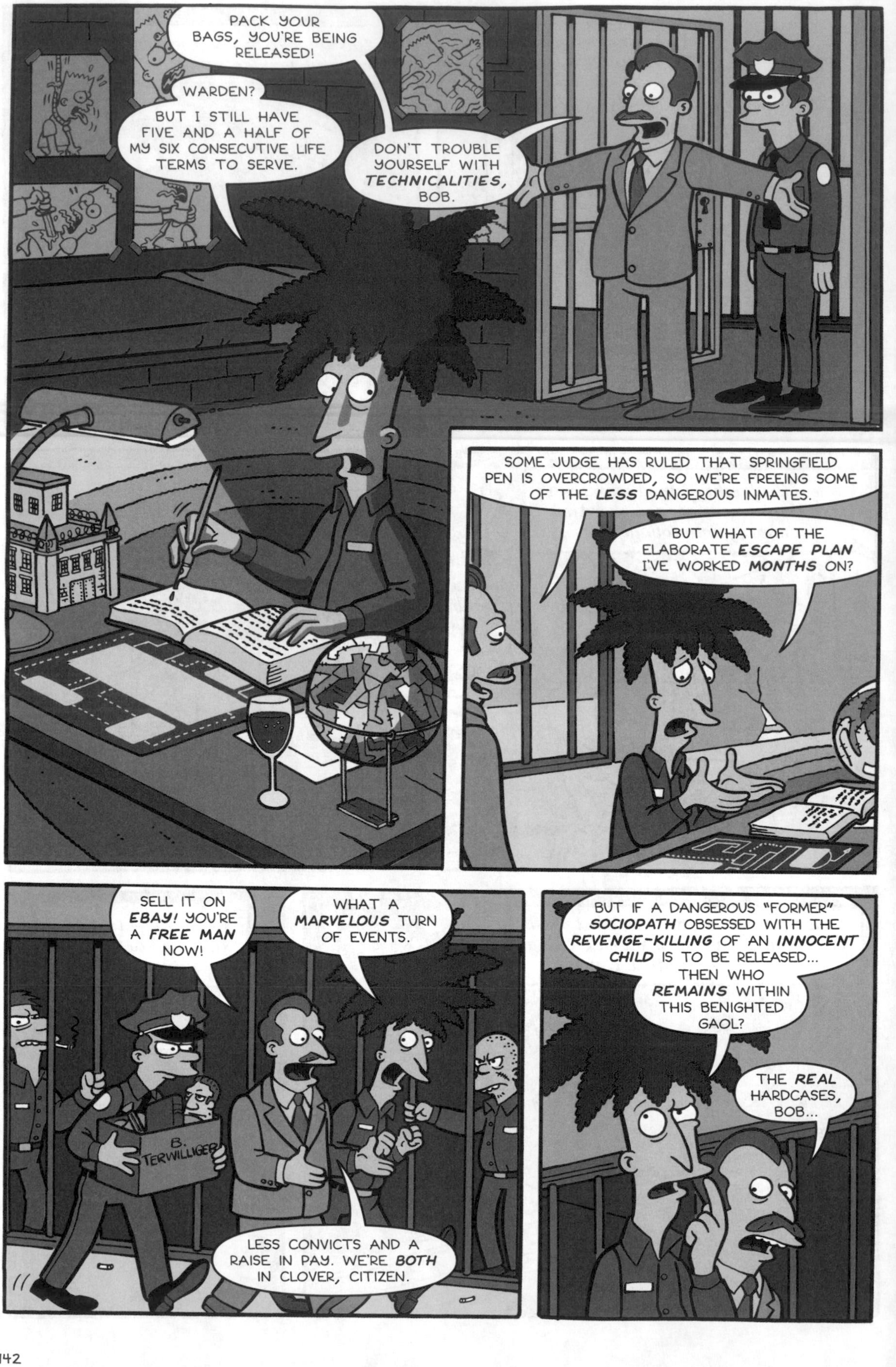
PACK YOUR BAGS, YOU'RE BEING RELEASED!
WARDEN?
BUT I STILL HAVE FIVE AND A HALF OF MY SIX CONSECUTIVE LIFE TERMS TO SERVE.
DON'T TROUBLE YOURSELF WITH TECHNICALITIES, BOB.
SOME JUDGE HAS RULED THAT SPRINGFIELD PEN IS OVERCROWDED, SO WE'RE FREEING SOME OF THE LESS DANGEROUS INMATES.
BUT WHAT OF THE ELABORATE ESCAPE PLAN I'VE WORKED MONTHS ON?
SELL IT ON EBAY! YOU'RE A FREE MAN NOW!
WHAT A MARVELOUS TURN OF EVENTS.
B. TERWILLIGER
LESS CONVICTS AND A RAISE IN PAY. WE'RE BOTH IN CLOVER, CITIZEN.
BUT IF A DANGEROUS "FORMER" SOCIOPATH OBSESSED WITH THE REVENGE-KILLING OF AN INNOCENT CHILD IS TO BE RELEASED... THEN WHO REMAINS WITHIN THIS BENIGHTED GAOL?
THE REAL HARDCASES, BOB...

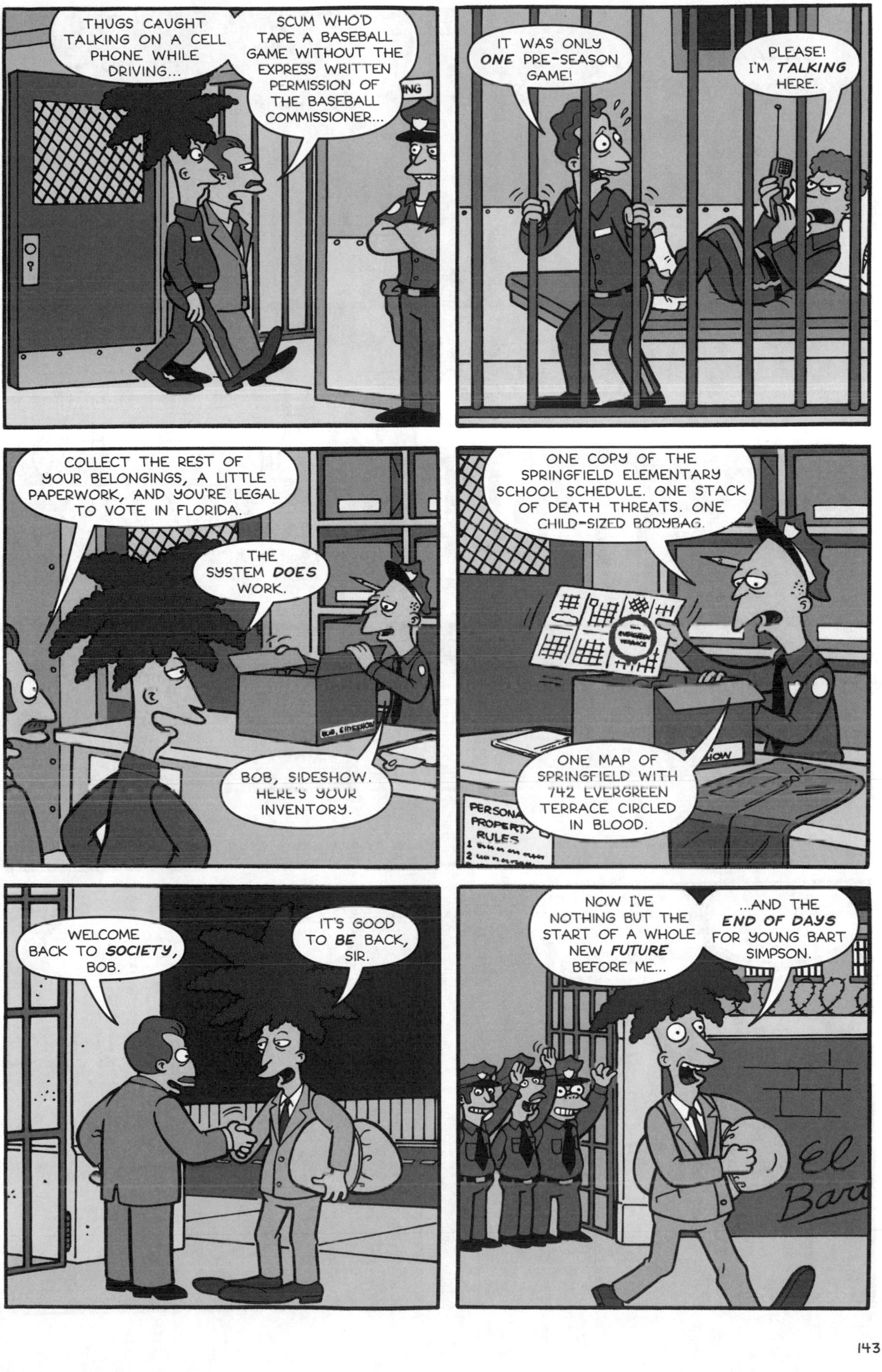
THUGS CAUGHT TALKING ON A CELL PHONE WHILE DRIVING...
SCUM WHO'D TAPE A BASEBALL GAME WITHOUT THE EXPRESS WRITTEN PERMISSION OF THE BASEBALL COMMISSIONER...
IT WAS ONLY ONE PRE-SEASON GAME!
PLEASE! I'M TALKING HERE.
COLLECT THE REST OF YOUR BELONGINGS, A LITTLE PAPERWORK, AND YOU'RE LEGAL TO VOTE IN FLORIDA.
THE SYSTEM DOES WORK.
BOB, SIDESHOW
BOB, SIDESHOW. HERE'S YOUR INVENTORY.
ONE COPY OF THE SPRINGFIELD ELEMENTARY SCHOOL SCHEDULE. ONE STACK OF DEATH THREATS. ONE CHILD-SIZED BODYBAG.
ONE MAP OF SPRINGFIELD WITH 742 EVERGREEN TERRACE CIRCLED IN BLOOD.
PERSONAL PROPERTY RULES
WELCOME BACK TO SOCIETY, BOB.
IT'S GOOD TO BE BACK, SIR.
NOW I'VE NOTHING BUT THE START OF A WHOLE NEW FUTURE BEFORE ME...
...AND THE END OF DAYS FOR YOUNG BART SIMPSON.
El Bart

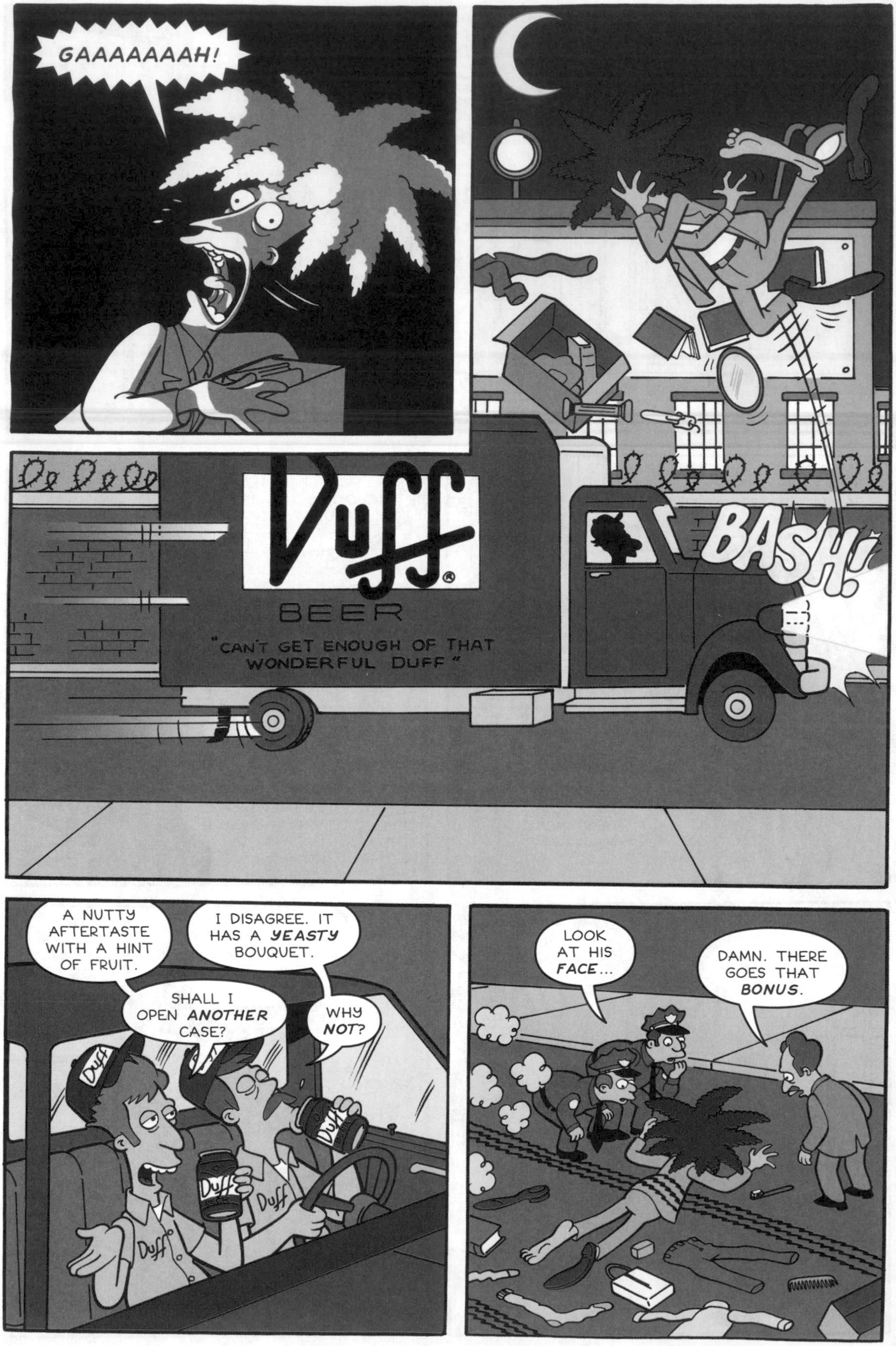
GAAAAAAAH!
Duff®
BEER
"CAN'T GET ENOUGH OF THAT WONDERFUL DUFF"
BASH!
A NUTTY AFTERTASTE WITH A HINT OF FRUIT.
I DISAGREE. IT HAS A YEASTY BOUQUET.
SHALL I OPEN ANOTHER CASE?
WHY NOT?
LOOK AT HIS FACE...
DAMN. THERE GOES THAT BONUS.

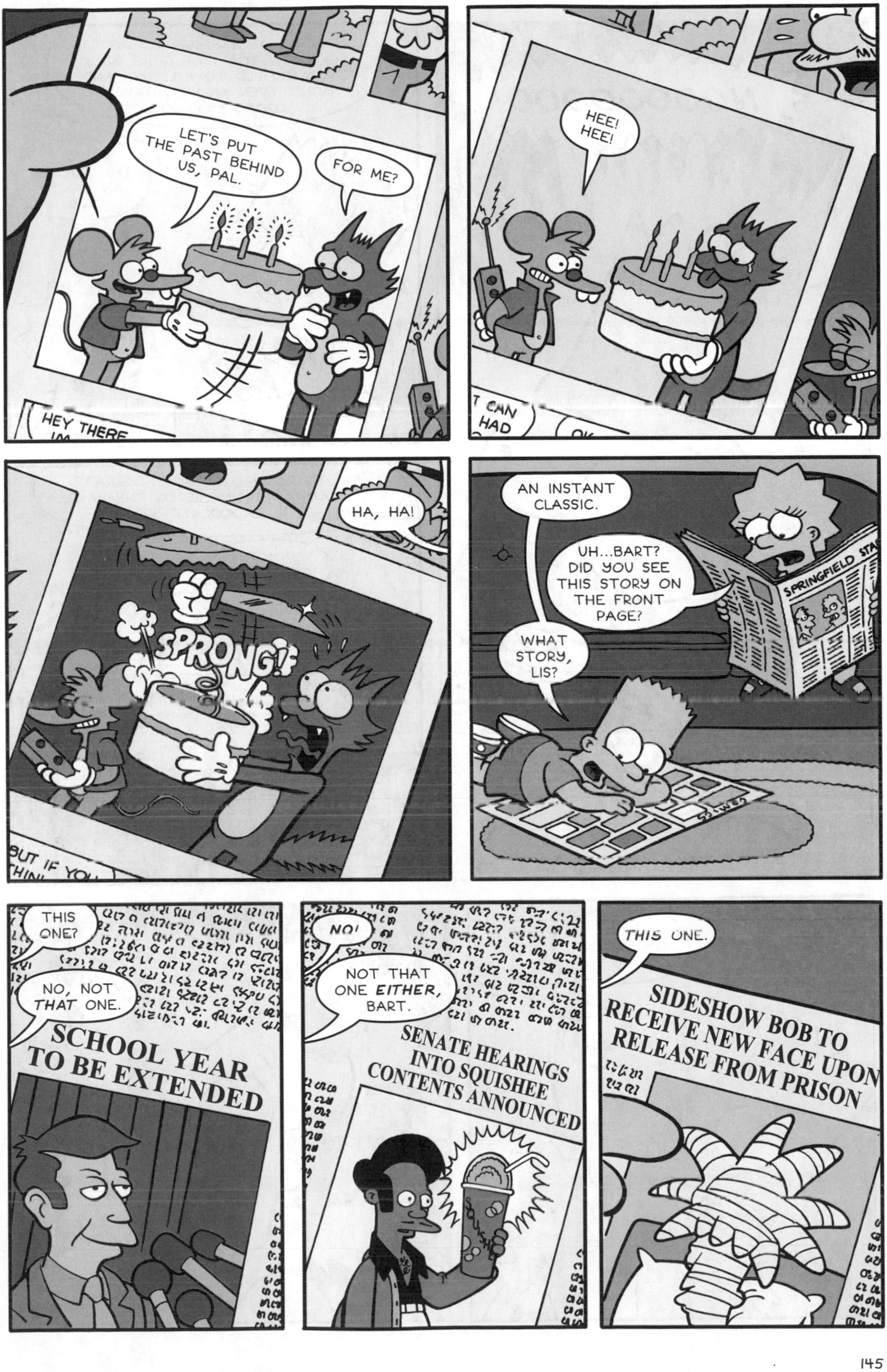

LET'S PUT THE PAST BEHIND US, PAL.
FOR ME?
HEY THERE
HEE! HEE!
T CAN HAD
HA, HA!
SPRONG!
BUT IF YOU THIN
AN INSTANT CLASSIC.
UH...BART? DID YOU SEE THIS STORY ON THE FRONT PAGE?
SPRINGFIELD STA
WHAT STORY, LIS?
THIS ONE?
NO, NOT THAT ONE.
SCHOOL YEAR TO BE EXTENDED
NO!
NOT THAT ONE EITHER, BART.
SENATE HEARINGS INTO SQUISHEE CONTENTS ANNOUNCED
SQUISHEE
THIS ONE.
SIDESHOW BOB TO RECEIVE NEW FACE UPON RELEASE FROM PRISON

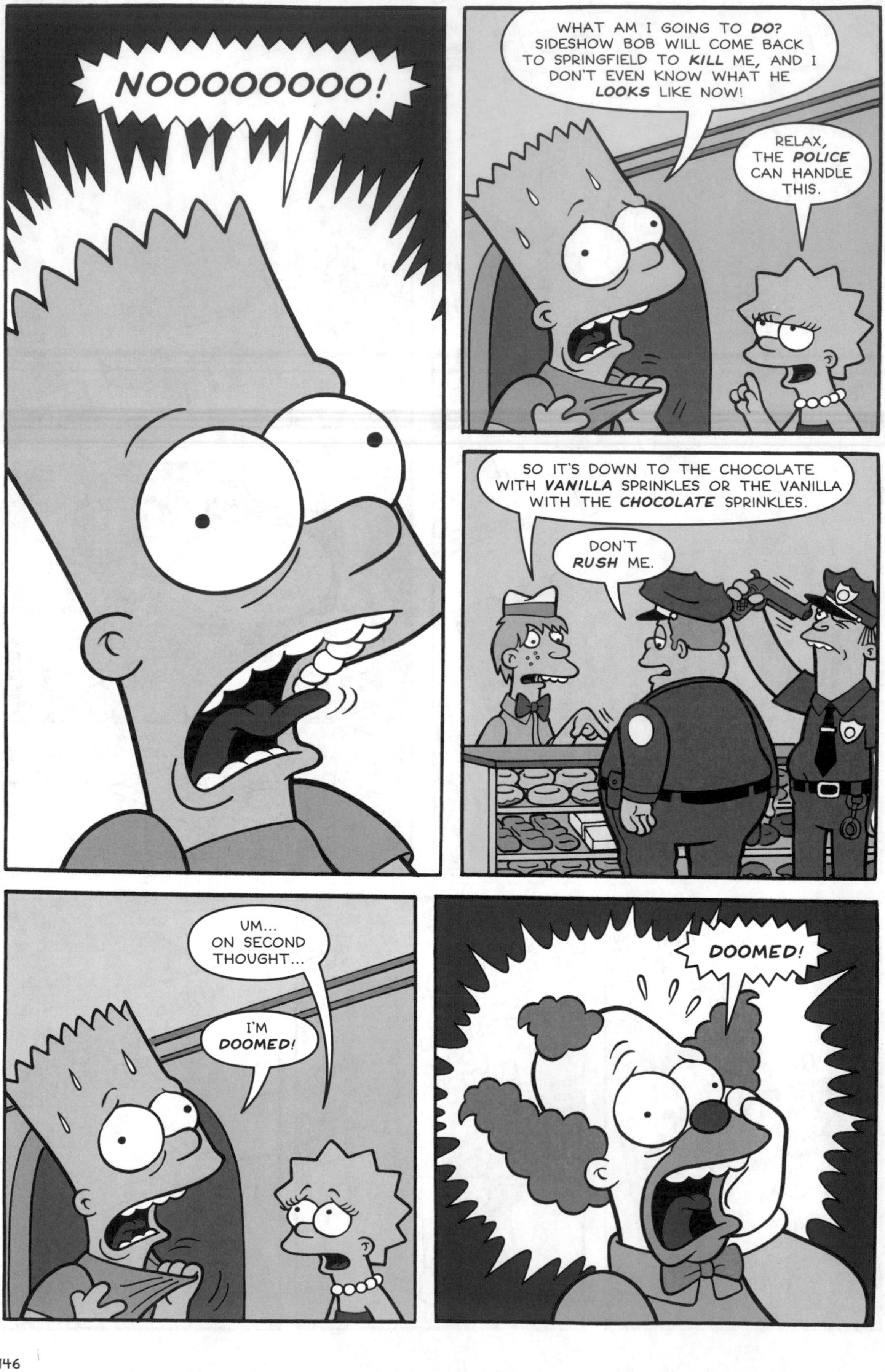
NOOOOOOOO!
WHAT AM I GOING TO DO? SIDESHOW BOB WILL COME BACK TO SPRINGFIELD TO KILL ME, AND I DON'T EVEN KNOW WHAT HE LOOKS LIKE NOW!
RELAX, THE POLICE CAN HANDLE THIS.
SO IT'S DOWN TO THE CHOCOLATE WITH VANILLA SPRINKLES OR THE VANILLA WITH THE CHOCOLATE SPRINKLES.
DON'T RUSH ME.
UM... ON SECOND THOUGHT...
I'M DOOMED!
DOOMED!

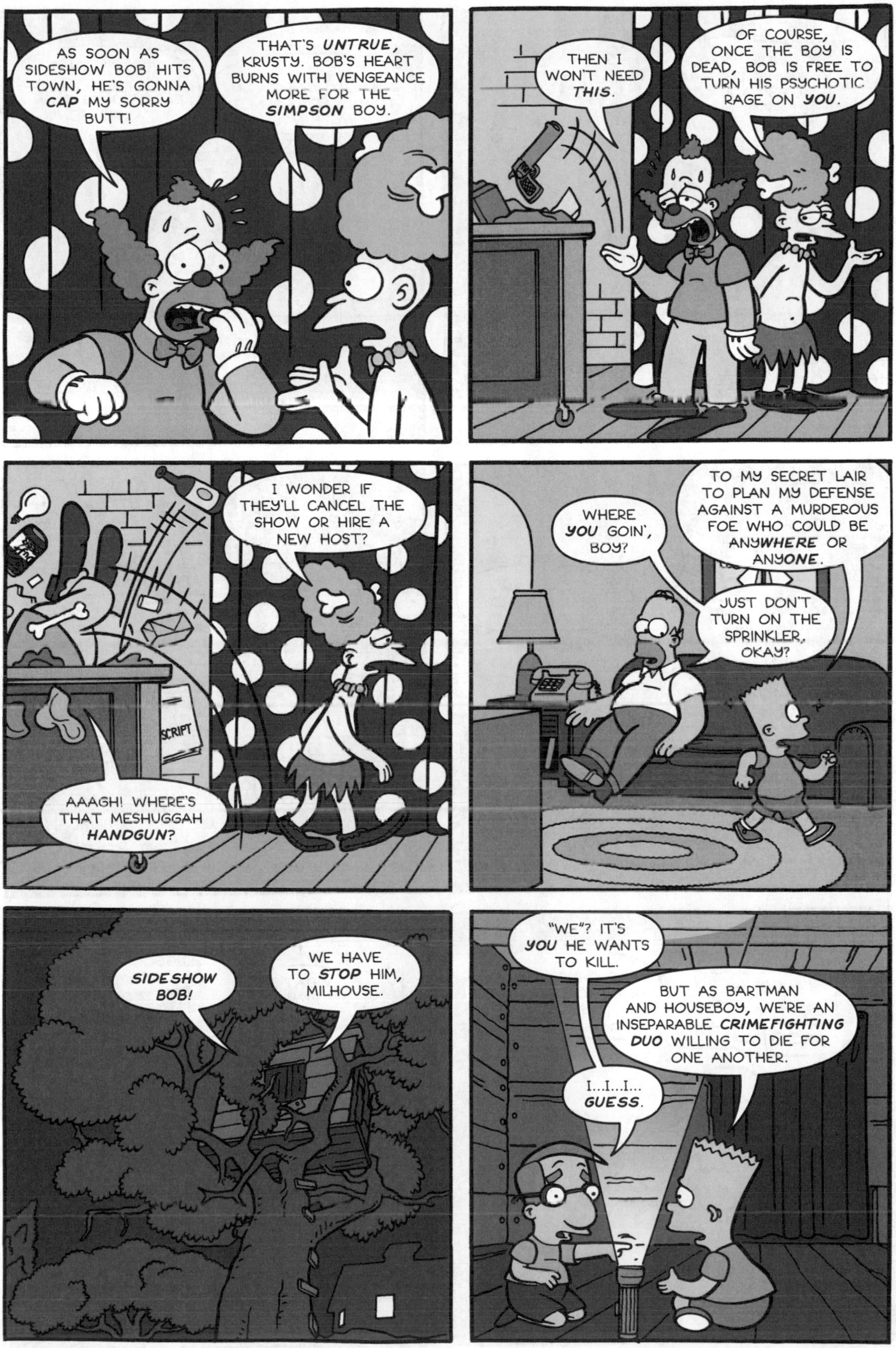
AS SOON AS SIDESHOW BOB HITS TOWN, HE'S GONNA CAP MY SORRY BUTT!
THAT'S UNTRUE, KRUSTY. BOB'S HEART BURNS WITH VENGEANCE MORE FOR THE SIMPSON BOY.
THEN I WON'T NEED THIS.
OF COURSE, ONCE THE BOY IS DEAD, BOB IS FREE TO TURN HIS PSYCHOTIC RAGE ON YOU.
I WONDER IF THEY'LL CANCEL THE SHOW OR HIRE A NEW HOST?
SCRIPT
AAAGH! WHERE'S THAT MESHUGGAH HANDGUN?
WHERE YOU GOIN', BOY?
TO MY SECRET LAIR TO PLAN MY DEFENSE AGAINST A MURDEROUS FOE WHO COULD BE ANYWHERE OR ANYONE.
JUST DON'T TURN ON THE SPRINKLER, OKAY?
SIDESHOW BOB!
WE HAVE TO STOP HIM, MILHOUSE.
"WE"? IT'S YOU HE WANTS TO KILL.
BUT AS BARTMAN AND HOUSEBOY, WE'RE AN INSEPARABLE CRIMEFIGHTING DUO WILLING TO DIE FOR ONE ANOTHER.
I...I...I... GUESS.

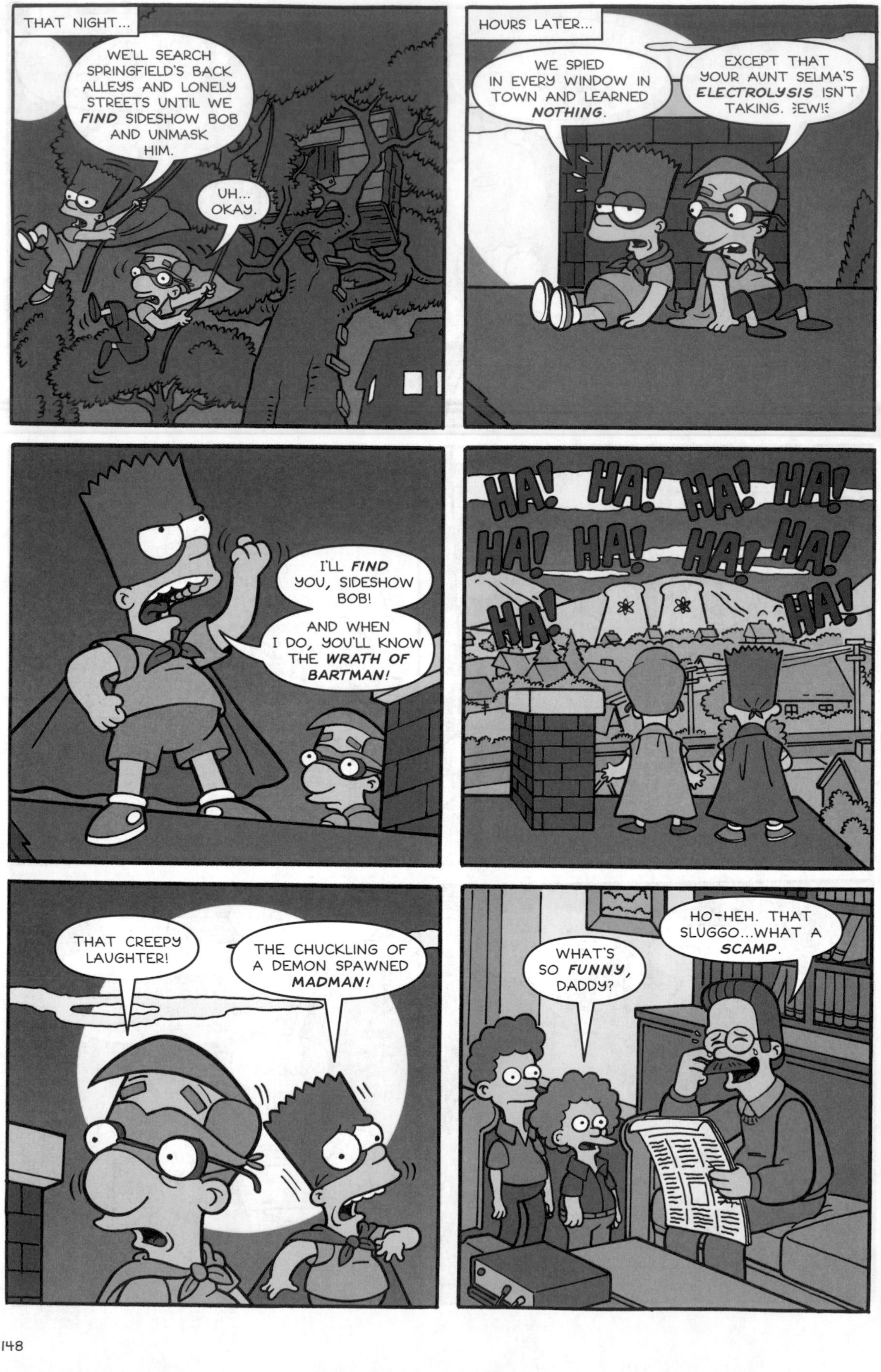
THAT NIGHT...
WE'LL SEARCH SPRINGFIELD'S BACK ALLEYS AND LONELY STREETS UNTIL WE FIND SIDESHOW BOB AND UNMASK HIM.
UH... OKAY.
HOURS LATER...
WE SPIED IN EVERY WINDOW IN TOWN AND LEARNED NOTHING.
EXCEPT THAT YOUR AUNT SELMA'S ELECTROLYSIS ISN'T TAKING. EW!
I'LL FIND YOU, SIDESHOW BOB!
AND WHEN I DO, YOU'LL KNOW THE WRATH OF BARTMAN!
HA! HA! HA! HA! HA! HA! HA! HA! HA! HA!
THAT CREEPY LAUGHTER!
THE CHUCKLING OF A DEMON SPAWNED MADMAN!
WHAT'S SO FUNNY, DADDY?
HO-HEH. THAT SLUGGO...WHAT A SCAMP.

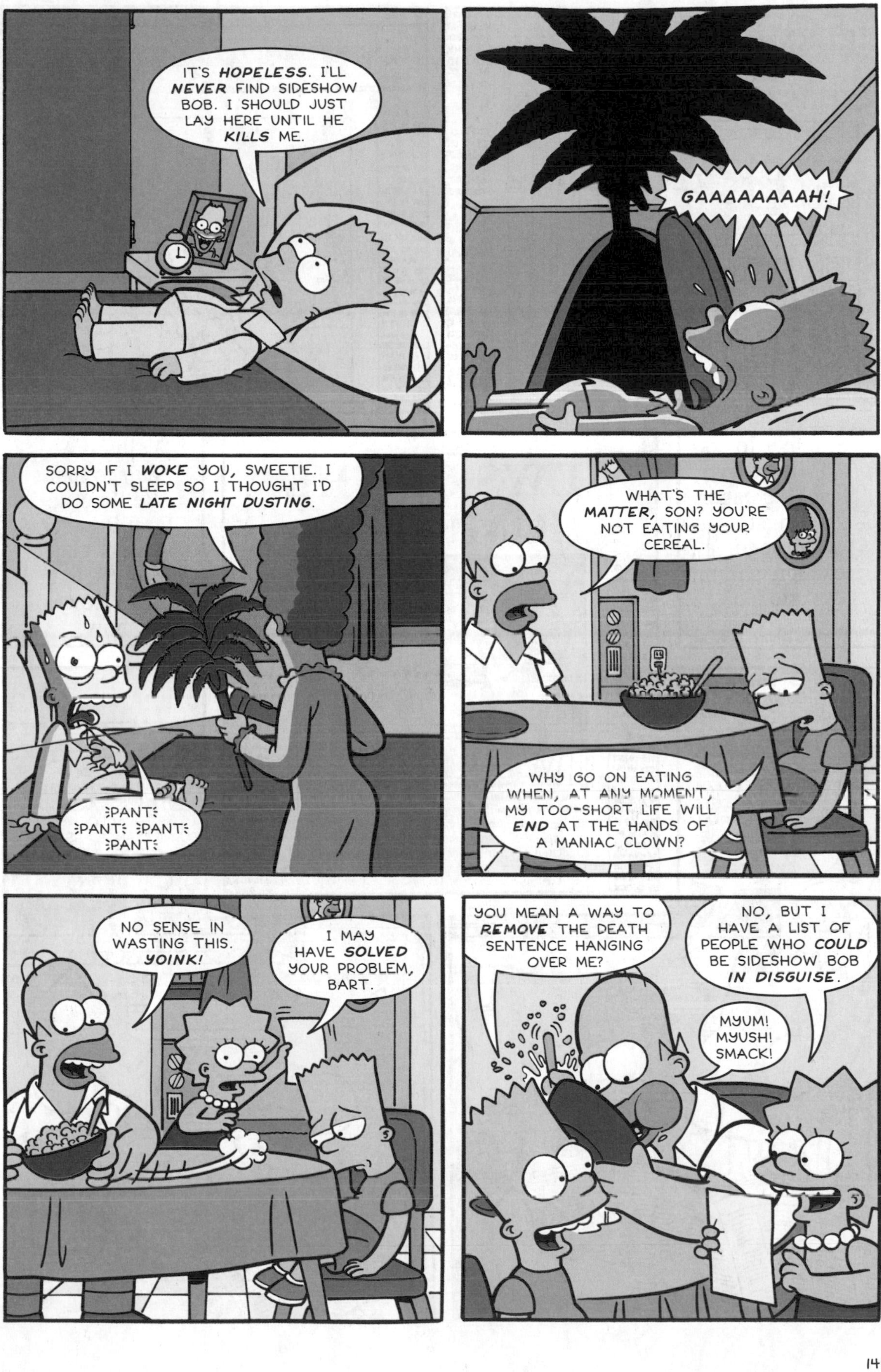
IT'S HOPELESS. I'LL NEVER FIND SIDESHOW BOB. I SHOULD JUST LAY HERE UNTIL HE KILLS ME.
GAAAAAAAAH!
SORRY IF I WOKE YOU, SWEETIE. I COULDN'T SLEEP SO I THOUGHT I'D DO SOME LATE NIGHT DUSTING.
PANT PANT PANT PANT
WHAT'S THE MATTER, SON? YOU'RE NOT EATING YOUR CEREAL.
WHY GO ON EATING WHEN, AT ANY MOMENT, MY TOO-SHORT LIFE WILL END AT THE HANDS OF A MANIAC CLOWN?
NO SENSE IN WASTING THIS. YOINK!
I MAY HAVE SOLVED YOUR PROBLEM, BART.
YOU MEAN A WAY TO REMOVE THE DEATH SENTENCE HANGING OVER ME?
NO, BUT I HAVE A LIST OF PEOPLE WHO COULD BE SIDESHOW BOB IN DISGUISE.
MYUM! MYUSH! SMACK!

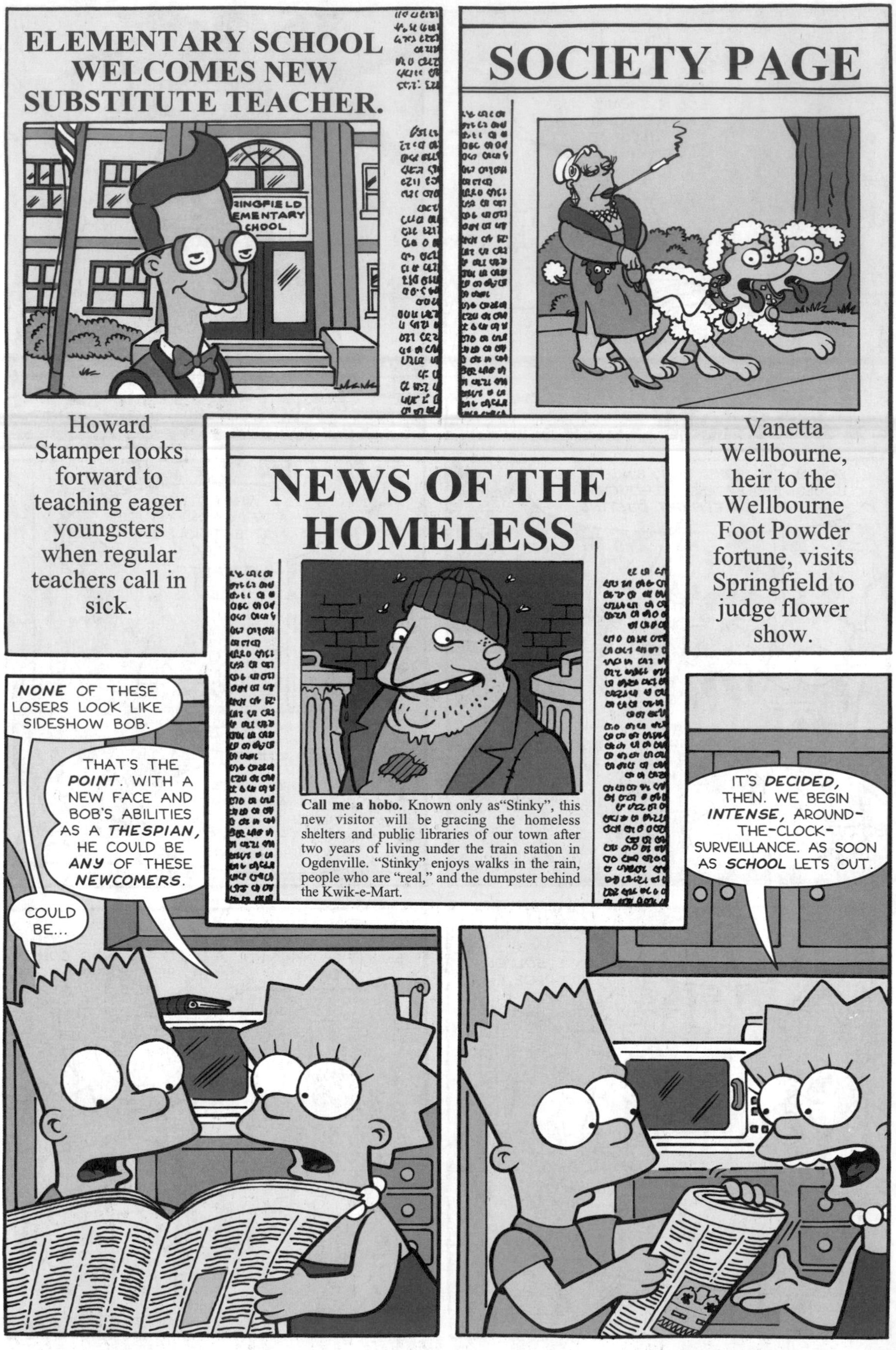

ELEMENTARY SCHOOL WELCOMES NEW SUBSTITUTE TEACHER.
SPRINGFIELD ELEMENTARY SCHOOL
Howard Stamper looks forward to teaching eager youngsters when regular teachers call in sick.
SOCIETY PAGE
Vanetta Wellbourne, heir to the Wellbourne Foot Powder fortune, visits Springfield to judge flower show.
NEWS OF THE HOMELESS
Call me a hobo. Known only as "Stinky", this new visitor will be gracing the homeless shelters and public libraries of our town after two years of living under the train station in Ogdenville. "Stinky" enjoys walks in the rain, people who are "real," and the dumpster behind the Kwik-e-Mart.
NONE OF THESE LOSERS LOOK LIKE SIDESHOW BOB.
THAT'S THE POINT. WITH A NEW FACE AND BOB'S ABILITIES AS A THESPIAN, HE COULD BE ANY OF THESE NEWCOMERS.
COULD BE...
IT'S DECIDED, THEN. WE BEGIN INTENSE, AROUND-THE-CLOCK-SURVEILLANCE. AS SOON AS SCHOOL LETS OUT.

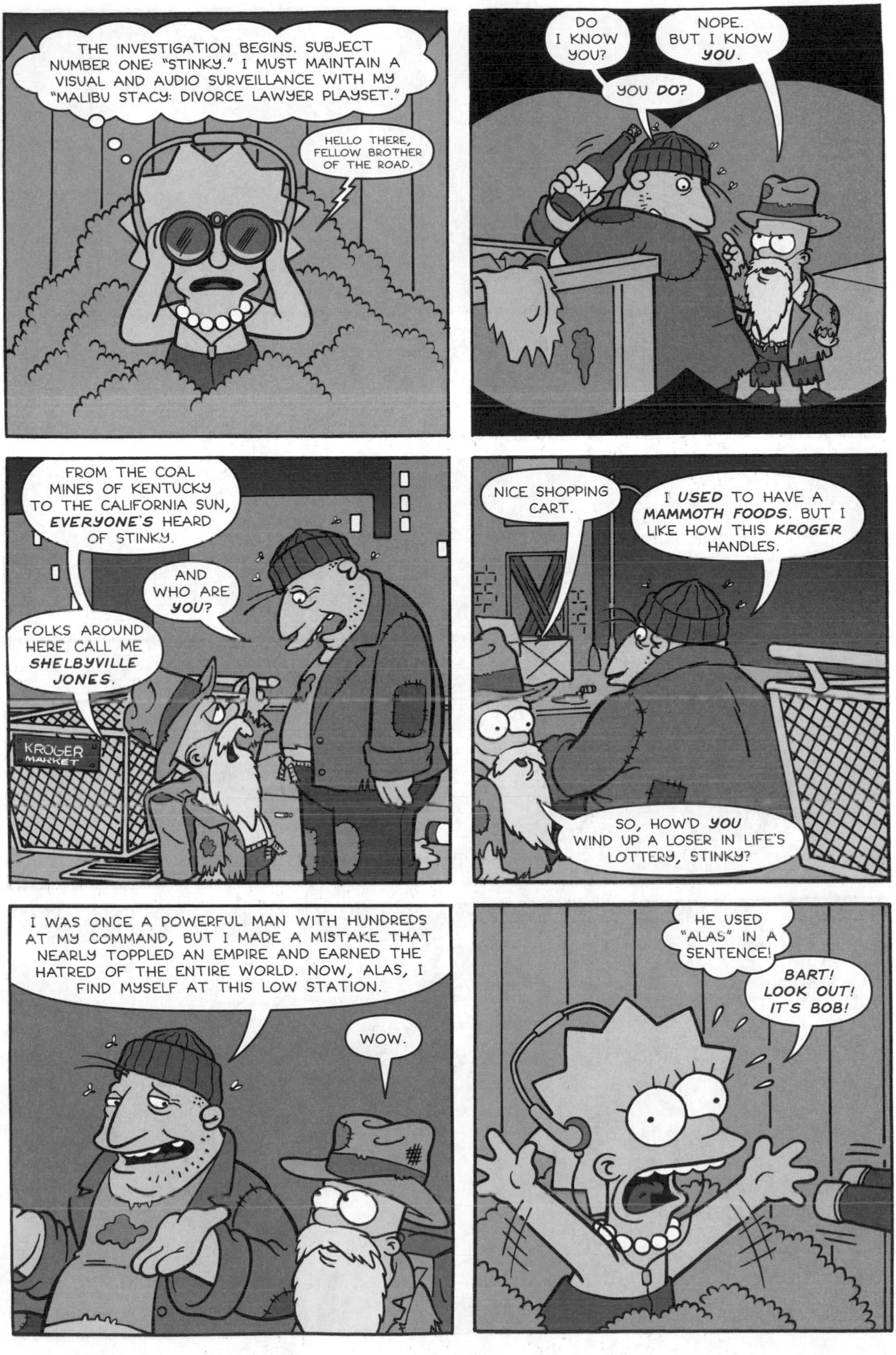
THE INVESTIGATION BEGINS. SUBJECT NUMBER ONE: "STINKY." I MUST MAINTAIN A VISUAL AND AUDIO SURVEILLANCE WITH MY "MALIBU STACY: DIVORCE LAWYER PLAYSET."
HELLO THERE, FELLOW BROTHER OF THE ROAD.
DO I KNOW YOU?
NOPE. BUT I KNOW YOU.
YOU DO?
FROM THE COAL MINES OF KENTUCKY TO THE CALIFORNIA SUN, EVERYONE'S HEARD OF STINKY.
AND WHO ARE YOU?
FOLKS AROUND HERE CALL ME SHELBYVILLE JONES.
KROGER MARKET
NICE SHOPPING CART.
I USED TO HAVE A MAMMOTH FOODS. BUT I LIKE HOW THIS KROGER HANDLES.
SO, HOW'D YOU WIND UP A LOSER IN LIFE'S LOTTERY, STINKY?
I WAS ONCE A POWERFUL MAN WITH HUNDREDS AT MY COMMAND, BUT I MADE A MISTAKE THAT NEARLY TOPPLED AN EMPIRE AND EARNED THE HATRED OF THE ENTIRE WORLD. NOW, ALAS, I FIND MYSELF AT THIS LOW STATION.
WOW.
HE USED "ALAS" IN A SENTENCE!
BART! LOOK OUT! IT'S BOB!

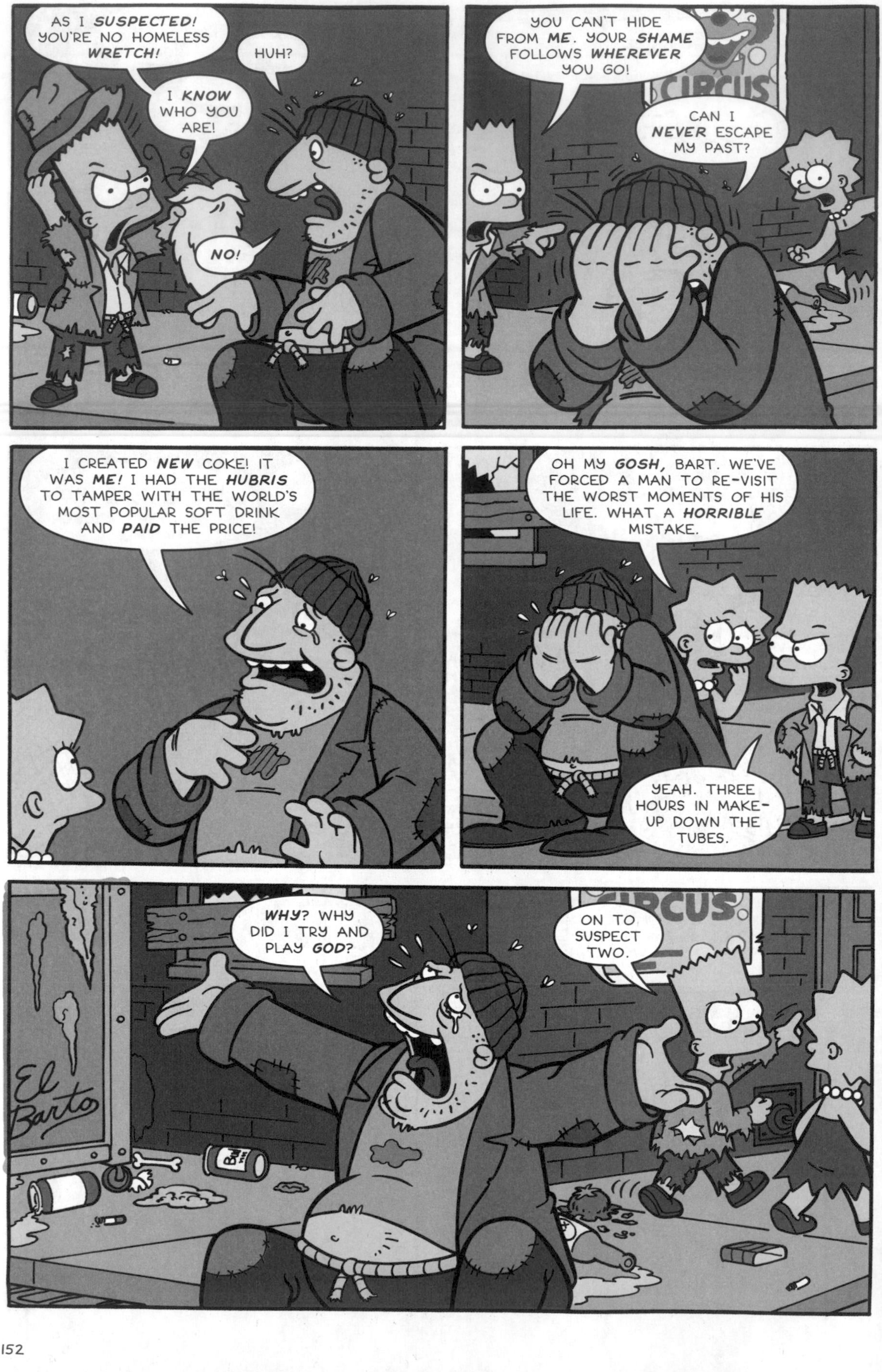
AS I SUSPECTED! YOU'RE NO HOMELESS WRETCH!
HUH?
I KNOW WHO YOU ARE!
NO!
YOU CAN'T HIDE FROM ME. YOUR SHAME FOLLOWS WHEREVER YOU GO!
CIRCUS
CAN I NEVER ESCAPE MY PAST?
I CREATED NEW COKE! IT WAS ME! I HAD THE HUBRIS TO TAMPER WITH THE WORLD'S MOST POPULAR SOFT DRINK AND PAID THE PRICE!
OH MY GOSH, BART. WE'VE FORCED A MAN TO RE-VISIT THE WORST MOMENTS OF HIS LIFE. WHAT A HORRIBLE MISTAKE.
YEAH. THREE HOURS IN MAKE-UP DOWN THE TUBES.
WHY? WHY DID I TRY AND PLAY GOD?
ON TO SUSPECT TWO.
El Barto

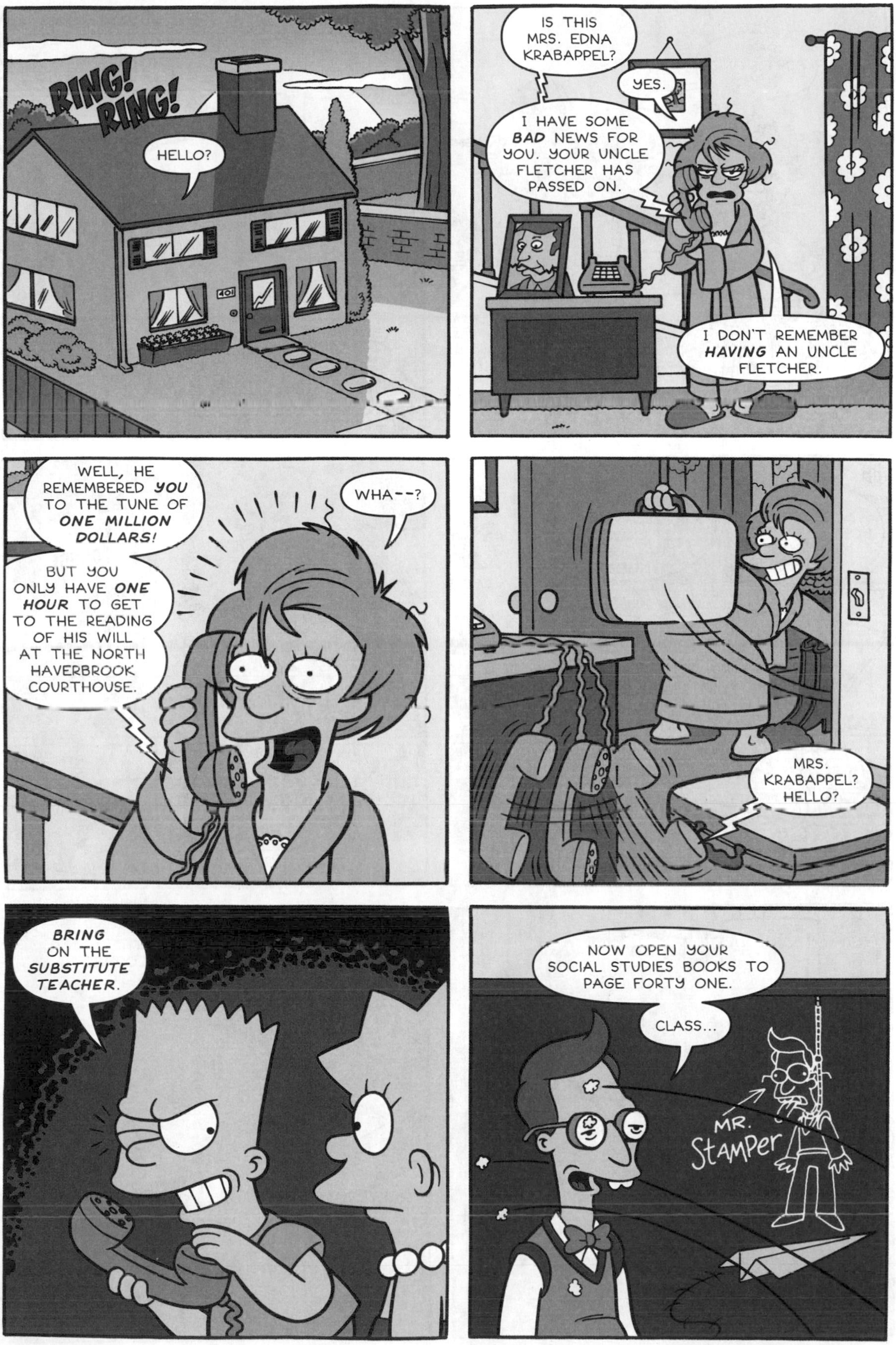
RING! RING!
HELLO?
IS THIS MRS. EDNA KRABAPPEL?
YES.
I HAVE SOME BAD NEWS FOR YOU. YOUR UNCLE FLETCHER HAS PASSED ON.
I DON'T REMEMBER HAVING AN UNCLE FLETCHER.
WELL, HE REMEMBERED YOU TO THE TUNE OF ONE MILLION DOLLARS!
BUT YOU ONLY HAVE ONE HOUR TO GET TO THE READING OF HIS WILL AT THE NORTH HAVERBROOK COURTHOUSE.
WHA--?
MRS. KRABAPPEL? HELLO?
BRING ON THE SUBSTITUTE TEACHER.
NOW OPEN YOUR SOCIAL STUDIES BOOKS TO PAGE FORTY ONE.
CLASS...
MR. STAMPER

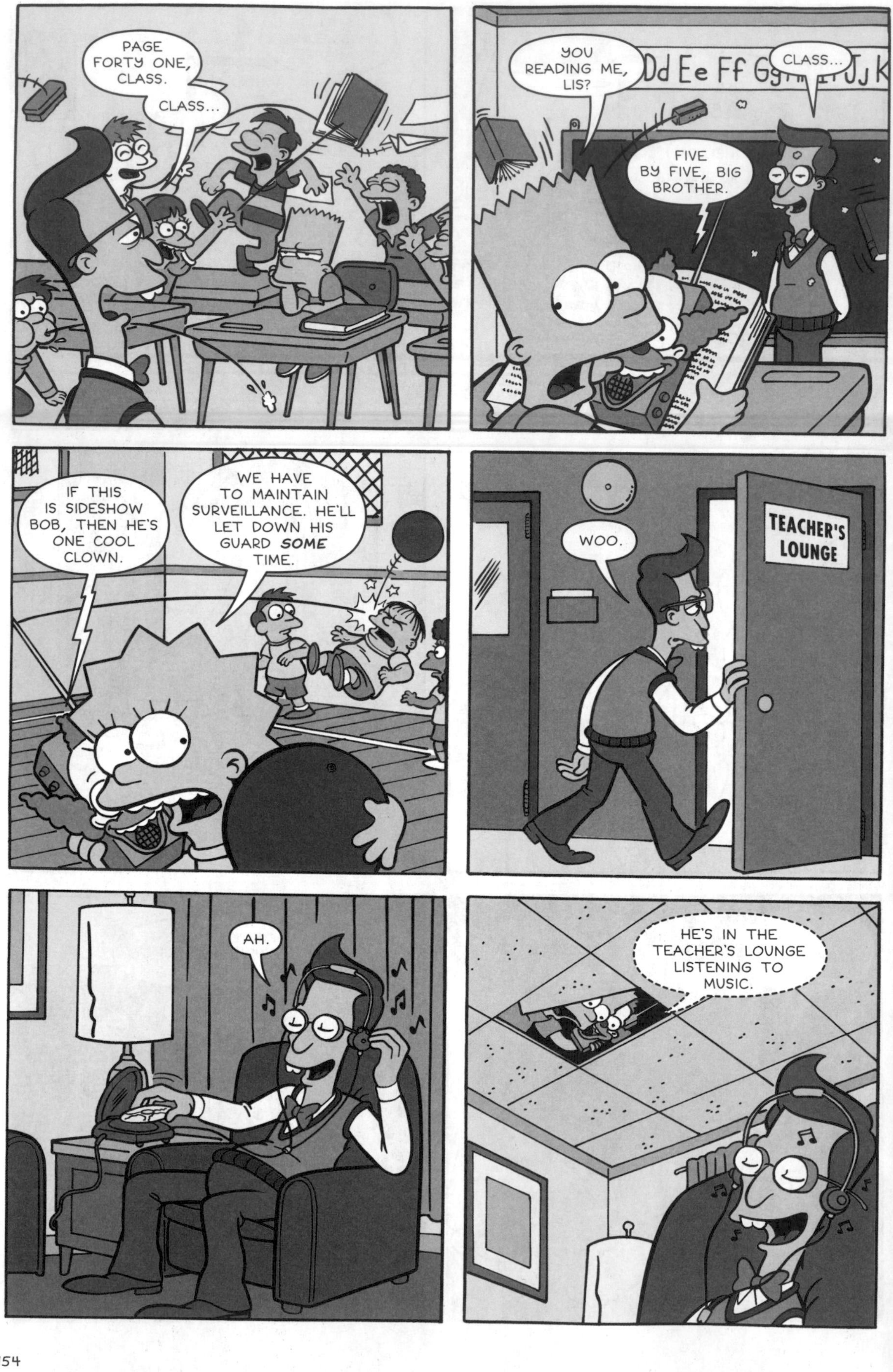
PAGE FORTY ONE, CLASS.
CLASS...
YOU READING ME, LIS?
Dd Ee Ff Gg
CLASS...
FIVE BY FIVE, BIG BROTHER.
IF THIS IS SIDESHOW BOB, THEN HE'S ONE COOL CLOWN.
WE HAVE TO MAINTAIN SURVEILLANCE. HE'LL LET DOWN HIS GUARD *SOME* TIME.
WOO.
TEACHER'S LOUNGE
AH.
HE'S IN THE TEACHER'S LOUNGE LISTENING TO MUSIC.

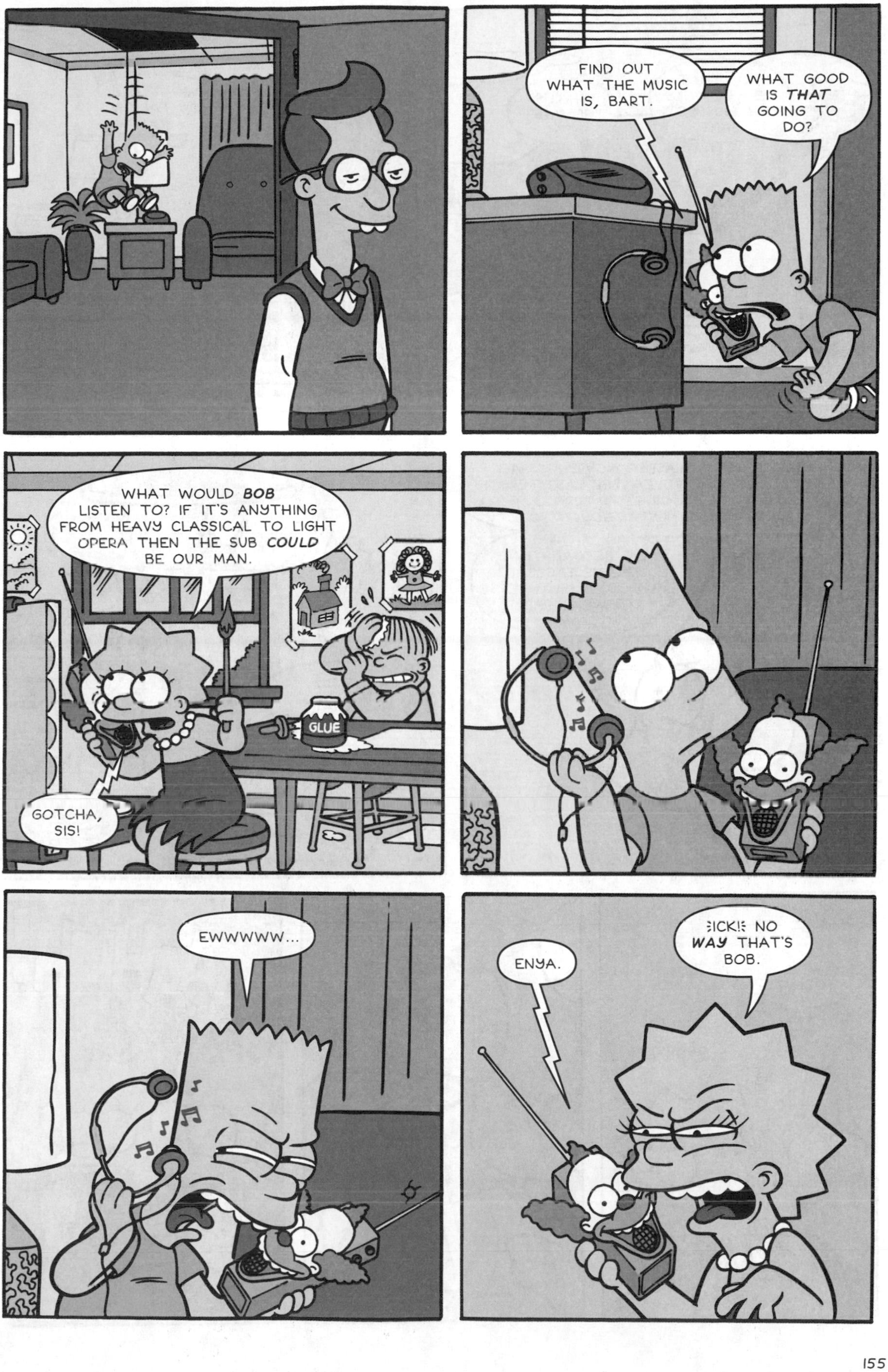
FIND OUT WHAT THE MUSIC IS, BART.
WHAT GOOD IS *THAT* GOING TO DO?
WHAT WOULD *BOB* LISTEN TO? IF IT'S ANYTHING FROM HEAVY CLASSICAL TO LIGHT OPERA THEN THE SUB *COULD* BE OUR MAN.
GLUE
GOTCHA, SIS!
EWWWWW...
ENYA.
ICK! NO *WAY* THAT'S BOB.

SO, THAT LEAVES ONLY *ONE* SUSPECT, BART.

WHAT'S THE *USE*, LISA?

YOU KNOW HOW THESE THINGS WORK.

MY AREA OF EXPERTISE.

WHAT ARE YOU *TALKING* ABOUT?

I'VE SEEN *EVERY* SLASHER MOVIE AND *ALL* THEIR SEQUELS. IT'S *NEVER* THE LAST PERSON ON THE LIST. BOB'S GOING TO TURN OUT TO BE SOMEONE WE NEVER *THOUGHT* OF.

AND *BEFORE* THAT, THE MESSAGES IN BLOOD, MISSING PETS AND WEIRD PHONE CALLS.

RRING!

HELLO?

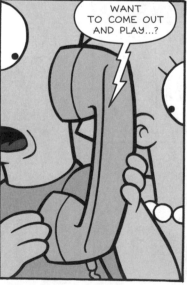

WANT TO COME OUT AND PLAY...?

AAAAHHH!

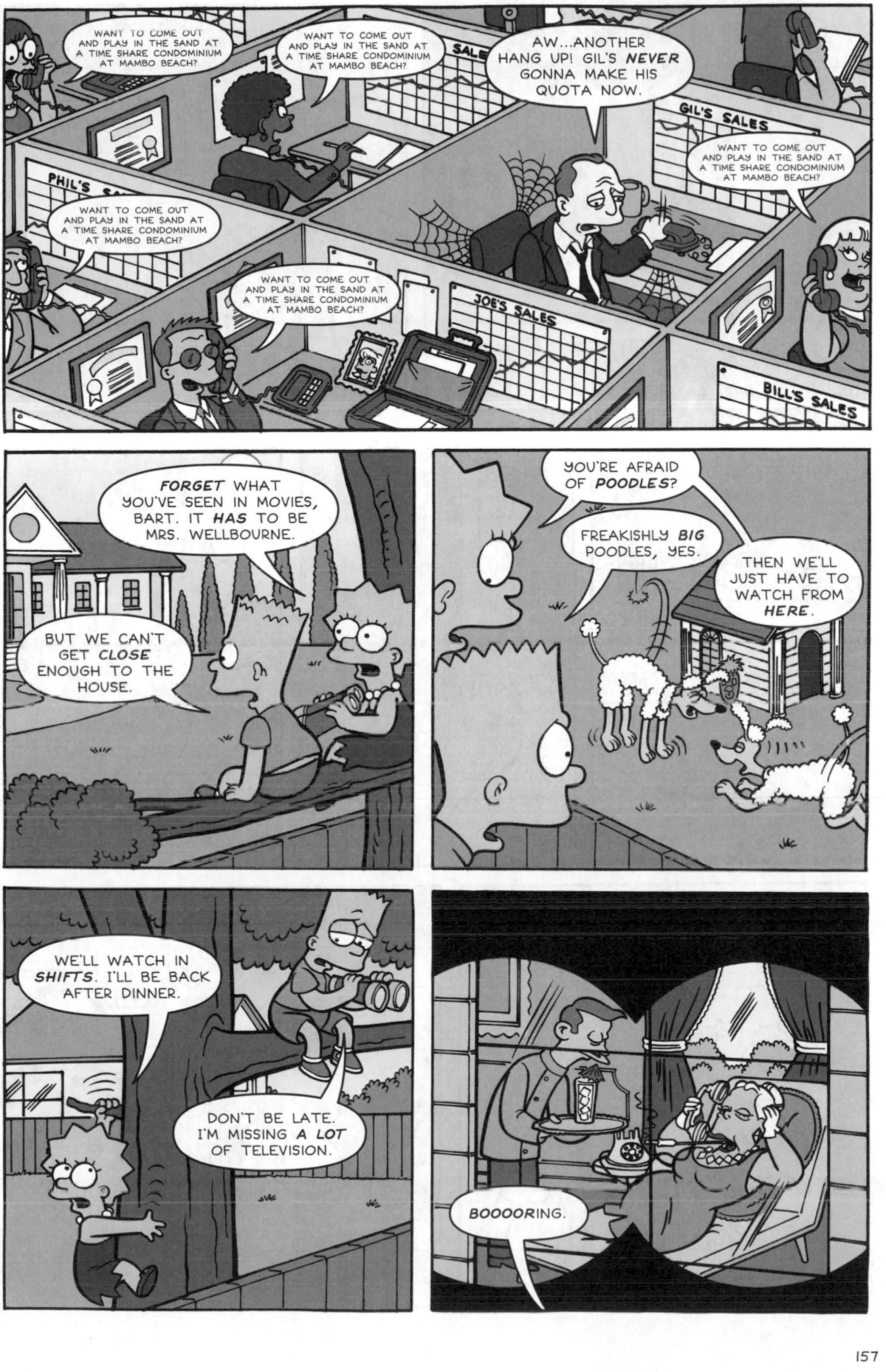
WANT TO COME OUT AND PLAY IN THE SAND AT A TIME SHARE CONDOMINIUM AT MAMBO BEACH?
WANT TO COME OUT AND PLAY IN THE SAND AT A TIME SHARE CONDOMINIUM AT MAMBO BEACH?
AW...ANOTHER HANG UP! GIL'S NEVER GONNA MAKE HIS QUOTA NOW.
GIL'S SALES
WANT TO COME OUT AND PLAY IN THE SAND AT A TIME SHARE CONDOMINIUM AT MAMBO BEACH?
PHIL'S SALES
WANT TO COME OUT AND PLAY IN THE SAND AT A TIME SHARE CONDOMINIUM AT MAMBO BEACH?
WANT TO COME OUT AND PLAY IN THE SAND AT A TIME SHARE CONDOMINIUM AT MAMBO BEACH?
JOE'S SALES
BILL'S SALES
FORGET WHAT YOU'VE SEEN IN MOVIES, BART. IT HAS TO BE MRS. WELLBOURNE.
BUT WE CAN'T GET CLOSE ENOUGH TO THE HOUSE.
YOU'RE AFRAID OF POODLES?
FREAKISHLY BIG POODLES, YES.
THEN WE'LL JUST HAVE TO WATCH FROM HERE.
WE'LL WATCH IN SHIFTS. I'LL BE BACK AFTER DINNER.
DON'T BE LATE. I'M MISSING A LOT OF TELEVISION.
BOOOORING.

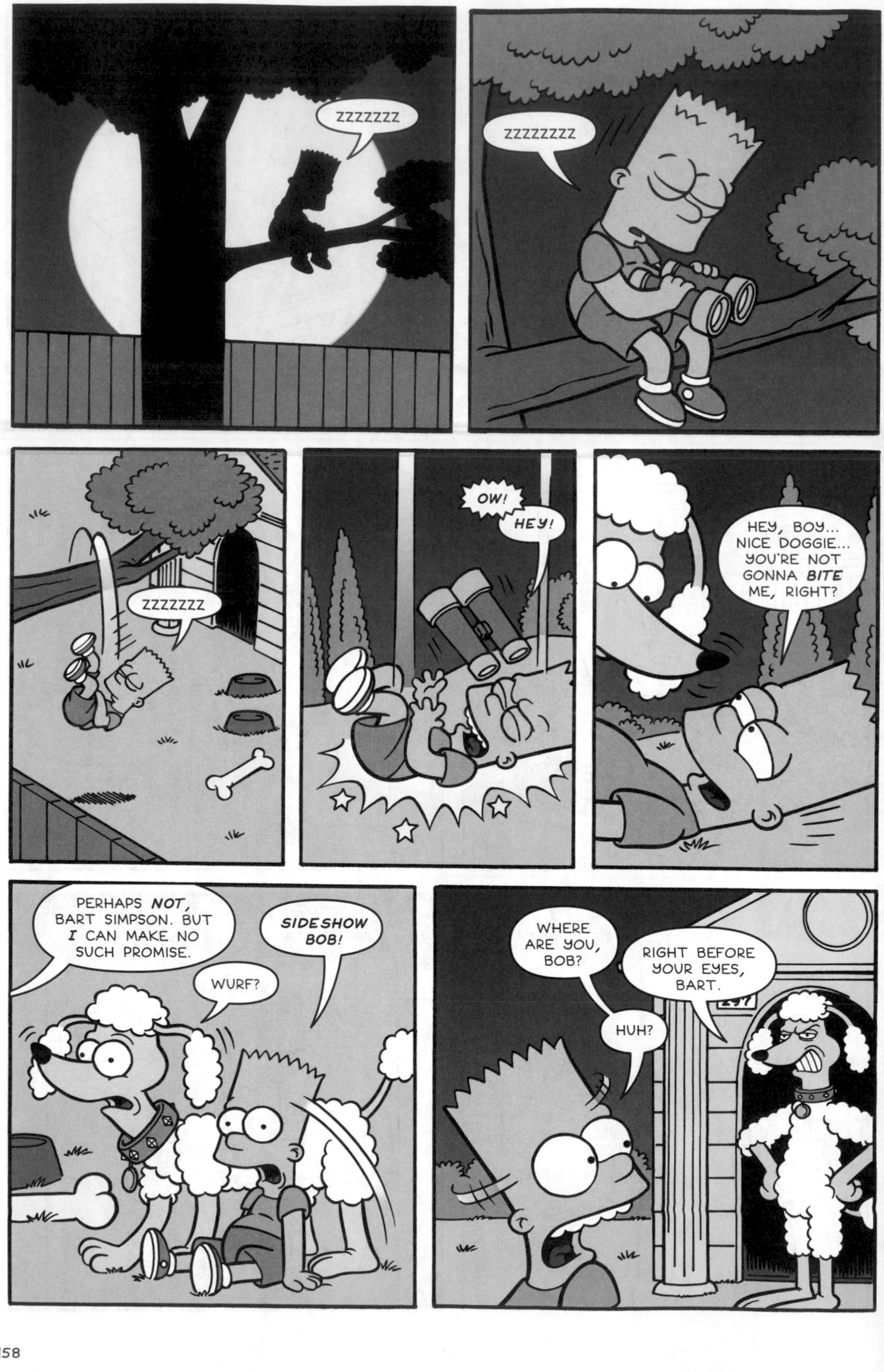

ZZZZZZZ
ZZZZZZZZ
ZZZZZZZ
OW!
HEY!
HEY, BOY... NICE DOGGIE... YOU'RE NOT GONNA *BITE* ME, RIGHT?
PERHAPS *NOT*, BART SIMPSON. BUT *I* CAN MAKE NO SUCH PROMISE.
WURF?
SIDESHOW BOB!
WHERE ARE YOU, BOB?
HUH?
RIGHT BEFORE YOUR EYES, BART.

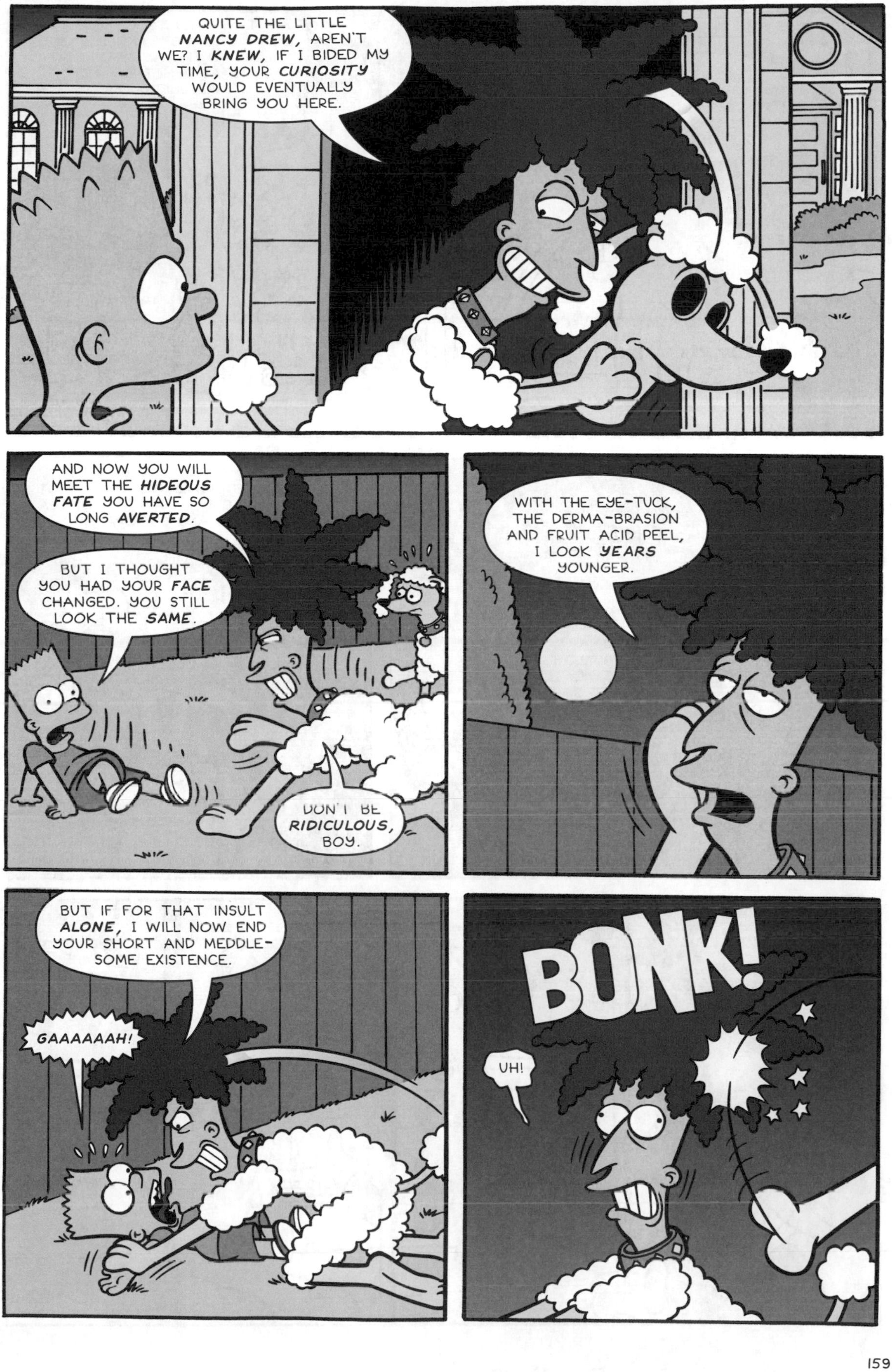

QUITE THE LITTLE NANCY DREW, AREN'T WE? I KNEW, IF I BIDED MY TIME, YOUR CURIOSITY WOULD EVENTUALLY BRING YOU HERE.
AND NOW YOU WILL MEET THE HIDEOUS FATE YOU HAVE SO LONG AVERTED.
BUT I THOUGHT YOU HAD YOUR FACE CHANGED. YOU STILL LOOK THE SAME.
DON'T BE RIDICULOUS, BOY.
WITH THE EYE-TUCK, THE DERMA-BRASION AND FRUIT ACID PEEL, I LOOK YEARS YOUNGER.
BUT IF FOR THAT INSULT ALONE, I WILL NOW END YOUR SHORT AND MEDDLE-SOME EXISTENCE.
GAAAAAAH!
BONK!
UH!

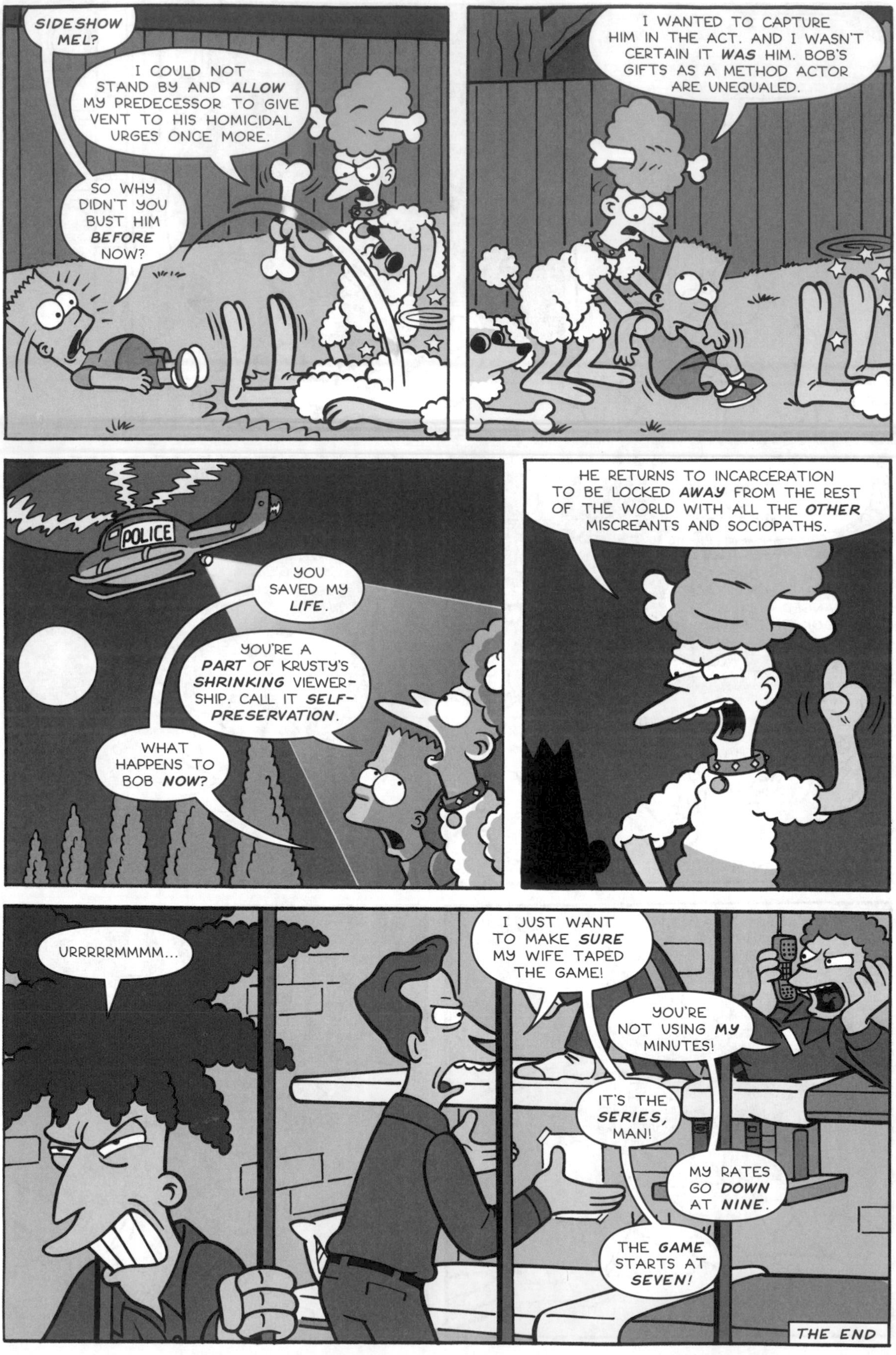
SIDESHOW MEL?
I COULD NOT STAND BY AND ALLOW MY PREDECESSOR TO GIVE VENT TO HIS HOMICIDAL URGES ONCE MORE.
SO WHY DIDN'T YOU BUST HIM BEFORE NOW?
I WANTED TO CAPTURE HIM IN THE ACT. AND I WASN'T CERTAIN IT WAS HIM. BOB'S GIFTS AS A METHOD ACTOR ARE UNEQUALED.
POLICE
YOU SAVED MY LIFE.
YOU'RE A PART OF KRUSTY'S SHRINKING VIEWERSHIP. CALL IT SELF-PRESERVATION.
WHAT HAPPENS TO BOB NOW?
HE RETURNS TO INCARCERATION TO BE LOCKED AWAY FROM THE REST OF THE WORLD WITH ALL THE OTHER MISCREANTS AND SOCIOPATHS.
URRRRRMMMM...
I JUST WANT TO MAKE SURE MY WIFE TAPED THE GAME!
YOU'RE NOT USING MY MINUTES!
IT'S THE SERIES, MAN!
MY RATES GO DOWN AT NINE.
THE GAME STARTS AT SEVEN!
THE END

HOMER VS. THE RACCOON

CRUNCH!

CLATTER!

CLANG!

...MUMBLE...GRUMBLE ...STUPID COCKTAIL WEENIES...WHAT KIND OF DRINK IS THAT?... MUMBLE...GRUMBLE...

TONY DIGEROLAMO	BRIAN ILES	MIKE ROTE	CHRIS UNGAR	KAREN BATES	BILL MORRISON	MATT GROENING
SCRIPT	PENCILS	INKS	COLORS	LETTERS	EDITOR	PEST CONTROLLER

¡YAWN!¡ HOMER, WAKE UP. I THINK THERE'S SOMEONE OUTSIDE.

CLATTER! BANG! CLANG!

MOM, I CAN'T SLEEP. AND I HAVE A BIG MATH TEST TO *FAIL* TOMORROW.

CRUNCH!

CLATTER!

YOUR FATHER'S TAKING CARE OF IT NOW.

HOMER, THAT NOISE IS WAKING UP EVERYONE IN THE HOUSE.

FLANDERS! WHY DON'T YOU GO THROUGH YOUR NEIGHBOR'S TRASH AT A *DECENT HOUR* LIKE *THE REST OF US!* FLANDERS?!

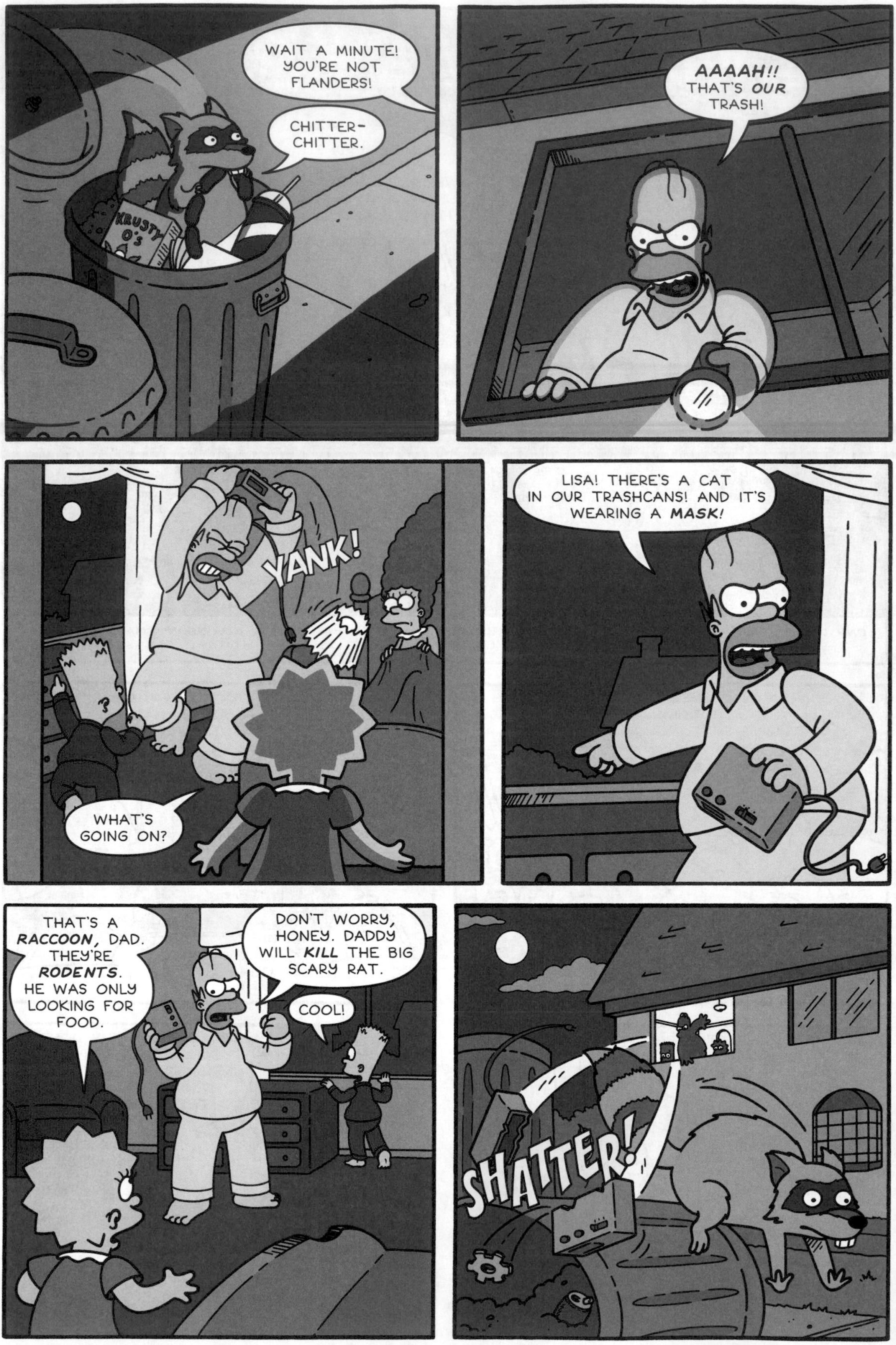
WAIT A MINUTE! YOU'RE NOT FLANDERS!
CHITTER-CHITTER.
KRUSTY O'S
AAAAH!! THAT'S OUR TRASH!
YANK!
WHAT'S GOING ON?
LISA! THERE'S A CAT IN OUR TRASHCANS! AND IT'S WEARING A MASK!
THAT'S A RACCOON, DAD. THEY'RE RODENTS. HE WAS ONLY LOOKING FOR FOOD.
DON'T WORRY, HONEY. DADDY WILL KILL THE BIG SCARY RAT.
COOL!
SHATTER!

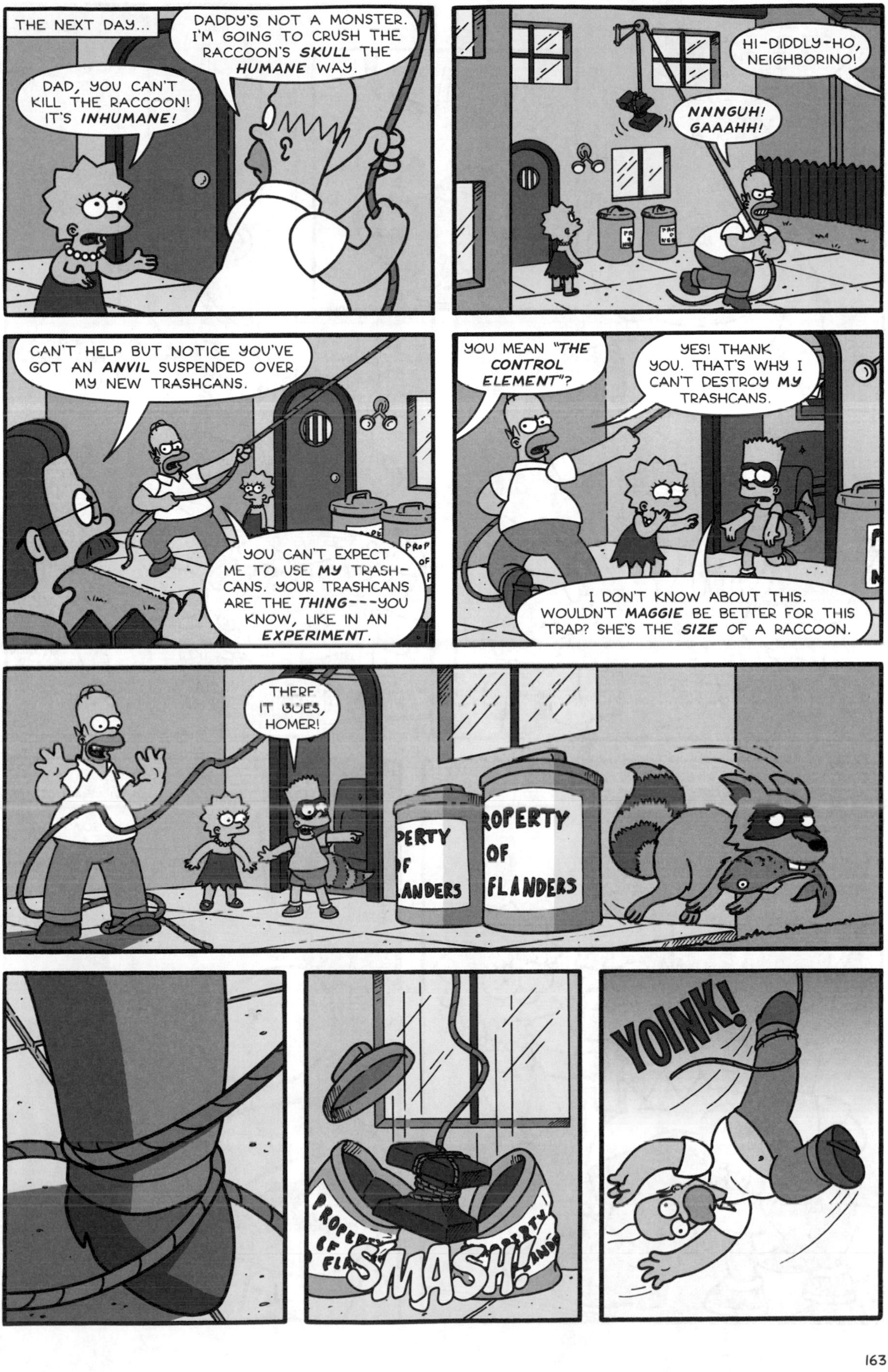

THE NEXT DAY...
DAD, YOU CAN'T KILL THE RACCOON! IT'S INHUMANE!
DADDY'S NOT A MONSTER. I'M GOING TO CRUSH THE RACCOON'S SKULL THE HUMANE WAY.
HI-DIDDLY-HO, NEIGHBORINO!
NNNGUH! GAAAHH!
CAN'T HELP BUT NOTICE YOU'VE GOT AN ANVIL SUSPENDED OVER MY NEW TRASHCANS.
YOU CAN'T EXPECT ME TO USE MY TRASHCANS. YOUR TRASHCANS ARE THE THING---YOU KNOW, LIKE IN AN EXPERIMENT.
YOU MEAN "THE CONTROL ELEMENT"?
YES! THANK YOU. THAT'S WHY I CAN'T DESTROY MY TRASHCANS.
I DON'T KNOW ABOUT THIS. WOULDN'T MAGGIE BE BETTER FOR THIS TRAP? SHE'S THE SIZE OF A RACCOON.
THERE IT GOES, HOMER!
PROPERTY OF FLANDERS
PROPERTY OF FLANDERS
SMASH!
YOINK!

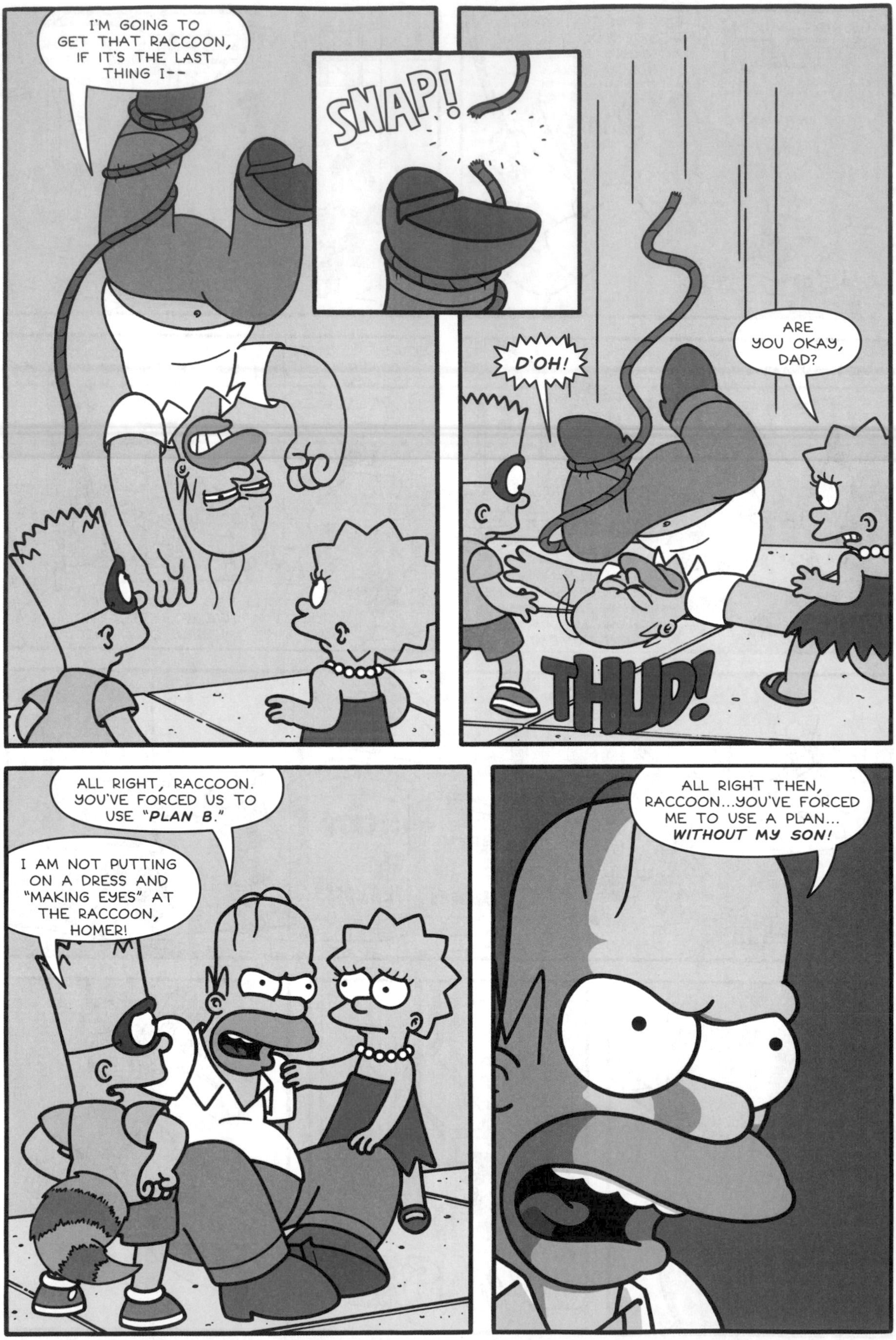
I'M GOING TO GET THAT RACCOON, IF IT'S THE LAST THING I--
SNAP!
D'OH!
ARE YOU OKAY, DAD?
THUD!
ALL RIGHT, RACCOON. YOU'VE FORCED US TO USE "PLAN B."
I AM NOT PUTTING ON A DRESS AND "MAKING EYES" AT THE RACCOON, HOMER!
ALL RIGHT THEN, RACCOON...YOU'VE FORCED ME TO USE A PLAN... WITHOUT MY SON!

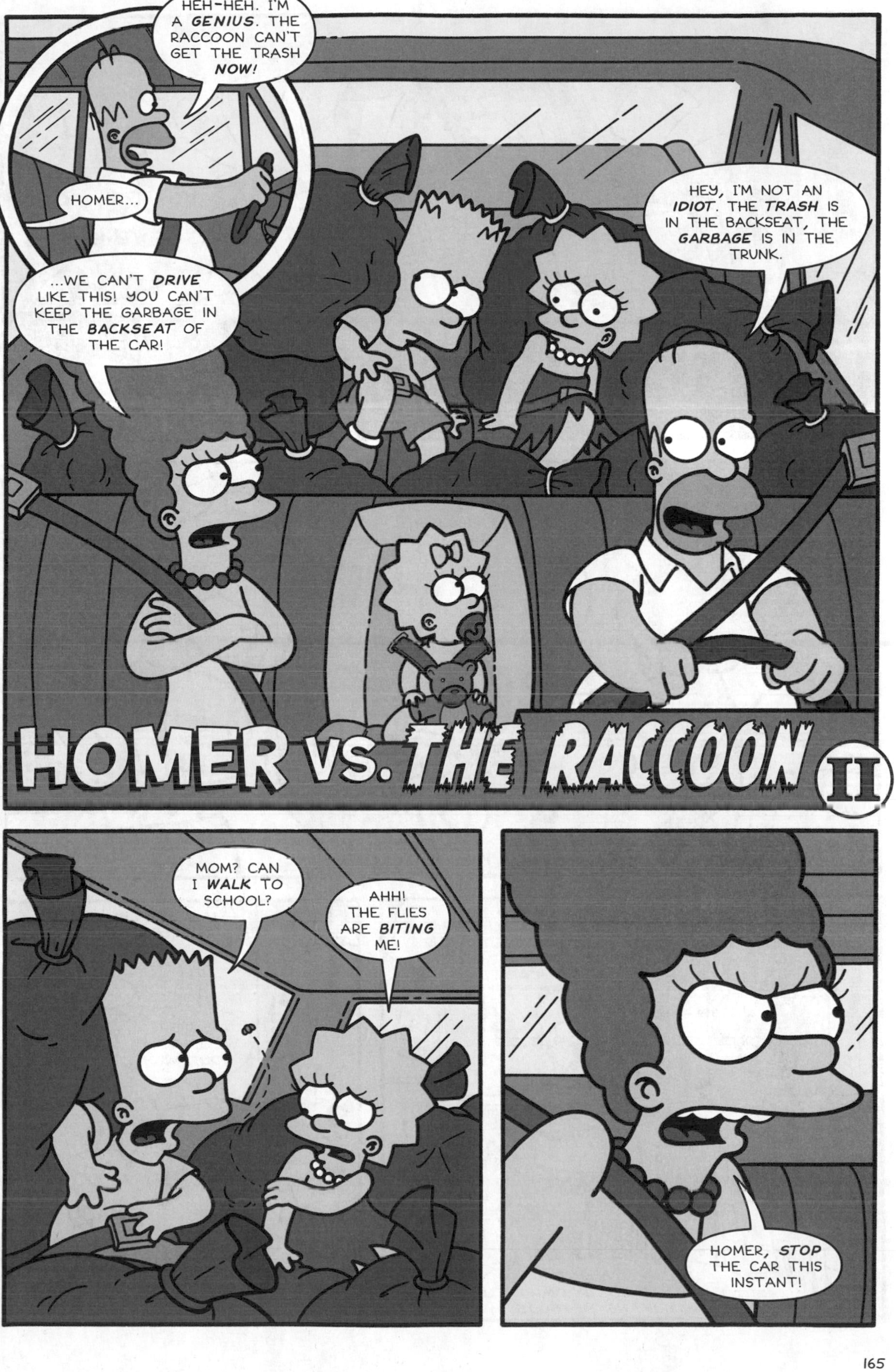
HEH-HEH. I'M A GENIUS. THE RACCOON CAN'T GET THE TRASH NOW!
HOMER...
...WE CAN'T DRIVE LIKE THIS! YOU CAN'T KEEP THE GARBAGE IN THE BACKSEAT OF THE CAR!
HEY, I'M NOT AN IDIOT. THE TRASH IS IN THE BACKSEAT, THE GARBAGE IS IN THE TRUNK.
HOMER VS. THE RACCOON II
MOM? CAN I WALK TO SCHOOL?
AHH! THE FLIES ARE BITING ME!
HOMER, STOP THE CAR THIS INSTANT!

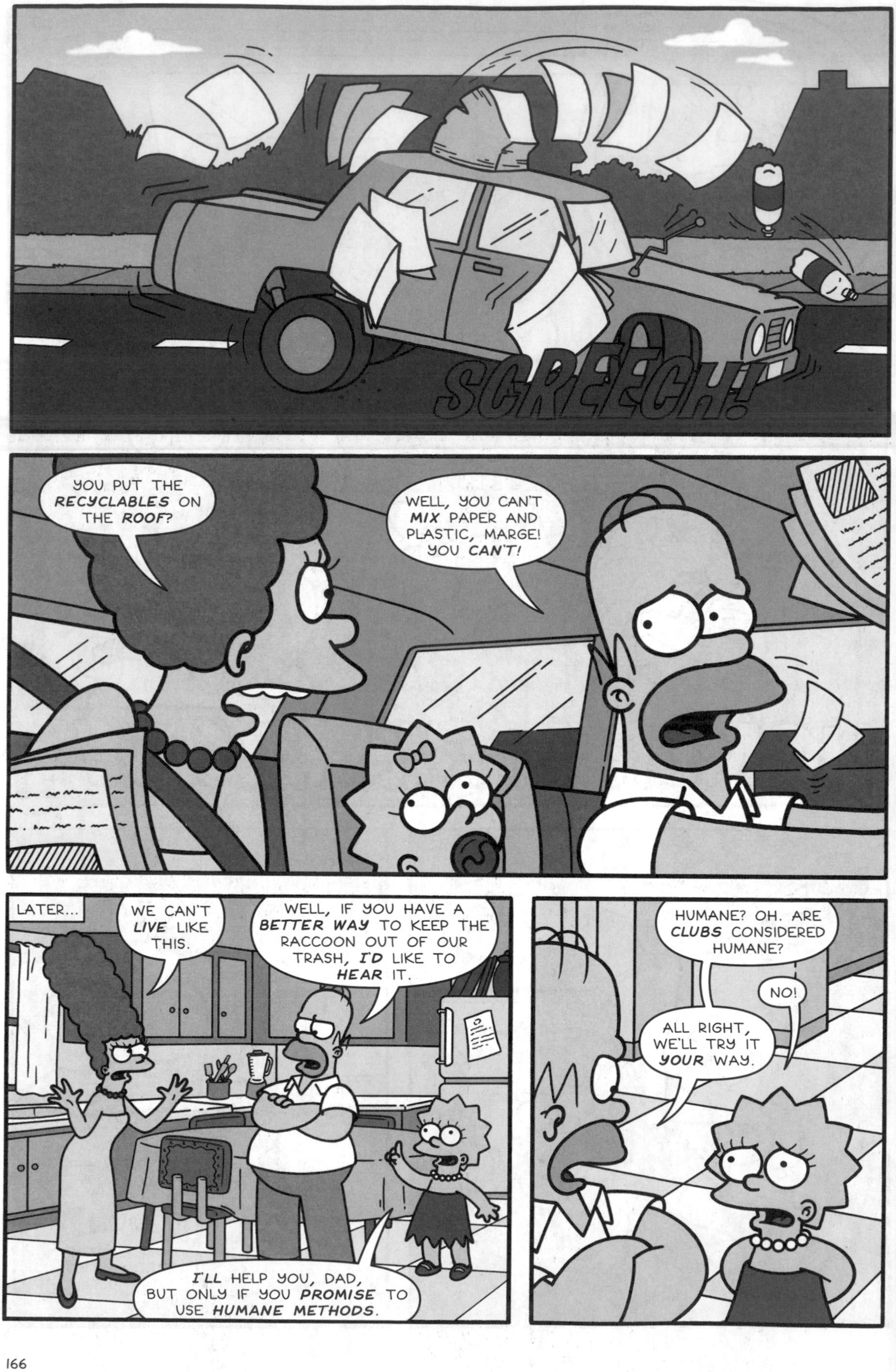
SCREECH!
YOU PUT THE RECYCLABLES ON THE ROOF?
WELL, YOU CAN'T MIX PAPER AND PLASTIC, MARGE! YOU CAN'T!
LATER...
WE CAN'T LIVE LIKE THIS.
WELL, IF YOU HAVE A BETTER WAY TO KEEP THE RACCOON OUT OF OUR TRASH, I'D LIKE TO HEAR IT.
I'LL HELP YOU, DAD, BUT ONLY IF YOU PROMISE TO USE HUMANE METHODS.
HUMANE? OH. ARE CLUBS CONSIDERED HUMANE?
NO!
ALL RIGHT, WE'LL TRY IT YOUR WAY.

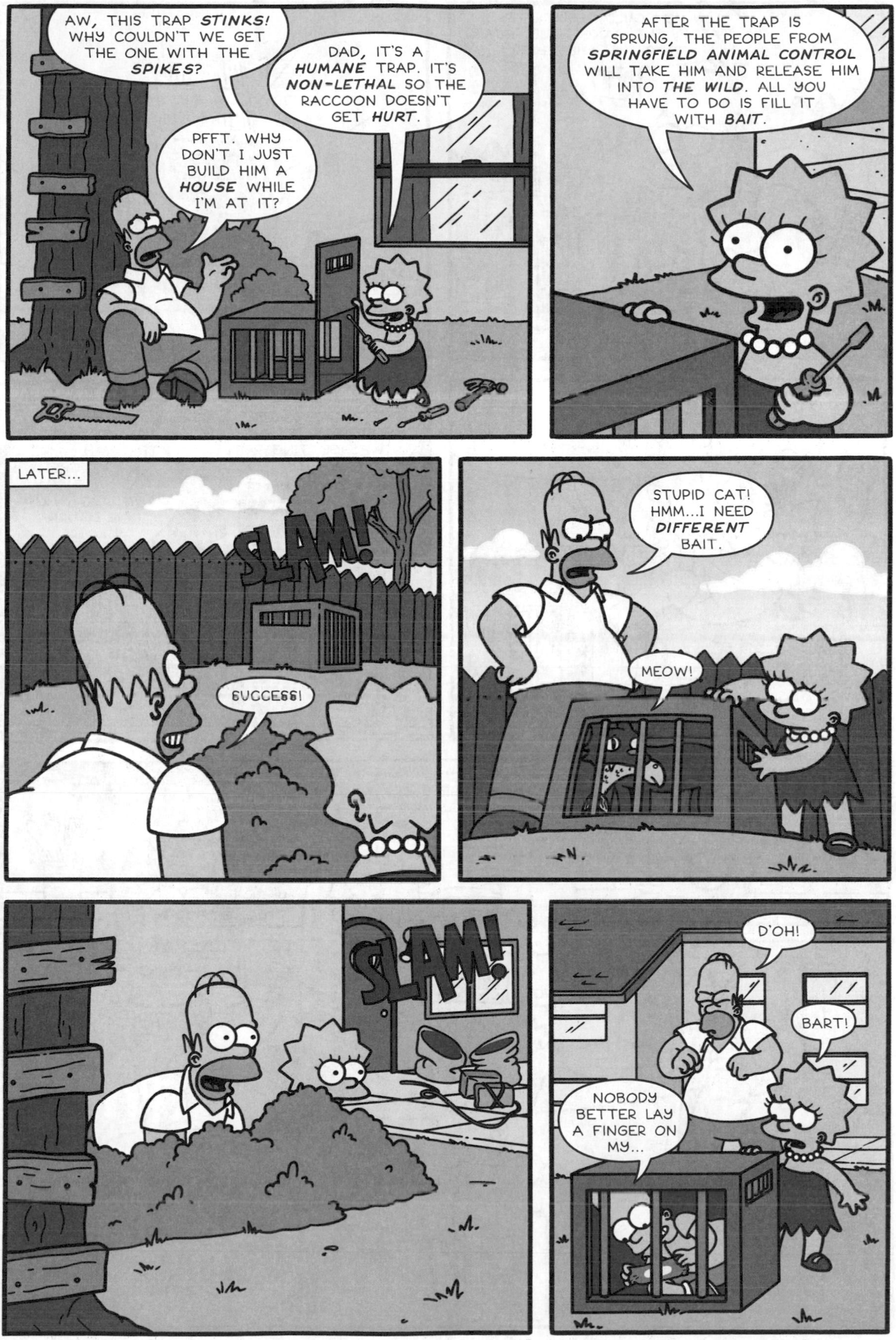
AW, THIS TRAP STINKS! WHY COULDN'T WE GET THE ONE WITH THE SPIKES?
DAD, IT'S A HUMANE TRAP. IT'S NON-LETHAL SO THE RACCOON DOESN'T GET HURT.
PFFT. WHY DON'T I JUST BUILD HIM A HOUSE WHILE I'M AT IT?
AFTER THE TRAP IS SPRUNG, THE PEOPLE FROM SPRINGFIELD ANIMAL CONTROL WILL TAKE HIM AND RELEASE HIM INTO THE WILD. ALL YOU HAVE TO DO IS FILL IT WITH BAIT.
LATER...
SLAM!
SUCCESS!
STUPID CAT! HMM...I NEED DIFFERENT BAIT.
MEOW!
SLAM!
D'OH!
BART!
NOBODY BETTER LAY A FINGER ON MY...

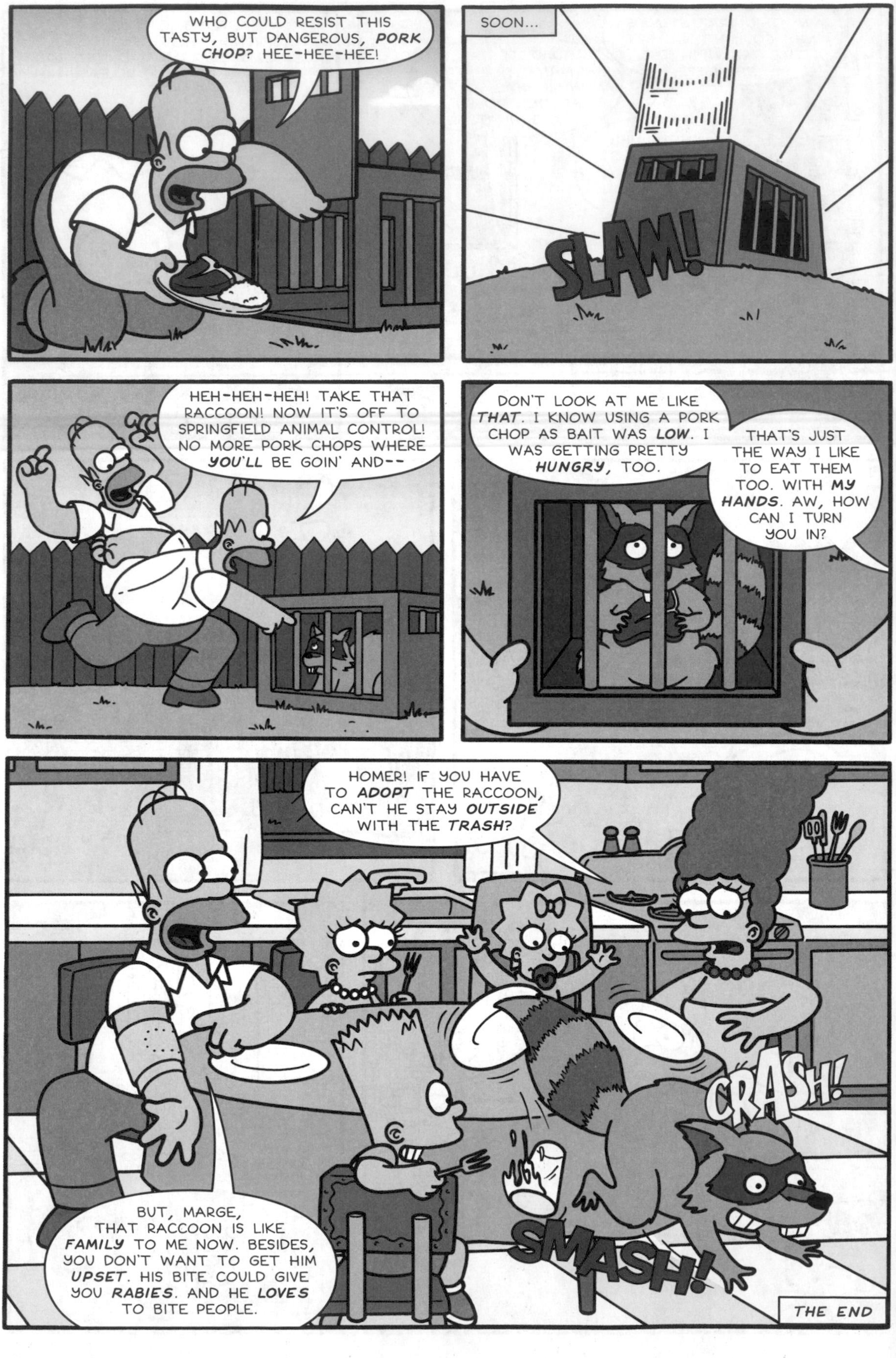
WHO COULD RESIST THIS TASTY, BUT DANGEROUS, PORK CHOP? HEE-HEE-HEE!
SOON...
SLAM!
HEH-HEH-HEH! TAKE THAT RACCOON! NOW IT'S OFF TO SPRINGFIELD ANIMAL CONTROL! NO MORE PORK CHOPS WHERE YOU'LL BE GOIN' AND--
DON'T LOOK AT ME LIKE THAT. I KNOW USING A PORK CHOP AS BAIT WAS LOW. I WAS GETTING PRETTY HUNGRY, TOO.
THAT'S JUST THE WAY I LIKE TO EAT THEM TOO. WITH MY HANDS. AW, HOW CAN I TURN YOU IN?
HOMER! IF YOU HAVE TO ADOPT THE RACCOON, CAN'T HE STAY OUTSIDE WITH THE TRASH?
BUT, MARGE, THAT RACCOON IS LIKE FAMILY TO ME NOW. BESIDES, YOU DON'T WANT TO GET HIM UPSET. HIS BITE COULD GIVE YOU RABIES. AND HE LOVES TO BITE PEOPLE.
CRASH!
SMASH!
THE END